WESTERN SOCIETY IN TRANSITION

WESTERN SOCIETY IN TRANSITION

Volker Bornschier

LONDON AND NEW YORK

First published 1996 by Transaction Publishers

Published 2017 by Routledge
2 Park Square, Milton Park, Abingdon, Oxon OX14 4RN
711 Third Avenue, New York, NY 10017, USA

First issued in paperback 2018

Routledge is an imprint of the Taylor & Francis Group, an informa business

Published in German as *Westliche Gesellschaft im Wandel* by Campus Verlag, 1988.

Library of Congress Catalog Number: 96-389

Library of Congress Cataloging-in-Publication Data

Bornschier, Volker, 1944–
Western society in transition / Volker Bornschier.
p. cm.
Includes bibliographical references and indexes.
ISBN 1-56000-227-1 (alk. paper)
1. Social history—20th century. 2. Economic history—20th century. 3. Social change. I. Title.
LB191.S652 1995
306'.09'04—dc20 96-389
CIP

ISBN 13: 978-1-138-51783-7 (pbk)
ISBN 13: 978-1-56000-227-7 (hbk)

Contents

Part III
Shaping Institutional Orders

Part IV
Convergence in the West?

Part V
Present Transformations and Future Competitive Edges

Preface to the American Edition

To explain what has been happening in the Western world a novel argument is advanced. The core countries, grouped around the triad formed by the United States, Japan, and the European Union, have experienced successive waves of change marked by phases of ascent, unfolding, and decay of societal models, generally over five to six decades. The latest model, based on Keynesian economic management, has been in its decaying phase since the 1980s. As a result, we are living through a crisis of legitimation characterized by acute contradictions. A new order, with a fresh basic consensus around an overarching set of norms that allows problems to be solved efficiently, has not yet crystallized.

A number of key areas, from the prevailing technological style, educational systems, power structures, the market, firms, and state-formations to modes of conflict and their resolution are examined in detail in a cross-national comparative perspective. These enable an order to be sustained, itself an indispensable resource from which the core countries derive many advantages. Much empirical evidence to support this case is presented, along with historical references going back several centuries. What the new order may turn out to be is as yet unclear, but there are certain indications of its probable shape. Since all core societies are now democratic, armed conflict between them is hardly likely. Nor will a single power dominate in future. Instead, there will be rivalry within the triad, distinguished by the relative decline of the United States, the competitive technological edge of Japan, and the attractions of the European welfare state, leading both to anticipated degrees of convergence and certain divergences as its world environment evolves following the collapse of the state-socialist counter-core.

This book is a completely reworked, updated, and extended version of the original German edition of 1988, *Westliche Gesellschaft im Wandel.* Many of the materials and empirical details included in the earlier edition had to be cut in order to create space for new materials covering recent developments. Therefore, citations of the German edition indicate that a more detailed empirical treatment of a particular point may be found there. The predictions of the original version, however, remain unchanged, although they seem much less controversial now than they did during the mid-1980s when I first proposed them in the original book.

ACKNOWLEDGEMENTS

My collaborators and many of my colleagues and friends have stimulated my ideas over the years and I owe a lot to them. A long list of their names acknowledging their valuable support is provided in the preface to the original German edition. The American edition, however, would not have been completed without the encouragement and help of Peter Lengyel, the former editor of *International Social Science Journal* and present co-editor of the *World Society Studies* series. His enthusiastic comments on the original manuscript in 1987 were a welcome encouragement after so many years of work. Even if his judgement, which appears on the cover of the German edition, was much too flattering, Peter Lengyel immediately thought it essential for this book to be translated into English. Other already promised publications, research, and teaching responsibilities, however, as well as my illness in 1990 prevented me from going ahead with that project. When it was resumed in 1993 it became clear that the result was in many ways a new book. In reviewing the original materials, cutting them down, and adding fresh materials from my ongoing lectures as well as my new articles, I enjoyed the help of Hanspeter Stamm—my collaborator at the Sociological Institute of the University of Zurich. Hanspeter Stamm then put together the new chapters of the English-language edition, which I reworked while they went back and forth to my friend Peter Lengyel in Paris. With his many valuable suggestions, Peter Lengyel considerably improved the clarity of argument as well as the English style. For the updating of data and figures as well as for formating I benefited from the help of Bruno Trezzini, another of my collaborators in Zurich. In implementing the many corrections and changes, as well as in subsequent proof reading Hildegard Köhler, also a collaborator in Zurich, was of great help. In doing this valuable work she was assisted in a first phase by Rachel Matthey. Finally, I benefited from the copy editing done by Richard Schauffler in Washington, who also offered many valuable suggestions and raised questions which pointed to shortcomings and thus helped to clarify and improve all the chapters in their latest stages. Simon Parker in Zurich read the proof of the whole manuscript with great care and competence, and was able to eliminate many errors that remained due to the various production steps, and for this I am grateful. Peter Lengyel, Hanspeter Stamm and all the others mentioned were essential for producing the present book, but the responsibility for the arguments advanced here, as well as any remaining shortcomings and errors, is mine alone.

1
INTRODUCTION AND OVERVIEW

THE PROBLEM

The past few years have witnessed such dramatic changes in Western and world society that it is appropriate to refer to the end of the postwar era. During the 1980s an enormous acceleration of history occurred, thereby radically changing world society in many respects. What seemed stable and predictable over decades came close to collapse or broke down spectacularly toward the end of the decade.

At the decade's outset Third World debt became acute; this resulted in vast immiseration and a veritable depression in large portions of the Third World, leading to the conclusion that, from a developmental point of view, the 1980s were a "lost decade." In the nation-states at the core, this period was marked by technological evolution and political turning points.

Core society found itself caught between the formation of a new *technological style* and the ongoing disintegration of its *politico-economic regime*. The consensual worldview that had solidified over decades dissolved, without any new frameworks having gained acceptance. In economic terms this decade was characterized by a short interim recovery that ended in a persistent recession at the beginning of the 1990s.

If the previous era had been marked by the economic doctrines of Keynes, the 1980s were dominated by those of Schumpeter. Against the background of the continued relative economic decline of the United States—the hegemonic power of the postwar era—the steady ascent of Japan was noteworthy. Furthermore, after years of "Eurosclerosis," the momentum toward further integration of the European Community picked up significantly and unexpectedly towards the mid-1980s, which compensated for the decline of the middle economic powers.

Finally, even more spectacular for Europe and the world were the consequences of the series of freedom movements in the revolutionary year of 1989. With the collapse of the Soviet Union, one of the stable coordinates of the bipolar postwar world disappeared overnight. With the end of the Council for Mutual Economic Assistance (CMEA) and the Warsaw Pact, the two means of domination over East Central Europe were abandoned.

Political orders that seemed to be rigidly fixed dissolved almost overnight. Such sensational examples of discontinuous social transformation astonished observers and drove home a severe lesson in humility to social scientists. A theoretically sound analysis of the events of the 1980s that puts them into an historical perspective has yet to be provided.

How does social order arise and why does it dissolve? This old puzzle is gaining new and special significance as a result of discontinuities and phases of revolutionary transition. A well-founded analysis would have to start by positioning the widespread instability within a recurrent pattern of social transition in Western society. Phases of crisis, like the one that started in the 1970s and continued into the 1980s, deprive societal institutions of their immediate acceptance. At the same time, the 1980s were characterized by a tentative search for alternatives, later on to be recognized as the beginning of "something new."

The long-term process of societal transition toward "something new" is the subject of this book. The perspective that will be sketched out interprets societal transition as the discontinuous evolution of *societal models,* which triggers long-term cyclical processes in different spheres of society. Therefore, societal transition is interpreted not only as continuous change but also as a discontinuous sequence of societal models. Even though new societal models are conditioned upon earlier ones, they are sufficiently different to justify both conceptions of evolution as well as of discontinuous social transition. Societal models are formulated and established as a result of persistent and deep crises. In the course of their unfolding they generate growing tensions, eventually leading to their dissolution and the search for a new model. Societal models may thus be identified as the basic units of social transition.

Two types of social transition will be distinguished. The first type encompasses the unfolding of a societal model, i.e., social change within a given order. The second type refers to the change of the order itself, i.e., a change of program that involves structural transformations in the organization of social life. We use the term *evolution* for this latter type of social transition.

The perspective we develop here avoids one-sided answers to the classic questions: What provides social cohesion? and What makes society progress? Such one-sided answers were suggested by the two predominant theories of postwar sociology: structural-functionalism and conflict theory. These two principal theoretical perspectives are commonly recognized as distinct in their answers to the question of what provides social cohesion. In structural-functionalist theory the importance of shared values and norms is stressed, whereas in conflict theory power relations are responsible for the integration of social entities. Both perspectives are of rather limited use in the study of social transformations. In opposition to such "absolutist" approaches, our view centers around the recurring transition from conflict to basic consensus, from basic consensus to conflict, and so on. The *trajectory* of a societal model is characterized by the change from basic consensus in its first phase to conflict in its second phase. It should be stressed, however, that the notion of basic consensus does not exclude disagreement and struggles *within* the accepted order in any way. Our approach combines elements drawn from both structural-functionalist and conflict theory and thus reconciles both research paradigms to a certain degree. As Seymour Lipset (1985) points out, conflict and consensus are just two faces of the same social process. Seen from this vantage point, it is hardly useful to exaggerate the differences between the two paradigms.

THE ARGUMENT

This book sketches out various elements of a theoretical perspective that we would like to call the *theory of conflictive evolution*. The primary focus of interest of this theory is not society as a whole, but on *societal models*, these being the units of social transformation. At a general level, societal models comprise the predominant basic consensus at a certain point in time as well as the institutional arrangements created to settle conflicts between leading values representing universal human aspirations and demands that arise from vested power. In our perspective, social structure is the result of the interaction of such conflicting principles, namely the striving after power, the striving after efficiency (self-determination and economic progress) and security, and the claim to equality. Societal models, on the other hand, represent the historical compromise among those principles. Against this background, a societal model can be interpreted as a renewed social contract that aims at producing legitimacy and thus social stability by realizing basic values. Because of the contradictions between leading values and power interests this is only possible for a limited time, however. Once it has been established, a societal model does not persist eternally without being changed. Rather, it runs through a particular trajectory that is characterized by a certain degree of regularity. Balancing and unbalancing processes as well as basic consensus and dissent mark the principal rhythms of this trajectory with the following stages: formation, unfolding, repletion, dissolution, and eventually decay and displacement by a new societal model.

Evolution is a feature of this process. Yet, rather than being a continuous phenomenon, evolution must be understood as long cyclical waves of structural construction and destruction. In each of these waves another societal model is spelled out. The societal model weaves together interpreted leading values (normative theories)—the most abstract components of culture—with two encompassing institutional complexes that differ in their functional logic: the *technological style* and the *politico-economic regime*. Originally coined by Carlota Perez (1983), the term technological style refers to a type of productive and administrative organization. The politico-economic regime, on the other hand, encompasses the shaping of the nation-state and the world market. On the basis of the above-mentioned principles and the institutional styles, the central institutions of modern times—i.e., the market, the firm, the nation-state and the educational system—are shaped, related to each other, and wrapped into a "package."

The social frame of reference of these processes is the world system rather than particular, territorially bounded societies. The social processes we are dealing with in this book are embedded in a capitalist system that is understood as a world-encompassing arena of market and interstate competition. It is not only firms that engage in market competition: in addition, governments of sovereign states are also competing in a "market" for optimal locations in the world economy, an economic competition outside of politico-military rivalry, the classical form of interstate conflict.

On the basis of the organization of the political and economic realm, different *societal types* can be distinguished, the *core* type being characteristically different from the *peripheral* type. Furthermore, the type of organization is marked by different societal models in the course of time, i.e., models spelling out the political and economic realms under normative guiding principles and relating them to each other.

Societal models represent not only an historical compromise between the previously mentioned principles. Since the legitimacy of social order is an important basis of competitive advantage in the world market, societal models also offer solutions to the problems of competition in the world system and the striving to attain or consolidate core status. If a given societal model succeeds in establishing an advantage in the competitive world system, it unfolds over national frontiers. As a result of the competition among different models and in spite of national particularities, societal models may thus cause convergence.

WESTERN SOCIETY AS A SOCIETAL TYPE

By using the notion of *Western society* we are claiming the existence of a *type of society* within world social structure that is constituted by sufficiently similar component societies. The evolution of typical features as well as the kind and extent of variations are the subjects of this book. The terms "Western" and "modern" are inadequate yet practical metaphors for the societal type under discussion. Within world social structure Western society holds a position which we propose to call the core. Western society is only a part of a totality that must not be forgotten, even though this totality is not the subject of this book. In our perception world social structure also comprises the rival counter-core (up to the end of the 1980s), the semiperiphery that is dependent on the core and the counter-core to varying degrees, and the marginalized and dependent periphery. For the sake of clarity it would be appropriate to start with an historical and comparative analysis of this set of societal types and their interrelations. This task would go beyond the scope of this study, however, and consequently only "Western society" will be analyzed.

For the postwar era the societal type in question can be delimited without problems. Not counting the very small societies of Luxembourg and Iceland, the following 18 countries were part of Western society during the postwar era: Austria, Australia, Belgium, Canada, Denmark, the Federal Republic of Germany, Finland, France, Ireland, Italy, Japan, the Netherlands, New Zealand, Norway, Sweden, Switzerland, the United Kingdom and the United States of America. These countries constitute the sample for the comparative analyses that follow. Greece, Portugal and Spain are not included because they are considered here to have only recently become members of Western society, since they did not exhibit all its typical features for the whole of the postwar era. Another candidate, Israel, will be excluded as a special case because it has been in an almost permanent state of war since its forced foundation in 1948 and a large part of its population was not born in the country. Presently, some other non-Western societies are pushing forward into the perimeter of the core. Apart from some city-states, mention should be made of South Korea and Taiwan, rare cases of upward mobility in world social structure for which Japan was the model.

The Western societal type is deeply rooted in Europe from which it spread early to North America and in the second part of the twentieth century—after the defeat of Japan in the Second World War—to East Asia. In spite of the considerable success of the early proponents of the capitalist project—Venice in the fourteenth and fifteenth centuries, and North Holland in the sixteenth and seventeenth—it remained confined to certain border regions in a very differentiated European environment for centuries. Only in the eighteenth century did the shift of leadership to England and the ensuing break-through of the English Industrial Revolution result in substantial adaptive pressure. Other European powers had to accept the superior institutions if they did not want to risk being outdone in the competition for core positions. Thus, the revolution of 1789 and even more so the liberal revolutions of 1830 and 1848 resulted in the constitution of a group of societies that promoted the project of the Western societal type.

This type of a society, which spread from 1830 and 1848 onwards, has two sociologically relevant and important features: 1) the constitution of market societies combined with an intense and complete unfolding of economic efficiency; 2) the political separation of power. The latter exhibits three additional features: 1) there is no full monopoly of territorial power in the overarching system; 2) different political power centers and parties exist within societies and compete for the same political power positions; 3) political dominion is forced to legitimize itself to non-elites, i.e., by means of elections non-elites dispose of at least one possibility to control leadership. This kind of political organization may be adequately described

by Robert Dahl's (1971) term "polyarchy." Currently, and as a result of gradual improvements in the separation of power in the political realm, the term "democracy" is also frequently used.

From an evolutionary perspective the historical success of this type can be linked to the separation of power and the differentiated institutionalization of countervailing power. This last aspect is stressed by John K. Galbraith ([1952]1967). In addition, success is a function of the enhanced possibilities of generating legitimacy and the superior learning capacity of this type. Superiority in the competition of societal types became particularly obvious in the revolutionary year of 1989. Two institutional solutions made this possible. First, market society is able to delegate a large part of the ever present problem of distributional fairness and justice to the market. Second, the separation of political power and its democratic control (elections, voting) can exist without a rigid pattern of truths or even Truth itself. In contrast to competing political systems, decisions can be made in a pragmatic way and in accordance with empirical problems.

In the periphery and the semiperiphery the central institutions of core society are only present in an incomplete or crippled form. Closely linked to the economic and politico-military dependency on the core, this fact also is an important reason for underdevelopment.

In the counter-core things are different. Here, a powerful state apparatus—as a precondition for this status—provides the necessary means to counteract pressure from the core and even threaten it. The basic condition for counter-core status is a counter-ideology that challenges the core's claim to cultural leadership. In the counter-core there is a tendency for the state, the economy, and the private spheres to amalgamate under the heading of a doctrine that claims to be absolutely true and attempts to regulate all realms of social life. In short, the counter-core is founded on the basis of the antithesis to the foundations of success in the core. In the postwar world system it was the state socialist model, with its claim to world leadership, that constituted the counter-core for over forty years until it succumbed and disintegrated in the competition of systems. Yet, counter-cores are a frequent phenomenon in decentralized world systems. For example, the absolutist projects of modernity were counter-cores to the outward-oriented economies of Venice, North Holland, and England, and presently, the revitalized Islamic fundamentalist model points to the possible formation of a new counter-core.

Market society and separation of political powers are two fundamental elements of the Western societal type. Together with the constitutional state they represent the *basic social contract* which was renewed at various times since 1830-48. On their basis and starting from general guiding principles, the political and economic realms are shaped and interwoven in a specific way. In our perspective, *societal models* are renewable social contracts. In this we agree with Ralf Dahrendorf's (1992: 50) assessment of the social contract as the central subject of history and his argument: "The social contract is rewritten on the basis of social conflicts." This is exactly the perspective advanced in our evolutionary conflict theory which aims at a more precise understanding and dating of the discontinuities in the renewal of the societal type. Two particularities of the theory merit some further comments in the following paragraphs. First, societal models are understood as cultural outcomes, and second, the importance of the competitive world system as a selective mechanism must be stressed.

SOCIETAL MODELS AND CULTURE

The notion of societal models as cultural outcomes deserves some clarification. As mentioned above, the principles that determine social structure—leading values on the one hand, social, economic and cultural power on the other—enter into a compromise within the societal model. This compromise mitigates tensions between leading values, universalistic demands and particular power positions. Four levels may be distinguished:

1. *Basic values*. In contrast to norms representing evaluative statements guiding behavior, values represent evaluative statements referring to the state of things. One might say that norms rule action whereas values rule being. In our theory basic values are at once the guiding lights of the cultural system and its compass. Such central basic values, which are anthropologically rooted, include equality, efficiency (self-determination and economic progress) and security.

2. *Normative theories*. These are more specific and selective than basic values insofar as they are historically formulated to determine what defines correct action. Normative theories interpret basic values, promote and convert them into leading values, and seek to mediate between incompatibilities of values or to override such problems by evaluation. Normative theories are influenced by cultural power and represent guidelines for

normative arrangements in various institutional areas of society. They are the result of a competition, a struggle for an adequate definition of reality. It is possible to distinguish phases in which normative theories hold a hegemonic position and are widely accepted from phases in which there is strong competition between different notions of reality.

3. *Blueprints for action.* These blueprints are practical prescriptions for conduct in institutional contexts. Thus, blueprints for action and institutional rules may be used as identical terms. Such institutional rules are not governed solely by universalistic leading values, transmitted by normative rules, but are also shaped by power interests. Blueprints for action represent the compromise between universalistic values and power interests. Yet, the more closely such blueprints adhere to interpreted leading values and power interests, the greater the legitimacy of a given social order—the legitimacy of social order being a key concept in the perspective advanced here.

4. *Action patterns.* These embrace social practice as well as the ensuing power distribution in society. They may be determined by blueprints for action as well as by specific power interests. The discrepancy between blueprints for action and action patterns constitutes deviant behavior with respect to normative rules and is thus illegitimate.

Legitimacy therefore acquires a dual character. On the one hand, it refers to the degree to which basic values mirror normative rules; on the other hand, it refers to the fit between normative rules and actual behavior, i.e., the extent to which leading values are respected in social practice.

Thus, the principles upon which social structure is built are: interpreted cultural leading values becoming guiding principles of society *and* particular power. To the extent that blueprints for action contribute meaningfully to patterns of action, a societal model emerges which legitimates social practice and the power expressed through it. If such linkages once existed but have lost their coherence and binding nature, then we can refer to the dissolution of a societal model that may even lead to its actual collapse.

The contention that principles structuring the social world are contradictory leads to a special kind of conflict theory. In contrast to functionalist assumptions, society without conflict is not possible. Yet, society can manage or suppress conflict. Management as well as suppression of conflict only work for a limited span of time. Against this background, the *function* of a societal model lies in its capacity to generate legitimacy by respecting basic values. Societal models generate societal power. Due to the contradictions between the above-mentioned principles, however, they can only do so for a time. From this follows a certain regularity in the course of a societal model, a *trajectory* with the stages: *formation, unfolding, repletion, dissolution* and *decay*.

THE WORLD SYSTEM AS A SELECTIVE MECHANISM

In view of the inevitable dissolution of societal models it must be asked why the attempt at instituting respected social order—generating legitimacy by means of renewed social contracts—is nonetheless a certain advantage. The answer is given by the second particularity of evolutionary conflict theory suggesting that the competitive world system of state societies is the fundamental selective mechanism.

Within this encompassing world system a more legitimate order is of considerable comparative advantage in determining the status of single countries. In a general perspective, respected social order—societal power—is a prerequisite for societies in a competitive environment; in addition, social order is also an often neglected factor of production.

Formation and decay of societal models cause cycles of order. If order is an economically useful factor, cycles of order trigger long waves of the economy. Furthermore, the quality and the extent of order determine the extent of social conflict resulting in a specific shape of conflict during the trajectory of a societal model. The present book scrutinizes these processes—long economic waves and changing levels of conflict as well as the institutional arrangements in the economic, political, and organizational realm including the division of labor in the educational system and social stratification.

Social order and the ensuing institutional structure are a lot less discretionary than it may appear at first sight. The above-mentioned principles—efficiency (self-determination and economic progress), equality, security and power—are partially incompatible. It is possible to imagine a large number of systems that link the conflicting principles with each other. As a consequence, often very different new beginnings are tried out after the decay of a hegemonic societal model. However, our theoretical perspective states that success in global competition will accrue to those societal models which optimize legitimacy in comparison to their competitors and challengers. Legitimacy, it should be stressed, is understood as the realization of basic values.

Positions are not rigidly and lastingly fixed in the world system. It has always been necessary to pay attention to legitimation demands during the evolutionary process of Western society in order to attain or preserve core status. If legitimacy poses a comparative advantage in the world system and thus leads to economic success in the long run, then coercion and illegitimate violence cannot be durable substitutes for the construction of order at the core of the world system. This is one of our central hypotheses and may appear quite questionable at first sight. Yet, as will be shown in this book, it becomes all the more plausible the more one consults the historical record regarding the long-term development of Western society.

THE KEYNESIAN SOCIETAL MODEL: AN ILLUSTRATION

Since the beginning of the nineteenth century three societal models can be discerned for the Western societal type that takes the core position in world society. These models will be briefly mentioned here before moving on to a detailed description of the latest societal model which will serve to illustrate the central points of our theory:

(1) The liberal societal model of the founding era, formed after the liberal uprisings of 1830-48 and dissolving in the late 1860s;

(2) The class-polarized model of the post-foundation era, originating following the widening of political participation and the extension of compulsory education in the 1880s and dissolving after the turn of the century;

(3) The societal model of the re-allocative market economy and welfare state era that integrated neocorporatist and Keynesian elements in varying degrees originating among pioneers (Sweden, United States, Switzerland) in the early 1930s and spreading after World War II. Since the late 1960s, this model has begun to dissolve and has, since the early 1980s, actually entered a phase of decay in certain countries (most obviously the United Kingdom and United States).

In order to further clarify the term societal model, it seems appropriate to discuss somewhat more precisely the three spheres—i.e., normative theories, politico-economic regime and technological style—that were linked to each other in the last societal model.

Normative Theories

The swing in doctrines related to economic policy was very important for the last societal model. The then emerging normative theory to solve economic and social problems may be summarized using the following formula: The state was regarded as the solution for the pressing problems that were the result of both the world economic crisis and a new technological style. Yet, the state was not only the solution; normatively fixed state intervention also allowed the integration of reformist socialism into the new societal model. Solidarity and redistribution, two socialist demands, no longer were in fundamental contradiction with a liberal position. The new guiding principles of economic policy in the welfare state era legitimized solidarity and redistribution as virtues that would stimulate economic growth. Yet the neoliberal and monetarist uprisings of the 1970s undermined the basic consensus regarding normative theories that had lasted for decades and introduced a new motto: Less State Intervention—More Freedom.

Politico-Economic Regime

The dominant normative theory of the neocorporatist-Keynesian societal model with its interventionist guiding principles created the possibility for a class pact for economic stability, social pacification and growth, thus promising a "democratization" of wealth. The past societal model was therefore characterized by two new linkages within the politico-economic regime: first, a new linkage between the economy and the state; second, a new linkage between capital and labor. From a comparative perspective the extent of cooperation and linkage of interests has differed among core countries, however. Despite similarities one finds different degrees of neocorporatist policy-making, i.e., of intermediation of organized interests coordinated by the state.

Technological Style

Procedural changes in the chemical industry were originally the key element of the technological style of that era. Using the new flow production it became possible to produce the key factor—energy (oil)—at diminishing relative prices for a long time. In addition, there were significant innovations in the shaping of formal organization. Mention should be made of "scientific management," the division of labor, and the reorganization of large corporations. The growth of the firm was conditional upon a far-reaching separation of ownership and control which in turn led to changes in the composition of the economic elite. By redistributing income and positions in favor of the distinctly enlarged middle classes, the renewed organization created mass demand, which reinforced mass production and the diffusion of the technological style. Finally, the new style offered a new mix of goods.

The 1970s announced the advent of a new technological style integrating and linking new productive, distributive and administrative elements. This style was formed during the 1980s by successively substituting information intensity for the material and energy intensity of the former style. The advance in productivity is a result of increasingly inexpensive micro-electronics and digital telecommunications. Computers are the new key product and chips the new raw materials. By changing the shape of organizations, the structure of jobs, and the patterns of consumption, the new style will alter the appearance of social life—the changes being possibly even more dramatic than those resulting from the former style.

ORIGIN, CULMINATION AND DECAY OF THE KEYNESIAN SOCIETAL MODEL

It is possible to date the formation of the two new linkages within the politico-economic regime—economy and state on the one hand, capital and labor on the other—quite exactly. The innovators of the historically victorious democratic variant started shaping the corresponding institutional arrangements between 1932 and 1934. As innovators we are referring to the neutral European countries Sweden (1932) and Switzerland (1934) as well as to the United States, the prospective new hegemonic power that saw its ambitions frustrated by a particularly severe economic crisis. When in the 1930s Franklin D. Roosevelt converted the new economic philosophy into a veritable state doctrine and began instrumenting the New Deal program salaries, the standard of living, and corporate profits exploded.

Mention was made of the victorious democratic innovators. It must be stressed, however, that the initial political answers to the world economic crisis differed between nation states of the West. In addition to the victorious democratic model one must also keep in mind the fascist, exclusive corporatist solutions with their stress on nationalist and strong anti-industrial elements (codeword: "Lebensraum") which flourished for some time on the continent after the assumption of power in the German empire by Hitler and his National Socialist German Worker's Party (Nazi party).

On the other hand, there were the democratically renewed neocorporatist social contracts that combined the integration of the working class into the system with a contract between the generations (old-age pensions and insurances). As mentioned above, these renewed contracts originated simultaneously in the United States based on the New Deal, in Sweden based on a social pact called the Folkhem (1932), in Switzerland where a 1937 'peace' agreement between opposing interest groups was concluded, and in the United Kingdom with its wartime welfare state. These regimes were compatible with the capitalist-industrialist logic and finally proved more successful in the economic and military struggle of the three war decades of the twentieth century (1914-45). Keynesianism thus became the dominant new model in the West.

As early as the Second World War the new regime became embedded within an international system of security and order that started with the Atlantic Charter of 1941 and was enforced jointly by the United States as the new hegemon in the world system, and the United Kingdom. Starting with the Atlantic Charter, not only a new world order—i.e., a new security policy—was laid out.; moreover, the world market was redesigned under the political, economic, and cultural hegemony of the United States, the institutional corner-stones for this process being the Bretton Woods agreements of 1944, the founding of United Nations in 1945, and the financial support of the reconstruction of Western Europe from 1947 onwards. World market and nation-state were newly shaped on the basis of the ideals of free trade, equal treatment, non-discrimination under the General Agreement on Tariffs and Trade (GATT), and the right of self-determination of nations (decolonialization) (Bornschier 1990).

The typical features of the last societal model have been the result of the conflictive interplay of the aforementioned principles. First, world market competition enforces fixing priorities with reference to economic efficiency. Furthermore, legitimacy of a social order is an important resource creating long-term advantages in this competitive environment. Not only business enterprises but also states as participants on the world stage are thus confronted with a logic that limits behavioral possibilities.

By defining membership and rightful claims the nation-state brought about a supply of legitimacy which would have been lacking had it only relied on the market process and the inequality resulting from the division of labor in formal organizations. In other words, the basis of equality in the population was raised by participatory rights and welfare state intervention. Beyond equality before the law, equality was also guaranteed by networks of social security and, in the sense of equal opportunities, by the distribution of formal qualifications. Thus, the educational system became more important than before under the Keynesian societal model. The educational system's efficiency at creating legitimacy stems from a combination of equality and equal opportunity, i.e., original and radical equality symbolized by the "zero hour" of the first day at school, with later differentiation symbolized by different educational degrees. Formal qualifications are normatively linked to hierarchical positions in formal organizations although full correspondence between qualifications and positions is impossible. This is the reason why economic growth also was of great importance in the "cosmology" of the last societal model: growth rendered possible a temporal interpretation of equality within social stratification. One could always rely on getting tomorrow what the upper strata as social groups of reference already had.

Economic performance with its key elements gross national product and mass consumption was the standard for measuring success and happiness during that era. Against this background the state received the authority to intervene *before* (school) and *after* (social security) the market thus ensuring the creation of societal legitimacy by offering more educational possibilities and a more equal distribution of income as well as stable economic growth with potential and actual gains for everyone: high profits for owners, full pay envelopes and mass consumption for workers.

These typical features of the last societal model, its "cosmology," are in no way deliberate results of modern functional necessities as suggested by adherents of the regulation school, but rather a logical result of a normative theory which assigns to income distribution a central role in the stabilization of society. This Keynesian argument may seem rather economistic at first sight, yet it was given a much more encompassing interpretation as an important cornerstone of the new social contract. This contract also included solidarity, elements of equality in outcome and a certain delinking of work and income, and it worked well for some time because mass consumption resulted in economic effects that supported the whole system.

Social integration in the neocorporatist-Keynesian societal model granted the remarkable peace and the low explosive power of political disputes even under conditions of mass democracy. When the societal model reached its apex, in many countries the powerful big interest groups, and particularly organized labor, were strongly bound to a politico-economic distributive alliance that administered the societal model. The growing crisis of the model during the prosperity of the 1960s thus resulted first in an intensification of the potential for intervention and an unprecedented agglomeration of power in the economy and the state.

Apart from the groups that were part of the circle of power there were no noteworthy let alone dangerous groups. Originally, the societal model came under strain from marginal positions. The starting point was the youth movement of the 1960s with the anti-authoritarian student revolt at its core. In the United States additional pressure was created by civil rights movements. These movements broadened during the 1970s into the alternative movements which integrated a growing proportion of the middle classes and constituted the basis for the so-called new social and political movements that managed to take hold within Western society and to affect the political landscape well into the 1980s.

The culmination of the societal model coincided with the fulfillment of the promises made to regulate conflict. There are good reasons to argue that the repletion of the model in Western core society has to be dated to the mid-1960s, i.e., earlier than is commonly supposed. During the 1960s the model reached the limits of its problem-solving capacity and thus exhibited the first signs of repletion. Still, these signs were not yet perceived as a downswing of the boom, rather the crisis became evident only after 1974 thus supporting the then popular interpretation of the oil shock as having undermined an "eternal" expansion.

There are a large number of possible sources of tension in the face of a diminishing problem-solving capacity of the model, some of which are illustrated in figure 1.1. With reference to technological style, mention should be made of the behavior of firms, i.e., the fact that growing industrial concentration hampers product innovations. In addition, market saturation poses a problem that is counteracted with export offensives which, however, lead to a destabilization of the world trade regime.

TABLE 1.1 Unfolding and Boundaries of Conflict Regulation in the Societal Model

UNFOLDING OF A NEW TECHNOLOGICAL STYLE					BOUNDARIES OF CONFLICT REGULATION BY:
Job structures	- possibilities of upward mobility and growing employment	(-) ——>	conflict	(+) <——	structural transition finished
Patterns of consumption and new goods	- diffusion of desired goods of mass consumption	(-) ——>	conflict	(+) <——	certain "democratization of consumption", yet no positional leveling out
Enterprises	- establishment of a new style	(-) ——>	conflict	(+) <——	concentration, market domination: mergers and struggles for take-over
UNFOLDING OF A NEW POLITICO-ECONOMIC REGIME					
Material infrastructure and additional demand/supply (induced growth, for example in road construction and expansion of state personnel)	- additionally: economic growth, services and public goods, possibilities for upward mobility in newly created professions	(-) ——>	conflict	(+) <——	structural transition finished
Intervention potential of economic policy	- economic fine tuning	(-) ——>	conflict	(+) <——	contradictions between different goals of economic policy
	- neocorporatist arrangement	(-) ——>	conflict	(+) <——	crusting of the distributional coalition, new issues are barely discussed politically
Social infrastructure	- welfare state programs and expenses	(-) ——>	conflict	(+) <——	financing problems, resistance against taxes
	- educational expansion and leveling out of educational possibilities	(-) ——>	conflict	(+) <——	problems in meeting legitimate claims on the basis of educational certificates
In general: consolidation of the interventionist state	- increase of state influence in economy and society	(-) ——>	conflict	(+) <——	concentration of state power, growing public sector and public debt
NEW COORDINATION OF THE REGIME IN THE WORLD POLITICAL ECONOMY	- formation and unfolding of international politico-economic regimes (Bretton Woods, GATT)	(-) ——>	conflict	(+) <——	decay of regimes (Bretton Woods, 1971) and tensions (in the GATT since the 1970s)

As time goes by the new technological style encompasses the whole society and thus radically changes the system of positions. One result is the enormous, structural possibilities for upward mobility, evidenced by the transition from blue to white collar jobs. Yet, these possibilities are diminishing, first in the manufacturing sector and later in the so-called induced sectors of the economy, particularly in services. Thus an important supplementary source of legitimation for the social structure is lost.

Among the population the diffusion of new products reduces their attraction and leads to a general trivialization of charisma so that the popular view is increasingly directed toward the unresolved problems of positional inequality in society. The promise of mobility on the basis of education reaches its limits because schooling is a positional good; in the formulation coined by Fred Hirsch (1976: 5): "If everyone stands on tiptoe, no one sees better." Finally, the change of values in the population induces retreat as well as criticisms of the system. At the level of the politico-economic regime mention must be made of state interventions that lead first to financial problems and later to tax revolts. In addition, economic fine tuning comes under pressure in view of stagflation: economic policy can neither solve the newly inflamed distributional conflicts nor can it overcome inflation.

In the world economy, the Bretton Woods system (which was established by the United States) with its fixed exchange rates became an "inflation machine" to the extent that the United States did not any longer keep to budgetary discipline. Consequently, following the first conflicts in 1969, the system broke apart completely in 1973. Finally, the change of the political economy of petroleum has to be noted. The societal model of the core had not regarded the periphery as an equal partner. For that reason, oil became a weapon that was used not only by the Organization of Petroleum Exporting Countries (OPEC) but also by the South in general in an attempt to overthrow the world economic order. Even though there was no substantial improvement in the position of the periphery, the oil wars of 1973 and 1980 nonetheless affected the system badly.

Societal models, it was said, are formulated in connection with long-lasting and profound crises. In the course of their unfolding they stir up growing tensions and dissolve, thus making way for the search for a new model. Looking back one can say that the last societal model was first established in the innovative countries Sweden (1932), the United States (1933) and Switzerland (1937), from which it spread over the Western world after the war, reaching its peak in the 1960s and dissolving in the course of the 1970s. Between the 1970s and the 1980s the previously respected normative theories were decaying. At the same time the new technological style crystallized, timidly accompanied by politico-economic arrangements which attempted to reshape society again.

The last stage of decay of the societal model can be dated with a similar degree of precision as its origin. Signs of dissolution could be observed at least since the beginning of the 1970s. The neoliberal and monetarist revolts of the 1970s broke up the basic consensus of the societal model. The motto "Less State—More Freedom" reflects the changed perceptions and can be interpreted as a reaction to the "social democratic century" (Dahrendorf 1983: 16ff.) on the normative level. Upon entering office in 1980, President Reagan announced "the state no longer is the solution but the problem", thus referring in a dialectical way to the starting point of the societal model which we have summarized under the heading: "The State is the Solution".

Ironically Reagan's statement that "The State is the Problem" was to become a quite correct assessment of the condition of things after eight years of his administration: The huge public deficit that Reagan left behind is indeed a problem. On the ideological level the formerly binding consensus of the societal model was successively destroyed, yet actual economic policy would have to be described as hyper-Keynesianism if one bears in mind the immense deficit spending and the ensuing consumptive boom that originated in the United States.

For that reason, the 1980s did not mark the beginning of a new societal model in the realm of the politico-economic regime, but rather the final stage of the former model. Its decay was not everywhere as dramatic as in the United States or the United Kingdom, however. Still, the transition from Keynesian demand management to supply side economics was felt everywhere. Thus, the neocorporatist, Keynesian societal model's decay reached well into the 1980s. The economic upswing that restarted in the course of the 1980s was primarily the result of a new technological style that was not yet accompanied by a new politico-economic regime.

Against this background, it can be asked how long a societal model lasts. Taking as our point of reference the innovator of the last societal model, Sweden, the origin of the societal model can be dated to 1932 and its end to the mid-1980s, when the awareness of the model's demise began to grow. "Sweden: The End of a Model" was the title of an article in the well-known German news magazine *Der Spiegel* (26/1991, p. 136ff.) when in 1991

TABLE 1.2 Stages in the Trajectory of the Last Societal Model Including a Tentative Dating for the Period after 1933/1945

	1933/1945-1957	1958-1967		1968-1979	1980-(1992) prognosis	
Politico-economic regime	formation	unfolding		repletion and dissolution	decay	
technological style	cristallization and diffusion	repletion of the diffusion process, first element of a new style		elements of the new style lead to heterogeneity	unfolding of the elements of a new style	
long wave of economic development	upswing	prosperity	prosperity recession	crisis	interim recovery	renewed crisis
dissent and conflict	dissent and conflicts are substantially reduced	dissent and conflicts are increas-ing again	dissent and conflict are diminishing again	dissent and conflicts are increasing violently	dissent and conflicts remain at high levels	

Note: Due to World War II the formation phase for large parts of the core—excluding the United States—was delayed (new beginning after the war). The new beginning is dated to 1944/1945 when the new world order of the postwar era was created (Bretton Woods, Yalta).
Source: Bornschier (1988: Figure 6.1, p. 150).

there was a shift of political power in Europe's model social democratic country. Traditional politics were at their end, the Swedish model, once praised as a prototype by social democrats, was "running out." Many people did not trust the ability of traditional political structures to cope with the shortcomings of the welfare state any more. Thus, taking the innovator and exponent of the social democratic variant of the last societal model, the societal cycle has a length of fifty to sixty years, this also being the time frame of the so-called long waves in the economy.

There were no signs of a homogeneous transition toward a new politico-economic regime during the 1980s, nor was such homogeneity typical for the transition to the neocorporatist, Keynesian societal model of the 1930s. The interim recovery of the 1980s, at the end of the decay of the model, did not stimulate a new beginning. Obviously the experience of a crisis at the end of the interim recovery is necessary to smooth the way for the establishment of constructive disenchantment. Yet, a new politico-economic regime and a new technological style are not established automatically. Rather, the necessary institutional arrangements are conditional upon courageous and imaginative actions.

The stages in the trajectory of the neocorporatist, Keynesian societal model are shown and dated in figure 1.2 which serves to summarize the above-mentioned structures and processes, and which are treated in more detail in the following chapters. The end of the decay phase is given as 1992, a date that represented a prognosis made in the mid-1980s when the German-language version of this book was first published. The dating was left as is because it is believed that from 1993 onwards changes in Western Europe, the United States and Japan will become visible that will later be interpreted as the formation of a new societal model.

Whether and how societal challenges are met is by no means fixed in phases of transition. Rather the outcome is conditional upon constellations of actors within and outside of society. From a short- and mid-term perspective, the theory does not neglect historical components causing variations in the institutional arrangements. For a dozen years or so groups that have been victorious in social conflicts may indeed enforce institutions that are tailored to their individual needs. In a long-term perspective, however, only those institutions will survive which serve the whole of society.

The sequence of societal models therefore is neither automatic nor fully determined. The establishment of a new societal model requires decisive action and attempts at shaping the order. For that reason, we as political persons cannot just sit back and wait for better times.

Plan of the Book

The book is divided into five parts. The *first* part contains three chapters that put forward the basic components of the theoretical model. Chapter 2 first addresses the basic principles—efficiency (self-determination and economic progress), equality, security, and power—while chapter 3 is dedicated to the regulatory impact of the competitive world environment. In chapter 4 the issue of the cyclical dynamics of social change is addressed and related to the sequence of societal models.

In the *second* part an historical line through the discontinuous development of the technological style and the politico-economic regime of Western society is sketched out. Chapters 5 and 6 take up the issue of long waves but extend the scope of the analysis beyond merely economically founded cyclical theories. In our theory, long-term fluctuations of the economy are regarded as the result of the development of the technological style and changes in the politico-economic regime. Following the analysis of the technological style and the politico-economic regime, the trajectory of the societal model and the accompanying changes in conflict levels and economic growth are discussed in a formal as well as historical perspective.

The *third* part scrutinizes the already mentioned institutional orders: the formal organization (chapter 8), the educational system (chapter 9), and the state and its relationship to capitalism (chapter 10). The world market, on the other hand, is discussed in connection with general regulatory forces in chapter 3. Rather than focusing on discontinuities between societal models, part three discusses the developmental trends that have resulted from various conflicts up to the present. In this connection social stratification and mobility in Western society should be addressed, but for reasons of space we had to refrain from including these materials in a special chapter (see, however, Bornschier 1991).

Part *four* contains an analysis of similarities and differences of institutional arrangements, social stratification, and mobility regimes during the postwar era among various countries. Chapter 11 treats Western society as a whole and chapter 12 offers specifications for the case of Japan. On the one hand, differences are explained on the basis of the positions of countries in the world system; on the other hand, they are related to political constellations and the institutional inheritances within countries. Processes of convergence will be discussed within the theoretical framework of the world market for social order and protection as a regulatory mechanism: Arrangements of social structure that bind together the conflicting principles with more legitimatory success, will prevail and set the standards, thus enforcing convergence. This mechanism is theoretically discussed in chapter 3, and is shown to have been at work during the process of nation building and the unfolding of capitalism (chapter 10) and is illustrated for the postwar era in chapter 13. The central questions are: Were there any location-specific advantages? If so, what were they? The theory of conflictive evolution as an explanatory framework points at the global environment that continuously enforces the creation of respected social order, i.e., societal power based on legitimacy, on the basis of so-called renewed social contracts. A more legitimate social order constitutes a competitive advantage in the competitive world system of nation states—an advantage that facilitates the explanation of long-term changes of the relative position of societies. The forces that stimulate social change therefore cannot be reduced merely to internal features of the societies under discussion. In addition, the functional logic of the world system creates an important degree of external adjustment pressure.

Part *five* finally addresses the present transitions in Western society and offers a look ahead. The transition of Western Europe towards political union is described and explained in chapter 14. The decay of the societal model and the transformations in the encompassing world social structure are the starting points for a discussion of the features of an emerging new societal model in chapter 15. In this connection, the concluding chapter analyzes the consequences of the changes for the future structure of the core. Although a change in hegemonic practices is in sight, we argue that, contrary to the predictions of mechanistic cycle theories, the transformations will not end with the emergence of a new hegemon.

PART I

THE ARGUMENT SPELLED OUT

Having provided an overview of the book and introduced the concept of the societal model in the introductory chapter we proceed in chapter 2 to a discussion of the continuous, conflictive principles of Western society: efficiency, equality and power, which we associate with the human demands for freedom, equality, and security. Through the different forms of power (social, cultural, and economic) a framework is constituted for the central institutions: the state, educational institutions, formal organizations and the market; these are embedded in the particular social form of the competitive milieu of the world system. The use of conflictive evolution theory is further established in chapter 3, which deals with the selective mechanism. With the interlinking of the political and economic spheres in the world political economy, competition arises for order and protection among nation-states. Through this world market for protection, the institutional arrangements that best compromise between capital expansion and supply on the one hand and the quest for legitimacy and entitlements on the other are selected. Those societal arrangements thus thrive which are in a position to best moderate social conflict and thereby create more legitimacy. In chapter 4 we introduce the notion of discontinuous social change. We differentiate between the innumerable social changes and a structural transition. The latter contains within it the new beginnings called forth by phases of crisis, that is, renewed social contracts. The rhythm of the ascendance and decline of social order brings about the interplay of economic expansion and stagnation, which are a central theme in the literature and generally discussed in terms of long waves of conjuncture.

2
PRINCIPLES OF SOCIAL STRUCTURES AND THEIR INSTITUTIONAL MANIFESTATIONS

THE CULTURAL FOUNDATIONS OF WESTERN SOCIETY

Societal models, as has been pointed out, are cultural outcomes based on a compromise between four principles of social structure: efficiency, equality, security, and power. Yet, the decentralized political system (Immanuel Wallerstein 1974) and cultural fragmentation of Europe (or heterodoxy, see Shmuel N. Eisenstadt 1987) cannot fully explain these cultural pillars.

One possible explanation could be drawn from the historical development of the West and its cultural roots. This is the path Max Weber chose. In historical terms the striving after efficiency and equality can be traced back culturally and ideologically to the common origins of the four central elements of the cultural pattern of modernity: universalism, individualism, rationalism, and pragmatism (Conze et al. 1975; Dann 1975). These building blocks of the modern cultural pattern derive from the ruins of antiquity; they were rediscovered during the early Renaissance in the twelfth century and have since been rearranged (Mühlestein 1957). The Judeo-Christian tradition constitutes another historico-cultural root in the sense that the Jewish idea of tribal brotherhood was extended to encompass a universal brotherhood of men (Nelson 1984). Here, universalism and a radical claim to equality have their cultural roots. Further bases can be found in ancient Greek logic and philosophy (rationalism) as well as Roman law, with its notion of the individual as a legal personality and party to contracts. Another Roman inheritance, bureaucracy, was mediated by the continuity of the Catholic Church. The secularization of these traditions during the early Renaissance and the Reformation, with their secular and pragmatic orientations, laid the basis for formal organization, which made its first appearance in the absolutist state and later in the modern business corporation.

With the emergence of the modern era, a new construction of society entirely different from the social organization of the Middle Ages began on the basis of these cultural foundations.[1] Two political movements and theories substantiated the notion of society as an organism: first, the theory of absolute state power and, second, the theory of individual natural rights (Coleman 1974). These two currents not only clashed with each other, but also contradicted the medieval idea of a fixed position for each social agent within the whole. Two new entities of social reality were thus created: the state and the individual. The individual was interpreted as a rational, purposeful, and autonomous actor. The individual's double claim to autonomy and to being the sole and ultimate source of power conflicted with all secular and sacred claims to leadership. State formation and the societal transformation of Europe took place in a particular structural context: a social system with a common cultural background and unfolding economic division of labor existed, yet there was no encompassing and centralized political order. Max Weber, in some of the lesser known passages of his work, was the first to point out this peculiarity and the ensuing dynamics of social change (see chapter 3).

It cannot be denied that the particular historical origins of the modern era are important. But the basic cultural principles can also be explained on the basis of universal subjectivism. This is Immanuel Kant's approach, and in what follows we will pursue this line of reasoning.

In our perspective the principles have an extra-historical and pre-social existence. Although subjective in nature, the pre-social element is universal. In this, our theoretical perspective is fundamentally different from Max Weber's conflict theory or structural-functionalism. Weber's ([1913] 1988: 428) "verständliche Erklärung" ("understanding explanation") is based on subjective criteria (individual motives for action), yet there is nothing universal, i.e., nothing meaningful, which is common to all men in the pre-social realm. Since Emile Durkheim, structural-functionalism as well as functional-structural theory use collectivist arguments: collective consciousness, normative integration, and systemic needs are the key elements of this perspective, but there are no goals and claims rooted outside the actual social self. Meanings and purposes are derived from social relations, which may even operate entirely without subjects in recent versions of system theory (Niklas Luhmann). This may lead to tautologies: the function of society is to perpetuate society. Hence everything perpetuating society seems functional—even tyranny.

Such perspectives neglect the fact that there is still another hypothesis, one that refers to subjective *and* universal pre-social forces. Neither social change nor social conflict can be explained without reference to such forces. In our own evolutionary conflict theory, the very conflict between basic claims and reality is the driving principle behind societal development. Though the specific social form of a historical society as well as that of the overarching social system determine how the principles are anchored, these principles are not created by an historical society. Society merely weighs principles against each other, suppressing one in favor of another or giving them equal weight. This is what is meant by extra-historical and pre-social.

The principles can be established anthropologically, in connection with those of natural rights. This reference to natural rights is not incidental. Basing our discussion merely on anthropological considerations could underestimate the power of these principles. There are different conceptions of natural rights, yet all of them include the idea that rights are not identical to the rules set by any existing power (Kohler 1979: 138f.). Here, "nature" in the sense of natural rights is understood as a metaphor for possibilities that exist independent of specific social conditions; further, "rights" goes far beyond a merely anthropological viewpoint—i.e., a description of human nature—in that people formulate claims even if they cannot be met in a specific historical situation. In such claims lies a utopian element, without which the development of Western society would seem quite difficult to understand. If we further interpret "rights" in a hyperpositive sense as justice, our notion also points to an antagonism between such claims and power (Kohler 1979: 139).[2]

If we see man as a consciously acting, reasonable and at the same time endangered and mortal natural creature, it is possible to postulate three basic human aspirations: a claim to autonomy, a claim to equality and a claim to security. These claims express corresponding basic values—liberty, equality, and security—that are not, however, equally pressing. For understandable reasons an ordering of priorities makes security most basic and thus most important (Maslow 1977). The fact that one always tries at least to stay alive explains why, under certain conditions, people can be forced to renounce their claims to liberty and equality. Security thus is a basic aspiration which overshadows the other two claims to a certain degree.

In this chapter we shall connect these aspirations with our basic principles (efficiency, equality, security, power) in order to derive social forces from them. The principles can be divided into basic values characterized by strict universalization, on the one hand, and different kinds of power, on the other hand. Even though there are various connections between basic values and the striving after power, the latter cannot be termed a basic value. The reason lies in the fact that nobody can admit to seeking power for its own sake. The striving after power must always be justified against a background of collective welfare or basic values which are supposedly promoted by its use. Yet only power in the sense of resources for action allows the implementation of basic values.

Like security, power is thus a basic principle. Hence, the important question in connection with power is not whether there is any, but how it is distributed. Whenever there is a lack of central control at the political and cultural level of a system, basic values become important. If in what follows some stress is laid on equality and efficiency this by no means implies that security and power are unimportant. This preoccupation rather points to certain particularities of Western society as well as to the fact that security and power are basic principles that have also determined the shape of earlier community formations.

A further problem we will have to address arises from the fact that the principles through which structures are constituted are not fully compatible and are in fact basically contradictory. This once more hints at a special kind of conflict theory: conflict exists not only at the level of interests, but already at the level of pre-social principles.

THE STRIVING AFTER EFFICIENCY

If one takes the term efficiency literally, a central aspect becomes evident: the Latin word *efficere* means "to bring about something." With regard to man this implies creating something that underscores individual differences. Such differences are not only rooted in varying talents, they are also a result of the autonomy of human will. The fundamental freedom of action of man as a reasonable being renders different actions and results possible. It leads to differentiation as a result of action—even beyond varied talents and even if the external conditions of actions (norms and opportunities) are strictly uniform. Of course, power may restrict or suppress the freedom of action for its object as well as its subjects, yet it can only conceal the claim to liberty.

A notion of efficiency that includes freedom—i.e., autonomous human action—implies dropping the concept of efficiency used in physics. In physics effort, earlier also called "effect," refers to the work performed as a result of a given force applied over a given time. Human action is more: the possibility and the claim to freedom—to autonomy of action. The process of human action is basic to human work (Bornschier 1981) as well as to the claim to liberty. The striving after efficiency thus covers an absolute claim which shapes social structure in the special historical system of Western society.

Ralf Dahrendorf (1979: 202) has argued that freedom signifies autonomous human action and that different actions do not differ in dignity or meaning. Like Aristotle before him, Dahrendorf distinguishes between two components of human action: work and activity. In this duality activity (vita contemplativa) refers to the individually chosen component and work (vita activa) to the externally determined component. For Aristotle this ordering also implied a hierarchy of social classes. In his conception the many were forced to lead a "practical" life in order to make a "contemplative" life for the few possible. Dahrendorf (1983a: 89) states: "This distinction has accompanied the passing centuries. No distinction has determined the formation of social classes more strongly than the one between 'those who must work' and 'those who do not have to work'."[3] Yet: "The claim to freedom is always absolute. Limitations of freedom occur, but this does not make them tolerable" (Dahrendorf 1983a: 91, our translation).

Freedom's various limitations cannot be detailed here. Rather, we shall now turn to some considerations concerning the important link between the striving after liberty and the striving after economic efficiency. Given a fixed time budget (24-hour day, limited life span) the claim to autonomy of action is limited by indispensable work which *has* to be done to secure survival. Autonomy of action can only increase if the time for necessary, i.e., existential work, is reduced. Time savings can either be used to reduce work time, thus rendering possible more free choice—true autonomy of action—or to improve the result of work so that consumption beyond basic needs becomes possible. No matter how time savings are used they are always inspired by an attempt to enhance the results of efforts. This leads straight to economic efficiency. Andreas Paulsen (1968: 9) advances a similar idea: "Like all creatures man needs a minimal amount of nutrition, clothing and housing to survive. If by his economic action he can only meet these basic needs, he lacks the true freedom of economic decision-making between alternative possibilities. Only a surplus sets activities free and renders possible the unfolding of all the values of civilization. Thus, one may say that economic action is oriented towards the acquisition and utilization of a surplus that goes beyond the basic needs of man as a natural being" (our translation).

Although the surplus from work as a consequence of increasing economic efficiency may be distributed quite unequally, the striving after liberty in the sense of self-realization and after economic efficiency are closely linked. The striving after efficiency includes individual realization and freedom as well as economic efficiency. The striving after greater freedom, namely autonomy of action, lies at the very core of the striving after economic efficiency (economy of time). Yet, the latter does not necessarily have to lead to more freedom for everyone. Any extension of the room for action is subject to, and is embedded in, social power struggles. For this reason, not only the claim to equality, but also the claim to liberty is very conflictive.

Under the modern capitalist division of labor the claims to freedom and economic efficiency are integrated in a special way. The use of energy for work, for activity, or any creative act must at least be compensated for by the exchange value of the outcome. Only this compensation justifies the use of energy under capitalist conditions. Here, the individual claim to efficiency must find a *compromise* with economic efficiency. The success of human creation is determined by its profitability. For this reason we may say that acts of creation that do not feed their creator either because they lack a market or because there is no effective demand for them, cannot be realized or, alternatively, must be subsidized (e.g., the arts). There is no possible resolution to his contradiction. Non-capitalist social systems, like traditional society, are organized around rigid normative structures. In such societies action is not subordinated to demands of economic efficiency, yet at the same time they do not admit individual claims to freedom.

THE STRIVING AFTER EQUALITY

The claim to equality is closely linked to the claim to liberty, yet it also oddly contradicts it. It can be derived from the basic equality that characterizes man as a thinking, speaking, rational, and meaningful being. Rational judgement is a precondition for freedom of will as well as for judgements concerning equality. In historical perspective one can point out that the claim to equality does not only appear in modern times. Already in the ancient concept of the *stoa* do we find the idea of equality of all men as natural beings endowed with reason, which reappears in the modern natural law traditions (Dann 1975). Interestingly enough, even outright pessimists in their judgement of man's nature, like Thomas Hobbes, assumed the natural equality of man. In *Leviathan* he writes: "Nature hath made man ... equal, in the faculty of body and mind" (Hobbes [1651] 1962: 110).

Granted the existence of a claim to liberty, equality in an "absolute" sense is a contradiction, because in this form it would admit no claim to freedom. We have to recall that freedom of will finally leads to inequality. Neither in the biological (genetic) nor in the social sense (and not even as a result of the freedom of will) is it possible to consider people as equals. At the same time, this paradox between the claim to equality and the multifaceted diversity of people constitutes a productive force, a contradiction, which historically made possible more equality in Western society. It is precisely the impossibility of realizing finally and fully the claim to equality which keeps this issue alive (Dahrendorf 1983b; Hondrich 1984).

The paradox can be resolved only by raising the problem of the *claim to justice.* If men are equal in principle, dissimilarity per se is not an argument for inequitable treatment or value statements that transform dissimilarity into inequality. Rather, justice demands that inequitable treatment or the assertion of inequality be justified. From an anthropological and natural rights point of view this justification is not discretionary. Rather, it remains linked to rational judgement and thus to equality in principle, despite dissimilarity.

The claim to equality thus arouses a striving after justice that, however, remains bound to the same source. Justice is always claimed in connection with distributional questions that affect the vital interests of people. The maxim here reads as follows: "Nobody shall be favored above another—*except that such treatment can be justified* (Kohler 1979: 143, our translation). Thus, even under conditions of uneven distribution strict adherence to the idea of equality in principle persists (Kohler 1979: 149). This argument points to Aristotle's linking of justice with equality, modernized by John Rawls (1972) as the principle of fairness. Still, justice is not equivalent to law. Rather, justice relies on the latter in a hyperpositive sense. Only thus can the striving after justice take a prominent place in the critique of legal conditions to become the impetus that has inspired different attempts to achieve justice through history (Kohler 1979: 136).

In what follows we will discuss three interpretational dimensions of the claim to equality: *equal treatment* (equality before the law), *equal opportunity,* and *equal value*. In other words: we will have to consider the transformation of the claim to equality into different kinds of the striving after justice that cannot be discussed without reference to the special circumstances of Western society.

The problem of formal equality before the law is well known: it is not necessarily fair to treat unequals (in the social sense) equally. The problems in connection with formal equal opportunity are also familiar: unequals (in a social sense) do not have the same starting conditions and opportunities. But even if there were equal starting points and opportunities one less obvious problem would remain. To allow maximum freedom, i.e., the full realization of individual efficiency, different outcomes of action would have to be of the same value. It is true that equal values would guarantee maximum freedom, yet society would become impossible because of the lack of a common measure of values. If, on the other hand, such a common measure exists and can be used to judge outcomes of actions, then different actions are not equally valid. Instead, one outcome is worth more than another. The transformation of dissimilarity into inequality despite equal starting points and opportunities supposes the existence of a value judgement. Without such a process of valuation society is inconceivable (Dahrendorf 1967).

Yet, there are ways to mitigate the inevitable valuation in society. In modern times the problem has been delegated to an anonymous and value-neutral institution: the *market*. The more abstract the central standard of values in society, the more freedom of action subordinates itself under this criterion. This is the case with market success measured in terms of money. The centrality of financial success therefore has an integrative function which partially eliminates the contradictions of the claim to justice that persist even under hypothetically equal starting points and opportunities. Still, freedom remains bound to the exigencies of economic efficiency. In addition, it must be stressed that the market is not a pre-social institution and thus does not qualify as a basic principle in our terminology. It is true that markets—i.e., price-regulated systems of exchange—have existed for a long time (since the Sumer civilization), but it would be wrong to conclude that they are "natural." Markets are and remain socially created and embedded institutions. This idea is encapsulated in Karl Polanyi's witty aphorism: "Laissez-faire was planned ([1944] 1978: 195)."

The problem of equal value can easily be discerned here. If there is a central measure of value and market exchange between unequal persons, equal value is difficult to achieve—even if all legal and economic reasons for inequitable treatment were to be removed. The market remains a mere device. Market society thus shifts the issue of justice to whether its special institutional mechanisms value results effectively. The attempt to achieve greater equality despite dissimilarity therefore supposes interventions into the interplay of supply and demand, i.e., the *redistribution* of opportunities measured in monetary terms. Such political interventions are conflictive because there are always winners and losers when compared to a situation without interference. Yet, the problem of equality as well as *distributional conflicts* can be mitigated in the following way: equal opportunities can also be interpreted in a temporal sense as a promise for the future. As this perspective posits growth and upward mobility as a result of structural change, it is conditional upon continuing economic development. In modern society, with its future-oriented notion of progress (Koselleck 1984), growth therefore attains a specific integrative function and thus acquires an important social role.

Here we are confronted with a last contradiction. Under an abstract measure of value a maximum of equal opportunity can lead to a maximum of economic efficiency. At the same time, however, maximal freedom is impossible and the claim to equality in the sense of equal value can only be met by resorting to redistributional means. Although these claims are fundamentally incompatible, it is nevertheless possible to imagine solutions that simultaneously provide for an improvement of equal opportunity, freedom, and equal value. In this context, mention can be made of the idea of providing a basic income for all and the achievement of a more encompassing degree of fully-fledged equal opportunity, which enhances economic efficiency and renders possible the redistribution of opportunities between individuals as well as between the realms of necessary work and freely chosen activity.

HISTORICAL CHANGES IN THE INTERPRETATION OF EFFICIENCY AND EQUALITY

The last remarks have pointed to possible changes in the interpretation of basic values. Before discussing the striving after security and power in the following section, the present section illustrates some historical changes of efficiency and equality over the past two hundred years.

Historically, the striving after efficiency became broadly embedded within the social structure of Western society during the expansion of the liberal project across the European continent after the French Revolution. The granting of civil liberties of economic action and political enfranchisement were the most important steps in this process. Christof Dipper, for example, emphasizes the changes in the interpretation of freedom during the first half of the nineteenth century: " 'Freedom' became such a legitimating feature of any rule that henceforth no regime could fail to call itself liberal (1975: 489)." Certainly, even after the broadening of the social conditions allowing for participation in "civil liberties," they remained connected to the predominant criterion of *economic* efficiency which, in turn, restrained the radical core of the claim to equality in the sense of universal individual development. Here, the radical basis of the striving after efficiency was merely concealed. However, across the trajectory of societal models it is possible to observe periodic shifts of closer, and then again weaker association of the two components of efficiency: individual development and economic efficiency. For the postwar era this is clearly shown by studies addressing value changes (see Inglehart 1977; Klages 1984).

With reference to the striving after equality we have mentioned three dimensions: equal treatment, equal opportunity and equal value. Equal treatment is anchored in the constitutional state's principle of equality before the law and has its historical roots in the homogenization of citizens during the modern nation-building process. Equal opportunity is expressed in the principles of freedom of the market and of trade. Here, the pioneers of capitalist development (particularly North Holland and England) took a certain lead even before equality before the law was formally established and before the liberal project spread to the continent in the past century. Further steps in the direction of a more encompassing guarantee of equal opportunity are also represented by opening access to schooling and the extension of the franchise, both begun in the second half of the nineteenth century. Equal value, finally, began with the construction of the welfare state in the first half of the twentieth century. The welfare state creates a minimal base of equal opportunity which is extended and guaranteed by citizenship and not conditional upon individual economic performances. The idea of equal value or equality in the outcome can be discerned in the award of a basic income, already partially guaranteed by old age pensions. Thus, proven performance in the market is not the only criterion for the value of a person, but also his or her wants and needs.

Beyond these broad historical lines it is also possible to identify different developmental phases within one and the same societal model. This can be illustrated using evidence for the trajectory of the latest societal model. In the formative phase there was strong identification with new creative opportunities opened up by the rising technological style. Even though there was a broad cultural consensus that efficiency primarily meant economic efficiency, the component of individual fulfillment was not eliminated from the dominant culture. Creativity or self-fulfillment at work resulted in high levels of work satisfaction—differences in these levels depending upon the kind of work, of course. In the repletion phase of the model, during the 1960s, a certain consolidation and institutionalization of the creative process was reached. It became increasingly formalized within ever-expanding organizations. The distribution of original and new identification objects (new products) led to their trivialization and to increasing marketing problems.

In this phase a split in the interpretation of efficiency began. Due to the persisting broad societal consensus the interpretation, in the dominant culture, of the formal structure was biased towards economic efficiency, whereas claims to individual fulfillment were increasingly relegated to leisure and various subcultures. As a result, work satisfaction began to dwindle, and this loss had to be made up increasingly by material rewards. Thus, split interpretations of efficiency coexisted in society. At a high level of material well-being a wave of self-realization with growing cultural diversity unfolded which collided increasingly with the market-related, "one-dimensional" interpretation of efficiency and thus served to weaken the societal model from within.[4] In the course of the dissolution of the societal model and the accompanying economic decline a loss of identity and ritualism became predominant. Conflict management is increasingly handled individually and via extremistic, oppositional marginal groups as well as new social movements (Meulemann 1983: 790).

As for efficiency, there have also been changes in the interpretation of equality in the trajectory of the societal model of the postwar era. At the outset, in the charismatic phase of the new products, a strong emphasis on the temporal aspect of the claim to equality can be expected: getting tomorrow those things some have already acquired today. On this basis social cohesion around common values became possible.

As in the case of efficiency, the formerly charismatic products of the new technological style (e.g., cars) became part of normal life as a result of their mass production. These products became a "common floor" (Dahrendorf 1983b) that was within reach of everyone and therefore lost any positional meaning (Hirsch 1976). As a result the temporal interpretation of equal opportunity reached its limits. The claim to equality shifted to positions that more or less secured the provision of a range of products. The typical middle-class issue at hand was one of equal opportunity in the filling of such positions and of equal starting points, mediated by the educational system. At the same time, and particularly on the part of the lower classes, the claim to equal value became more accentuated to level positional privileges in the distribution of material rewards. The accent on equal value in the lower class—as opposed to equal opportunity in the middle classes—arose because socially defined prerequisites for participation in the competition for positions, i.e., educational and occupational qualifications, were lacking. This was the time of reforms aimed at greater justice. The reform of the educational system aimed to create more equal opportunity whereas equal value was tackled by extending the redistributive welfare state.

On the one hand, society's positional structure came under increased legitimatory pressure during this phase. On the other hand, competition for the privileged positions in the social division of labor became "frustrating," to use Fred Hirsch's (1976) terminology. The lower classes lacked the social prerequisites (formal education beyond compulsory schooling) to take part in that competition and in the middle classes the promise of equal opportunity led to an excess of socially defined prerequisites for profitable positions. Furthermore, the central measure of value—money—progressively lost its integrative power as formerly charismatic products became part of normal supply as a result of market saturation.

For these reasons claims to equality became increasingly radical and finally exceeded the adaptive capacities of the societal model. Conflict management and articulation remained confined to class-specific contexts, the command over educational resources being the central variable. The middle classes frequently articulate radical claims to autonomy whereas the lower strata are preoccupied with redistributional issues. Since those possessing higher educational qualifications have easier access to alternative measures of value the conflict takes the shape of a conflict of measures. As a result of a radical claim to equal opportunity the claim to autonomy requires that the outcomes of individual action be equally valid. This would not only imply maximum freedom, but also the end of society, since different outcomes without any common measure of value result in "indifference." The increasingly privatized individualism of groups and persons in the downswing is but one expression of this indifference that further undermined the original cohesion of the model. People lacking higher educational qualifications articulated their claims to equivalence, thus intensifying the distributive conflict.

The downswing was thus marked by a somewhat paradoxical coincidence: the spread of post-materialist value priorities with their emphasis on self-fulfillment on the one hand, and an intensifying distributive conflict that affected the value dimension of money, on the other hand.

THE STRIVING AFTER SECURITY AND POWER

Whereas the striving after liberty and equality can be attributed to universal human features, the characteristic element of power is not its universalism but its exclusiveness. Certainly, freedom supposes the existence of power, i.e., will power. At the same time, the limitation of power imbalances constitutes another condition for freedom. The problem of power is thus essentially a problem of distribution, i.e., of the exclusiveness of power.

What then is power? The question refers to a central, yet strangely obscure analytical dimension of sociology. To be sure, Max Weber's (1964: 152) classic definition of power is widely known: "'Power' is the probability that one actor within a social relationship will be in a position to carry out his own will despite resistance, regardless of the basis on which this probability rests." Such a definition of power does not explain what it is, however. Rather, it makes a prediction at the level of action that reads: if two social actors have different amounts of power, the stronger will eventually prevail in a confrontation. Thus, the definition contains assumptions it would have to explain: power and strength as well as their distinction.

The problem of strength and enforcement is known from nature. In a formal perspective, the problem of power therefore is something that man shares with all creatures that engage in any transactions. If we conceive of society as the regular interaction of people it becomes clear that without power structures a multitude of relational patterns would be the result of mere chance. For any person it would be possible to be sometimes the stronger and sometimes the weaker partner in confrontations. Against this background the ever-present striving after power can be explained by an attempt to create a stock of potential resources for action so as always to be stronger, no matter what the circumstances. The creation of such a stock, the accumulation and preservation of resources for action, has costs in the form of outlays of energy and strength: power thus has to be reproduced to fulfill its function as a resource for action.

The striving after power is a principle exactly analogous to the striving after efficiency and equality. That power becomes a social force is due to the *striving after security*. It is typical for the human striving after security that the resulting power—as the social manifestation of the striving after security—is in fundamental opposition to the striving after efficiency and equality. With reference to the first principle power means lack of freedom, whereas it implies inequality—at least between groups—in terms of the second principle. Yet, power also represents a stock of opportunities for action and it therefore is a condition for the realization of basic values. On the one hand, power (in the sense of such a stock) is a necessary condition for autonomous action, i.e., for achieving one's self-interest. If, on the other hand, the power thus employed interferes with the opportunities of others, there is conflict with the claim to security. Power therefore is not just positively connected to the striving after security: power aspirations without a social frame of reference and without social responsibility are illegitimate.

There are a multitude of culturally shaped ways to transform the striving after security into power. The striving after power can be manifested in different ways and thus may lead to different distributions of power. The following are three ideal-typical ways to achieve security and continuity:

1. Reciprocity: Opportunities for action are not used exclusively for oneself but some are shared within a group in order to claim reciprocity if needed (principle: insurance).

2. Redistribution: Opportunities for action which actually belong to others are used for oneself (principle: skimming off).

3. Accumulation: Precautions are taken by not grasping existing opportunities but saving them instead for later use (principle: economy).

The different patterns of the striving after power are not identical with the various sources of power. Rather, different sources can be combined in the striving after power. In the following section three kinds of power will be discussed: social power, cultural power, and economic power.[5]

SOCIAL POWER

Groups and associations are an important and frequently neglected basis of power. In the first instance, social power is power that is institutionalized *within groups*. This statement refers to reciprocal networks of relationships that create solidarity and thus systems of insurance. In the private sphere as well as in formal organizations, the maintenance of reciprocal networks involves considerable expense (Bourdieu 1983). Group solidarity creates societal power in which members participate and which can be mobilized in their interests, although it does not "belong" to members individually. A member of the group may symbolize the power and represent it internally as well as externally. This would be the prototype of *political power* that was originally social power. Participating in group power has a price for individuals that goes beyond the mere maintenance of exchange relationships based on reciprocity. Such groups or communities are characterized by a common culture. Compliance with its norms is an additional price that usually appears quite acceptable because the individual is deeply rooted within the group's norms and interpretation of the world. In addition, the group has the power, i.e., the means of compulsion, to enforce conformity.

One important feature of groups is the maintenance of boundaries that discriminate between the internal and external sphere. This boundary is expressed by membership. Since expulsion of a group member implies a loss of power for this person, the mere threat of it creates pressure to conform. If, apart from persons, there are no other resources to be concentrated and monopolized by the group, only limited differences of power between various groups are possible. This was the case over most of the history of mankind. To be able to reproduce their accumulation of power constantly, groups were compelled to remain small; the extent of sociability being limited, people could only maintain a limited network of social relations based on reciprocity. Such limitations of power differentials between groups no longer exist in more complex societies, however, because of the division of labor, professional specialization, technology in the form of tools and weapons as well as more complex systems of coping with the world intellectually. As a result, groups may specialize along the lines of such resources. Professions are the normal starting point of specialized groups, as well as the social intercourse of members who see themselves as equals. Such circles try to stay exclusive in their control over the resources that are the shared basis of their power. Stringent rules and conditions of admission—closure—characterize these groups, which sometimes even resort to marriage regulation to keep the group closed over time.

This type of striving after social power based on the deliberate closure of groups to maximize solidarity has been present throughout history. The resulting power differences between groups were conditioned by the functional importance of the resources brought together by the members. Apart from classic professional associations, the comparatively new professional groups of top managers of big corporations spring to mind as examples. In their attempt to secure their own and their organization's fortunes they accumulate social power by engaging in a multitude of group relationships that stretch beyond their own corporation. This is shown by the multitude of interlocking directorates in present-day society.

To sum up, social power is power generated by solidarity and/or closure and shared through membership. In modern times, however, this has not been confined to aggregating social power by limiting group size (exclusivity). Rather, mechanisms have arisen to expand group size to advance collective social power.

The *modern state* is the most powerful expression of social power by *expansion* of the group (see chapter 10). The expansion of a group to become a national public requires an administrative apparatus and the delegation of joint action to this apparatus.[6] This in turn leads to the emergence of political power and a partial formalization of the group. Social power thus becomes the aggregate of an apparatus (formal organization) and a national public. Yet, it is not only the modern state but a variety of other, quite diverse agglomerations of power in terms of their social basis which fall under this type of social power. Examples are trade unions or car clubs whose attempt to broaden their bases distinguishes them from typical professional associations.

The lasting and stable increase of social power by group expansion depends upon an administrative apparatus to manage group power. In a historical perspective this apparatus—the *formal organization*—was not only the result of the concentration of economic power but also due to the expansion of societal power which, however, to a certain degree, is always economically motivated.

Social power is extended by the group. It unites the striving after equality and power in the following way: social power enforces internal conformity with the group's norms so that the group becomes a more or less intimate community or, even more frequently, an association of interests. The elements of the social distribution of power are therefore conditional upon internal equality. The preservation of homogeneity and thus solidarity as a source of power may even imply a certain redistribution of resources. This internal ethic of equality is in contrast to an ethic of inequality in the realm external to the group. According to this ethic it is quite normal that internally equal members enjoy privileges in prestige, economic opportunities, and political access not shared by others.

Societal power institutionalized within nation-states is therefore an important dimension of the distribution of power in the world system. In the next chapter the dynamics of the world system and the world political economy will be addressed in more detail. Here, it is important to note that the distribution of power within large groups may be affected by countervailing power. A classic case of countervailing power is the coalition of the many against a certain power that originated in comparatively small groups which managed to effectively monopolize resources. The coalition of those who only own their labor power (trade-unions) against entrepreneurs is an important example of recent origin. Freedom of worker association was a late but decisive step towards the modification of the societal distribution of power (see also chapter 6). A further example from the postwar era is the developing countries' coalition within the Group of 77.

CULTURAL POWER

Culture begins with the manner of thinking and therefore with the imagination of *alternative* worlds as well as its intersubjective mediation, i.e., communication. Culture is a stock of positive knowledge and concerns values, norms, customs, technologies and modes of procedure. It has an ideal component relating to human consciousness as well as an objective expression in cultural artifacts and objects (e.g., books and machines).

Within any given culture there is a tension between the knowledge of everyday practice that produces identity and meaning and the fact that it is possible to imagine alternatives. Despite such alternatives a group's culture is forced to establish its manner of confronting the world as the only correct, admirable, and reasonable way. The self-evident behavior of groups is based on this cultural principle. Groups normally live simultaneously under a kind of "democracy" concerning participation in the common culture and a "dictatorship" concerning positive knowledge. The cultural power arising from this ranks group power ahead of individual power.

In simple cases cultural power is not separated from social power but part of it. Yet, even in simple societies cultural power may already be singled out, for example in the person of the magician or the judge. Separated from social power, cultural power may itself become the power basis of a group. Thus exclusive groups may claim a monopoly for interpreting the world (religion, art, science) and for practice (professional wisdom). Examples are castes of priests, professional associations, groups of scientific experts, or research institutes that play a role in the formation of public opinion. Such groups are often internally structured as communities.

If the interpretation of the experienced world as well as the exploration of alternative worlds becomes the privilege of certain groups, domination results. In an evolutionary perspective, however, this has also favored a long process of calling cultural power into question: as a differentiated system, culture necessarily had to become more abstract to integrate the various realities of groups based on it. The written word and systematization were important bases for cultural symbols which could, in principle, become accessible by learning.

Religion, art, and science (jurisprudence, philosophy and natural science) are the arenas newly shaped at the beginning of modernity. As a result of Europe's decentralized social structure the Catholic Church lost its unquestioned authority over what is right, beautiful and thinkable. Truth, virtue and beauty were emancipated and secularized. The media of cultural exchange, namely written language and printing technology, made possible a universalistic broadening of culture, i.e., beyond the certainties of particular groups. On this basis the modern universities, intellectuals and professionals came into existence.

Under modern conditions the appropriation of cultural power takes place at two separate levels: first, at the level of acculturation, i.e., socialization concerning existing cultural knowledge; second, at the level of the exploration of alternative worlds, i.e., expansion of cultural power by placing particularistic experiences of the world into perspective. This process is governed by a specific modern institution: the school.

The modern *educational system* is an important, though not the only, place of controlled appropriation of knowledge (secondary socialization) partially independent of primary groups. As the school homogenizes the accumulation of knowledge it adapts itself to cultural integration beyond groups. This feature of the school system points to its importance in the process of nation-building to be discussed more fully in chapters 9 and 10. At the same time, the educational system segregates stocks of cultural knowledge according to grades and thus creates cultural power differences.

In the modern school system the basic cultural tension between common knowledge and reasonable exploration of alternative worlds is regulated in a specific way. We are referring to the fact that both elements are integrated within one overarching school system from kindergarten to university. Although different elements are stressed at different stages, segregation is not complete. Schooling thus leads to cultural power differences smaller than they would be without formal education. The modern school hence promotes equal opportunities—even though historically there have been differences in the degree to which this was the case.

The school transforms education into graduated formal training and also generates cultural power. This is done by an objectification of knowledge formerly bound to persons. Degrees and certificates as the expression of this objectivation are tradable so that exchange rates between different kinds of power can be established within the societal structure. At first sight and independent of the pool of talents in society, the gradation of formal education established by the school system appears to contradict the principle of equal opportunities entirely. This problem becomes less pressing, however, if one remembers that schooling only renders possible exchange rates between different kinds of power, thus creating a certain amount of *equivalence* in the horizontal dimension of societal stratification. Equality in the access to higher schooling would be of modest instrumental value if there were no norms of equivalence between school certificates and degrees on the one hand and societal positions on the other hand. Thus, the extent of equal opportunities at school remains bound to the state's and the economy's occupational structure, which in turn is conditioned by the technological style.

The distribution of cultural power is subject to processes of change, too. During the trajectory of the latest societal model the modern mass media (press, radio, television) have contributed to a distribution of cultural power within present society that is more homogeneous than it would have been if schools alone had been responsible for cultural power. The mass media are a countervailing power against established cultural power (particularly the sciences), and the change in the distribution of power is based on a broadening of participation in the cultural discourse.

In a functional perspective, the mass media are for culture what trade unions are for social power. Both are systems of countervailing power and both are criticized by the established elites of societal and cultural power. The rejection of television by sections of the educational elite is a case in point.[7]

ECONOMIC POWER

Anybody owning economic means, the so-called factors of production, has power. There are two questions attached to this simple statement. First, what exactly are factors of production?; and second, who owns them? Normally attention is directed towards two factors of production: financial power and labor power. In their pure form both have one thing in common: they are *potentialities*. In their abstract form, they can do anything and nothing: financial power is merely an action resource measured in monetary terms and labor power is simply everybody's work potential.

Only the *organized combination* of both results in economic power. It is not only money and pure labor power that interact in this organized combination, however, but also objectified forms of cultural power (use of energy, tools, and machines), personalized cultural power (know-how), and the environment structured by social power: institutional regulations and infrastructure—in short the social order, which may possess different degrees of legitimacy. The combination of various sources of power results in a structure that only thus combined can be truly termed capital—capital because it is *the* economic factor and *the* economic power. Capital then refers not only to things one can own as, for example, objectified forms of cultural power or real estate, but also to the combination of many components. Some of them cannot be acquired or transferred to other owners. They can only be "rented" or procured as public goods. Therefore private property in the sense of personal ownership must be distinguished from capital. Not only analytically, but also in reality, ownership and control are to a considerable degree separated under conditions of present-day capitalism (see below).

At the level of economic enterprises the components of capital are only potentialities. Structured components represent organizational effort in which the discrete elements do not simply add up. Rather, there is an outcome from the interaction under organizational effort: synergy. Those who engage in working with factors of production are called entrepreneurs. Further, it is important to note that there are not only economic but also social, political, and cultural entrepreneurs.

Organizations do not have to be built from scratch every day. There are standard solutions for the formal organization of economic enterprises—cultural patterns which undergo long-term changes and therefore are part of the transition of the technological style. The shaping of formal organization as a standard solution for an epoch is the result of the diffusion of innovations. To the extent that organization is consolidated it may, however, become a barrier to further innovative activity. Technological styles are cultural products and for that reason they, too, exhibit the contradictory features of culture: the tension between positive knowledge and practice, on the one hand, and the alternatives that can reasonably be imagined, on the other hand. For that reason innovators do not appear regularly; they turn up more frequently when a technological style reaches its limit of saturation due to formalization, standardization, and routine. This phase of change in the technological style in opposition to settled power constellations in the cultural, social, and economic realm is the heyday of entrepreneurship, whereas the phase of standardization is marked by the exploitation of the newly formed organizational power sources by established societal groups, as for example finance capital, trade unions, or the state.

The economic logic of formal organization is a result of the fact that aggregate power is greater, i.e., of more value, than the sum of its parts (the aforementioned synergy effect). Such surplus value may result from the undervaluation of the contributions of the component parts of power to the total product. Yet, undervaluation is not absolutely necessary and thus not the only source of surplus value (see chapter 8). Surplus value may simply result from of a combination of factors of production more efficient than an alternative combination. The modern corporation marks the rise of a new entity in the social realm, an artificial person, which not only produces this surplus value but also owns it. Individual persons, on the other hand, are restricted to claims on output. Ownership in the classic sense and control as well as claims on output have thus been separated in a complex way.

The various sources of power can be combined to intensify each other's effect. In addition they can be transformed so that one source can be used to attain another. In so doing, energy is spent. If such a process of transformation is subject to an assessment of utility leading to a valuation of power expenditures and gains in monetary terms we can speak of *economies*. Mediated by money—the universal measure of value—financial power plays a central role here.

It is important to note that the economy is only apparently a closed system and thus not distinct from other societal domains. This is shown by the aforementioned transformation of different kinds of power. The economy is the sphere of economic action, yet it is permeated by economically motivated behavior (see Weber [1921] 1972, and chapter 3 for a discussion of this distinction). The latter happens if social power is used to gain economic advantages. Trade union power, for example, can be used to achieve or expand participation in financial and organizational power, wage increases, and joint management in plants. Social power can also be used to influence legislation that concerns economic action as, for example, regulations about working hours and safety. Associations of firms, so-called cartels, can be used in a similar fashion. Their activities are thus not confined to mere mutual agreements concerning markets, quality, and prices.

In many important respects, cultural power is also economically motivated. In connection with the educational system we have already pointed to the fact that gradations in formal education form the basis for establishing exchange ratios between cultural power and the remaining positions in society. In addition, state power as a political form of social power is, after all, economically motivated. States tax economic activity and produce public goods, i.e., prerequisites for action. These themselves constitute factors of production; "protection" enters the economic process at varying degrees of quality and cost and will be discussed in the following chapter.

Capital is unfolded by organization and factors of production. This leads to organizational power. In addition, formal organization also led to the emergence of a new entity in the social realm. Modern society began with two new entities: the *individual* and the absolutist state as a predecessor of the modern *state*. In the course of its evolution a third entity was created—the artificial person bearing various names: limited liability company, business corporation, trust, stock company. The natural person as the bearer of property and sovereignty rights—one of the leading ideas of Western society—is confronted with a new organizational form, the artificial person (Coleman 1974). In the twentieth century the artificial person began a triumphal progress around the globe only paralleled by that of the modern states. Further, the artificial person's progress is not confined nationally; rather, it merges together economic activities beyond states. What are presently known as *transnational corporations* may later on well be seen as the predecessors of a new global reality—quite similar to the absolutist states that were the predecessors of the modern states. Every day the newspapers are full of reports on how this new system expands by take-overs and big corporate mergers.

This is another phenomenon that points to the relevance of the international dimension, which will be addressed in the following chapter. Three central institutions that serve the production, differentiation, and administration of power (firms, schools, and states) have been mentioned in this chapter; they will be discussed further in chapters 8 through 10.

NOTES

1 Medieval society saw itself as a hierarchically structured whole of entities which were subordinated to each other and held specific positions with associated functions (bellatores, oratores; laboratores; see Duby 1981, 1984; Bloch 1982; Ganshoff 1977). According to James Coleman (1974) this organic structure broke up under pressures that originated at both ends of the hierarchy. The peak of the hierarchy (the monarch) as well as the bottom layers (individuals) gained in power and functional importance. For further comments on the institutional structure of modernity see also Münch (1984).

2 The declaration of the rights of man as such (Süsterhenn 1961)—the so-called human rights—began a long time before the American and French revolutions. The first declaration of human rights on the basis of natural rights can be found in the preface to a law enacted in 1289 in Florence: "Because liberty as the basis of will cannot be conditional upon alien criteria but must be based on self-determination; because personal freedom derives from natural right—the same that protects peoples from oppression, that protects and elevates their rights—we are determined to preserve and enhance it" (quoted in Raith 1979: 29, our translation).

3 Dahrendorf (1983a) points to a similar distinction in the writings of Karl Marx who combines Aristotelian and Kantian elements to set the empire of necessity against the empire of freedom.

4 Daniel Bell (1976) interprets this cyclical process as a trend which will eventually lead to the disintegration of capitalist society: A "new hedonism," always present in capitalist culture, thereby undermines the Protestant ethic.

5 Pierre Bourdieu (1983) has addressed the distinction of social, cultural, and economic "capital." Although we do not subscribe to Bourdieu's use of the term capital, we nonetheless must acknowledge the inspiration we have derived from his contribution. In addition, John K. Galbraith (1984) also lists three instruments or methods to exert and enforce power, namely condign, compensatory, and conditional power. Furthermore, he points to three sources of power: personality, property, and organization. Although his model is somewhat similar to our own perspective it is not identical.

6 In our perspective another reason for the sweeping career of the modern state as a generator of social power via the nation-state lies in the fact that it uses the gap in social ties that the differentiation of modern society necessarily brings about for the accumulation of its power. Individuals participate in a large number of groups so that the feeling of community (we-feeling) diminishes. Societal differentiation results in a reduction of solidarity because people participate necessarily, but only to a limited degree, in different spheres. With the emergence of an apparatus, politics, in the sense of the competition of parties, arise (Weber [1921] 1972: 539, 837ff.). Parties are themselves social groups that compete in order to capture the apparatus. The homogenization of the national public to produce a we-feeling and limited competition in the occupation of the apparatus historically preceded mass-democratic participation and control of the state apparatus by the people (see also chapter 10).

7 Further evidence for such a perspective can be found in the way the elites of both countervailing powers are recruited. A 1972 study of 3,500 elite positions in the former Federal Republic of Germany shows, for example, that in the trade unions and the mass media only two or three out of ten position holders had a higher educational degree—the average for all elite positions being seven out of ten holding university degrees (Bolte and Hradil 1984: 187).

3
THE REGULATIVE IMPACT OF THE WORLD MARKET

THE WORLD POLITICAL ECONOMY AS A SELECTIVE FRAMEWORK

According to historical settings, efficiency (self-determination and economic progress), equality, security and power—the four basic structuring principles—are related to each other in changing institutional frameworks and represented by different actors. Since these principles are contradictory and not fully compatible, one must ask why one of them did not triumph over the others in the long run.

"Realists" would immediately think of power as the probable candidate for survival in the process of social evolution. Yet, why did the two central values of modernity—the striving after equality and efficiency—not vanish? Apart from some erratic ups and downs, the ideals of modernity have a stronger hold in social structures today than they did several centuries ago. In fact, there has been a trend towards convergence (see chapter 11), supporting the success of these. What is the reason for this? We are used to viewing civilization as a rising or unfolding process, but what are the conditions underlying this development?

The answer advanced here lays stress on the *world market for social order and protection*. Pivotal to the notion of a world market for protection is the idea that the historically possible (although not necessarily maximal) mooring of the central values of modernity in social structure led to comparative advantages in the competitive world milieu. The theory underlying the world market for protection argument is inspired by the work of Frederic C. Lane (1979) and emphasizes that social order, also termed *protection*, is a territorially bounded public utility. Production, trade, and financial transactions are conditional upon social prerequisites. They require protection. Property rights must be respected and people have to be motivated or forced to engage in exchange relationships. Protection is by no means a secondary factor of production but at least as important as labor, knowledge, organizational resources, financial means, and credit (Hintze [1929] 1964: 431). In our perspective, protection is a neglected element of national economic production functions. Governments, which can be understood as political undertakings, produce "order" and sell this public utility to capitalist enterprises as well as to citizens under their rule. By means of supplying this utility, governments affect the locational quality of their territory in the framework of the world economy.

In this connection it is possible to take up an idea advanced by Lewis Coser who bases his considerations of the functions of social conflict on notions developed by Georg Simmel (1908: chap. IV). According to Lewis Coser (1956: 95) conflict with another group leads to increased cohesion of the group. This idea can also be used for large groups at the level of the world system. Societies in an encompassing and competitive system tend to temper internal conflict to increase cohesion within society. This may be done by measures promoting solidarity whereby the function of cohesion would be international competitiveness.

Thus, states not only engage in politico-military competition but also in genuinely economic competition within this world market for social order. This is the case not only because capital and labor are to a certain extent mobile between states, but also because different social orders imply varying degrees of long-term economic success. Governments normally react quite sensitively to this world market for social order. In an attempt to keep their political and military equilibrium they are forced to produce the political preconditions for economic success. If they fail or only perform unsatisfactorily, they can neither attain nor preserve core status in the world economy.

In this sense the world economy must be understood as a *political world economy* that relates economic and state action as well as economic and politico-economic competition to each other. On the one hand, the world economy causes societal adjustment pressure that must be tackled by state political institutions. On the other hand, state action feeds back on the domestic as well as the world economy. As shown in figure 3.1, this feedback mechanism has three dimensions.

FIGURE 3.1 Elements of the World Political Economy

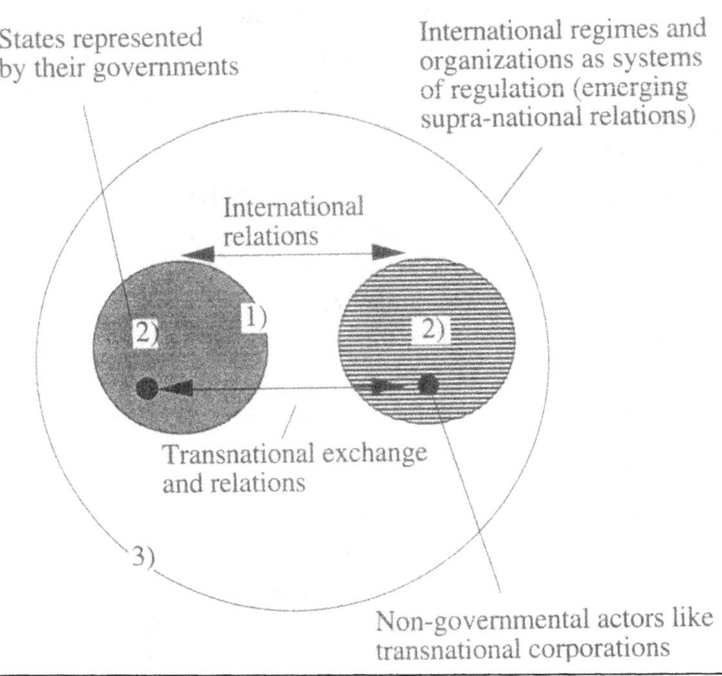

Source: Bornschier (1992: 329).

(1) First, given states determine the permeability of their boundaries by reference to economic transactions (e.g., regulation of trade, capital movements, or the migration of workers). (2) In addition, states create social order as a public, yet territorially bounded utility (e.g., by the legal framework in general and, for example, by way of an educational system with a certain degree of equal opportunities and special contents or a social security network). (3) Finally, states create social order by way of regulation systems which may be based upon mutual agreement between them or enforced by hegemonies. As a result of such international cooperation and constellations, public utilities come into existence which in this case are *transnational* utilities (e.g., trade systems like the GATT, the monetary system of Bretton Woods which, however, did not survive the hegemonic

decline of the USA).[1] The notion of a world market for protection stresses the second of these dimensions: the domestic social order as a means to achieve a favorable position in international competition.

THEORETICAL PERSPECTIVES ON THE LINKAGE OF POLITICS AND ECONOMICS

As mentioned above, comparative advantages must be viewed against the background of a world of economic and economically motivated competition which is frequently discussed in world-system analysis.[2] At a more general level, the relationship of the state and capitalism is central to this discussion. Thus, one must address a problem recently revived by Niels Steensgard (1981: 272): the somewhat strange coincidence of two unique phenomena—the emergence of the modern state and the development of capitalism.

The relationship between the modern state and capitalism has been discussed in quite different ways for a long time. Early notions stressed a common determination of one by the other. Interestingly, the idea of the influence of state action and non-action on the economic process is shared by mercantilists and liberals. Yet, the prescriptions for state action derived from this insight are entirely different (absolutism versus liberalism). Orthodox Marxism, on the other hand, typically stresses a reversed, one-sided causal relationship. The economic unfolding of the means of production brings about the state. In the materialist perspective, the state is capitalism's ideal super capitalist that does what is needed anyway: it secures capital utilization and the maintenance of class rule. Finally, Joseph Schumpeter's idea of an opposition between nation-state and capitalism—one being bound to territorial and particular orientations and interests, the other taking the whole world as its sphere—must be noted.

Another line of reasoning on the relationship between state and capitalism was pursued by such as Max Weber, Otto Hintze and Werner Sombart. The latter (Sombart 1928) stressed the common spiritual roots of capitalism and the modern state. For Sombart, one and the same "spirit" created capitalism, the new state, the new religion and science as well as technology at the end of the Middle Ages.

After the turn of the century Max Weber added an interesting new idea to the long history of thinking about the relationship between state and capitalism. Weber's ([1921] 1972: 815) reasoning is that the continuous, peaceful or belligerent struggle between competing states provides the choicest opportunities for modern capitalism. Any given state has to compete for the free-flowing capital that dictates conditions under which it is prepared to help state power develop. According to Weber, this constellation of competing states is the prerequisite for the development as well as the perpetuation of capitalism. Capitalism will only last as long as no world empire arises.

The idea that both important processes of the modern world system, i.e., state formation and capitalist development, are inextricably interrelated—representing but two sides of the same underlying social process (Hintze, [1929] 1964: 428)—was not fully elaborated by Max Weber due to his early death. Yet it has influenced various other theorists and recently received a new and very interesting interpretation by Christopher Chase-Dunn, who regards capitalism as a system in which political and economic processes can be understood to have a single, integrated logic (Chase-Dunn 1981, 1989). In similar fashion, Kennedy (1987) sees the political and military rivalry of states and the world economy as a mutually interdependent unity subordinated to an embracing overall logic.

Equally seminal was Max Weber's notion of economic behavior. He introduced the analytical distinction between *economic* and *economically motivated* action (Weber [1921] 1972: 31). Later Frederic Lane (1979: 51f.) further elaborated on the notion of economically motivated behavior which uses force as a means and suggested that violence, under certain conditions, may be productive. Max Weber's seminal ideas thus laid the ground for two further developments. On the one hand, there is the distinction between two types of enterprises that developed in modern times and which do not differ in their ends, but only in the means to achieve them: tribute versus profit logic—the *tribute* logic of the state being subordinated to the *profit* logic of capital in the modern world system. While Weber seems to imply that this is a characteristic of the world system as a whole we would rather suggest that it is the condition for attaining or maintaining *core* status in the world system (see below). On the other hand, the notion that not only economic activity in the narrow sense, but also force may be productive, and that "violence-controlling" elements must be included in economic analysis, is important.

It was Otto Hintze, however, who first formulated the idea of two enterprises. According to him the process of modern state formation can be regarded as a political undertaking alongside the economic one. In the long run the political undertaking can only be successful in striving after power if it is at the same time able to satisfy the vital needs of its citizens. Service to the public lies in the creation and supply of power for security and rule of law (Hintze [1929] 1964: 431f.).

In the work of Frederic Lane (1979) these ideas in the tradition of Max Weber and Otto Hintze reappear. Lane, a specialist on the history of Venice, sees both the notion of two types of enterprises and state power as a basis for utility and profit. This is clearly evident in the very title of his recent collection of essays *Profits from Power: Readings in Protection Rent and Violence-Controlling Enterprises* (1979). In the opening section, he asks: "Why did some groups of merchants prosper more than others, at some times and places? Why those of Venice more than those of Genoa?" (1979: 1).[3] As an answer, Lane formulated his *theory of protection rent*. He distinguishes two kinds of enterprises in the modern world system: "(1) those that produce protection and are called governments and (2) those that produce goods and other services and pay governments for protection" (1979: 2). The theory suggests that success in the world system is determined by a certain symbiosis between these two kinds of enterprises. In addition, Lane initiated a systematic treatment of the problem in comparative perspective. What are the consequences of protection if it is at certain times and in certain places produced with greater ease or at lower cost?

In order to fully understand Lane's theory of protection rent it must be acknowledged that not only are capital, land, labor, and technology factors of production, but so is protection. Protection, although politically created, shares certain characteristics with land, insofar as it is also *territorially bounded*. Thus, there exist not only land rents but also protection rents (Lane 1979: 25).

The theory can be stated from the point of view of states or capitalist firms: (1) That those states would be the strongest "which could combine a moderate tribute with effective protection conducive to innovation and investment" (Steensgard 1981: 271).

(2) That those capitalist firms would prosper the most which could choose or were fortunately placed in a network of economic transactions effectively protected at low cost. Advantages thus accrue to both sides: higher returns due to lower protection costs provide protection rents for

capitalists and enhance their accumulation, and higher returns due to more taxable income also provide a larger resource base for the state.

What we may add to this line of thought is that it is not the capitalist state *per se* that is most favorable to economic success, but the state that reconciles capitalist profit logic with claims to *legitimacy* among the citizens, based on demands for security, equality, and efficiency. Although legitimacy is attached to a social order, we suggest that its enduring effect does not rest on ideology but on features of the social structure which reflect the meeting of such demands.

In what follows, these extensions are to be spelled out more precisely.[4] Apart from introducing the world market for protection, two alternative factors of production—violence and legitimacy—are discussed. In addition to protection at the level of the world system, the issue of protection within territorialy bounded states must be adressed. This aspect was not formally excluded from Lane's work, yet not fully addressed. His examples refer to protection of the external sphere (e.g. the convoy protecting the Venetian trade fleet) and tariff policy in the strict sense.

THE WORLD MARKET FOR PROTECTION ARGUMENT

Three actors are relevant in the social system interpreted as the world market for protection. Political undertakings—which we normally call governments or states—are ultimately defined by their claim to territorial monopoly of physical force, which is also the basis for their capacity to raise resources (taxation being the modern form). This is called the *tribute logic.* Capitalist firms combine factors of production and sell products and services on markets in order to make profits. They are thus subject to the *profit logic.* The large majority of citizens sell their labor power either to political or economic undertakings to gain an income and to make a living. Yet, although subject to political and economic power, citizens have a unique option to invest a social order with various degrees of legitimacy. They are subject to the *logic of legitimization*. The degrees of legitimacy invested in a social order we see as depending on the extent to which claims to security, equality and efficiency are *fulfilled.* The compromise between these contradictory orientations of the three actors is regulated in the long run by the world market for protection.

Since various political undertakings offer social order, an important condition for characterizing the constellation of actors as a market is fulfilled. Nevertheless, consumers of social order are to varying degrees restricted in where they can buy that public utility because migration between territories incurs costs: transfer costs, loss of economic and social capital, and devaluation of cultural capital, to mention only material costs.

Despite such (sometimes significant) market imperfections, the actual or threatened shift of consumers to alternative supplies of effective social order forces different producers of that territorially bounded public utility into a competitive relationship. This may also be the particular outcome of the long-term economic consequences of different types of social order.

Since social order is a product with attached utilities, it must be produced. In principle, government can produce social order either by means of coercion, which rests on *force* as the ultimate means of state power, or it can adopt measures which change the social structure in such a way that capitalists and/or the population subject to the state's rule attach greater *legitimacy* to the social order. It may be argued that many different factors enter the production function of "protection." Thus, "violence" and "legitimacy" only refer to the two most abstract factors of the production. At a conceptual level they are independent (external force versus domestic agreement with an order) but, like capital and labor, they are also alternatives within a certain range. At the concrete level, however, there is a large and historically variable number of factors of production. The actual mix of factors in a given historical situation can be called "social technology."

Under the heading *force* we subsume all actual or threatened acts that aim at obliging actors to behave in a specific way or to avoid certain behavior, by any measures (threat of physical harm to persons and property, curtailment of freedom to act, to move, to express opinions, or to trade). Insofar as force is exercised on the basis of laws, we speak of a state under the rule of law or of an international order based on international law. Legality and democracy within a state territory substantially narrow the application of force. *Legitimacy* is extended by actors according to the degree to which they acknowledge and accept the rules of social action and their *results*.[5] Perfect legitimacy would occur if perfect consensus about values, norms and procedures existed. There are links between legality and legitimacy. But even under conditions of democracy these links are neither perfect nor must they necessarily be substantial. The missing congruence of both terms is reflected in the semantic meanings of *legal* (according to law) and *recognized* (legitimate). Even if the subjection to laws is based on majority vote, legality and legitimacy may not be congruent.

It must be stressed that even the most legitimate society cannot fully renounce the use of force (see Dahrendorf 1967). A certain minimum of coercion is necessary. On the other hand, the use of force stands in need of some kind of consensus, at least by certain sections of society. At a minimum, those responsible for actually using or threatening the use of force—and not only those who deliberately profit from it—must accept their task, i.e., they must be coopted. In other words: even if a maximum of force is used, legitimacy in the population cannot reach a value of zero.

These facts are reflected in figure 3.2 which shows the protection curve, i.e., the trade-off between force and legitimacy in the production of protection. From figure 3.2 it is evident that force and legitimacy cannot be wholly substituted for each other. Possibilities for substitution only exist in the zone delimited by the asymptotes in the coordinate field of force and legitimacy. This is shown in figure 3.2, which assumes an elasticity of substitution of -1.

Although *force* and *legitimacy* are partly alternative measures to produce social order, the world market for protection argument maintains that it is only *effective* social order which secures a competitive advantage in the long run, i.e., that which rests on legitimacy attached by citizens to it. This proposition needs further comment.

Social order is not a homogeneous product: it is of different qualities depending on whether protection is produced by *force* or by attached *legitimacy*. In the latter case we speak of high quality or effective social order. We must now introduce points on the social basis of preferences for social order of different qualities, applying the triple distinction between political undertakings as suppliers of social order, capitalist firms, and citizens as consumers of that territorial-bounded public utility.

Suppliers of protection are in general clearly not indifferent to the quality they produce. Legitimacy as a source of protection limits their power and thereby that portion of "taxation" they can consume as the ruling class. The political ruling class comes under different pressures. Private firms demand cheap effective protection, and their threat to invest abroad may force government to supply protection almost at cost. Thus the political elite has to renounce part of its potential income, a part of the income-generating capacity of the state being eventually shifted from the luxury consumption of political elites to protection rents for capitalists. This historical shift has of course accompanied democratization, but in comparative perspective such an outcome was not the rule, being largely restricted to core countries.

FIGURE 3.2 The Protection Curve

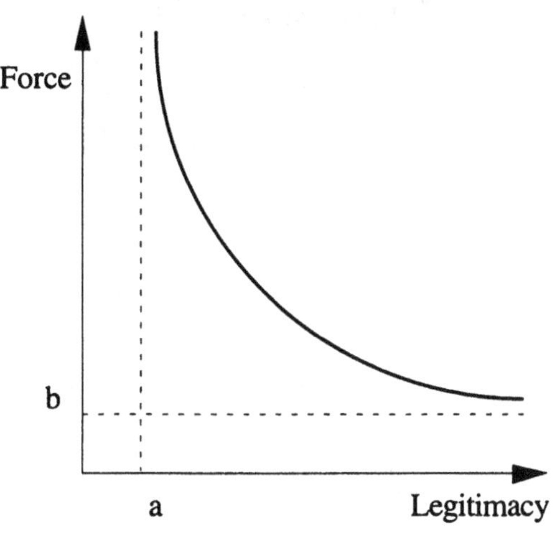

a: necessary legitimation minimum (asymptote)
b: necessary force minimum (asymptote)

With regard to the preferences of consumers of protection, we consider first those citizens who are clearly not indifferent. The majority prefers a social order of high quality. Citizens have three broad measures of resistance at their disposal in order to combat an illegitimate regime: (1) politico-military opposition to government; (2) political protest or votes against office holders; and (3) subtle measures of refusal by reduction of commitment. The opposition of citizens to a regime raises the costs of control and suppression for those in political power. They need to raise taxes to break or hold down resistance, which increases the costs of the state *without* improving the level and quality of protection.

Refusal as a more subtle form of resistance seems unspectacular, but should not be underestimated. It is probably among the most powerful weapons at the disposal of citizens, at least in the long run and in the competitive world environment. A reduction in commitment seriously impairs productivity since a lack of consensus about the social order reduces motivation in general, and work motivation in particular. In economic terms such losses may well outweigh working days lost through strikes.

As employers capitalist firms are thus also not indifferent to the kind of protection they can buy. In the first place they naturally prefer protection at low cost. But subsequently, pressed by world competition, they are interested in a motivated and loyal work force. It would be naïve to assume that the behavior of employers in general is characterized by a search for low costs *per se*. Primarily they optimize profit, and this may be easier to achieve if the factors of production they buy are of good quality and thus worth their price.

If a state tries to break resistance in a population by means of force, capitalist firms suffer from two disadvantages. First, they cannot rely any longer on a motivated work force, and, second, they must pay more for protection. Under such conditions capitalist production is clearly not impossible, as we know from numerous historical and contemporary examples, but such social formations are neither able to attain nor maintain *core status* in world production.

The hypothesis is, then, that on the world market for social order and protection sufficiently high quality protection is preferred. However, protection of high quality effective social order which is based on legitimacy given to it by the citizens has not always been the actual outcome of the world market at various places and times. Other solutions exist for other societies, but these for the lack of high quality protection are not the topic of this book and will thus only briefly be addressed here. Another reason is that the reaction of the world market even at the core of the world system is slow and does not penalize alternative solutions immediately, but only in the longer run.

The long run in more successful social formations at the core has always been characterized by protection options that favor legitimacy. This should be understood in comparative-historical terms, i.e., as compared to contemporary competitors. Only because of this were they successful and, for a while, leaders in capitalist development. Freer arrangements of wage labor, greater opportunities for larger parts of the population, and more liberal institutions were typical for all the industrial leaders of the modern world system. Over time this option, typical for ascending social formations, became even more urgent due to increasing levels of industrial complexity. Those who tried to wander along other paths never reached the peaks of the world industrial pyramid.

This pattern, however, applies to ascending social formations, as well as to those that manage to keep on top. Declining ones, and declining hegemonies in particular, lose their position partly because they gamble away their earlier competitive advantage in the protection market. External protection rents of hegemons may mask the decline for a while but will intensify it later since they cause the elites to neglect the claims of domestic legitimacy. This can be illustrated using historical and comparative data.

Before doing so, it seems appropriate once more to review certain analytical dimensions of protection within the framework of the protection curve described above (see figure 3.3). Three aspects of protection merit attention: the quantity of protection, its quality, and its price. The higher the price, the more costs are incurred by the consumers of protection.

FIGURE 3.3: Summary of the Analytical Dimensions of Protection

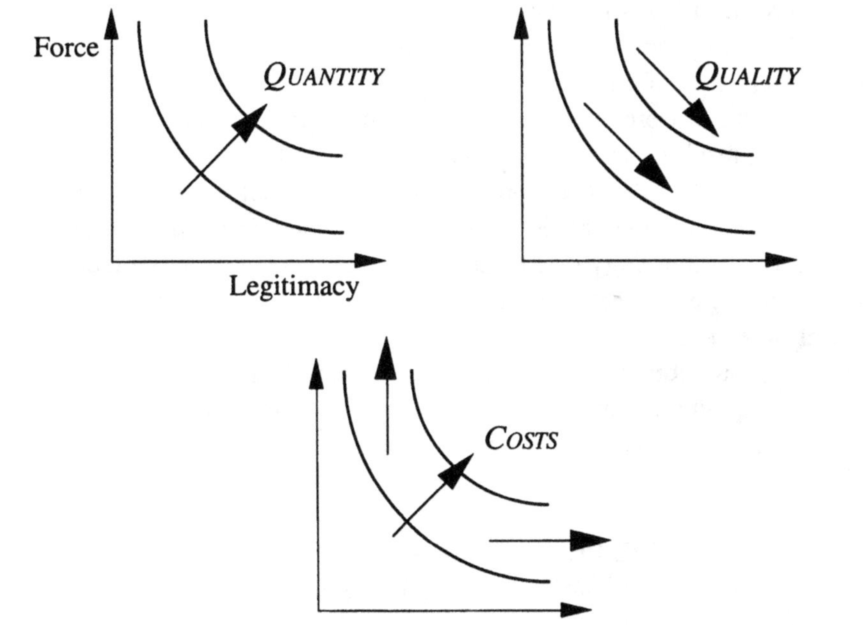

If an increased quantity of both factors is used, or if one factor is held constant and the other's use is increased, the result is a higher *quantity of protection*. In other words, we are leaving our protection curve for another protection curve situated at a higher level. This is shown schematically in figure 3.3. We can thus distinguish cases according to their location at different levels of protection.

At a *constant* proportion of factors of production the cost increases further with the quantity of protection produced. In addition, cost increases in both directions in the asymptotical parts of the respective curves. This can be deduced from the law of non-proportional returns which states that the return (here: the quantity of product), which is dependent upon the combined input of different factors, does not increase or decrease proportionally with the input of only one of these factors if the other inputs are held constant (Paulsen 1968, 2: 77).

The same quantity of protection of a given quality can imply different costs for its consumers. Lower cost is the function of a higher efficiency of production, which in turn leads to a protection rent for the consumers. Basically, there are three reasons for such an improved *efficiency* of production. A superior social technology may be used and/or less production factors may be expended and/or protection may be provided at cost. From an historical perspective, social technologies as well as the typical agents producing protection have changed. The class controlling the state, frequently of aristocratic origin, or the princes, who initially governed the state as if it were a family business, were forced to yield to professional managers, resulting in the market provision of protection at cost.

If we move in the direction of a substitutive increase of legitimacy on each protection curve, this implies an improvement in the *quality of protection* in our terminology (see figure 3.3). The reason lies in the fact that the same amount of protection is coupled with more domestic consensus on the social order and therefore with a higher level of motivation. Although the various protection curves represent situations of identical protection (so-called isoquants), protection is not a homogenous utility. In the eyes of consumers, the isoquants therefore are *not* indifference curves.

THE PROBLEM IN HISTORICAL AND COMPARATIVE PERSPECTIVE

Over the long run Western core society has shifted considerably on the protection curve. Compared to earlier times, violence has been exchanged for legitimacy to a considerable degree. But this process was neither linear nor identical in different countries.

During the first phase of modernity, i.e., until the beginning of the nineteenth century, European states became more dissimilar; this polarization was accompanied by a dramatic process of concentration reducing their number from about 500 to 25 (Tilly 1975: 27). The *absolutist state project* with its attempt to create a *world empire* included a movement towards greater violence on the protection curve. On the other hand, decentralized social systems of the *world economy* type—important predecessors being Venice, the Hanseatic League, North Holland, and later England and the United States—were positioned on the protection curve at a lower level, characterized by a higher degree of legitimacy. In the framework of the extended theory of protection rent it is no historical coincidence that the modern guise of state monopoly of physical force at the core can be traced back to this second developmental tradition.

At the beginning of modern times enterprises that differed substantially in their methods but not in their goals of creating wealth began to prosper. One institutionalized method was the tribute logic founded on domestic violence and external military conquests ("mergers" by marriage alliances were also typical).

The absolutist projects (Habsburg Spain, France) were subject to tribute logic. The profit logic, on the other hand, dominated in the decentralized world economy projects. Yet, it would distort the picture if the absolutist projects alone were viewed as war-like and violent whereas the later projects were interpreted as peaceful. Even Venice, the early example of the second type, was permanently entangled in military actions—for example against its arch-enemy Genoa, itself not an absolutist antipode—and became very competent in the military organization of its trade ventures.

The symbiosis of the two kinds of enterprises with their different traditions in the modern, territorial nation-state has only slowly and discontinuously emerged. Initially, long-distance merchants organized their own protection. To this end they often founded cooperatives, the prototype of the minimal state. The governments of the emerging territorial states earned profit for their family enterprises *("L'état, c'est moi")* and thus laid the foundations of mercantilism. The lack of clear-cut specialization at the level of the firm was first clearly noticed during Europe's overseas expansion (Lane 1979: 2). The big chartered companies were conglomerates of military, industrial and trade enterprises. King Henry the Navigator of Portugal acted after the fashion of state-trade countries later. The bulk of the receipts from the spice trade with the Eastern world went into his own purse, out of which he had to pay for the protection of the sea routes to India and its trading ports (Lane 1979: 17).

But how did the subordination of the reasons of state to the profit logic that eventually led to symbiosis and the supply of high quality protection at cost come to pass in the type of European state that was later to become dominant around the world? Usually how the monopoly of physical force as a source of tribute is organized within a territory is assumed to depend upon economic development and internal power struggles (see Lipset 1960, Lenski 1966). Yet, such a perspective is too limited. The history of nation building is not only a history of *internal* struggles but was also determined by the competition *between* territorial power monopolies. Certainly, this induced internal struggles and also helped to determine the positions of domestic adversaries (see also chapter 10).

The monopoly of physical force is territorially bounded and the world is limited. For this reason the competition for sources of tribute resembles a zero-sum game: one actor gains what the other loses. This is the motivation behind attempts to found world empires—the maximal extension of the mass of tribute, i.e. the world as an empire on which the sun never sets and which belongs to the sun-king. Yet, these attempts lead to immeasurable costs of protection. The financial needs of the armies are enormous and the adversarial armaments race leads to a waste of potential wealth. Examples can easily be found in the vast financial distortion and economic misery left by Charles V and Louis XIV. Yet, it is surprising that, despite these examples, attempts to create world empires continued throughout modern history up until the twentieth century.

The second line of competition is dominated by the profit logic. Competition is founded on relating protection cost to products and to improving their quality. Historically, this strategy can be traced back to modern concepts of social contract. It attempts to limit the cost of territorial power and international order by an enhanced and substitutive input of consensus. This seems reasonable enough, and it is no wonder that such notions of a world order made their first appearance during the European Enlightenment, and were rooted in humanism (see chapter 10). But how can reason prevail if one does not trust Hegel's "world spirit"? If the reduction of cost by way of order is retroceded to the consumers in the form of lesser tribute (taxes), this results, as already mentioned, in comparative advantages in accumulation, i.e., the development of capital and innovations are given a free hand.

Historically this process was initiated and perpetuated by the unbroken continuity of the world economies which successfully resisted attempts to create world empires. Such success was not only due to many world economies' geographical locations in marginal maritime zones or their fortunes in war, but also to the fact that they always had clear *economic advantages*. They were dominated by elites that were, despite recurrent tendencies towards aristocracy, primarily interested in profit rather than tribute. In due course, the economic logic and the existence of these societies in modern times (Venice, the Hanseatic League, North Holland, England) forced a new logic upon the European state system (see Weber 1923: 288f.).

The world market for protection is nothing less than the very structural peculiarity of the encompassing social system of modern times. Our observations thus explain an important linkage: the coincidence of the emergence of the modern state with the development of capitalism. These processes are coupled: mediated by market processes they are complementary. Capitalism cannot exist without protection, yet it can only develop in an accelerated fashion if the tribute exerted for protection is invested according to capitalist logic instead of being consumed by parasitical elites.

Still, the manner in which both logics were merged into a symbiotic relationship at the core is more complicated than would be expected on the basis of Max Weber's somewhat functionalistic arguments. Weber's model describes the final result, but only marginally examines the way leading to it. The phase of convergence and gradual amalgamation that began in the nineteenth century was preceded by centuries of conflict: the systems of North Holland and England, on the one hand, and the absolutist projects of Habsburg Spain and France, on the other hand, are the important historical protagonists of this process. At the same time they also serve as examples for another structural feature of the modern world system: the opposition of core and counter-core.

To sum up, we have proposed that the merger of tribute and profit logic during the emergence of the modern Western state was not a continuous and linear process. Rather it was quite conflictive and first led to the polarization of core and counter-core: world economy versus the absolutist state project, the latter connected with mercantilism. The capitalist logic only became dominant after the English Industrial Revolution because the leap in industrial productivity only left two alternatives to the counter-core: it could either fall back or adjust to the social structure of the leader in the world economy. A first wave of adaptation manifested itself during the liberal project around 1830 (see also chapter 7). To be sure, the broadening of the democratic and liberal movements also profited from the newly dominant logic.

Thus, the structure of social systems belonging to the *world economy* type fosters the emergence of *core states* that subordinate tribute logic to profit logic. As mentioned, this also favors the optimization of consensus and legitimacy within current historical alternatives These, for example, include the integration of populations without discrimination within a technological style, with its typical occupational and distributional structures as well as legitimation claims depending on population mobilization (Zwicky and Heintz 1982: 268). Against this background, the postwar societal model can be conceived as a specific step towards the world market for protection at the core. Governments were forced to behave as capitalist states, i.e., to renounce tribute logic, and to ensure internal legitimacy to compete in the world system so as not to be economically penalized in the long run. Under such effective social order capitalist firms and populations eventually share in the advantages of a territorially bounded public utility. What firms seem to surrender in not resorting to cheaper solutions than the welfare state they recuperate through a loyal and motivated work force and by widening their markets.

Constraints at the Periphery and the Semiperiphery

Even though periphery and semiperiphery are not the themes of this book, it is useful to briefly point to the constraints responsible for the unsatisfactory functioning of the world market for protection in these regions. Due to structural constraints the peripheral and semiperipheral states cannot attain the same levels of legitimacy as their counterparts at the core. Thus, protection provided by the state at the periphery is necessarily based more strongly on violence and society as a whole is normally less legitimate. The result is an indirect advantage for the rich core countries. Many possible competitors in the world economy are handicapped for structural reasons.

At the *periphery* the constellation of the three important groups—state class, capitalist firms and population—is quite different from the ideal type described above, upon which core status depends. The particularity of the state class at the periphery is due to the fact that its preferences can be articulated without being substantially modified by other actors. Even though the preferences of the three groups of actors are similar at the periphery and the core, the result of their interaction at the periphery is quite different from the historical development at the core, ending in the taming of the former state and democratic control of the new state class.

At the periphery, open popular resistance to the state class can easily be suppressed, and subtle forms of opposition very successful at the core—as for example the holding back or denial of services—are normally irrelevant. Finally, influential capitalist firms take an interest in the "law and order" function of the state without concern for the broader legitimacy securing such order. This constellation has only been possible because peripheries do not compete on equal terms in the world system. Rather, they specialize as producers of raw materials. In addition, the competition of systems as between core and counter-core resulted in considerable advantages for the state class at the periphery until recently. Only on this basis was it possible for the state class to behave in a way that gave preference to violence.

In this constellation the state class earns an income that can primarily be used for the consolidation of its own power because popular resistance cannot seriously threaten the sources of such income. In an enclave economy oriented towards raw material exports popular resistance is not very dangerous since neither as labor power nor as consumers are populations of substantial functional relevance for the economic system. These core-dependent raw material economies are the basis for the skimming off of tribute by the state classes. For capitalist firms, too, the mass of the population is irrelevant because it is not integrated either as workers or as consumers.

Among the easily taxable and abundant sources of income from which tribute for the state class as well as the maintenance of its tyrannic rule can be derived, *raw material rents* occupy first place. The role of raw materials is stressed by Hartmut Elsenhans (1987: chapter 1) who argues that the development process is blocked by their abundance. According to Elsenhans and contrary to "extra profits" in industrial production, which must be reinvested because competitors will start to imitate successful production sooner or later, raw material rents can be appropriated by the state class without having to disappear in the long run.

The economic resources stemming from raw material rents are further supplemented by easy access to credits, development financing from the core, and—very important for repressive purposes—military support from the core and the counter-core for the state classes. The latter in particular puts governments of peripheral countries in a good position to break popular resistance by applying or threatening to apply violent measures.

With reference to the situation at the *semiperiphery*, the case must be qualified substantially for the two basically different types of countries to be found here. First, there are semiperipheral countries which dispose of *raw materials*. These have begun industrializing during the postwar era; their access to the semiperiphery will most probably not be transitory but quite durable. Examples are Mexico, Brazil, Argentina (agrarian raw materials) and South Africa, cases which can be found in the standard listings of so-called newly industrializing countries (NICs). The arguments applying to the periphery still hold to some extent for these countries since they are still predominantly integrated into the global division of labor through raw materials and semi-finished products. Dependent industrialization protected by tariffs has been a special feature of their postwar industrializing process. From tariffs and customs duties additional sources of wealth were created which the state could skim off through taxes or directly through state enterprises. Unlike raw material rents, these tariff protection rents must partially be invested in the creation of the infrastructural prerequisites of industrial production. The taming of the state is thus accelerated because it must be legitimized in the face of at least part of society and of transnational corporations. The "abnormality" of the periphery is thus partially perpetuated, but at the same time the logic of state action must be subordinated to capitalist logic. In addition, the range of political options not based on ethnic origins increases: national and transnational raw material interests as well as industrial interests and the predominantly urban labor "aristocracy" within the integrated sector play new roles. Yet, these potential elites are still opposed by the large group of marginalized urban and rural groups.

One feature of continuing abnormality is the division of society along the line of an integrated segment versus a marginalized majority. In the integrated part a conflictive coalition of interests between state class, transnationals, and local business elites (see Evans 1979) perhaps extended by a labor aristocracy can usually be observed. In spite of all the differences of interests, this integrated segment needs the state to protect the industrializing "island" against the marginalized majority. The functional irrelevance of the majority of the population for the circuits of the dominant economy persists, yet the dimensions are different from those found at the periphery proper because only very limited numbers of people are tied to export enclaves.

Mention must also be made of those countries lacking any substantial stock of raw materials. They used to be very poor, even poorer than several peripheral countries, but have developed from poor agrarian situations to newly industrial ones within as short a time as a quarter of a century. In such cases, location at the semiperiphery must be regarded as a transitory stage. Due to the competition for industrial production locations, the world market forces governments to create the social and political preconditions for successful competition. Even though democratization presently confronts many problems, these countries are slowly resembling core countries. Examples are the Republic of Korea, Taiwan, Thailand, and the city-states of Hong Kong and Singapore. Their model was Japan, which successfully managed the transition from an agrarian economy to become one of the leading industrial countries of the world.

Factors fostering these developments have been the lack of raw materials, ethnic and religious homogeneity, and successful agrarian reforms that equalized the distribution of income. Here, members of the state class can turn into economically motivated political entrepreneurs, join forces with private capital and thus become the motor of development. The followers of this developmental path feature a combination of a centrally planned economy and a private market society that eventually leads to the emergence of a "guided capitalist economic order." Not laissez-faire, but a development pattern combining private capitalism and official planning have paved the way to the top for Japan. For some decades now Korea and Taiwan have been following this same route. The state class neither has to mediate between raw material and industrial interests, nor does it take part in the management of economic enterprises. The contrast with the behavior of the state classes in Latin America and Africa is marked. Park Chung Hee is an example of a leader who drew his strength from patriotism. The Korean economic miracle was the result of his efforts, the ascent of Japan after the Meiji Restoration of 1868 being his inspiration.

COMPETITION AMONG GOVERNMENTS

In the perspective advanced here, the behavior of states is disentangled from the narrow focus on power policy. States, we have argued, do not engage only in politico-military rivalry. In addition, the world market for protection leads to genuinely economic competition between states because different social orders lead to long-term differences in economic success. Governments have always had to react to this imperative if they did not want to be driven out of the race for core positions. This became most evident with the end of the great systems rivalry in 1989.

Since it is not centrally organized like a world empire, the modern world system makes flexibility possible, i.e., rivalry between different social arrangements shaped by a multitude of conflicts internal to its constituent societies. At the same time, conflict in the external sphere—competition within the encompassing world system—reduces the possibilities for social arrangements and thus work as a selective mechanism for societal evolution. In the short run, groups that have prevailed in social conflicts may set up a variety of institutions. In the long run, however, only those institutions which offer their societies good starts to attain or preserve status in the competitive world milieu will survive.

Although we stress the sociological lineage in our argument, we must point out that the effect on government behavior of competition among governments for mobile resources has also received attention in economics. A recent example is Stefan Sinn's (1992) article "The Taming of Leviathan." Although economists often tended to identify the domain of competition in the realm of politics with competition among political parties for support (see, for example, Stigler 1972: 91), intergovernmental competition already received attention in the work of Friedrich List (1841) reflecting the role of governments in promoting national industry. Long before that, Adam Smith addressed in his *Wealth of Nations* (1776) a core mechanism of the world market for protection by reflecting on the consequences of the state's power to tax.[6]

Several recent contributions address certain specific spheres of government policies, such as international coordination of monetary policies (Scheide and Sinn 1989) or strategic trade policy (Bhagwati 1989), while our argument stresses a whole package of "locational factors" created and supported by governments. Such a more encompassing approach can also be found in recent economic thinking. In his *The Competitive Advantage of Nations,* Michael Porter (1990) points to the relationship between industrial structure, institutions, and people in explaining why some nations triumph and others lag. He radically rejects classical thinking about comparative advantages that only emphazises natural resources and other cost factors.

As we have argued, such classical comparative advantages were never realistic nor sufficient in explaining industrial predominance. Institutional, i.e., politically created factors, were relevant for economic competition from the onset. Our notion of a world market for protection supplements the theoretical apparatus to explain state action in one important instance: the economic motive of political undertakings, or even more pointedly, the implied view that states and their rulers are producers of economic utilities. Even if they have often been neglected by analysts of the political system, such motives early on claimed their place beside classical power and security policy.

The economic motives of state agents become pre-eminent once the world economy becomes central for the status allocation process. This was not the case to its present extent at the inception of the modern world system, but rather occurred in thrusts, one of these being the English Industrial Revolution. In the present century, the globalization of the economy under the initial predominance of U.S. enterprises has created a situation in which transnational corporations increasingly forced states into competition to become choice locations.

As a result of the globalization of production by the transnationals the market and therefore competition have changed. Due to imperfections of the world market for protection, reaction patterns were incomplete and the pace of adjustment was slow. Still, even in its incompleteness, this selective mechanism was very powerful in the long run, and competition for locations has once more become keener in the postwar era. In addition, new semiperipheral countries have become locations for industrial production. If Adam Smith stressed the role of mobile capital as early as 1776, it did not play a major role for the interactions of suppliers of protection at that time. Only the more intensive stage of globalization led to greater competition for industrial locations which must initially be prepared socially and politically. The importance of preconditions becomes particularly clear by reference to the technological style. Political entrepreneurs must "construct" the surrounding societal conditions to suit it. We shall discuss this in more detail below.

The notion of a world market for protection is by no means merely a scientific abstraction as shown by statements by leading figures in the world economy. For example, Robert A. Jeker (1991: 9), a top manager of Crédit Suisse, declared in an article titled "Global Economy and National Politics": "Countries compete with each other. Any country must strive to create true advantages over competing countries in the race for locations." For Jeker, there is now "also keen competition between the host countries of transnational corporations, their economies and the surrounding conditions" (our translation).

CONCLUSIONS

The perspective developed here is based on sociological approaches addressing the nexus of state and capitalist development. Such approaches can be found in the works of Max Weber, Otto Hintze, Frederic Lane and Christopher Chase-Dunn, to name but a few. There are some important extensions, however: first, our notion of a world market for protection goes beyond Lane's theory of protection rent. In addition, our concept of legitimacy in connection with protection and the extension of protection to the domestic sphere of the state monopoly of physical force are noteworthy.

Protection can be represented by a production function that features force as only one factor of production. The other, alternative factor is legitimacy, measured in terms of the actual fulfillment of the principles of efficiency and equality in social structure. In other words, we stress the quality of protection. The fact that protection of good quality was and remains a business is the reason for the survival of the leading values of modernity in the process of social evolution.

Varying conditions at the periphery and the semiperiphery as well as the dimension of time must not be neglected, however. Certainly, there have been and still are totalitarian regimes that have had considerable economic success over the short run. In our perspective, however, such regimes cannot maintain themselves in the long run because the striving after efficiency and equality lead to increasing opposition so that ultimately they succumb economically in the competitive world milieu.

Thus, we may give the following answer to our opening question: "Why did the power principle not prevail at the expense of the striving after efficiency and equality?" Over the centuries, the existence of a world market with its particular logic of competition has led to a situation in which the striving after economic efficiency was never without support. Due to the market-mediated quality requirement of protection as an input factor for low-cost capitalist production, the claim to equality and freedom did not remain a mere historical episode. Rather, it always found support because the legitimacy of an order is conditional upon guaranteeing these principles. And legitimacy is also, as we have seen, a factor of production positively influencing the quality of protection.

NOTES

1 Regulations between political entities are the starting points for supranational authority. They are frequently discussed under the heading of "international regimes." Yet, transnational utilities are normally only partially public as countries not taking part in the given international regimes can be excluded (see Krasner 1983, Kohler-Koch 1989, Effinger et al. 1990).

2 It is not possible to give an extensive bibliographical overview of this theoretical approach here. For overviews see for example Shannon (1989), Wallerstein (1979, 1984), Chase-Dunn (1989).

3 Elsewhere, Lane (1979: 75) formulates this in the following way: "Imagine a case of various enterprises competing in the same market and having the same costs except that they pay different costs of protection. The sale price of their product will be high enough to cover the highest protection cost, namely that of the marginal producer whose offering is needed to satisfy the demand. The profits of the enterprises enjoying lower protection costs will include the difference between their protection costs and that of the marginal competitor. *This difference I will call a protection rent.* Just as differences in the fertility of land result in rents to owners of more fertile fields, so differences in the ease of securing protection result in returns to enterprises which enjoy cheaper protection" (emphasis added).

4 It should be stressed that elements of the "world market for protection" argument are also compatible with some of the ideas expressed in the work of Parsons (1964), Spencer ([1880] 1969), and Buchanan (1980). Parsons (1964) suggests that evolutionary universals provide an edge to those societies which develop them first. Among such evolutionary universals he points to legitimization as an explicit societal task. Furthermore, the difference between the tribute and profit logic are also mentioned by Parsons, although in different terms. The same is true for the distinction between military and industrial society in the work of Spencer ([1880] 1969). Recently a dualism of orientations appeared in the new political economy under the labels of "rent seeking" and "profit seeking" (Buchanan 1980; Tollison 1982). Originally rent-seeking action was seen as a feature of individuals who wish to manipulate the state. Lately this perspective has been extended to the behavior of the state itself.
In contrast to Parsons, Spencer, and Buchanan we analyze the two distinct logics within the framework of a specific overarching historic social system that emerged at the core of the modern world system and triggered thrusts of social changes within individual societies dictated by the need to increase legitimacy as a resource in the competitive world system. Davis (1961) also points to the selective effect of the international system for social change. In addition to earlier theoretical work mentioned in the text our argument covers explicitly also the welfare state era. In terms of economic growth implications of the welfare state we differ from Olson (1982) who seems to imply that any attempt at coordinating economic action other than through "pure" market forces retards economic growth (see also Korpi 1985).

5 A collection of recent contributions that reflects the ambiguities and problems associated with the term legitimacy in sociological thought can be found in Cipriani (1987).

6 *The Wealth of Nations* ([1776] 1981: 848f.): "The proprietor of stock is properly a citizen of the world, and is not necessarily attached to any particular country. He would be apt to abandon the country in which he was exposed to a vexatious inquisition, in order to be assessed to a burdensome tax, and would remove his stock to some other country where he could, either carry on his business, or enjoy his fortune more at ease. By removing his stock, he would put an end to all the industry which it had maintained in the country which he left. Stock cultivates land; stock employs labour. A tax which tended to drive away stock from any particular country, would so far tend to dry up every source of revenue, both to the sovereign and to the society."

4
WAVES AND CYCLES AS MODES OF CHANGE

SOCIAL CHANGE AS A CHANGE OF PROGRAM

Some 500 years before Christ, Parmenides remarked that there is nothing new under the sun. In fact, he went on, there is neither evolution nor movement, but only unchangeable, persisting being. Our senses, which convey a world in motion, are deceiving us. Yet, at about the same time, Heraclitus asserted that everything is flowing, nothing lasts. His dialectical theory interprets the law of development as the evolutionary flow of the continuous interaction of opposing forces at different levels (Störig 1961).

The positions of Heraclitus and Parmenides are less contradictory than may appear at first sight. If one reads Heraclitus as saying that the continuous interaction of opposing forces at *different* levels constitutes social transition in the true sense, whereas the process at the same level only leads to variations, then transition or change only occurs between the levels. In other words, there is only variation, but nothing really new under the sun, as asserted by Parmenides, i.e., unfolding contradictions at a given level lead to variations, but not to true changes.

We may link this to our notion of *societal models*. As will be shown in some detail in later chapters, a societal model is a complex yet only temporarily successful attempt to resolve social contradictions. The model unfolds and thus causes a multitude of changes. But these form part of the model and only become manifest during its unfolding process. The societal model as a program is strange, since it is prospective and present at the same time. At first, it is more oriented towards the future, but in the course of its trajectory it becomes increasingly preoccupied with the present, the problems of which it can solve less and less satisfactorily, thus making a change of program necessary.

Strictly speaking, social change is thus the change of program. In the course of its unfolding a program regularly goes through different stages, which can be understood as the *trajectory of societal models*. This sequence of stages implies variation but not social change in the strict sense. In different programs, the various stages are similar, not in content, but only as structural processes.

Programs or societal models are therefore the basic units in social change. For this reason we can distinguish between cyclical processes of variation within periods, on the one hand, and program changes, on the other. Such transitions in the societal realm are "historical" phases in which a variety of further developments becomes possible. Thus, from time to time action becomes possible, represented by different solutions to one and the same contradiction. We will discuss such functionally equivalent solutions to contradictions more fully in chapter 7.

LEARNING AND CHANGE

Here, we propose to discuss in somewhat greater detail why societies do not learn continuously. Why do innovational thrusts in the techno-economic and the politico-institutional spheres occur? One possible answer is that societal power, intended to cope with uncertainty, hinders innovation.

It is possible to understand social relationships as attempts to come to terms with uncertainty. Society can be thought of as a *Problemlösungsgemeinschaft* (a problem-solving community) (Giesen 1980), whose task it is to provide security in a physical sense (safety and ensuring basic needs) as well as security for action, i.e., the meeting of expectations. Such functions are reflected and institutionalized in a sanctioning apparatus that punishes wrong and rewards correct behavior; in a production apparatus that regulates how things are to be done; and in outlooks that define the perception of the social world. A common understanding of the world is made possible by encompassing and binding conceptions (Giesen 1980: 98).

This is what a societal model does. By way of a system of institutional routines it meets expectations and regulates action. Societal routines relating to how the world is seen—normative theories—and how it is engaged—technological style and politico-economic regime—constitute societal power to cope with uncertainty. Although such power favors certain groups, it is not the attribute of any particular group or person. Why then is social power so persistent?

The persistence of societal power can be explained by applying conflict as well as learning theory. Conflict theory would have it that as certain actors are privileged by societal power, they develop a vested interest in maintaining the existing order. They combat opposing interests and do not react innovatively or invent novel situations within the framework of a given politico-economic regime. This argument can be extended by distinguishing, for example, between two further types of interest: interest in the distribution of material wealth and interest in different conceptions of the world.

Learning theory stresses the more abstract conflict between meeting expectations and autonomy for action. Thus societal institutionalization of power is greatest if no alternative action possibilities exist at all because then the meeting of expectations is at its maximum. There is thus an exchange relationship between meeting expectations and alternative action possibilities. In this perspective the routinization of institutions and conceptions of the world create maximum certainty, yet at the cost of restricting alternative actions (Giesen 1980: 96).

Societal power—rooted in a societal model—resists change and alternatives because power stems precisely from restriction. For this reason, power is an advantage and a disadvantage at the same time. Societal power creates strong social cohesion—solidarity—and suppresses conflict of interests. But as Bernhard Giesen (1980: 99) has pointed out in another context, routines and a rigid conception of the world can lead to a crisis of interpretative knowledge. If the contradictions between conventionality and reality exceed a certain threshold, social power enters a crisis and begins to dissolve.

The opposition of certainty and autonomy of action can also be put in terms of Schumpeter's notion of statics and dynamics in social life. In order to refute the critique of Schumpeter that statics are characterized solely by traditional behavior and not by rationality, two kinds of rationality must be considered: 1) bounded, traditional rationality which does include rational elements even though embedded within conventional wisdom and institutional routines representing social power; and 2) free rationality. As the latter's means and ends are not bound to conventional wisdom, it can radically open up new perspectives and future-oriented scenarios.

Even in our individualistic societies there are times when signs of a new basic consensus and a mobilization towards a new program arise. Yet, what seems voluntaristically possible during given historical phases on the basis of a certain power constellation is not necessarily viable over the long-term. Despite voluntaristic space for manoeuver in certain phases, there is a long-term selection of programs. In addition, even though changes of program occur, there is also a great deal of continuity, so that one must not think of program changes as being too drastic. There is a simple reason for this: the social process and therefore the generation of programs is embedded within the world-encompassing process of economic and military competition. This setting, the core of which has remained unchanged in modern times, is decisive for the survival of programs.

TIME LAGS, DISCONTINUITIES AND CYCLES

To speak of program changes in our societies seems doubtful, for changes do not happen simultaneously in different social domains. Let us assume two social areas whose stages of change are characterized by a phase displacement. When does change in a strict sense, i.e., the change of program, happen? When one or the other area has reached the beginning of its cycle?

The fact that changes or social transitions do not occur simultaneously in different realms of society has been part of the theory of social change since William F. Ogburn (1964) coined the term "cultural lag." In fact, Ogburn's cultural lag referred primarily to asynchronous change of the material and non-material components of culture. Yet cultural lag can be applied more generally to asynchronous change of all cultural components. Naturally, technology and its application are also part of culture because even the "hardware" is embedded within mental constructs. To define technology as part of material culture is therefore quite questionable.

If there is asynchronous change in different spheres, three questions must be asked:

1. How can such spheres be distinguished meaningfully?;

2. How can asynchronies in these spheres be explained?;
3. Can one speak of change in general if changes in different albeit related spheres of society are timed differently?

However, before addressing these questions and giving more complete answers in the following chapters, we have to ask whether asynchronisms in social change have temporal limits, or whether and under what circumstances they become a lasting concomitant of the continuous interaction of opposing forces at other levels of society (Heraclitus). Unlike Heraclitus, Ogburn did not regard cultural lag as a fundamental part of his theory of social evolution: "In the long perspective of history (. . .) lags are not visible because they have been caught up" (Ogburn 1964).

Yet, within the limited human life span, medium-term, epoch-making asynchronisms are very important because they decisively influence destiny, happiness, and suffering. In addition, modern change is itself repeatedly discontinuous. In fact, over the whole span of modern society change *cannot* be represented as an equilibrium originally displaced and later meant to recover permanently its initial state. Quite the contrary: for reasons to be discussed in chapter 7, equilibria can never be fully attained. As soon as a situation of approximate equilibrium is reached, processes of decay in the social structure and fresh disequilibria set in.

Continuous discontinuity of social development leads to the expectation of waves in the transformation of social structure. Since the beginning of this century and despite periodic shifts in attention, *long waves* have been a research issue of growing importance. Yet the notion of long waves does not necessarily embrace discontinuities in social change. If one understands waves as harmonious oscillations, they may also imply the periodic return of past situations, as defined by Parmenides.

Our own perspective on discontinuities in social change is also characterized by waves. Yet it does not stress only *cyclical phenomena*, but also *program changes* at the boundary between periods. Gerhard Mensch (see below) has tried to capture this kind of change, going beyond mere notions of waves (such as those proposed by Schumpeter and Kuznets) with the term "metamorphosis." This conception of waves formed by discrete units of social change constitutes an unquestionable conceptual advance.

To identify a program change, a clear-cut beginning is required—a recognizable fresh definition of problems in social life and new ideas for their solution expressed in novel regulatory mechanisms and institutions. In the introductory chapter we already introduced two spheres related to each other but characterized by asynchronous program changes. These are the spheres defined as *technological style* and *politico-economic regime*. But how can one possibly speak of *a single* program change for a period (wave) if changes do not occur simultaneously?

A program change occurs if both spheres—technological style and politico-economic regime—are deliberately related to each other; that is, the two are consciously forced together in praxis in an adaptation that is collectively reconciled in a renewed social contract. Thus, our notion of social change strictly refers to a process with a clear beginning, and in which the unit of social change persists from the beginning until the decay of the societal model. The "historical" phase, lasting about two decades, lies between the dissolution of the old order and the inception of the new.

Here, we can explain why program changes in technological style and the politico-economic regime do not occur simultaneously. The first elements and components of change in the technological style already emerge in the late peak of the long economic conjuncture. Despite all attempts at monopolization typical for this phase, reaction to market law sets in only after the old technological style has been saturated and the high growth rates and substantial gains in productivity, which arose with the introduction of that technological style, have already become things of the past.

But such changes in style are gradual and at first only spread slowly. Thus, no *collective* program change is stimulated because change works in a decentralized fashion. Actions are based on individual calculations of utility directed towards an impersonal market and can thus be made in a value neutral way. These individual, market-oriented, and value-neutral decisions in the formative phase of a technological style are in conflict with the decision-making logic of collectives formulating, interpreting, and enforcing a given politico-economic regime. Such political processes are not value-neutral because they affect different actors with specific interests who must agree upon a basic consensus for a new start. Under democratic conditions this implies a long process of communication and negotiation; it not only takes time but is also more clear-cut, leading to a new societal model that binds and crystallizes the technological style.

A further point has to be added: the first signs of a new technological style can be perceived in the "late summer" of the long economic cycle. Who wants to think ahead in this phase? People are fascinated by the late bloom and expect it to produce the much dreamed about fruits of the prior program change. Experience, however, teaches that the economic sky begins abruptly to become overcast after this late summer. As interest-bound viewpoints become rigid during this phase even more time is lost, the conservative stress on conflicts of interest not being conducive to a new beginning and mutual agreement.

These are the main reasons for asynchronisms of social processes in the transition of technological styles and politico-economic regimes, occasioning time lags of one to two decades in duration. Deliberate new beginnings, i.e., the amalgamation of technological style and politico-economic regime, create a *societal model*. Such societal models are the special units of social change. Within a societal model there are, as we have seen, also variations and changes in the sense of inception, unfolding, and growth, but these are already part of the original program and are thus merely fulfilled. Such variations are also characterized by regularities which we shall describe as the "trajectory of societal models."

Finally, we may already point to fluctuations in the economy—the economic cycle. In the approach taken in this book economic fluctuations are part of a complex social process. By contrast to conventional perspectives, the economic cycle is thus endogenized.

Economic fluctuations—reflected, for example, in growth rates, output, prices, and employment—are normally regarded as the cause of social and political phenomena.[1] But economic activity is itself a part of the social system. It is embedded within the processes we have called the trajectory of the societal model. In other words, it is at least plausible to reverse the conventional assumption and to assume a causal relationship running from social and political processes to the economy. The idea that the economic cycle is a result of the entire social process is central to our thesis. In the following chapters the elements of this perspective will be elaborated step-by-step in order to bring them together at the beginning of chapter 7. Yet the basic idea is quite simple and can already be set out here.

A certain level of economic activity is the result of different conditions. We may point to only two of these: growth depends, first, upon progress in the diffusion of the technological style and, second, on the shaping of the politico-economic regime. Thus, economic growth is endogenously determined. Since Keynes, the availability of financial resources has not been the only factor determining the propensity to invest. This point is taken into account in our model. Availability of financial resources and thus a low rate of interest and low labor costs are not the central, and in certain periods maybe not even be important determinants of the growth of production. Instead, the most important determinants are to be found in societal patterns.

Value priorities change during the trajectory of the societal model, and social conflict takes on different shapes and occurs at different levels at successive stages of the model (chapter 7). Differences in the kind and frequency of conflicts are not a mere reflection of economic fluctuations. Rather they depend upon the legitimacy of the social order in the eyes of its members—legitimacy in turn being a function of the phase of a societal model with respect to the unfolding of the technological style and the politico-economic regime.

LONG WAVES

For many, repetitions in social development processes hold a certain fascination, but also cause much confusion. Why indeed should social phenomena recur?

Social phenomena are in fact unique and cannot be repeated. The preoccupation with comparatively vague categories such as growth rates or price changes leaves open the question of the grounds on which they are founded. Even if—in a strict sense—events cannot be repeated, it is possible that comparatively constant conditions and causes periodically result in similar if not identical phenomena.[2] If this is the case, we can speak of a *structural cycle*, meaning that certain clearly distinct events succeed each other regularly and recur without interruption. Timing plays no part in structural cycles. Events can be spread in any order over time without affecting the cyclical character. Only succession without interruption or intervening episodes is essential, not any regular phasing over time. An example of a very simple conception of the structural cycle is represented by the two-phase model of successive upswings and downswings (as in Rostow 1978). A *temporal cycle* is quite a different matter: "War breaks out every fifty years" is an example of such a cycle.

A conceptual analysis of structural and temporal cycles is, however, hardly to be found in the literature. Social, political, and economic reality is much too complex and the definition of cyclical phenomena is too unstable for any simple temporal cycle to be identified. Nevertheless, most authors adopt analyses of cyclical conceptions which contain elements of temporal cycles of sorts.

The literature examines a large variety of cycles. Schumpeter (1939) distinguishes three types with different lengths in his theory of economic development and business cycles: the *Kitchin cycle* lasting three-and-a-half years (also known as the inventory cycle); the *Juglar cycle* lasting 8-10 years, and the *Kondratieff cycle* lasting 45-60 years. Simon Kuznets (1930) pointed to cycles of between 18 and 25 years later known as *Kuznets cycles.* These refer principally to the cyclical incidence of investment in construction. Apart from such mainly economically grounded cycles one must also mention the approximately century-long world political *hegemonic or power cycles* of the rise and fall of world powers (see Wallerstein 1974; Modelski 1978; Kennedy 1987).

Since the 1970s there has been a revival of concern with Kondratieff cycles, and hegemonic cycles have equally aroused growing interest in various social scientific domains. As they are of importance for our theoretical perspective, we shall deal with them in somewhat greater detail below.

DO KONDRATIEFF CYCLES EXIST?

The ample research literature provides many partly contradictory conceptions of the existence of Kondratieff cycles. This arises essentially for two reasons. Firstly, very different methodological approaches have been adopted. The spectrum extends from simple visual testing to complex procedures of time-series analysis (like spectral analysis) and polynomial regression analysis. In the second place, the various studies examine Kondratieff cycles in very different domains such as prices, industrial production, investment, innovation, foreign trade, indebtedness, social inequality, social and political conflict, wars, value hierarchies, and cultural production.

Several authors argue that Kondratieff cycles are purely a price phenomenon and cannot be observed in other domains. This critique of Kondratieff and Schumpeter was already formulated by Kuznets (1940) and Garvy (1943). Forty years later Eklund (1980) repeats the old objection that long waves are so far only conclusively discernible through price data. And in fact, the empirical evidence for the existence of Kondratieff waves in *real production* is contradictory. Several authors who have calculated the growth rate of industrial production in certain core countries both in upswing and in downswing phases after about 1850 have been able to confirm fluctuations of the Kondratieff cycle type (Mandel 1980; Bieshaar and Kleinknecht 1984; Screpanti 1984; Kleinknecht 1987). The manner of calculating growth rates in these studies is, however, not free of problems (see the criticism of Goldstein 1988: 185-188 and Reijnders 1990). From the theoretical point of view further problems are raised because the definition of upswing and downswing phases of real production (product cycles) is generally linked to the peaks and troughs of the empirically observed price series. In addition, cycles can be artificially generated or erased when cyclical fluctuations are filtered out together with the trend (see Metz 1984; Gerster 1988; Eisner 1990, 1991).

In the past few years new work has appeared which examines Kondratieff cycles in the domain of real economic activity by other methods (Goldstein 1988, van Duijn 1983; Gerster 1988). Despite the undoubted methodological advances of recent years, the empirical verification of Kondratieff-type long waves remains uncertain, particularly as concerns product cycles.

Still, the mixed evidence at national levels does not necessarily preclude the existence of the phenomenon. At any rate, the evidence since the end of the last century suggests a synchronisation of cycles at the national level. Thus deviations from the cycle of the world economy at large have become smaller in the course of time. For this reason we have to start from the assumption of cycles in the world economy. Before turning to a short overview of theoretical explanations, we will shortly discuss the syntax of long waves in the following section.

THE SYNTAX OF THE LONG WAVE

The phases of the long wave are reminiscent of the four seasons. Prosperity, recession, depression, and recovery are the four phases commonly applied in the description of cycles. In what follows we shall anticipate features of our theoretical model to suggest a somewhat more complicated syntax of the long wave. In our perspective, each wave has two peaks: an actual *prosperity* phase and an *interim recovery*. In chapter 7 we will turn to theoretical deduction as well as to the argument that the two peaks differ in underlying social processes, even if growth rates are identical in both cases. As a structural formula the syntax reads as follows:

U – P – PR – C – IR – D

with:

U: Upswing phase, starting from a low point with high, yet erratically oscillating growth rates.
P: Prosperity, with the highest and only slightly oscillating growth rates of the cycle.
PR: Prosperity-recession, with slightly diminishing growth rates interrupted by recessions. Growth starts to oscillate more strongly.
C: Crisis, with an abrupt decrease of growth rates.
IR: Interim recovery, with high growth rates.
D: Renewed crisis and depression.

In figure 4.1 the growth rates of world industrial production since the spread of the liberal project of the Industrial Revolution in the second third of the nineteenth century have been depicted. The complicated syntax in the sequence of different phases can be noticed without interruption three times since 1835/50 in figure 4.1.[3] The above remarks concerning oscillations anticipate results of a detailed observation of the past long wave (see chapter 7) that does not appear in figure 4.1 but is nonetheless advanced as a general hypothesis here.

The syntax of the long wave can be seen three times in figure 4.1:

1st wave (1835)-1882	2nd wave 1883-1932	3rd wave 1933-1993
(U-P)-PR-C-IR-D	U-P-PR-C-IR-D	U-P-PR-C-IR-D

The beginning of the sequence cannot be observed directly in the time-series data but can be presumed on the basis of estimates (see endnote 3). The same holds for the end of the sequence: recovery can be discerned after 1982, yet the coding of this phase as "IR" assumes a renewed decline of growth rates. As mentioned above, considerations concerning the duration of distinct phases, as well as the whole cycle, do not play a role in structural cycles. Only the correct and uninterrupted sequence of phases is important. Figure 4.1 thus substantiates the argument.

FIGURE 4.1 Average Annual Growth Rate of Industrial Production in Different Periods, 1835-1993

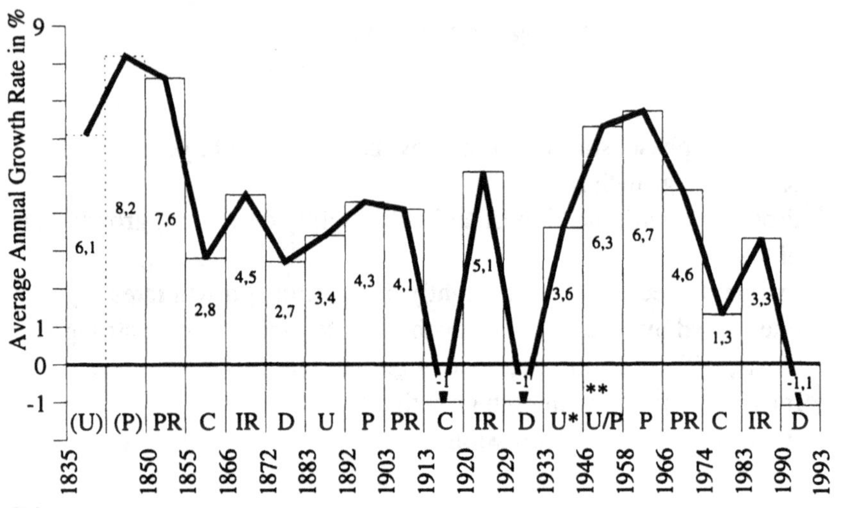

*) 1933-38: 6.7% p.a., 1938-46: 1.6% p.a.
**) Renewed upswing in the countries affected by the war; prosperity in the other countries.
Sources: 1835-1850 Crude estimate, see endnote 3. 1850-1929 From peak of one Juglar cycle to the next (van Dujin 1983: 154). 1929-1986 Compilation from different volumes of the *United Nations Statistical Yearbook and the Monthly Bulletin of Statistics* of the UN. The data since 1929 refer to the growth rates of world industrial production in the "capitalist" part of the world. If socialist countries had also been included the result would have been quite similar because their share in world industrial production is comparatively small (Bornschier 1988: table 3.1).
Periodization with regard to contents: 1929, in this year's autumn the decline into depression began. 1933, measured in terms of industrial production, the low point of the depression is overcome. 1946, the first full year of peace. 1958, free convertibility of currencies in the West. 1966, the year before the recession of 1967. 1974, the last year before the great post-war decline. 1983, the year in which recovery set in. 1990, the year marking the beginning of the newest depression. 1993, last year for which data are available.
Note: The line is not based on real data but only serves to visualize the wave-like character of the process.

The two great wars have not had a decisive impact on the syntax of the second and the third wave. World War I may have aggravated the downswing after 1913, yet it was not the reason for the decline in industrial production that can be observed as early as 1903 in the aggregate. The United States was briefly engaged in the war (1917-18) and did not suffer any domestic destruction. The growth rate of industrial production in the United States declines continuously after 1900 from about 8 percent p.a. to minus 6 percent in 1921 (Rostow 1978: 390). The war years 1915-17 did not bring about any decline for the United States but a slight recovery of growth in the middle of a twenty year phase of diminishing growth rates (see Ogburn and Adams 1964: 274).

World War II occurred in an upswing phase, which it delayed for the countries most affected—thus the coding "U, U/P" in figure 4.1. The low point of the depression of the world economic crisis was reached in 1932. Until 1937 there was an accelerated recovery which brought industrial production to generally higher levels than it had been before the decline into depression (1929). In 1937, the index of industrial production was higher than in 1929 for 10 out of 14 core countries, the leaders being New Zealand, Sweden, Finland, Ireland, Norway and Denmark. These examples illustrate that the general upswing cannot have been a mere reflection of war preparations. Between 1937 and 1948, the United States and countries not deeply involved in the war exhibited strong growth of industrial production. At the same time the countries deeply affected by the war stagnated and the losers even suffered losses. The historical phase of the 1930s will be discussed in chapter 7. There we will also explain the syntax of the long economic wave on the basis of the interaction of the technological style with the politico-economic regime over the regular trajectory of the societal model.

AN OVERVIEW OF LONG CYCLE THEORIES

Cycle theories have existed for a long time. We owe a classic formulation of a true cycle theory to the Maghrebian civil servant and historian, Ibn Khaldun (1332-1405). His approach is an early example of a strong formulation of a sociological cycle theory. Ibn Khaldun's basic purpose was to explain the rise and decline of an empire. Against the background of the history of the Arab people, Ibn Khaldun suggested a cyclical theory of social development that encompasses and links environmental factors, social processes, and societal structures. His argument is paraphrased by Dieter Seibel (1980: 57): "A society whose energy stems from the strong cohesion of the powerful members of the tribe as well as from the environment begins in the desert. The powerful Arab tribe succeeds in conquering an urban culture. The tribe is strong enough to give this urban culture important developmental impulses after conquest. Yet, by living in an urban surplus society social cohesion and martial abilities are reduced. Structures of domination are consolidated as dynasties in hierarchical formations. Finally, the ruling dynasty succumbs to the aggression of a new tribe and vanishes" (our translation). Even though Ibn Khaldun's theory is bound to specific ecological and historical conditions, it points to several mechanisms that are still relevant. Phenomena of saturation and institutionalization as well as differing action patterns in different social spheres and the competitive milieu in which they are embedded.

Cycle research in this century has been centered around the already mentioned Kondratieff waves, connecting price and product cycles with other cyclical processes in the economic, political, and sociocultural domains. The explanation of long waves of the Kondratieff type in the literature is predominantly couched in economic terms, fluctuations in economic activity being related to economic processes themselves. More recently, sociocultural approaches and the notion of hegemonic cycles have also received greater attention. As we cannot go into any detail on these different perspectives here, we have to confine the following discussion to a brief sketch of major explanations. A more complete overview can, however, be found in Bornschier and Suter (1992).

Economic Explanations

Economically based theories can broadly be divided into three main strands: innovation theories stemming from Schumpeter (1939), the Marxist-oriented capital accumulation theories in the tradition of Kondratieff (1926), and sector theories as suggested by Forrester and Rostow (see references below).

Innovation theories accept the intermittent appearance of innovations as the central explanation of long-term alternation between boom and depression. Current innovational approaches (Mensch 1975; Freeman et al. 1982; van Duijn 1983; Kleinknecht 1987) are rooted in Schumpeter's (1939) work concerning the crisis of the 1930s. It was he who distinguished between inventions (i.e., the discovery of new products or production techniques) and innovations (i.e., the commercial application of scientific inventions). Innovations occur in intermittent batches depending on the attitudes of entrepreneurs who initially shy away from risky investment in inventions. Once innovations have proven profitable, more and more entrepreneurs are attracted to them; the few highly perceptive pioneers are followed by a swarm of mediocre imitators as the upswing, initiated by the pioneers, broadens into a boom. The most prominent contemporary representative of innovation theory is Gerhard Mensch to whose work we will return.[4]

Empirical evidence concerning the appearance of innovations is mixed (see Mensch 1975, Kleinknecht 1987; Goldstein 1988; Clark et al. 1981; van Duijn 1983). Differences in the findings of these authors may essentially be due to different categorizations of innovations. As for the timing of innovations within the Kondratieff cycles, the empirical evidence tends to support Mensch, according to whom they are concentrated in the downswing or – depending on the periodization – in the early upswing phases of these cycles.

In another strand of theory long waves are understood as the result of long-term shifts in capital accumulation. This line of argument above all forms the core of work in the Marxist tradition (see Altvater and Hoffmann 1980, Mandel 1980 and Poletayev 1989). According to Mandel (1980), the most prominent defender of capital accumulation theory, an economic upswing is occasioned by a sudden rise in the rate of profit, while on the other hand the downswing of a Kondratieff cycle is connected with a long-term decline therein. In Marxist theory, the main determinant of profit rates is the organic composition of capital (the ratio of fixed to variable capital, i.e., that between the costs of fixed capital investments and wages), the surplus rate, and capital circulation velocity (Mandel, 1980: 14). Thus, the rate of profit rises when the organic composition of capital (i.e., the proportion of fixed capital investments in relation to wage bills) sinks and/or the surplus rate and the velocity of circulation of capital rise. Sinking profit rates (enhancement of the organic composition of capital, stagnant surplus rate, and a slowing in the velocity of circulation of capital) implies excessive capital accumulation, which means that it becomes impossible to find investment opportunities promising adequate profit returns.

The passage from an upswing to a downswing phase may be linked with the developmental dynamics of the capitalist accumulation process (the trend towards diminishing profit rates). One of the major flaws of this approach is the fact that Mandel sees the start in a rise in the rate of profit as determined by external factors. In addition, Marxist capital accumulation theories have only slim empirical grounding. There are but few, and these are hardly convincing studies dealing empirically with profit rate cycles.

Neo-Marxism and neo-Schumpeterism are not irreconcilable. One emphasizes a profit rate cycle, the other an innovation cycle. The first suggests an explanation of why innovational thrusts occur—because profit rates are endangered—the second why the capitalist process is not necessarily oriented towards decline—because the structures, on which profit expectations depend, renew themselves. Mandel, as a proponent of the profit cycle, has already incorporated the significance of basic innovations into his model. On the cusp between the two schools of thought lies the work of Rod Coombs (1984), who investigates the connection between long waves and innovations in the labor process. He refers to the models of Mandel (1980) and Freeman (1979) and identifies steps of mechanization: primary mechanization (rigid power and tool machines); secondary mechanization (flow technologies between processing points), and tertiary mechanization (flexible control technologies).

In addition, there are certain other noteworthy theories. The System Dynamics National Model developed by Jay Forrester (1976, 1978, 1983) and his colleagues (see Graham and Senge (1980) and Sterman (1986) among others) is a sectoral model embracing the consumer goods and the infrastructure and capital goods sectors. The initially delayed and subsequently exaggerated reaction between the two sectors leads to long waves of economic activity. The tendency of individuals and firms to amplify demand especially for capital goods is reinforced through a wide range of positive feedback mechanisms. Forrester's simulations led him to the discovery of 50-year cycles. He is thus one of the few who can actually explain the assumed length of Kondratieff cycles (Wagner 1981). Although the model focuses on economic forces it also takes into account socio-cultural factors like employment, social and organizational innovations, and political and social values.

Van Duijn (1983) combines the asynchronic features of the two sectors with basic innovations and thus arrives at a theoretical explanation of long waves. The delayed overexpansion in the infrastructure and capital goods sector follows the multiplier-accelerator principle which in economics plays a prominent role in the explanation of shorter cycles of the Juglar type (see Samuelson 1939).

Rostow's terms of trade approach (1975; 1978: 103-304; 1985) must also be classified amongst the sectoral ones since he explains cyclical movements through shifts in the relative prices of agricultural and industrial raw materials as well as industrial products. Rostow attempts to connect "terms of trade cycles" with two other wave-like processes: the sequences of major technological innovations and the domestic and international flow of migration connected with cyclical fluctuations of economic growth. These three forces govern successive trends through complex interactions. The upswing of a cycle is marked by rising raw material prices, rapid expansion of agricultural production, high interest rates, and a distribution of income which favors the agricultural sector and profits as against real urban wages. The downswing, by way of contrast, witnesses falling raw material prices, low interest rates, and a distribution of income favoring urban wage earners (Rostow 1978: 109-110). Because of the low raw material prices during downswings, the prevailing leading sectors can expand more rapidly and with fewer constraints during this phase (Rostow 1978: 299-304).

Rostow explains the rise in the relative prices of primary products through greater demand pressures on raw materials, occasioned on the one hand by expanded aggregate demand and on the other hand through diminished supply. The downswing of a cycle is caused by tendencies towards sector-specific excess investment and production occasioned by the temporal lags inherent in the investment process and by "follow-the-leader" behavior by investors. The price movements analysed by Rostow finally reflect cycles of relative shortage (upswing) and glut (downswing) of raw materials. A certain investment pattern is closely linked to the movement of relative prices: rising prices channel investment capital towards the raw materials sectors. The rising profitability of primary production directs capital exports and migration flows towards raw material-producing countries.

Sociocultural Factors

In addition to the dominant economic explanatory models, a number of sociocultural and socioeconomic approaches have recently appeared (see Eisner 1990, 1991). Apart from the explanation of economic cycles in terms of sociocultural factors, these approaches often deal with the social consequences of economic cycles.

David Gordon's (1980) theory, for example, proposes a step-by-step transformation of social structure in connection with long waves. Crisis trends in the economy and contradictions in the social structure reinforce each other. Social conflicts become increasingly oriented towards structural problems and thus engender a need for structural change, that is to say the creation of new social institutions to resolve the crisis. The upswing is based on the stability of the new social structure of accumulation. It is followed by a slowdown of accumulation: falling profits along with more acute social conflicts result in crisis. Apart from the chronic class conflict, the problematic factors in the crisis are, according to Gordon, cycle-specific.

The regulatory approaches advanced by Lipietz (1984), Boyer (1984) and Mistral (1982) consider the depression of the 1890s as a crisis of the model of extensive accumulation, characterized by competitive capitalist production, the "night-watchman state," and low wage levels. This depression was resolved by the success of a new developmental model, that of Taylorism, i.e., the breakdown of work and the rationalization of production processes coupled with the deskilling of labor. Since aggregate purchasing power remained stagnant, Taylorism led to the crisis of the 1930s, the first crisis of intensive accumulation. The new model of the postwar era became Fordism, based on higher real wages consistent with advances in productivity, that is to say, on a constant ratio in the organic composition of capital coupled with a stable rate of profit.[5] Further institutional characteristics of Fordism were the centralization of capital in the hands of multinational corporations and a new definition of the state as an entity supporting the new model of social partnership.

A further perspective stresses the importance of the technological style and its institutional safeguarding. "Technological style," as advanced by Perez (1983, 1985), has already been mentioned several times and is to be understood as a paradigm (in the sense of "common sense practices") for the most efficient organization of production in a given historical phase. Such a style is diffused through the profit motive. The crisis occurs as a result of the breakdown of complementarity between the economic and the socioinstitutional sub-system. The inception of a new technological style is dated from the zenith of the old economic cycle. A new technological style is characterized by a "quantum jump" in productivity, caused by a key novel factor.

Freeman et al. (1982) focus on the employment effects of technological innovations. Product innovations introduced at the outset of an upswing are labor-intensive and stimulate employment. Labor shortages and the associated wage increases then make labor-saving innovations attractive. During the downswing the pressure of competition increases on firms which invest their capital chiefly in material- and labor-saving process innovations. Leading industries, which originally created jobs, thus lay off workers by adopting rationalizing processes. An upswing can only occur if a new technological style breaks through so that the excess labor pool of the depression can be absorbed.

Tylecote (1984) is concerned with the connection between economic growth and social inequality. He argues that growing domestic and international inequalities lead to a slowing down of economic growth and to the transition from upswings to downswings. Only the narrowing of inequalities can help the breakthrough of a new technological paradigm, thus occasioning a new upswing. Nollert (1989) in his model emphasizes the mutual relations and feedback mechanisms of three dimensions: equality, economic performance, and political conflict. He demonstrates empirically that, in the postwar era, the extent of inequality and the intensity of political conflicts are decisively influenced by the degree of neo-corporatism. The relationship between inequality and long waves not only domestically but also at the level of the world system is discussed further by Grimes (1985).

Attempts to analyze the connection between economic cycles and discontinuities in the intensity of social conflicts and movements are closely connected with those which seek to integrate social inequality with the cyclical notion (Barr 1980; Cronin 1980; Hobsbawm 1981; Screpanti 1984; Silver 1989; Brand 1990; Kowalewski 1991). It is argued that, during phases of high economic growth, social and political conflicts occur relatively rarely. During an economic upswing, however, individual material expectations and needs also rise. Towards the end of an upswing, as stagnation sets in, it becomes increasingly difficult to meet these higher demands. This leads to the accumulation of latent tensions and frustrations, manifested in the form of social and political conflicts and protests by underprivileged groups (especially workers). The argument is essentially based on the idea that societal stability and legitimacy depend largely on economic growth. While Cronin (1980) understands social conflicts to be determined by the course of economic cycles, Screpanti (1984) argues precisely the opposite: social conflicts are, for him, a cause of Kondratieff cycles.

Finally, de Greene (1988) approaches the phenomenon of Kondratieff cycles from the perspective of general systems theory and suggests an evolutionary model of logistic cycles. Sequences of Kondratieff waves are considered as a succession of societal structural changes. Each structure is characterized by a specific mix of social institutions, technologies, and ways of life, as well as psychological forces. System evolution is described as successive bifurcations along alternate pathways. Emphasizing the multi-causal and coevolutionary nature of the driving forces behind long waves, de Greene links ideas of Kondratieff, Mensch, Forrester, Perez and others, thus providing a framework for the integration of different economic and sociocultural approaches.

Hegemonic Cycles

The theorizing on long cycles does not stop here, however. In addition, there is a growing body of literature taking up the issue of hegemonic and leadership cycles. Still, there is a certain lack of consensus about the periodization and structure of hegemonic cycles in early modern times. Modelski considers Portugal the hegemonic power in the sixteenth century, while Wallerstein proposes Habsburg Spain; other authors mention no early hegemonies. There is, however, widespread agreement concerning the last three hegemonies. Thus, North Holland achieved world economic power in the seventeenth century. After the Napoleonic wars and for the greater part of the nineteenth century, Great Britain assumed the hegemonic position (though Modelski sees England as hegemon already in the eighteenth century), losing its dominance towards the end of the century. The resulting rivalry finally resulted in the two world wars. The United States emerges from the Second World War as the dominant power in the world system. Its hegemony lasted until around the end of the 1960s, when global economic and political power became more equally distributed between the United States, the European Community and Japan while the military superiority of the U.S. over the Soviet Union was relativized. Every hegemonic power disseminates its specific ideology of freedom: freedom of the seas (North Holland), free trade (Britain) and freedom of investment (United States) (see Research Working Group 1979: 499; Modelski 1978: 225; Wallerstein 1983).

There are essentially two theoretical strands to explain hegemonic cycles. Authors in the tradition of world-system analysis emphasize the economic logic and stress the close linkage of political hegemonic cycles and economic Kondratieff waves (Chase-Dunn 1978; Research Working Group 1979; Bousquet 1980; Goldstein 1985; Boswell and Sweat 1991). According to this approach, hegemony is based on productivity advances due to the early introduction of basic technological, organizational, and social innovations. However, as such innovations are adopted by other core countries, and even by those at the semiperiphery, the advantages are narrowed and eventually disappear altogether. The comparative advantages of hegemonic power are further reduced by the trend toward higher labor costs and the growing (military) outlays required to shore up the world order. Thus, hegemonic power is a multi-centric structure which assumes economic and political power worldwide.

By contrast to these conceptions, which emphasize economic power, the representatives of a second, more politically oriented theoretical current underline the autonomy of politico-military processes (Modelski 1978; 1987; Rasler and Thompson 1983). Modelski stresses the importance of the (unpredictable) outcome of global wars. Through victory in global conflicts, hegemonic powers triumph over their rivals and create a new world order to secure their position, which enables them to enjoy monopoly profits. The decay of hegemony results particularly from the high and rising costs of maintaining the world order. Modelski's cycles of hegemony are thus essentially determined endogenously by the dynamic laws of the global political system. Yet, in more recent work, one can detect a convergence of these two fundamental approaches. As discussed in chapter 3, economic power and political power are increasingly seen as mutually interwoven processes which influence each other, or as two sides of the same coin (see Chase-Dunn 1981, 1989; Väyrynen 1983). Kennedy (1987) arrives at the following generalization as a result of his detailed historical studies: nation-states expand their military power depending on their economic basis to secure their economic interests; the cost of such military responsibilities, however, in the long run exhausts even the strongest economies, hence their inevitable decline.

How Kondratieff cycles fit with hegemonic cycles has yet to be entirely clarified. The Research Working Group (1979) argues that hegemonic cycles stretch over two Kondratieff cycles, each half the length of the latter (i.e., the upswing and downswing phases) coinciding with one of the structural periods of the hegemonic cycle. This simple model has been rightly criticized by Bousquet (1980) on the grounds that particularly the ascendant hegemonic phase does not fit the periodization of Kondratieff half-cycles. In her view, phases of rivalry for hegemonic status last considerably longer than those of established hegemony.

Väyrynen (1983) has attempted to relate cycles of hegemony, Kondratieff waves, and war cycles since 1825. He adopts the division of hegemony cycles into four phases that occur concurrently with Kondratieff cycles, as mentioned above, and finds a bunching of wars in the phase of ascendant hegemony during a simultaneous upswing of the Kondratieff cycle (for the period 1892-1929: the Russo-Japanese war, the First World War, the Russian Revolution and civil war). Contrary to his expectations, however, numerous wars also occur in the phase of hegemonic maturity that indeed also coincides with an upswing of the Kondratieff cycle (in the period 1845-1872: the Crimean War and the Franco-Prussian War, amongst others; in the period 1948-1973: the Korean War).

LOOKING AHEAD

In this chapter it was possible to establish empirically secured cyclical phenomena in the long-term economic process with a duration of about two generations. We have suggested a structural formula for describing the syntax of the long wave, which will be discussed in chapter 7. There is a multitude of theories postulating structural cycles. The two main currents—profit rate and innovation cycles—have been partially integrated in recent approaches. In addition, there are some more encompassing approaches which also take political and societal factors into account Yet, these theoretical sketches still assemble the additional factors around the economic cycle of the Kondratieff type. Exceptions are notions of hegemonic cycles and the theory of change of technological styles, both of which are able to establish theoretical independence from the economic cycle.

In the following chapters we will pursue this line of more encompassing theories. We shall try to explore discontinuous social processes that cause economic cycles more completely. Thus we shall be continuing the discussion of ideas already addressed in the theories sketched out above. By way of an extension of existing theories, however, so-called cycles of order are postulated. The cyclical alternation of consensus and dissent around the trajectory of societal models is seen as the reason for long economic waves. A societal model is said to possess three components: leading cultural values, interpreted by normative theory and intended to legitimate power; technological style; and the politico-economic regime. In the formative phase, these three elements are related to each other; in the unfolding phase the promises of the societal model are partly met. The repletion phase is marked by the exhaustion of the model's capacity to overcome contradictions, which is why it collapses.

In the framework of these notions, the contradiction between growth and equality is an index of dynamics. Following a period of expansion, the growth processes initiated after the formulation of the structural model increasingly encounter the barriers of a constant inequality in income distribution. The egalitarian aspirations embedded in the model can no longer be met on account of economic stagnation, and the social consensus supporting the model falls apart.

NOTES

1 Classical examples of such perspectives can be found in Emile Durkheim's *Le Suicide* (1897) addressing the connection between economic situations and suicide rates, and in William F. Ogburn's *The Influence of the Business Cycle on Certain Social Conditions* ([1922] Ogburn and Thomas 1964). In addition, Vilfredo Pareto discussed the social and political consequences of long waves as early as 1913. The line of research that regards the economic cycle as the causal factor of social and political phenomena has continued until the present time.

2 See for example George Modelski's (1978: 214) definition of "a cycle as a recurrent pattern in the life (or functioning) of a system." Alfred Kleinknecht (1981: 107) regards the cycle as a regular recurrence that is caused by a historically constant complex of conditions and causes.

3 The data before 1850 are based on estimates. In Great Britain, the precursor, one can discern a high growth rate in capital but not in consumer goods. Britain generates the broadening industrializing process but seems to neglect national consumption (annual growth rates: 1836-45: 4% in capital goods and 2.9% in consumer goods; 1845-57: 5% in capital goods and 2.3% in consumer goods (van Duijn 1983: 151). In the U.S. industrial production exhibited extreme peaks of up to 24% annually (Rostow 1978: 390). In all core countries, industrial production grew substantially between 1830 and 1860. Their share in world industrial production (industry and manufacturing) advanced from 39.5% to 63.4% (see table 3.1 in Bornschier 1988 and Bairoch 1982: 292ff.). This leads to the conclusion that a general wave with high growth rates of world industrial production must have begun around 1830/40. For a newer detrended data series on world industrial production for a long time-span (1770-1979) see Metz (1992).

4 The literature concerning long waves, which has appeared in recent years under the influence of the Schumpeter revival, is extensive. Apart from Gerhard Mensch one must mention Freeman (1979), Clark et al. (1981) as well as contributions by Freeman (1983) and the University of Sussex circle. Jacob van Duijn (1983) who links innovational thrusts with delayed and exaggerated reactions in the interconnection between infrastructure and capital goods investment and the consumer goods industry may also be included. The work of Carlota Perez (1983, 1985) also falls under this

category, although she perceives the innovational process to be much more deeply embedded within a sociocultural and institutional framework. Finally, Alfred Kleinknecht's contributions (1979, 1981, 1983, 1987) belong to the same theoretical school.

5 This model of institutional linkage between the trajectory of real wages and advances in productivity (i.e., a constant ratio in the organic composition of capital) contradicts Mandel's argument, at least in the postwar era, for he sees precisely the fluctuations in the organic composition of capital as the principal determinant of long waves.

PART II

DISCONTINUITIES AND THEIR LINKS

This section aims to elaborate and link the notion of discontinuous social change with the concepts of the technological style and politico-economic regimes. In chapter 5 we discuss the development of the technological style. At the peak of the life cycle of a societal model, at the moment of its greatest economic expansion, the old style begins to dissolve and elements of a new style surface. These new elements begin to unfold during the interim recovery following the first crisis, but they only crystallise into a new societal model following a renewed crisis, at which point they diffuse with powerful momentum. Consideration is given to the form of politico-economic regime in chapter 6. The two social spheres—the technological style, and the politico-economic regime—are regarded as interconnected in a societal model. This begins when they are interrelated in the form of a new social contract. The linking of technological style and regime is further elaborated at the beginning of chapter 7, in which the central theme is the interplay of these two elements throughout the career of a societal model. The rise of a societal model to hegemonic practice and its subsequent decline bring about a long cycle of conflict (the interplay of consensus and dissent) and a long economic wave. The latter consists of a long phase of upswing and downturn, the latter interrupted by an interim recovery, which in the end calls forth a renewed crisis. The formal treatment of these themes is followed by an empirical elaboration of the economic dynamics and of cycles of conflict in the Keynesian societal model.

5
Technological Styles

Concept and Phases

Following Carlota Perez (1983), technological style here refers to a complex cluster of components, including basic materials, industrial procedures with their typical patterns of mechanization, the division of labor, organizational structure, corporate structure with its division of property rights, the supply of goods with its specific patterns of distribution, consumption, lifestyle and leisure behavior. Beyond the components of this cluster there are various complex and discontinuous processes which tend towards an unstable equilibrium during the upswing phase. Only by combination of the different elements during a crystallization phase does a growth surge become possible. The technological style then spreads to permeate all economic and social spheres. Finally, the spread leads to saturation and the coherence of a technological style begins to dissolve; new elements of a coming technological style then emerge.

Four stages can be discerned:

1. During the prosperity-recession phase (PR phase, see chapter 4) new elements of heterogeneity in the technological style appear, their dissemination remaining restricted.

2. During the interim recovery phase (IR), an accelerated unfolding and linkage of the new elements of the style takes place, but their diffusion remains restricted.

3. Full crystallization of the new style with an innovative range of products occurs only at the outset of the upswing phase (U); old products are produced in a new way and new products emerge in large numbers. Still, the upswing only succeeds in connection with matching investments in economic infrastructure and social regulations within the framework of a novel politico-economic regime.

4. The new technological style spreads quickly during the upswing and prosperity phases (U and P). During prosperity this permeation process tends towards saturation. No later than during the prosperity-recession phase new elements of an emerging style appear, thus completing the cycle.

Now, the coherence of the technological style begins to dissolve as soon as the economic peak is reached, i.e., when the permeation of the style, with its specific range of products, reaches the saturation point and induces a surge of investments aimed at rationalization. In fact, to reach an equilibrium of production and consumption two kinds of inventions are necessary. Innovations aimed at saving labor in the productive apparatus alone (i.e., innovations which increase output with the same work-time input) lead to disequilibria if they are not linked to inventions which fascinate people so that they want to spend their leisure consuming these goods and services, for which they are even prepared to work overtime to acquire. In the recent societal model, flow technology and Taylorism were examples of process innovations, whereas television sets and cars represented the second type of invention leading to the supply of hitherto unknown goods and services.

During the alternation of technological styles these two types of inventions do not occur simultaneously. This is a built-in disequilibrating mechanism which increases disparities and delays the emergence of a new style. Disparity only slowly produces effects because initially induced industries continue to expand. To take the example of the automobile, the induced growth effects consisted of the army of mechanics and gas station employees, the new tourist industry, and public investments in roads, bridges, and tunnels. Still, the downswing triggered by the mismatch of production with consumption gains momentum and is reinforced by entrepreneurs who act defensively in the face of crisis. They rationalize their production through new methods which already incorporate elements of the coming technological style. The widening gap between process and product innovations during the transition from the 1960s to the 1970s has been demonstrated empirically by Alfred Kleinknecht (1987). Only the crystallization phase brings about a fresh range of products and services and thus a new match between productive opportunities and consumption that leads to the unfolding of a new technological style.

By the fascination of novel goods and services we mean inventions which put people under their spell because they complement human capacities. They render possible things that people would not naturally be able to do. Thus their fascination stems from an amplification of human action and experience. It is therefore not surprising that changes in transportation and communications have been key projects lending substantial impulse to the development of technological style. Railways were the key project of the development of technological style during the first wave following the liberal revolts of 1830/48, whereas it was electrification during the second and cars during the third wave. Finally, the informatization of society is the key project of the coming technological style.

RECURRENT LIMITS TO GROWTH FOR ENTERPRISES

A technological style unfolds in the alternating play of organizations and markets. Joseph Schumpeter, though he mentioned industrial organization and capitalist enterprises in his theory of long waves, stressed the role of the capitalist entrepreneur. But, "new entrepreneurs" normally "reanimate" and redirect already existing enterprises. During their evolution enterprises mutate in response to recurring limits of feasibility in organizational and technological development. This merits special attention because the innovation literature favors spectacular changes on the product side.

Expansion in the scale of enterprises is a central feature of the development of formal organization. Not only have leading enterprises grown enormously, but also the average size of firms has increased dramatically over approximately two centuries of industrialization. At any given time, the dominant large firms normally grew at a faster rate than the bulk of the remaining ones. Do firms then grow to an unlimited scale?

In an attempt to explain enterprise growth, organicist growth models have drawn on biological analogies and models of nuclear division (Haire

1959; Starbuck 1965). In this perspective there are two factors hampering development and finally leading to stagnation after a phase of exponential growth: organization and the market. In the long run, however, the unlimited expansion of scale suggested by such theories do not stand up because organizations do not have a genetically determined developmental potential. Rather, they can mutate. Organization theory stresses management and communication problems. One limit to further growth of already large enterprises is organizational-administrative adaptation to their increasing scale. In this perspective, growth decreases if there is no adaptation because, in the absence of structural adjustment, continued organizational growth leads to growing inefficiency. Edith Penrose (1968: 44ff.) has pointed to the temporarily limited enhancement of firm performance through the scarcity of the entrepreneurial and managerial services after a period of rapid growth (see also chapter 8).

Yet, it is not the scarcity of entrepreneurial capacity alone but a more general problem of control that lies at the core of management and communication problems. Even under conditions of appropriate enhancement of entrepreneurial capacity and management, a loss of control as a result of the bureaucratic-hierarchic structure is unavoidable at any given level of administrative technology. Arguments along such lines have been advanced by Oliver E. Williamson, R. Joseph Monsen and Anthony Downs (see Bornschier 1976: 81, 104). Williamson for example, points to "a great deal of evidence that almost all organizational structures tend to produce false images in the decision-maker, and that the larger and more authoritarian the organization, the better the chance that its top decision-makers will be operating in purely imaginary worlds." (1967: 123)

For Williamson, the loss of control results from "serial reproduction distortion that occurs in communicating across successive hierarchical levels" and becomes even more extensive if goals differ between hierarchical levels (Williamson 1967: 135). Costs and loss of control announce the delay and finally the cessation of expansion. But then, how did large modern corporations ever evolve from the family enterprises of early industrialization? The answer, of course, is: organizations mutated. It is not correct to posit constant administrative technology. Edith Penrose has pointed to the differences in administrative structure between very large and very small firms, which "are so great that in many ways it is hard to see that the two species are of the same genus" (Penrose 1968: 19). In addition, her observation holds not only for small and large enterprises but also for the leading firms in different eras of organizational development.

Interestingly, changes in organizational structure always emerge in clusters. They begin when expansion stagnates and economic growth on the basis of conventional strategies of market monopolization encounters limits. Organizational changes are elements of the technological style, but they only emerge after a new technological style has crystallized and—supplemented by general societal innovations on the basis of a revised consensus—trigger a fresh general wave of expansion.

Mention can be made of certain quantum leaps in the solution of the organizational efficiency problem. In the course of the railway boom around the mid-nineteenth-century, the classical family-owned firms ran up against their limits. The enormous amounts of capital needed could no longer be mobilized through family accumulation alone. The institutional solution to this problem was the joint-stock company, i.e., the modern corporation, whose limited liability greatly favored its expansion. After making its first appearance in the 1860s and 70s, it gained acceptance during the upswing phase of the 1890s and became the typical organizational form of leading firms. In fact, the wave of monopolization at the turn of the century only became possible because the joint-stock company considerably facilitated vertical and horizontal integration through mergers and takeovers.

But the typical large firm of the turn of the century, the highly centralized corporation, raised new problems of inefficiency. The organizational solution was the modern corporate structure: a multisectoral structure with overall corporate management and special staff functions for long-term planning at the top. At the subordinate level corporate sectors are structured multi-functionally according to products and/or regions, which include a division of management functions into sectoral and operational management. This transition, which initially only took effect within a small group of American corporations during the 1920s, has been studied and described by Alfred Chandler (1962, 1977).

A further control problem of the turn of the century boom arose out of an intensifying class struggle. While corporations had grown large, the processes of manual operation had not basically changed. Workers and their foremen were in control of the work process. Their growing organization and resistance meant increasing loss of control for management and thus inefficiency. The organizational answer was "scientific management" or Taylorism—a new kind of division of labor which secured control by dividing work into planning and executive activities, introducing precise time and processing schedules and standardizing tasks and tools. Around the turn of the century, Frederick Taylor (1911) experimented with his "scientific management," and by the 1920s several leading firms had already applied the new methods of work organization. Still, the real breakthrough of Taylorism occurred only during the general upswing after World War II.

At the level of organization the new work methods created an enormous proliferation of detailed planning, coordination, and communication. The resulting increases in planning and coordinating costs became a problem during the 1960s. Only the expanding markets at the semiperiphery and monopolistic profits of oligopolies were able to offset this organizational inefficiency which became intensified by a new control problem: the increasing refusal of the workforce to fully engage themselves, particularly at the level of routine work (see also chapter 8). Here, the organizational answer was computer-aided planning, surveillance, and communication.

The multisectoral structure of the leading corporations also reached its boundaries. Individual sectors grew very large themselves and required decentralization. The new system, "management by control," exhibits a fresh element: control now consists of decentralized, cybernetic regulations of independently responsible decision-makers combined with step-by-step, centralized surveillance of net profit contributions. Behavior and success control are decentralized, while marketing and planning are merged into a new system within the corporation and measured through the so-called profit centers.

MONOPOLIZATION AND THE NEGLECT OF BASIC INNOVATIONS

In the course of product development and market penetration, firms regularly enter into conflict with their environment, the markets. During the upswing phase those firms grow fastest which have new ideas, launch new products, and thus create new markets. An innovative range of products emerges and gradually spreads during the upswing. Around such products, as for example the automobile, new or changed lifestyles emerge, first only accessible to the upper strata. Yet, the lower strata also wish to participate in the new lifestyles; during the upswing this goal becomes increasingly realistic. The new range of products as well as their use become an element of the social structure. The products and their corresponding lifestyles become social imperatives as status symbols develop a close relationship to social stratification.

If competition was originally centered around innovations and risky market launchings, it now shifts to the consolidation of consumption patterns (by way of advertising), refining innovations, and finally to sham innovations (fashions). Mass becomes essential even if its appearance is avoided by differentiating products. Firms producing great quantities at low prices to supply broad markets grow. The big beat the small. Concentration and the power of large firms grow and bureaucratic standardization as an organizational principle parallels increasing product standardization.

Once the fascinating products have penetrated from the top to the bottom of the social pyramid saturation becomes a problem. At first, wealthy consumers turn their backs on the mass market and begin to experiment with alternative lifestyles. This is the era of the cultural revolts against the institutionalized material mass culture that began during the 1960s in Europe. That the world market is still large and profits are quite attractive prevents a rethinking of the giants which had grown so large during the expansion process. This contradiction between organization and the market defines the limits to growth, which in the history of the industrial system has been overcome only by depressions and the ensuing reordering of industry and the gamut of the range of products.

The growing organizational problems resulting from increasing size can initially be contained by administrative reorganizations, i.e., by concealing lack of efficiency. Further growth and diversification are still possible by takeovers and acquisition of other firms. However, such external growth gradually changes the organizational power center towards a financial holding company which participates less and less in the industrial system's characteristic task of creating value. This affects the vital functions of the industrial system, which is based on the courage to launch risky basic innovations. After a while, the dominance of financial capital implies the end of industrial dynamics and encourages speculation.

The outcome of this development is a deficit in industrial ideas for new breakthroughs. This deficit cannot be offset by bureaucratic institutionalization of research and development, because such activities are mostly of a defensive nature. They are less preoccupied with basic innovations of new products than with improvements of existing ones, and, later, with sham innovations. Risk aversion, market dominance, and fear of the destruction of invested capital by new products and processes are the reasons for the absence of basic innovations. Competition in quality in the interest of the consumer is neglected as a result of market dominance and tacit agreements. This perspective is reflected in the work of Gerhard Mensch (1975: 219).

According to Gerhard Mensch (1975: 121), stagnation has "its roots in the exhaustion of the improvement potential of the old technologies and the resulting concentration of supply and saturation of demand. Both factors express the unwillingness of the well-off to purchase mass goods satisfying formerly 'advanced' needs in quantities which the existing capacities in growth industries would be able to produce." (our translation). This recurring situation constitutes the limit to growth for firms. Yet, according to past experience, a further upswing favors new industries where firms are larger than average; established firms are not often members of this new elite, however.

Gerhard Mensch refutes the idea that the economy evolves in cycles. In his perspective, economic activity is characterized by thrusts of succeeding S-shaped cycles, each of which resembles a logistic curve. In his book he has presented impressive historical material for 1745-1965 that shows that so-called basic innovations have, in fact, occurred discontinuously in the past (Mensch 1975: 142). Further, he shows that the discontinuity of basic innovations (their first industrial applications) cannot be attributed to discontinuous scientific discoveries (Mensch 1975: 176-178). According to him, basic innovations occur suddenly and in clusters during the depression phase. As their gestation requires some time, however, they cannot immediately become the source of a new economic upswing.

THE CRYSTALLIZATION THESIS

While Gerhard Mensch's material is very impressive, a closer look reveals that the data only refer to basic innovations in new products. This is too restricted a perspective. In his discussion of the dynamics of investment, Joseph Schumpeter mentioned not only new consumer goods but also new production and transportation methods, new markets, new forms of industrial organization, and new resources (e.g., oil). Our notion of technological style is much broader than Mensch's definition of basic innovations.

In order to clarify this, one might compare technological style to a botanical plant able to regenerate itself. The plant draws through its roots energy sources and basic materials, of which it can assimilate both improved old ones as well as new ones. The basic materials are the forces that pulsate through the whole plant. The stem channels and multiplies these forces according to laws of mechanization, division of labor, and organizational structure. Different industrial sectors would be the plant's branches—some half dried up, others sprouting, some springing directly from the stem, others growing out oddly. Finally, the leaves and flowers stand for the different products that emerge from old as well as new branches. Although this analogy should not be overdone, one thing becomes clear: if we concentrate too much on "leaves" and "flowers," we can lose sight of the whole plant, i.e., the technological style.

Each particular component of a technological style must be harmonized with the others to allow for a quantum leap in productivity. Yet, without renewal of the range of products, the plant cannot "bloom," and the possible quantum leap does not induce a closed circular flow of employment and consumption. For that reason, a renewal in the range of products is of crucial importance; around it a technological style definitely crystallizes and forcefully unfolds.

Gerhard Mensch's argument regarding clustered basic innovations that occur during a depression and lead the way out of a crisis as well as his data have not gone uncriticized, as the following reappraisals show.

First, basic innovations do indeed occur in clusters. Thus, they take place in a discontinuous fashion. Alfred Kleinknecht (1986, 1987, 1992) has compiled data from various sources to eliminate the idiosyncrasies of particular classifications. His data for 1900 - 1974 can be found in Table 5.1 where they have been grouped according to our own structural formula advanced in chapter 4. It is easy to see that basic innovations per year exhibit a clear temporal concentration in all four columns during the short time span 1935-1939. This deviation is statistically significant.

Second, the innovation peak does not occur during the depression phase as suggested by Mensch, but during the early upswing. This has been postulated and verified by John Clark, Christopher Freeman and Luc Soete (1981) and by Jacob van Duijn (1981). Table 5.1 also shows that the peak of radical innovations falls within the early phase of the upswing. We have further demonstrated that there was a general upswing in industrial production from 1933 onwards which, however, was dramatically curtailed by the war in several countries (Bornschier 1988: 161). It would be wrong to explain this upswing by war preparations, however (see chapter 7).

TABLE 5.1 Basic Innovations According to Different Sources, 1900-1974

Phases according to our structural formula (see chapter 4)		Periods according to Kleinknecht, correspondingly collapsed	Radically new products (a) #	per year	Basic innovations (b) #	per year	Basic innovations (c) #	per year	Basic innovations (d) #	per year
parts of	P	1900-1904	0	0	1	0.2	5	1	1	0.2
	PR	1905-1914	1	0.1	7	0.7	8	0.8	6	0.6
	C*)	1915-1920	0	0.1	1	0.2	2	0.4	1	0.2
	IR	1920-1929	6	1.2	3	0.6	10	2.0	7	0.7
	D	1930-1934	5	1.0	6	1.2	5	1.0	6	1.2
early U	U†)	1935-1939	11	2.2	8	1.6	15	3.0	12	2.4
war	U	1940-1944	5	1.0	6	1.2	7	1.4	10	2.0
cont. U and	P‡)	1945-1959	13	0.9	12	0.8	22	1.5	15	1.5
	P	1960-1964	7	1.4	4	0.8	9	1.8	1	0.2
	PR	1965-1974	5	0.5	2	0.2	8	0.8	3	0.3

Note: All series taken from the compilation in Kleinknecht (1987); Series (a): radically new products (including scientific instruments) according to Kleinknecht. Series (b): Basic innovations according to van Duijn. Series (c): Basic innovations according to Hanstein and Neuwirth. Series (d): Basic innovations according to Mensch but supplemented by Kleinknecht and revised according to the critique by Clark et al. (1981). Basic innovations 1965-1974 may be an underestimate because the time frame may have been too short for the authors to recognize radical innovations. For details of sources see Kleinknecht (1987).
*) Sets in before World War I (about 1913).
†) The upswing begins in 1932, after the trough.
‡) For some countries the period immediately following the war was already one of "prosperity" (see Bornschier 1988: 161).
Source: Kleinknecht (1986: 375; 1987).

The crystallization thesis explains the clustered occurrence of basic innovations during the early upswing, the elements of the new technological style having been consolidated and linked to each other during the interim recovery. What was lacking for full crystallization was the extended range of products, which make their appearance during the recovery *after* depression, when the politico-economic regime emits clear signals of a new beginning. Therefore, growth after depression is more than mere recovery; it is in fact the beginning of a long upswing.

Third, the clustering of basic innovations refers more to product than to process innovations. Jacob van Duijn (1981) suggests instead, that process innovations are initiated during the downswing (our PR phase), whereas product innovations occur during the upswing. Alfred Kleinknecht (1986) not only finds empirical peaks of process innovations during his "depression phase" (our early upswing phase), but also during late prosperity (our PR-phase). His empirical material on Great Britain confirms that process innovations have the two above mentioned peaks. In addition, it is evident for different phases of our structural cycle that during interim recovery (1920-29), process innovations are more important than product innovations. Both types of innovations are equally important during depression (1929-1932), the total number of innovations being very low, however. During the early upswing (1932-1945) as well as during its continuation until 1960-62, product innovations are more frequent than process innovations; however, the latter become more important close to the prosperity-recession phase. Consequently, process innovations grow more frequent after 1962, while product innovations decrease (see Kleinknecht 1987: 137).

The empirical findings referring to the discontinuous occurrence of radical innovations in industrial production are thus in accordance with the notion of a sequence of technological styles. Process innovations start during the saturation phase of a technological style whereas product innovations occur during the early upswing phase, thus leading to the crystallization of a technological style.[1]

BASIC MATERIALS AND MECHANIZATION

Although basic materials and mechanization have already been mentioned, their importance has not yet been fully assessed. Basic materials used to produce tools have lent their names to whole eras of human history (Stone Age, Bronze Age, Iron Age), and for this reason they must not be omitted from a discussion of technological styles. In our botanical analogy basic materials are drawn through the "roots" of the plant. Apart from working materials, energy sources are equally important basic materials.

Energy and working materials mark the limits of possibilities in mechanizing work processes. The triad composed by energy source, the strength and additional properties of materials, and the form of mechanization has repeatedly encountered limits of feasability over the history of industrialization. But these limits were always overcome by path-breaking innovations in all three components. There is no reason to suppose that this will fail to recur in the future.

Three events of the historic years 1765-1767 before the definitive upswing of English eighteenth century industrialization can be taken as illustrative examples.[2] In 1765 James Watt built the first low-pressure steam engine, for which he took out a patent in 1769. The result was a new and more flexible power source being made available for nascent industry. Further, the first blast furnace in England able to produce larger quantities of iron was built in 1766. This alleviated the scarcity of iron, but problems persisted because the raw iron was brittle and not easily malleable due to its high carbon content. Between 1785 and 1796, during the peak of the English wave, there were substantial improvements in smelting on the basis of coke. Finally, in 1767, James Hargreaves constructed the first spinning machine. "The machine reduces the price of yarn but destroys many jobs" is how this was perceived in terms of societal evolution. Of course, the former is the outcome of the latter and could already be observed in milling, the factories of the Middle Ages in Europe (Gimpel 1975). At that time, the problem of job loss seems to have been less pressing as low levels of productivity in agriculture recruited almost every available hand for the production of food. In 1775, the spinning machine was improved and propelled by hydraulic power. A further and decisive step in the mechanization of the then leading textile industry was the introduction of the mechanical loom in 1822.

These three examples of process innovations at the beginning of the definitive breakthrough of industrialization show that its history was from the outset not merely that of mechanization. Rather, it was the melding of mechanization, materials, and energy sources that was of decisive significance.

Rod Coombs (1984: 677), referring to the work of Martin Bell (1972), suggests viewing mechanization as more than just a single unilinear process. For the study of the mechanization process, three dimensions are important: 1) Mechanization in the transformation of workpieces (termed primary mechanization); 2) Mechanization in the transfer of workpieces between transformation sites (termed secondary mechanization), and 3) Mechanization in the control of the above mentioned transformation and transfer (termed tertiary mechanization).

Mechanization thus means that human labor in transformation, transfer, and control is executed by machines. But we tend to speak of automation if the control process in transformation and transfer is executed by machines only. However, automation itself can be fixed or flexible (Coombs 1984). Numerical control machine tools (NC) are examples of fixed automation, and computer-aided numerical control machine tools (CNC) are examples of flexible automation of the same type of primary mechanization. Similarly, flow technologies with mechanical switchers or sensors are examples of fixed automation in secondary mechanization. Computer-aided manufacturing (CAM) would be a corresponding example for a flexible technology.

The three stages of mechanization suggested by Coombs can be assigned to the three past technological styles in the following manner. The first wave, encompassing large parts of the core, was characterized by primary mechanization in connection with the railway boom. This was amplified by the appearance of machine tools. During the next wave, the electrification boom, elements of secondary mechanization were already present, but primary mechanization remained dominant, however. Within the framework of the third wave, the automobile boom, secondary mechanization becomes predominant as is evidenced by the introduction of flow and assembly-line technologies. This kind of mechanization of transfers exhibits some features of fixed automation. In the coming technological style (discussed below) flexible control technologies in the framework of tertiary mechanization are to become predominant. In this connection it can be remarked that the corresponding findings of Coombs (1984) fit the thesis that new elements of a future technological style begin to appear during the prosperity-recession phase.

While Rod Coombs' stages of mechanization may be helpfully employed as a classification system, his perspective on mechanization does not sufficiently stress the important role of energy sources and of those materials which render surges of mechanization possible in the first place; they also constrain mechanization because the limits of feasibility with respect to energy use and the qualities of the materials are reached sooner or later. This extended perspective is advocated by David Landes (1969) and was also extensively discussed in the original German version of this book. For reasons of space, however, we cannot go into further details here concerning the technological developments which have occurred since the early nineteenth century.

TAYLORISM AND PROCESS PRODUCTION

The history of mechanization tells only one side of the story, for the dimension of work organization is often neglected. Work organization under the technological style of this century consisted of two analytically separable features: the new forms of work organization, i.e., scientific management or Taylorism[3], on the one hand, and a further stage of mechanization, i.e., secondary mechanization or process and flow technology on the other. Both create substantial thrusts and together with the other components of the technological style they are responsible for the quantum leap in productivity. But it must be stressed that these productive thrusts happen especially during the transition to the new model of work organization. On the whole, progress in productivity is considerable while the new style spreads. Once everything has been organized according to the new model, the dynamics of the productivity cease.

Taylorism (Taylor 1911) was characterized by the separation of planning and execution, on the one hand, and the detailed division of labor for production work. This was not only accompanied by cost cuts but also by a change in the job structure to favor office and technical personnel. At the same time, income distribution changed correspondingly. The remaining workers earned a lot more than before and a new group of middle income earners expanded substantially.

Yet improvement in income distribution only has a positive aggregate effect if workers made redundant succeed in finding comparably paid jobs elsewhere. If this is not the case or if too many people lose their jobs, aggregate income distribution does not improve. Instead, the outcome is a dual structure with corresponding income differences between those within the new work organization and those excluded from it.

In fact, from long-term data for Germany between 1882 and 1970 it is evident that the transition to Taylorism led to an extension of the middle class (see Kleber 1983: 70f.). During the technological style which peaks at the turn of the century, the increase of clerical workers is moderate and unable to compensate for the decrease in self-employment; the middle class as a whole was shrinking according to the data for the German empire. At the transition from the old to the new technological style the share of clerical workers is clearly higher and compensates for the decline in self-employment. There is a stabilization in the magnitude of the middle class, which includes about equal shares of members from the old and the new middle class. During the diffusion phase of the new technological style (after 1950), the share of employees increases again and more than compensates for the loss of self-employment. The middle class as a whole expands considerably and finally includes more than half the working population; within the middle class, its "new" segment becomes most important.

FIGURE 5.1 Clerical and Technical Workers as a Percentage of all Industrial Workers, Grouped According to Plant Size, German Empire and Federal Republic of Germany, 1907 - 1970

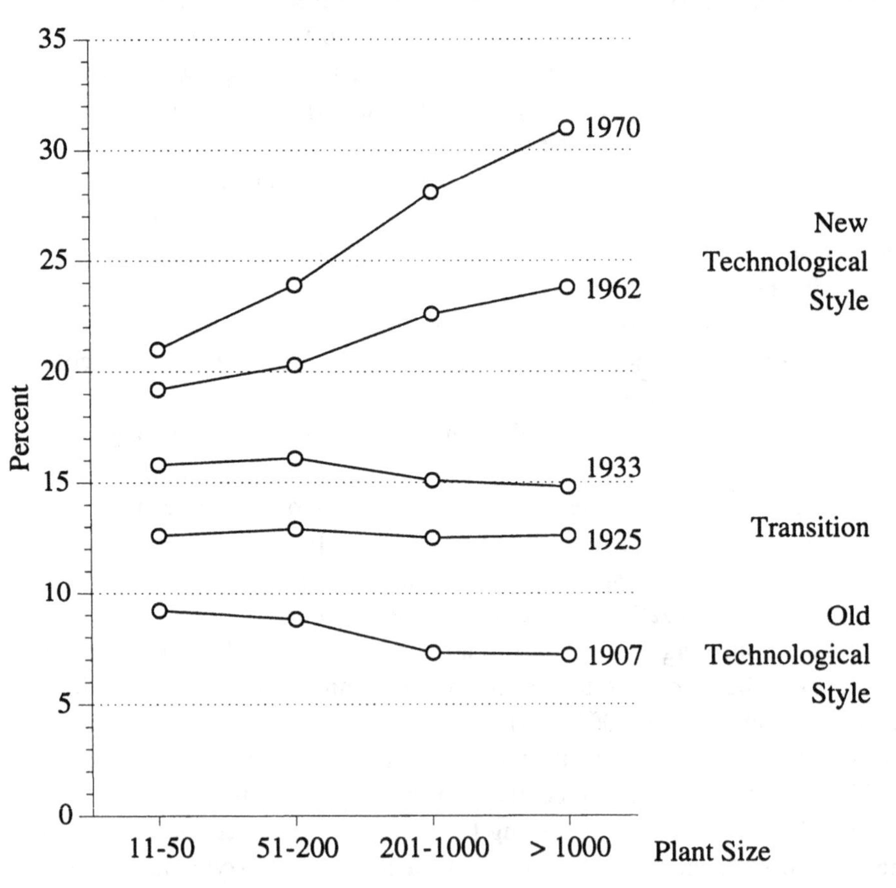

Source: Stockmann (1981: 109) and Stockmann et al. (1983).

Apart from Taylorism, the rise of process production must be stressed. New technical production processes are also independent contributors to quantum leaps in productivity during the transition from one technological style to another. In the production of sulphuric acid, for example, flow technology made its appearance around the turn of the century. Over the following 70 years (1895-1963) the personnel necessary for producing sulphuric acid was reduced from 100 to 7 persons per unit. As this reduction occurred in a strongly discontinuous fashion, the example substantiates our hypothesis that new technological styles begin during the downswing phase of the economic cycle (see Kern and Schumann 1984: 247f, 253; Bornschier 1988: 112f.).

As elements of the new technological style, flow technology and Taylorism brought about a change in work organization during this century. After the diffusion of the new style, this change also became evident in the class composition of society and in income distribution. In figure 5.1, the changing work organization in German industry as a whole is shown as a comparison of the changes that the shares of technical and clerical workers underwent in relation to the share of production workers.

During the previous technological style, the administrative component was reduced with growing plant size. The bigger the enterprises, the more office personnel was saved. This relationship certainly promoted the corporate mergers that took place before and after the turn of the century. Under the new technological style, the administrative component (particularly technical employees) increases substantially because Taylorism and secondary mechanization call for more supervising, communication, and technical personnel while making many production jobs obsolete.

THE AUTOMOBILE AS THE KEY PRODUCT OF THE PREVIOUS TECHNOLOGICAL STYLE

The central projects of the joint waves of industrialization at the core have been the railway boom during the wave which peaked in the second third of the nineteenth century, electrification during the wave peaking around the turn of the century and automobiles during the wave which peaked during the 1950s (in the United States) and 1960s (in Europe). These projects are the key to understanding the corresponding epochs and lifestyles. In addition, they are central to identity, guarantees of job security, and the dynamic of the industrial movement. The automobile is a good example of the fact that technological style changes do not fit the economic wave perfectly but exhibit a phase displacement. The change in style has altered the automobile.

Cars could already if only rarely be seen on the roads during the peak of the foregoing wave (see Fondin 1969). Apart from the new methods of mass production, important technical improvements from the 1920s (interim recovery) until the 1930s made a new product out of the car as we know it today. At the outset of the 1930s, the "package" for one element of the upswing was ready: the pioneering automobile had changed into a new product which would soon become the key project.

While data for general economic development between 1925 and 1935 do not exhibit substantial changes, the diffusion of the range of products did change. In the mid-1930s important products are on their way to becoming the cornerstones of new lifestyles, particularly during leisure time. Leisure and individualization propel the ensuing further broadening of consumption. At the same time, average household size decreases during the new wave of industrialization.

If one chooses to use information on only a single product to describe the growth of global industrial production during the postwar period, the very number of cars produced would be a good indicator since every fourth job in the Western industrial countries was directly or indirectly linked to the car.

The reasons for the current stagnation of petrochemicals, the basic industry, and car production, the key industry, are obvious. In Western core society the saturation point of car traffic has been overstepped, physically as well as ecologically. In 1980, the density of cars was 400 to 540 per 1,000 inhabitants in North America and Oceania. Apart from some exceptions, the corresponding figures for Europe lie between 300 and 400. Only Japan, with its 200 cars per 1,000 inhabitants, has a somewhat lower car density. Even though there is an enormous theoretical potential in other countries, a similar density of cars there would cause a gigantic global environmental catastrophe if the current technology were used.

The global situation requires a future-oriented and integrative solution for this and comparable problems. A new, "softer," and less resource-intensive technological style is an ecological necessity. At the same time, such a style would allow the participation of broader segments of the world population in its technological potential, impossible under the past style.

INFORMATION AND LEAN PRODUCTION AS ELEMENTS OF A NEW TECHNOLOGICAL STYLE

It was suggested that a change of technological style lays the basis for a revolution in resource productivity during its later diffusion. At the outset of the long downswing of the postwar era (prosperity-recession phase, in Europe from 1967 onwards, in the United States from 1958 onwards) important initial elements of a future technological style appear. Tertiary mechanization, i.e., flexible and programmable automation of integrated work places, which lays the foundation for full automation in several industries, is once again bound to pathbreaking advances in basic materials. If, during the past style, petroleum was the most important basic material and the car was the key project, the new style's central project is the computer as a vehicle for informatization; the chip becomes the basic material.

The revolution in the productivity of factors, now under way, is based on cheap (and progressively cheaper) microelectronics and digital telecommunications, aptly described in some of its dimensions as early as 1985 by Carlota Perez (1985). Computers and cabled or wireless networking are its components. The energy and raw material intensity of the previous technological style are replaced by information intensity at ever-diminishing cost. Robots begin to produce with unbelievable speed, even undertaking quality control; they reduce wastage, are quick and precise, suffer no fatigue, and require no motivation. Stocks are reduced or even junked in accordance with the "just-in-time" concept. Materials and their unnecessary flows are economized by, amongst other things, recycling, while energy conservation results from the use of microcomputers to control processes. Mass production is no longer the high road to greater productivity, as Perez shows. It can equally be achieved through a diversified range of production in limited runs. Flexibility in production becomes the watchword, tending towards the fashioning of single items, as once was done by hand. Nor is production alone in undergoing a revolution. People become more productive because they can communicate through networks, obtain information faster and more comprehensively and have access to almost unimaginable software. Other innovations are the use of artificial intelligence, translation software, combinations of audiovisual media and a markedly closer association of global hubs.

Against this background, a revolution in the productivity of resources of all kinds is under way: labor, capital, energy, and raw materials are all subject to it. Productivity is here defined as value added per unit of resource input. This revolution—Carlota Perez's quantum leap in productivity—not only saves labor. Potentially, capital invested in inefficient plant labor, in raw materials and land, as well as in flexible machines is also saved. The revolution not only economizes but also makes capital and labor more productive in a hitherto unknown way. As a result, economic flows can broaden and generate an increasing need for skilled workers. Still, it would be wrong to stress only the revolution in production: distribution, traffic and communications (telebanking, electronic fund transfers at the point of sales etc.) are undergoing substantial changes, too.

The present change of technological style leads society into the age of information. Information technology is the key, consisting of semi-conductors, computers, communications, entertainment electronics and automation. The information and communication (I&C) technologies put people into a position to store, handle, and globally convey as well as receive quantities of information unheard of to date. The outcome is a transition from the traditional industrial economy to an information economy (Seitz 1991: 8).

Without further analysis, the catchword "information society" only encompasses the phenomenological level, however. In our perspective, I&C technologies must be further analyzed as the most important cornerstones of the emerging technological style. This is also the perspective of Freeman and Soete (1991) who report the findings of the Maastricht Economic Institute on Innovation and Technology (MERIT), (see also the survey on the *New Technologies in the 1990's* by the OECD 1988). Information technology in such a perspective refers to a new variety of products and services as well as to a technology that is bound to revolutionize production and distribution in all branches of industry and the services. The I&C complex has emerged over the past two decades as a result of a series of closely associated basic improvements in microelectronics, spun glass technology, software development and communications and computer technology (see Freeman and Soete 1991: 6).

Viewing the I&C technologies as core elements of a new style stresses technology and not only information. The new technology (often also called cross-cutting technology) is pervasive, i.e., one that permeates each and every sector. In this perspective, it is not only new industries and services but also the reshaping of old ones which have important societal impacts (Freeman and Soete 1991; Freeman 1989; OECD 1988). As policy strategies, diffusion methods aimed at applications and training are designed. Thus, it is not only the development of software, but also basic and continuing training for software users which forms part of necessary societal activities. The implication for technology policy is the need for general technology programs with particular stress on the user side. I&C in the new technological style not only affects different services and industries, but also each particular functional task within these sectors, such as for example research and development, manufacturing, marketing, transportation, and administration. In this perspective, I&C can be understood as a name for systematization surpassing automation insofar as the different, formerly separated departments and tasks are joined together systematically within the framework of organizations.

Apart from information technology, four further constituents of the new technological style analyzed by Konrad Seitz (1991) must be mentioned (see also Bornschier 1988). First, there is biotechnology which is very ancient (wine fermentation, brewing beer, leavening dough, as well as animal breeding and grafting plants) but has been radically transformed by one of the most dramatic discoveries in research history leading to the birth of genetic engineering: the ability to decode the DNA molecule.

Like information technology, biotechnology, or the "information technology of life", is also a cross-cutting technology that fundamentally affects a series of industries and services. It leads to a new science of medicine and a new agriculture and it transforms mining as well as the oil and chemical industries. According to Seitz's (1991) prognosis, the revolution in information technology of the 1980s and the 1990s will most probably be followed by a revolution in biotechnology at the outset of the twenty-first century.

Other important constituents are new technologies in connection with materials (see Bornschier 1988; Seitz 1991). The sequence of Stone Age, Bronze Age, Iron Age and Steel Age leads us into the age of synthetic materials. High-performance working materials with incredible properties are appearing. Semiconductors are a basic material like petroleum, and together with hydrogen (or methanol) they may well become the "oil" of the turn of the millennia. They make possible the production of photovoltaic solar cells and microelectronic chips which are basic for information technology. New giant industries, such as for example the computer industry, are based on the chip. In the shadows of this technology a new one is already emerging that may well drive out the old one at the end of the century: *optical* computers and *supra*conductors.

Energy technology is a further important element. Neither petroleum nor nuclear fission are likely to be the energy sources of the future. Currently, various renewable sources, as for example batteries powered by solar energy, are being studied and improved. Apart from novel accumulators, hydrogen and substances containing hydrogen are of particular interest (Bornschier 1988: 105-109). Finally, space technology must be mentioned, but since it will only affect the distant future but not necessarily the next technological style, it will not be discussed further here (see Seitz 1991: 18).

A technological style based on modern physics, chemistry (semi- and supraconductors, catalysts) and biotechnology may well generate path-breaking thrusts before the turn of the millennium. This may go hand in hand with a blurring of traditional boundaries between physics, chemistry, and biology and the emergence of interdisciplinary research and technology development. Methods adapted to environmental and resource-saving requirements are just two of the already perceptible directions which the transition will take.

As mentioned above, basic materials and new avenues of mechanization constitute only part of the technological style. "Technology" includes, as we have seen, not only artifacts but also the way they are used or the way people act in a transformed environment. Some new management techniques and forms of work organization may thus now be discussed.

A system evolved in Japan some time ago has affected manufacturing in the Western world for several years. It is known as "lean production"—or sometimes as "Japanization." Lean production stands for a whole organizational complex as "Taylorism" once did (Womack et al. 1990). The basic idea is to replace fixed and dull work (for example on the assembly line) with work in teams. Each team executes a whole set of work processes and is responsible for the highest possible product quality. For this reason, the teams are also called "quality circles" (Imai 1992). The Japanese lead has trigged a debate on quality management and new organizational forms in order to meet the challenge (Jürgens et al. 1989; Jürgens 1992, 1994; Roth 1992; Weber 1994; Zink 1994).

Compared to Fordism and Taylorism, lean production has two decisive advantages, which are also mentioned by Womack et al. (1990) and Seitz (1991: 170): "First, it requires less of everything—half of the workers in manufacturing and development, half the production space, a tenth of the inventories of components, etc.; defects can already be remedied during production and do not later have to be detected in the repair area; the standard of quality thus is considerably higher than in conventional assembly line production. Second, lean production is flexible and renders possible the cheap production of short runs; it is not only possible to produce different variants of one car on the same production line, but even different models" (our translation).

According to Japanese experience, the outcome is a cooperative relationship between management and trade unions at the level of industrial relations. Lean production is a procedure that favors consensus in decision-making and enhances the identification of workers with their enterprise. Joint responsibility for quality also leads to intensive cooperation and solidarity within the teams. A team of experts from the Massachusetts Institute of Technology (MIT) (Womack, Jones, and Roos 1990) even claims that "lean production will truly change the world." The corresponding tools are computer-integrated manufacturing (CIM) and just-in-time (JIT) production—two key concepts of new management practices to be discussed briefly.

Under the JIT concept, components are only produced and sent to the production location if they are really needed. In that way, production becomes optimally flexible. Large inventories are no longer necessary. According to Womack et al. (1990) it is wrong to attribute the success of the Japanese to a massive output of standardized products. Quite to the contrary, under JIT the Japanese have managed to customize their production.

Just-in-time *(kamban* in Japanese) is not a mere means of rationalization and increased productivity. It extends beyond production, sales, and marketing into all areas of management and decision-making (Holl and Trevor 1988). Thus, a Volkswagen executive familiar with the system points out: "In speaking of just-in-time, we mean a management philosophy that has spread through the managerial system like an ideology. (. . .) If we view the just-in-time system as the opposite of functionally differentiated plant organization according to Taylorist principles, then it becomes clear that just-in-time is a reversal" (Höhn 1988: 85, our translation), the end of the old system and a transition in the direction of post-Taylorism. One needs to add that *kaizen* (continuous improvement process) is also a key element in the Japanese concept of lean production (Imai 1992) which—due to its emphasis on "humanware"—offers a competitive edge.

The "humanization of work" movement had already originated in the 1970s in order to escape from the dead end of Taylorism. But it was the demonstrated economic success of the Japanese that helped make the new human-centred methods of work the model for management.

The new management philosophy leads to a flattening of the hierarchical pyramid because computer-aided information systems and partly autonomous groups can coordinate and control what used to be the responsibility of lower management. More autonomy and responsibility are shifted to teams. At the same time, there is a growing interpenetration of functional spheres. At the level of the employees this requires multiple skills so that employees can oversee the whole production process. Conventional hierarchies and management practices thus become increasingly questionable.

The coming amalgamation of management philosophy with the hardware and software of the I&C technologies can be demonstrated by the example of computer-integrated manufacturing (CIM). This new concept of production can be interpreted as systematization, i.e., a new stage of automation. Freeman and Soete (1991) have pointed out the difference between automation and systematization, CIM being an example of systematization—the networking and coupling of flexible, i.e., computer-aided, automation.

CIM means the integration of what has, in some instances, existed for years. Computer-aided numerical control (CNC) machine tools of the third generation, computer-aided engineering (CAE), computer-aided development (CAD) and computer-aided manufacturing (CAM) are all integrated under CIM. CIM is an ideal example of technology because it is not a machine or a fixed system of production, like the assembly line, but a concept.

CIM technology embraces some substantial innovations. First, mechanization and automation make mass production obsolete. Flexible manufacturing of small quantities becomes possible, unit production being the ultimate goal. Second, the new technology renders possible production according to the just-in-time principle. There are no stocks, everything is produced to order. Thus, it is possible to adapt quickly to individually differentiated and rapidly changing demands. Third, the new technology not only saves work, an aspect very prominent in the public debate, but also capital. Machines can be reprogrammed in a flexible way and may therefore be used for different tasks. In addition, under JIT ordering, warehousing and controlling stocks are needed no longer.

SUMMARIZING AND CONCLUDING REMARKS

This brief prospect should not be misunderstood as an attempt to spread misguided technological optimism. Experience shows, however, that much more was possible in the past than was believed by contemporary observers, particularly during the pessimistic phases that always accompanied transitions of technological style. Yet we may ask a new question today: can or should we do everything that is possible? The risks of new technologies must be considered and controlled. But potentials must not be neglected in the discussion of risks. The new technological style does not necessarily imply greater conventional consumption for Western society. There are also possibilities of broadening the market. By overcoming current environmental and resource limits, world population may be able to participate more fully in what has become a matter of course in the "rich North". In order to make, however, information society generalizable and workable, a new source of energy is required with which the insecurities of previous petroleum-based development can be put aside (see chapter 15).

The new technological style, the contours of which can be recognized today, has the following features, which represent the components for the development of a technological style referred to at the beginning of this chapter. These features are summarized again briefly here.

The central element of the new basic materials is the chip, through which the computerization of wide areas of the economy and society is possible. The computer, with its pervasive applications, becomes the key product. The industrial modus operandi and typical forms of mechanization go beyond what up to now has been understood as flexible, tertiary mechanization, i.e., automation. Together with the new information and digital communications technologies and aided by the decline in prices of the basic material and key product (chips and computers), a new level of automation—systematization—will be achieved. CIM is the concept that represents this development.

With respect to the type of division of labor and organizational structure we can say the following. The new arrangement that organizes the creative abilities of people in groups with the goal of quality improvement—not only of the product, but also of the workplace—represents a departure from Taylorism. At the same time, it drives process production forward to a new form, one in which the human factor is more highly valued in comparison to technical devices. The concept of total quality control, i.e. *kaizen* (Imai 1992), represents the notion of extensive quality control and continuous improvement, in which all employees (executives and members of groups) are brought together in enterprise-wide efforts.

Ending the waste of materials, energy, and human effort in the firm was a concern of Taiichi Ohno of Toyota, and became the heart of the concept of lean management. Along with the improvement of productivity in individual firms, this points the way from today's wasteful economy to a new one that carefully economizes all resources, one which can be made compatible with ecologically sustainable growth (see chapter 15).

Consumer-oriented management breaks apart the economic integration of conventional organizational forms. In the same way, the market directly approaches individual workplaces. The flexibility that is thereby achieved leads to decentralization, networking, and reciprocal penetration of previously hierarchical and functionally differentiated domains of the enterprise. The centrally organized, multifunctional firm becomes enclosed and absorbs into itself elements of the market, which are also articulated in the form of so-called profit centers.

Taylorism achieved a layering of income through the differentiation of the workplace, which in the aggregate was partly compensated for by the widespread filling of middle positions. Group-centered organizational structures also recreate income differentiation at the level of the firm, but they do it in the form of differences between productive groups and less productive groups, or jobholders and those without jobs. Just as in the previous societal model measures of poetic justice became necessary, so measures of political justice must accompany the new model in order for it to gain broad acceptance. This will be necessary for a number of reasons, not the least of which is the high level of unemployment that will become a big social problem in the transition to the new technological style.

Finally, the new technological style opens up new consumer and leisure patterns, addressed by the concept of the information society. The acceptance of such a future will depend not least of all on whether it succeeds in developing an environmentally sustainable development path. Although the new style is in principle much more environmentally workable than the previous one, this task remains to be solved in the future. This will require the simultaneous presence of a politico-economic regime. We enter into this complex in the next chapter; we will also return to the dovetailing of style and regime again in chapter 15.

NOTES

1 It should be pointed out that all data are based on patent statistics examined for more and less important innovations. The law, however, only allows technical procedures leading to a certain product to be patented. This creates a gap in the data for some pathbreaking innovations in the transition of technological styles because certain important steps such as, for example, new models for corporate structure or a new work organization (e.g., Taylorism) cannot be patented and do not appear in the usual innovation statistics. Yet, such innovations become very important during intermediate recovery after a technological style has been saturated, and they contribute to the quantum leaps in productivity.

2 Basing the assessment on changes in basic materials or mechanization makes a difference of about half a millenium in dating the industrial revolution. The sudden spread of mechanization displacing manual work and thus leading the way from the manufacturing to the industrial system occurs during the eighteenth century in England—the so-called English Industrial Revolution. But it is also possible to adopt an earlier dating of the industrial revolution, assigning the transition to the change in the energy balance and the use of the forces of *inanimate* nature during the "industrial revolution of the Middle Ages" (see Gimpel (1975) on milling).

3 To be exact, the rationalization process generally referred to as Taylorism has made its way in two waves. The first wave was influenced by the "works management movement" (Jenks 1960/61) in the framework of which Frederick Taylor conceived and popularized his ideas, particularly after the turn of the century. Important rationalizing processes—completely in Taylor's direction—set in as early as during the wave of the 1880s and were carried through by works management as a heterogenous yet very active rationalizing movement (Nelson 1975; Haber 1964; Kocka 1969; Jaun 1986). The second wave is generally called "Taylorist" and has two special features. On the one hand, rationalization of the economy was markedly intensified in the U.S.A. At the same time, following the American model, Germany and Switzerland, among others, introduced various rationalizing measures in work organization. On the other hand, trade unions began to take up and include Taylorist ideas into their positions. This in turn laid the ground for the enormous expansion of rationalizing ideas in the wave that began in the 1930s (Nadworny 1955).

6
Politico-Economic Regimes

A politico-economic regime is a cluster of institutions that regulate social behavior, build consensus, implement compromises, and manage conflict. A regime or regulating system is political because it applies to territorially bounded and collectively binding processes. And it is economic because it deliberately affects economic decision-making and the outcome of economic behavior. Yet, politico-economic regimes do not only hold sway over territorial states but also among them, in the form of international regimes (Krasner 1983; Keohane 1984). The "world market," for example, did not emerge spontaneously, but is essentially a social construct consisting of a variety of regulating systems in the framework of the world political economy (see chapter 3).

Politico-economic regimes do not spring into existence spontaneously and have no end in themselves. They mediate the contradictions of social structure and influence social practices. Their function is to enhance the legitimacy of society, or, in other words, to limit conflict. Basic values and their interrelations are interpreted by means of politico-economic regimes through normative elements transformed into institutional rules. As politico-economic regimes are selective with reference to the interpretation of basic values and the regulation of the power structure, they are independent determinants of social practice. Thus, regimes mediate between basic values and social practice as well as between power structures and social practice. Through a functioning regime, power structures reproduce themselves differently in social practice than would be the case if they alone were to influence patterns of action.

In short, a regime constitutes a compromise between basic values and power interests. It encompasses the complex of basic societal ideas, normative theories, and their transformation into institutional rules (see also figure 6.1 below). In what follows we shall offer a brief sketch of the various dimensions of the concept of a regime as well as some empirical illustrations of long-term discontinuities.

To simplify the analysis, the various components of a politico-economic regime which are bound together into a single package can be assigned to four complexes:

1. *The degree of popular political and economic participation* which a regime tolerates. The two types of participation do not necessarily have to coincide. Rather, participation refers to two different problems:

a) The definition of political participatory rights: Who can participate in political decision-making and in what manner?

b) The definition of economic participatory rights: Who can make economic decisions and use economic resources, on what basis? This refers to the definition of prerequisites for participation in economic decision-making, as for example property rights (claims to decision-making and use of resources) but also to mere claims to participate in the outcome of social production on the basis of quasi-property rights (social security claims) as well as claims to participate in economic activity in general (the right to work), and, finally, claims to participate in the prerequisites of economic action (e.g., the right to education, the right to free choice of job) (see also Marshall 1965).

2. A further important aspect of a regime is the *demarcation of the market sphere and the realm of collective decision-making*. This also includes the definition of duties of private and public actors. Apart from the demarcation of the market and the state this also refers to how the state is to be allowed to intervene in market processes (e.g., by setting basic wages, regulating prices for politically sensitive goods, controlling cartels, etc.).

3. Further, mention must be made of the *complex of collective formation of will and forms of conflict management*. The political power structure on which a regime is based—i.e., such institutions as, for example, direct or representative democracy, presidential systems or the centralization and decentralization of administration—does not establish all significant rules.

Further regulatory systems beyond a parliament's guiding conflict management, as for instance "pre-parliamentary" consultations in Switzerland or institutionalized neocorporatist arrangements,[1] are also important.

4. Finally, the very politico-economic *power constellation* which would also be present in the absence of a regime must be kept in mind.

POLITICO-ECONOMIC AND MORAL REGIMES

"Realist" approaches to politics see political action as the outcome of power constellations. For this reason it is important to stress that a power constellation as such does not yet constitute a regime. Although power constellations do influence regimes, the latter are, for as long as they function, much more: they are regulations with a normative basis and corresponding institutional arrangements subject to a logic of legitimation.

The notion of a regime includes the idea that action is not exclusively and perpetually based on pure power relations and that conflict does not result in a permanent and insurmountable polarization of politically opposed groups. Rather, regimes are characterized by a "common understanding," i.e., an agreement on basic matters and on the way in which conflict is to be resolved "peacefully." Such a basic consensus represents social peace, which in turn is more than the mere absence of conflict in which each party tries to gain advantages at the expense of the others and uses force. In other words, a regime is based on a social contract (Rawls 1975, Moore 1978).

In the framework of a regime, rules of action result from the interplay between power relations and rationales that go beyond particular power interests (Habermas 1983). These rationales legitimize regulations on the basis of moral judgement, and for this reason we speak of a regime.

Morality is rooted in culture. It refers to the theoretical side of culture and prescribes correct behavior. In addition, culture is practical because it prescribes how one is to act in different situations, and it is pragmatic because the actual power constellation along with a coherent rationale influences rules and institutions (see figure 6.1).

Values may be described as the navigational lights of the cultural system. As pointed out in chapter 2, however, they offer contradictory orientations. We advanced the notion of only three leading values in modern society: the striving after efficiency, the claim to equality, and the claim to security,

FIGURE 6.1 Rationales, Assessments and Influences on Regulations: the Politico-economic Regime and the Relationship between Cultural Levels, Power Structure and Social Practice

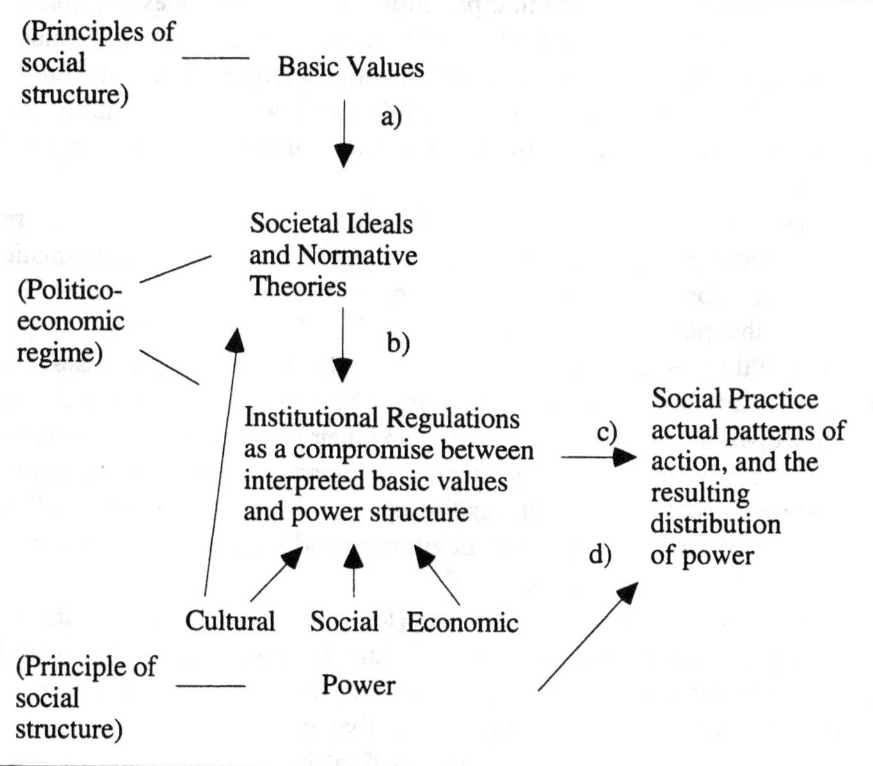

Legend: The two assessment processes

I) Assessment of social structure by actors lacking power

a) To what degree are basic values anchored in societal guiding principles and what degree of agreement with normative theories can be found?

b) How complete and coherent is the transformation of normative theories into institutional rules?

c) What does the relation between ideals and reality look like? This also depends on the degree to which power interests can determine social practice.

The consequences of this assessment can be: attribution of *legitimacy* (agreement), mere tolerance of a social order, withdrawal, or refusal.

II) Assessment of social structure by powerful actors

d) Do the institutional rules serve one's own interests? The consequence of this assessment can be: attribution of legitimacy, or refusal of the existing order together with recourse to uncontrolled use of power.

Illegitimacy of an order leads to deviant behavior or to the articulation of interest in socio-political change—depending upon the political possibilities and resources any given social movement has at its disposition.

which oppose the striving for power. Other values, such as freedom, are closely linked to these. In chapter 2 we further demonstrated how the striving after freedom and after economic efficiency are closely related. In addition, leading values are subject to interpretation, so that it becomes possible to construct an entire system on the basis of normative theories, which are much more specific than leading values. Such theories interpret values, attempt to mitigate value conflicts for different social realms, and establish normative rules of behavior. Cultural power has a direct effect on such normative theories.

Normative rules as well as the institutions that guarantee them are practical because they prescribe behavioral patterns, and they are pragmatic because their form and content are not only subject to values (mediated by normative theories) but also to group (political) and economic power.

Against this background, figure 6.1 shows two assessment processes. On the one hand, legitimacy is important. The more social practices are embedded within cultural leading values and their historical interpretation by way of normative theories, the greater the legitimacy and thus mass loyalty to an existing order. The greater the legitimacy, the less probable violent conflict and the use of force to suppress it. Legitimacy and force are thus substitutes for one another (see chapter 3).

The other evaluative process refers to whether a regime is of use in achieving particular ends. This is important for power elites that would possibly do better without the regime, i.e., on the basis of a return to pure power politics. If both assessments are negative, mass as well as elite loyalty decreases. The result is the erosion and final breakdown of the regime: "peace" collapses.

Basically, our notion of a politico-economic regime refers to a multitude of different processes, namely the conscious separation of the market from political authority, the way in which economic interests (corporations) organize themselves, the constitution of the political sovereign (political participation), and the coordination and mutual penetration of politics and economies.

The manipulation of the political economy is also a central issue in regulation theory, inspired by Marxism and particularly popular in France (Lipietz 1985; Boyer 1986; Aglietta 1979). Although it originally proposed an anti-economistic research agenda, the theory is currently being elaborated in an economistic fashion. The theory is based on a phase concept of capitalist development; the term "mode of regulation" refers to the sum of institutional forms, networks, and explicit and implicit norms that guarantee the compatibility of behavioral patterns within the framework of a regime of accumulation and in accordance with societal relationships and even transcending their conflictive properties (Lipietz 1985: 121). Generally, regulation of social relationships means "the way in which this relationship reproduces itself despite its conflictive and contradictory character" (Lipietz 1985: 109, my translation).

There are some differences between the regulation school and our approach here. First, regulation theory has largely remained economistic. Second, and more important, regulation is not linked to leading and basic values which are mediated by normative theories. According to the theory's Marxist inspiration, the contradictory nature of social relationships evident in the citation above refers mainly to the relation between capital and labor. In our perspective, on the other hand, the relationship of principles (basic values and power) is already a conflictive one. Normative theories offer interpretations aimed at mitigating these conflicts and proposals for institutional rules. Such theories must allow for generalization; the basic consensus that they envision is similar to an implicit social contract.

INTERNATIONAL REGIMES

Economic and political spheres are necessarily linked to each other at the national as well as the international level. An intense discussion around international regimes has emerged within American political science circles over the past few years, as already mentioned in chapter 3. During the 1970s, the notion of international regimes was originally advanced by John Ruggie (1975) (see also Keohane and Nye 1977; Krasner 1983). Since that time, a veritable "regime school" has emerged that is quite unanimous in its definition of international regimes. These are defined as "sets of implicit or explicit principles, norms, rules and decision-making procedures around which the actors' expectations converge in a given area of international relations" (Krasner 1983: 2). Although the exact significance and mutual delimitation of principles, norms, and procedures for decision-making is not stated clearly, it seems that these terms refer to behavioral rules at varying levels of specification. Thus, principles and norms are understood as general characteristics (structures) whose specific realizations are rules and procedures (Cohen 1983: 323ff.).[2] In this perspective, a regime's particular appearance can change without its basic principles and norms being affected.

In a comparison of the regime perspective with our own notion of the politico-economic regime, the following points of agreement emerge. International regimes are understood as social institutions and regulating systems. Guiding principles and normative theories in our perspective correspond to "principles and norms" in Krasner's (1983: 2ff.) treatment of international regimes. His rules and procedures, on the other hand, are identical to our institutional arrangements. In addition, Krasner also stresses the fundamental difference between principles and norms, on the one hand, and rules and procedures on the other hand. Guiding principles and normative theories (principles and norms) are fundamental to the characterization of a regime. There may well be different institutional arrangements (rules and procedures) which are compatible with the same leading values and normative theories (principles and norms).

Thus, there are pattern differences over time as well as between different societies within one and the same regime. In this case, different institutional arrangements (rules) are applied. These differences must be distinguished from regime transition in which guiding principles and normative theories (principles and norms) actually change.

An example of different regimes can be found in orthodox and social or embedded liberalism (Krasner 1983: 4). Orthodox liberalism seeks to assign the regulation of social relationships to the market, whereas social liberalism advocates state intervention to counteract social and economic disequilibria resulting from market forces. Thus, "orthodox and embedded liberalism define different regimes" (Krasner 1983: 4). The transition from prewar orthodox to embedded liberalism was a fundamental regime transition which has even been described as "revolutionary" (Krasner 1983: 4; Ruggie 1983: 201-214).

In addition to the difference between "change within a regime" and "regime transition," another feature must be mentioned: the weakening, disintegration, and dissolution of regimes. Here, too, Krasner's perspectives (1983) and ours are in agreement. Weakening and disintegration become a problem if (1) a regime's components become incoherent; or (2) if there are inconsistencies between the regime and action resulting from it.

Finally, mention must be made of the similarities between Krasner's perception of causal relations mediated by regimes and ours. Regimes intervene systematically and are more than mere adhoc arrangements and agreements, rather their purpose is to facilitate agreements (Krasner 1983). Still, the concept of international regimes stresses formal institutions somewhat single-mindedly. Weakly institutionalized international regimes, such as the world market, are often not regarded as true regimes in this perspective (Pfister and Suter 1987; Strange 1983: 338ff.).

Within the regime school there are two competing but increasingly converging theoretical perspectives aimed at the explanation of the emergence and decline of international regimes. The functionalist or institutionalist approach (Haas and Young in Krasner 1983) is based on the traditional functionalist theory of international relations (Mitrany 1976; Haas 1964) and argues that increasing international interdependencies and the growing density of interactions lead to a more urgent need for international cooperation in the long run. Conversely, realists or structuralists stress the role of power and hegemony in the creation and maintenance of international regimes (Krasner 1983; Keohane 1984). Correspondingly, the disintegration of regimes is linked to the decline of hegemonies.[3]

However, actual reality differs from that imagined in these two perspectives. Regime development is characterized by breaks, discontinuities, new beginnings, and the disintegration or dissolution of regimes. To explain this, an integration of regime and hegemony theories is in order, for international regimes are closely linked to some of the questions raised by hegemony theory. Under conditions of a world political constellation still dominated by nation-states, hegemony refers to the ordering and leadership function of one big nation which, for the sake of all or at least many, assures certain common functions and thus renders possible ordered exchange relations. In this perspective, hegemony must be distinguished from imperial rule, which is enforced by military means and colonizes or patronizes alliance partners. Further, hegemony is distinguished from dominance. Hegemony, at least at its culminating point, refers to legitimate leadership. Hegemonies differ from particular regimes in that hegemons are functional leaders for many different regimes at the same time. Hegemony is an interlinkage of economic, political, and military leadership.

Hegemony theory stresses that the benefits of hegemonic politics accrue not only to the hegemon, but also to all others in its orbit, particularly small states that may act as free riders. Yet, the long-term mismatch between benefits and costs for the hegemon eventually leads to its decline, an argument advanced by Paul Kennedy (1987) for example.

An important link between regime and hegemony theories is the theory of hegemonic stability first advanced by Charles Kindleberger (1973, 1986; see also Keohane 1984; Gilpin 1987) in his analysis of the global economic problems following the crisis of 1929. In this perspective, particularly popular in the United States, single hegemons fulfill their leadership role better than groups of states. Thus, during the nineteenth century, Great Britain had a positive function as economic hegemon. Conversely, the world economic depression at the outset of the 1930s was the result of the reluctance of the United States to assume the leadership role. Though the United States accepted this useful role after World War II, according to this theory, many current problems of the world economy can be traced to its partial loss of leadership capacity. In this perspective, hegemony is not identical to oppressive dominance, but as already mentioned, consists of a cooperative leadership role exercised with the consent of other states.

In the perception of hegemonic stability theory, hegemons establish international regimes, i.e., orders as a public utility, which dissolve with the decline of hegemony. The neorealist position in the formulation of Keohane (1984: 32) has modified this thesis. Although the construction of central regimes depends upon a hegemon, once they have become institutionalized they may well survive hegemonic decline. In fact, despite the decline of U.S. hegemony, important international regimes have not come apart completely, although they experienced profound crises. An example of an international regime that has come under pressure during hegemonic decline without fully disintegrating, is the General Agreement on Tariffs and Trade (GATT), which suffered setbacks during the 1970s and 1980s; within its framework ever more acute economic tensions are played out between North America, Western Europe, and Japan. An example of actual disintegration is the Bretton Woods system of fixed exchange rates which came under pressure after 1969 and was abandoned in 1971.

In chapter 16 we will return to the debate on hegemonies. On the basis of the sequence of societal models which will be discussed in the following chapters, we will suggest a distinction between hegemonic social practice (societal model) and the hegemon's position within such a structure. While it is possible to see regularities in the rise and dissolution of hegemonic social practice, the rise of hegemons—Great Britain during the nineteenth century and the United States during the twentieth—was bound to sets of conditions which will most probably never recur.

DISCONTINUITIES IN INTERNATIONAL REGIMES

International regimes are characterized by a multitude of discontinuities. Stephen Krasner (1976: 330) has presented material concerning the openness of the international trade regime that shows the following fluctuations:[4] The period 1820-1879 is characterized by increasing openness of the trade regime. Tariffs are reduced (with the important exception of the United States which remains strongly protectionist), while the shares of foreign trade are high and keep rising.

The period 1879-1913 is characterized by moderate closure in the world trade regime, i.e., tariffs rise. Although the regime reopens somewhat during the period 1900-1913, tariffs do not decrease. The importance of foreign trade first decreases (until 1900) and then increases again (until 1913). During the period 1918-1939 a short closure follows. Tariffs are raised in two waves during the 1920s and the 1930s, and the share of foreign trade decreases so precipitously that one is tempted to speak of the breakdown of world trade.

As a result of the Bretton Woods agreements, institutionally secured by the GATT, the period 1945-1970 is characterized by a large degree of openness, which reached its peak in 1960-1968 (the Kennedy Round of the GATT). Tariffs are reduced and the share of trade increases. Beyond the data presented by Krasner, it is possible to observe a renewed closure of the trade regime and a rise in protectionism from 1970 until recently.

The following regularities can be discerned. During phases of unchallenged hegemony, namely during British and American hegemony, the world trade regime is liberal. Competitive phases with regard to leadership, on the other hand, are characterized by "mercantilist" trade regimes. In addition, a further generalization can be made: Independent of the hegemonic situation, regimes are more mercantilist during the downswing phases of the long waves than during their upswing phases. During the peak phase regimes are more liberal.

We can conclude this section with the hypothesis that international regimes emerge as a result of the interplay of the rise of hegemons and the establishment of new hegemonic politico-economic regimes. The decisive role of hegemons in establishing new politico-economic regimes was very evident during the nineteenth and twentieth centuries. This, however, may change in the future (see the concluding chapter).

REGIMES IN THE SOCIETAL MODEL

A politico-economic regime forms part of a larger context: the societal model which also includes the technological style. Figure 6.2 illustrates the most important relationships between normative theories, the politico-economic regime, and technological style.

FIGURE 6.2 Relationships between Normative Theories, the Politico-economic Regime and Technological Style

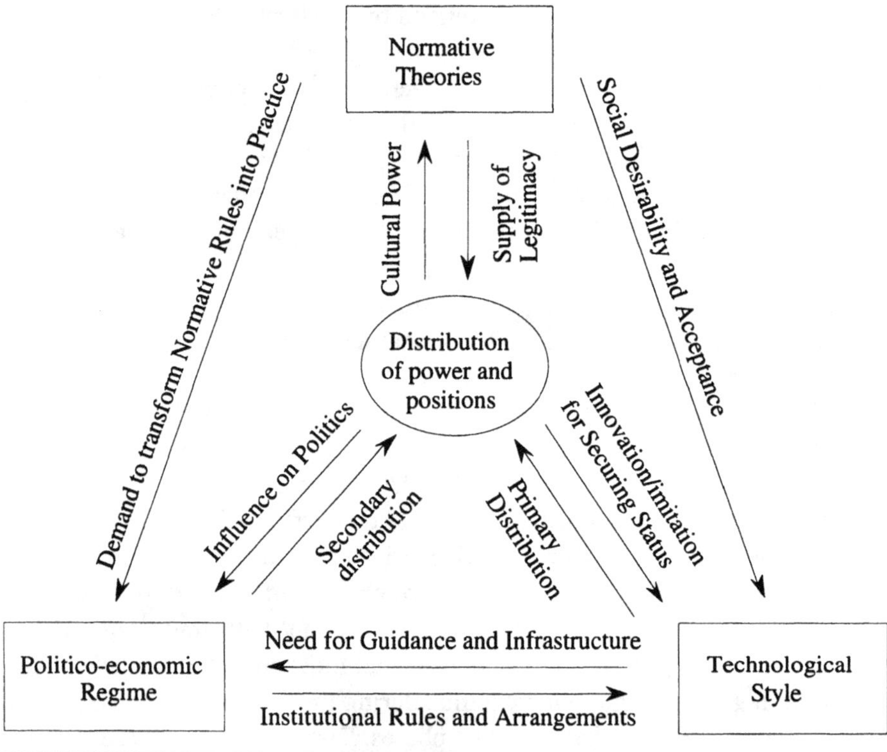

The moral regime (or normative theories) plays a key role in this connection. If a politico-economic regime has eroded, and elements of a new technological style have already unfolded, a prolonged theoretical debate takes place between sharply divided camps of pessimists and optimists. Although the critique of modernity has always been very strong, the "friends of progress" have normally prevailed in past debates. This is no coincidence. Western society necessarily has utopian traits because its internal contradictions do not allow for any better solutions than "returning to the future." And in the past this return has always brought about greater awareness of basic values in the social structure of Western society.

If normative theories pointing to a positive future prevail, the next step is a demand to create institutional arrangements in the framework of a renewed social contract (for example, management of transitory unemployment, creation of new infrastructures, regulation of the economy, measures for protecting the environment, etc.) which make the future under a new technological style not only acceptable but also desirable.

A renewed basic consensus—a renewed social contract—and the formation of a changed politico-economic and moral regime constitute the beginning of a new societal model whose institutional arrangements are quickly implemented. The trajectory of such a new societal model and the sequence of conflicts accompanying it will be the theme of the following chapter. At this point we will merely anticipate that the new basic consensus or social contract coming into effect after a phase of intensive dissent and perplexity only constitutes a truce at first. A "letter of credit" concerning the future is agreed upon, the quality of which decides whether and how the new technological style and politico-economic regime unfold. The redemption of the promises and fascination with the novel variety of products and attached lifestyle may then lead to broad consensus around the new model.

At the outset, the shaping of the new social contract, i.e., the new basic consensus, is capable of extension and is aimed at the future. After the great growth surges associated with the unfolding of the new technological style have passed, when the future has reached the present, dissent begins to spread. In response, and in order to rescue the model, the politico-economic regime can be extended according to the principles of the moral pattern. This may be referred to as legislative reforms (Rawls 1975; Moore 1978) during the peak phase. Such reforms concern the improved redemption of promises already part of the originally renewed social contract and its principles but not fully implemented due to the resistance of interest groups.

After the model has been saturated, when its capacity for solving problems has failed, first signs of disintegration appear, leading finally to dissolution. Not only do conflicts become more intense, but "peace" can also be challenged by groups, and in the interstate system the probability of sharp conflicts increases, which in the past has led to an accumulation of classical warlike activities.

Is there any empirical evidence for important phases in the renewal of the politico-economic regime before the upswing, legislative reforms during the peak phase, and violent conflicts during the downswing phase? In a preliminary overview of different waves of societal transition we must examine whether the hypothesis regarding the development of politico-economic regimes is worth maintaining.

EMPIRICAL EVIDENCE FOR DISCONTINUITIES

In what follows, we examine the three common waves of societal evolution in the core. The first wave begins with the spread of industrialization and its accompanying societal framework from England to the European continent, North America, and (with a time lag) Japan. The structure of these waves with regard to the rate of expansion of world industrial production has already been presented in chapter 4 (figure 4.1).

Renewal of the Social Contract

The following general observation can be made: each industrial upswing is preceded by a significant renewal of the politico-economic regime.

Prior to the first wave, liberal revolts preceded the onset of the spread of the societal model in the core. These revolts and movements fought for political liberalization, the guarantee of open markets, and the freedom of economic action. Free trade was the key project. Although free trade was institutionalized over a period of several decades in different Western European countries (Alber 1982), a clear diffusion of this project, only temporarily interrupted by the restoration period, is discernible (see also Bornschier 1988: 305).

If one omits the two late cases of nation-building (Germany and Italy) as well as the case of Finland (under Russian rule until 1918 and thus not sovereign), the median value of diffusion in Western Europe had already been crossed in the period 1830-1839. The arithmetic mean for the introduction of free trade in ten Western European countries is 1833. The general upswing in world industrial production began 1835-1845. Yet, the proportion of the core population able to profit from the new freedoms was comparatively small because free economic and political activity was confined to a minority. The mass of the population remained outside the model; the social contract thus only affected a minority. For only a small proportion of Western European countries was compulsory mass education part of the first model; by 1842, only three out of fourteen countries had introduced compulsory schooling (see chapter 9, table 9.3).

Prior to the second wave, at the outset of the 1880s, a new and broadened basic consensus was sought by substantially extending political participation. Important extensions of the franchise in twelve Western European countries took place before the upswing (Alber 1982: 39).[5] The mean year of introduction is 1883, and by 1888 this process had taken place in eight out of twelve countries (see also Flora et al. 1983: 460f.). Even where there had already been broad participation before, as for example in Switzerland, where men had been enfranchised since 1848, civil rights were once more extended during this period. In Switzerland, the referendum was introduced in 1874 and the constitutional initiative in 1891. The founding of labor parties took place in the decade 1880-89, when parties in seven out of eleven countries came into existence. By the end of the 1880s, labor parties existed in nine out of eleven Western European countries (Bornschier 1988: 305).

Compulsory education generally formed part of the new politico-economic regime. In nine countries which did not already have compulsory schooling, it was introduced around 1880 (for example, in England in 1880, in France in 1882, see table 9.3 in chapter 9). In other words, around 1880 there is an accumulation of three elements of a renewed politico-economic regime: extensions of the franchise, self-organization of the working class, and generalization of compulsory mass schooling. According to our data, the upswing of world industrial production starts after 1883 (figure 4.1 in chapter 4).

Prior to the third wave, substantial changes taking place in the political economy can be summarized as follows: a new and active role of the state in economic matters; a social solution to the unemployment problem; the transition to Keynesian economic policy (demand-oriented and anticyclical), the emergence of neocorporatist arrangements of interest mediation; and the redistributive welfare state, the core elements of which are compulsory forms of social insurance. At the same time, around 1932-33, significant regime changes occurred in Sweden, the United States, and Germany. These historical variants will be discussed more fully in the following chapter. The democratic (social-democratic and social-liberal) variants triumphed after World War II and became standard solutions. The upswing of the third industrial wave starts after 1932 and for some countries, where it was interrupted by the war, only after 1945.

The extension and generalization of the welfare state between 1930 and 1950 can be demonstrated on the basis of data for thirteen Western European countries (Alber 1982: 65): In 1930, the cost of the four basic forms of social insurance equalled about 2.8 percent of gross domestic product. By 1950 this proportion had risen to 4.9 percent. Even more important than this rise is the decrease in cross-national differences: the coefficient of variation of the cost dropped dramatically from .75 (1939) to .31 (1950) (see Bornschier 1988: 308).

Legislative Reforms

Significant reform attempts aimed at rescuing the model occurred three times during the peaks of the waves. During the peak of the first wave, reforms concerned the freedom of organization, a logical complement to free trade, whose introduction was, as we have seen, centered around 1833. For freedom of organization, a wave can be observed during the period 1850-59 (see Bornschier 1988: 305). For nine Western European countries (excluding Italy, Germany, and Finland; see above) the mean year of introduction is 1856, a year that still lies within the prosperity-recession phase (see figure 4.1).

During the peak of the second wave, there was a "landslide" to the left in most political systems during the recession phase 1903-13 as a result of a wave of class struggles, including mass and general strikes (Wolfgang Mommsen 1969: 96, 178ff.) Still, the overall reform capacity of the societal model remained weak.[6] For both capital and labor, the utilization of the existing order for their own interests seems to have resulted in a general resistance to reformist policies during that phase (see also figure 6.1). Some attempts at reforming the model must be mentioned, however. After the 1906 landslide victory of the Liberals in England (a social-liberal coalition; Mommsen 1969: 179) there is a split into two camps; one specific reform is the curtailing of the House of Lords' powers (1909-11). In France, a socialist government experimented with forms of voluntary social insurance but the resistance of the capitalists was substantial (Mommsen 1969). Still, voluntary social insurance emerges during the peak of the second wave (Flora et al. 1983), and there is a stronger responsibility of government to parliament, even under authoritarian regimes as, for example, in Imperial Germany (Mommsen 1969).

During the peak of the third wave, around and shortly after 1960, a surge of educational reforms in Europe aimed at higher permeability and less class-specific recruitment in higher schools can be observed. In the United States, the civil rights movements that led to the Civil Rights Act prohibiting racial discrimination in 1964 must be mentioned. In addition, it is possible to observe a wave of incipient legislative reforms in the debate around equal rights for men and women, for example in marriage law (see Bornschier 1988: 325). Finally, in all Western countries the role of the state increases after 1960; the redistributive activities of the state are strengthened and social insurance is extended (see also chapter 10).

Collapse of Social Peace

During the crisis phase, violent conflicts, which include the collapse of peace between groups as well as between states, accumulate three times. During the crisis phase of the first wave, around 1856-1866 (see figure 4.1 in chapter 4) warlike activities become so frequent that one is tempted to speak of a "world war." There are three wars between states and three civil wars.[7] Nine of the countries that currently form part of the core were engaged in interstate or civil wars. During the crisis phase of the second wave, which according to our structure sets in after the prosperity-recession phase of 1903-13, World War I starts and a large proportion of core states become engaged in war.[8] After the Russian Revolution in 1917 and until the mid-1920s, Europe witnesses a wave of revolutions and a surge of guerilla wars (Coackley 1986: 5). During the crisis phase of the third wave, from 1973 onwards there is also a surge in violent conflict. Fortunately, world war is no longer a rational strategy due to atomic deterrence. But the Western hegemonic power was engaged in a long and bloody war.[9] Although never formally declared, this war in Asia slowly became a classical one, which can be dated at the latest from the time when the United States extended the war to Cambodia in 1970 and opened an air war on North Vietnam in 1972.[10]

Further, at the peak of 1973-74 there is a North-South confrontation which assumes the character of world class struggle.[11] In fact, some phases of this struggle clearly exhibit warlike features, as for example the oil embargo of the Arab countries against the United States and the Netherlands ("the oil weapon").[12] Finally, a further indicator of the collapse of social peace is the wave of domestic and international terrorism that starts around 1970.

Two important wars of this century, those in Europe and Asia that begin in 1939 and in 1937 respectively and soon become World War II,[13] do not fall within any crisis phase but rather in the beginning of an upswing phase when compulsory-corporatist regimes (dictatorships) challenged the new liberal-corporatist regimes (democracies).[14] The new hegemonic social practice arose after the hard-won victory of the democracies under the leadership of the United States.

The prediction of increasing and continuing interstate conflict during the decay phase of a politico-economic regime as well as new beginnings must not be misunderstood mechanically as a theory of war cycles. The fact that during the second half of this century the core has consisted exclusively of democratic states and the counter-core has been eliminated from competition through the collapse of the Soviet Union has changed the parameters. An empirically well-founded rule says that democracies do not engage in war against other democracies (Russet 1993, 1994). For this reason, intensifying conflicts in the core do not lead to military conflicts. Instead, wars are conducted with politico-economic means, a contemporary example being the trade-related disputes among the triad (United States, Europe, and Japan).

SUMMARY AND OUTLOOK

In a comparison of the three past societal models, the second—the class-polarized societal model of the post-foundation era—was clearly the weakest. Correspondingly it offered somewhat unstable conditions for economic success. The result can clearly be seen in a comparison of the economic success attaching to each of the three societal models.

What might be the features of the coming societal model? Although we will discuss this in the final chapters we may briefly anticipate the discussion here. A new societal model will not shape society from the bottom up, but will reshape it significantly. The evolution of societal models exhibits features of cumulative social progress in the sense that the essentials of earlier features that have already demonstrated a high capacity to solve problems remain intact. The most important examples are market economies and the political form of democracy.

After the wave of free-market fundamentalism at the outset of the 1980s, the debate about what markets can and cannot do has led back to greater realism. The new economic doctrines place more trust in the self-regulating capacity of the market than the formerly dominant doctrine of Keynesianism. Yet, the renaissance of the market also calls for a new definition of state responsibilities and how they can be met.

The novel human claim to greater ranges of choice—to more freedom—may be reconciled with the flexible concept of "lean production." In order to achieve this, a lean state is needed. The rebuilding of the state and the cutting down of neocorporatist-Keynesian structures needs time, however. Everywhere consciousness is growing that the time for reforms has come. A new model involves the role of quality, the setting of priorities and the communication of visions which are capable of fascinating people. In all likelihood the size of the government's role will no longer be a sign of strength; instead, impulse programs and strategic planning will move to the fore.

The new and leaner state will also assume formerly private tasks, for example, the development of technology as a factor of production and the protection of the environment as a scarce resource. If this rebuilding process attempts to avoid any further expansion of the state in the traditional manner, elements of its former tasks cannot help but be delegated and privatized. Such a move still meets with much resistance, not least on the part of public officials.

Strategic changes that seek to improve both "supply and entitlements" simultaneously (Dahrendorf 1992: 8) are typical for the beginning of a new societal model. If, as we hold to be the case, the aim of progress is to create legitimacy and guarantee stability, the welfare state cannot be dismantled but rather needs to be rebuilt in order to engender support among society for the newly extended market sphere. A simple and not too bureaucratically complex guarantee of equitable life-chances through a minimum income would be one possible solution.

Before going on to consider in the next chapter the interplay between the technological style and the politico-economic regime in the framework of the societal model, which is characterized by a trajectory and linked to a growth and a specific conflict sequence, the material concerning discontinuities presented in this and the previous chapter are summarized for the politico-economic regime in table 6.1 and for the technological style in table 6.2.

TABLE 6.1 Summary of the Development of Politico-economic Regimes

Periodi-zation	Structural formula for world industrial production (see figure 4.1)	Societal projects prior to the general upswing	Legislative reforms during the peak	Grave con-flicts during the crisis, collapse of social peace	International trade regime
	Discontinuities in the development of politico-economic regimes				
First wave					
~1835-50	Upswing and prosperity	Free trade			
1850-56	Prosperity recession		Freedom of organization		Free trade growing liberalization of the inter-national trade regime
1856-66	Crisis			Wars and civil wars	
1866-72	Interim recovery				
1872-83	Depression				
Second wave					
1883-92	Upswing	Marked extension of political participation, compulsory schooling			Mercantilist period
1892-1903	Prosperity				
1903-13	Prosperity/ recession		Certain strengthening of government responsibility to parliament; voluntary social insurances		
1913-20	Crisis			World War I, revolutions, guerilla wars	
1920-29	Interim recovery				Hyper-mercantilist period
1929-32	Depression				collapse of world trade

<u>*Third wave*</u>

1932-45	Upswing	State intervention in the economy; welfare state		International elimination and demarcation struggles until the Korean war	
1945-58	Renewed up swing, or prosperity	Bretton Woods agreements			Liberal trade regime, high degree of openness (Kennedy round of the GATT)
1958-66	Prosperity		Educational reforms; civil rights; equal rights for women (beginning)		
1966-74	Prosperity/ recession			U.S. war in Asia, North-South "war" using the "oil weapon," terrorism	
1974-82	Crisis				Neo-protectionism; non-tariff trade barriers
1982-87	Interim recovery				Bilateralism; trade wars
1987-	Crisis				

from 1992? upswing?

............................***Speculations***..................................

Solution of conflicts along the lines: East-West, North-South, Humankind-Nature. New conception of a liberal welfare state: basic income for all *and* greater market freedom	A social liberal world trade regime, explicit anchoring of special and preferential treatment of Third World countries

Source: Bornschier (1988: 133f.).

TABLE 6.2 Summary of the Development of Technological Styles

	Discontinuities in the development of the technological style (see chapter 5)				
Periodization	Structural formula (see figure 4.1)	Basic materials and "key project"	Mechanization	Division of labor	Organization and property
First Wave					
~1835-50	Upswing and prosperity	Coal and steel; railways	Power engines, primary mechanization	Artisan operation of machines	Modern family enterprise
1850-56	Prosperity/ recession	Refined steel emerges			
1856-66	Crisis	Oil industry emerges			First investment trusts
1866-72	Interim recovery		machine tools	First assembly lines	
1872-83	Depression				Cartels
Second Wave					
1883-92	Upswing	Steel and electricity; electrification	Flexible machines: primary mechanization (power and machine tools) on the basis of electric motors	Operation of machines	Beginning of trust and firm formation
1892-1903	Prosperity				Merger wave
1903-13	Prosperity/ recession		Secondary mechanization, flow and assembly-line technology, continuous process production, chemicals and petro-chemicals	Beginning of the spread of Taylorism, 1912: Taylorist society	

1910-20	Crisis				
1920-29	Interim recovery	Cheap oil derivates emerge	Beginning of the spread of secondary mechanization		2nd merger wave, modified corporate structure, public stock companies
1929-32	Depression				
Third Wave					
1932-45	Upswing	Petroleum and synthetic materials			
1945-58	Renewed upswing, or prosperity	"Automobilization"			
1958-66	Prosperity	Chips emerge	Computerization starts		
1966-74	Prosperity/ recession	Chips are improved and become cheaper	Beginning of tertiary mechanization, control technologies, wave of automation	Debate on humanization of work	Merger wave
1974-82	Crisis				
1982-87	Interim recovery	Superconductors, optical semiconductors, energy alternatives	First fully automated plants	Reduction of Taylorism	Merger wave between global corporations, markets within corporation
1987-	Crisis				
from 1992? Upswing?		***Speculations:***			
		Superchips, new energy: photo-voltaic generated hydrogen "information society"	Fully automated plants, interventions into living nature: industrial biotechnology on an industrial base	Computer-aided and more encompassing work beside full automation	Global corporations that make "a village" out of the world on the basis of new information techologies

Source: Bornschier (1988: 135f.).

In the mid-1980s, when work on the first edition of this book was finished, we estimated that the fourth wave would begin in the second third of the 1990s. This prognosis is not modified for this new edition (see figure 6.3). As it is impossible to make precise predictions on the basis of our theories, it would be wrong to claim an accuracy that does not exist. Our prognosis still holds, although the upswing is not coming as quickly as we had hoped. After three years of stagnation, it becomes clear that a more fundamental new beginning is in order.

The economic downswing that set in as early as the 1970s fuelled a political impulse toward conservative and business-friendly policies. These policies can also be labelled "conservative" because they are one-sided with respect to costs and profits and thereby accommodating to unemployment, and because global management by financial means ignored the problem of legitimacy and created the illusion that there was no decay of the societal model but only a disequilibrium of the money supply. Crisis management on this basis did not bring about a stable new upswing. Still, it may have had an effect in the sequence of societal processes of learning in the sense that, at the end of the interim recovery, it became evident to all that more fundamental problems await their solutions.

The interim recovery is not only characterized by the policies mentioned but also by the unfolding of elements of a coming technological style. But only when a future-oriented pragmatism has taken strong hold of society and politics can the preconditions for social innovations facilitating an acceptably renewed social contract arise. In their absence a stable upswing along with a new technological style is impossible. Not investment capital, but rather basic consensus, societal solidarity, and optimism about the future are the truly scarce resources during the long downswing phase. Interim recoveries always (1866-72, 1920-29, 1983-90) seem to have given rise to false hopes, for growth during them is spotty, uncontrolled, and speculative, and in most cases ends quite abruptly.

During this interim cycle of irrationality, time passes without being used. Obviously the experience of a new crisis after interim recovery has been and still is always required. This crisis we call a depression and differentiate it from other crises not because it brings even smaller growth rates than the preceding crisis phase or even a veritable crash as after 1929, but because it occasions even deeper helplessness and despondency. At the same time, this may also become a kind of constructive disenchantment; the various changes that were tried throughout the West since the late 1970s have not offered a new starting point.

A new technological style and a new politico-economic regime are not established spontaneously. The institutional arrangements needed call for brave steps that point far into the future. Under current conditions, such steps must lead towards a persuasive world model. The renewal of the social contract has to be conceived on a world scale. It must be aimed at reducing the tensions along the fault-lines humankind-nature and North-South.

NOTES

1 Schmitter and Lehmbruch (1979) define neocorporatism as an institutionalized form of social interest mediation. Interest associations and other corporations negotiate power compromises on the basis of their position in the system of societal reproduction with the state as the organizational core. The exertion of power becomes objectivized within an institutional arrangement. Thus, the notion of corporatism encompasses at least two dimensions. An important variant interprets corporatism as an arrangement between state and interest organizations in the formulation and implementation of politics (Lehmbruch 1984). This kind of incorporation of associations is often referred to as "concertation". In this perspective, corporatism is contrasted with the liberal model of pressure politics that neglects the role played by extra-parliamentary associations. The other important variant of the argument depicts corporatism as a certain type of structure of organized interest mediation (Schmitter 1981). Ideally, one can speak of corporatism if both entrepreneurs and workers are each represented by only a single organization that has been endowed with unique decision power by the state. This model of interest mediation primarily contradicts pluralistic concepts that stress the spontaneous formation and potentially unlimited number of politically relevant organizations (see Nollert 1992: 61ff., 181ff.).

2 Krasner (1983: 2) defines principles, norms, rules, and procedures for decision-making as follows: "Principles are beliefs of fact, causation, and rectitude. Norms are standards of behavior defined in terms of rights and obligations. Rules are specific prescriptions for action. Decision-making procedures are prevailing practices for making and implementing collective choice."

3 Recent findings from analyses of the change of international regimes during the 1970s and 1980s—i.e., the period of the decline of US hegemony—have led to some changes in the realist position. On the one hand, it became evident that international regimes did not vanish completely despite the decline of American hegemony. On the other hand, new but only weakly institutionalized international regimes, as for example the debt regime, emerged during this period (see Pfister and Suter 1987).

4 His indicators are: protectionist tariffs, the share of trade, and the concentration of trade in certain regions or colonial empires.

5 A further important surge of expansion took place before World War I (see also chapter 10 and Stein Rokkan and Lars Svåsand 1978).

6 The meager reform efforts of the peak phase of the second wave can also be explained by the shift of internal tensions to the international level. Such a transfer of tensions certainly occurred in the framework of the then dominant social imperialism.

7 The following events have been taken into consideration: The Crimean War 1854-56 (Britain, France and Sardinia against the Russian Empire; Austria only mobilizes its forces, Prussia stays neutral); the war of Austria and Prussia against Denmark 1864; the war of Prussia against Austria 1866. *Civil wars*: Italian unification wars 1859-61; American civil war 1861-65; civil war (with revolution) in Japan 1861-67. The German-French war of 1870/71 has not been included as it falls into the intermediate recovery phase of world industrial production.

8 In addition, the Russo-Japanese war of 1904/05 and the Japanese-Korean wars of 1905 and 1910 must be noted.

9 In addition, the 1982 war of Britain against Argentina must be mentioned.

10 The first phase of the Vietnam War begins in 1957, the second in 1961 with the United States becoming one of the war parties. Recession in the United States set in earlier than in the rest of the West (see also chapter 7).

11 The date of the coming into effect of the declaration of a New International Economic Order (NIEO) on May 1, 1974, was deliberately chosen: it was aimed to link the struggle of the South with the historical struggle of the working class in the North.

12 This happened as a result of the Yom Kippur War. The Netherlands was included in the embargo to affect the oil spot market in Rotterdam.

13 With the Japanese invasion of China the wars begin in 1937 in Asia. In Europe, the wars start with the German-Austrian union, the annexion of the Sudeten regions of Czechoslovakia by Germany and, finally, the German war against Poland that starts the world war in Europe (1939). Further mention must be made of the war of the Soviet Union against Finland (1939).

14 Bruce Russet (1988a, 1988b) has investigated the causes of international military conflict of varying intensity during the nineteenth and twentieth centuries. His results point to a quite complex causal pattern. One finding, however, merits special attention: the difference of democratic and non-democratic governments. For democratic countries, participation in international conflicts became more probable if per capita income had decreased previously. In non-democratic countries, things worked in the opposite direction: they exhibited a higher propensity to engage in international conflicts after periods of economic prosperity.

7
The Societal Model and its Career

Societal models are the units of social change. Each constitutes an *attempt* to integrate a technological style with a politico-economic regime. We underline the word "attempt" here. For reasons already discussed in chapter 4, changes in societal realms as defined by technological style and politico-economic regime take place with phase displacements. For this reason, precise equilibrium is impossible. Rather, developments are characterized by successive imbalances which, however, can go through a phase of more or less successful coupling of the politico-economic regime with the technological style within every model.

A societal model going through different phases—which we call its "career"—presupposes a beginning and an end. The beginning consists of a change of program which includes a consciously new start with a fresh social contract. In what follows, we will try to show that our points of societal models have been clearly defined historically. For the last model, for example, the years 1932-33 were the key years during which institutional innovators became active.

The end of a model first becomes evident by the limits and finally the breakdown of the problem-solving capacity of a politico-economic regime. Once the problem-solving capacity of a regime reaches its limits and the coherence of its cluster of arrangements collapses, phenomena of dissolution appear and social peace is increasingly broken. Yet, the decay phase is more than mere dissolution. Parts of the cluster of arrangements are abandoned or replaced without the emergence of recognizable new coherence. Examples from the last model are the retrenchment of the welfare state and the transition from Keynesian policies to monetarism.

In what follows we will first address the general theoretical model and then go on to an empirical demonstration of fluctuations in economic growth and conflict over the career of a societal model. Finally, we will discuss the range of arrangements during the historical phase of the 1930s and the features and dynamics of the victorious neocorporatist, Keynesian societal model for purposes of illustration.

THE FORMAL TREATMENT

For technological style as well as politico-economic regime we distinguish between four phases. For the *regime*, these phases are: (1) formation; (2) unfolding; (3) saturation and signs of dissolution; and (4) decay. The social impact of the politico-economic regime oscillates between growing and diminishing problem-solving capacity:

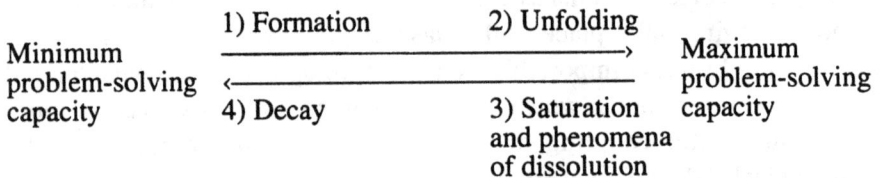

	1) Formation	2) Unfolding	
Minimum problem-solving capacity	———————————→		Maximum problem-solving capacity
	←———————————		
	4) Decay	3) Saturation and phenomena of dissolution	

For *technological style* the following phases can be distinguished: (1) elements of a new technological style become linked; (2) the style crystallizes and diffuses; (3) the diffusion process becomes saturated as elements of a new style emerge; and (4) the technological style becomes more heterogeneous. The social process of the technological style oscillates between decreasing and increasing homogeneity. Once a new style has been fully diffused, homogeneity reaches its maximum:

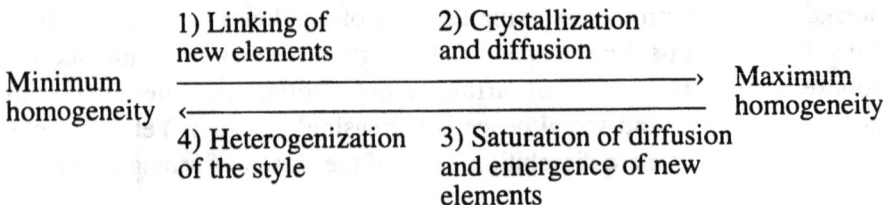

	1) Linking of new elements	2) Crystallization and diffusion	
Minimum homogeneity	———————————→		Maximum homogeneity
	←———————————		
	4) Heterogenization of the style	3) Saturation of diffusion and emergence of new elements	

Thus, we have two social processes which are related to each other and oscillate between two states in four phases. Both social processes are decisive for economic management processes and for the conflict cycle during the course of the societal model.

The problem-solving capacity of a politico-economic regime refers to the institutional infrastructure of economic processes and is thus an important aspect of the macroeconomic production function. It creates the preconditions for economic growth. The phases of the technological style, on the other hand, are decisive for profits and industrial expansion. During the linking phase (1) quantum leaps in productivity lead to increased or renewed profit margins for certain groups of enterprises, but not for all. The reinvestment of profits for a harmonious dissemination of the style remains modest, however, because the expansion of consumption is limited. During these phases, there is a tendency to favor financial against industrial investments.

This changes during the crystallization phase (2). Cumulative upward processes result from the expansion of consumption and the reinvested earnings accruing from the quantum leaps in productivity. Still, it is important to note that the gains and industrial reinvestments as a whole result from the adoption of the new technological style because this includes the quantum leaps in productivity. Thus, the more the style has diffused, the weaker the aggregated growth surges.

For our purposes we assume that the two unfolding processes oscillate regularly between lesser and greater problem-solving capacities of a regime, on the one hand, and between lesser and greater homogeneity of the economic units with respect to the technological style, on the other. "Regular" means that we are *positing* a constant rate of the social process.

If the phases follow each other at a constant rate, harmonious swings like those of a sine function result. Thus, problem-solving capacity and homogeneity can be represented as functions of time. Yet, this image of harmonious swings must not be misunderstood as an occurrence of one and the same thing. Rather, we interpret them in the following way: although each technological style and each politico-economic regime is historically unique, they follow similar *processes of emergence and decay* in the course of time.

We must keep in mind, however, that the processes arising from the technological style and the politico-economic regime do not occur simultaneously. In terms of harmonious swings there is a phase displacement. The foregoing theoretical argument explaining this refers to different logics of social management. Decisions affecting the components of the technological style are made in a decentralized way, guided by the market, on the basis of actors' *individual* utility calculations. However, decisions concerning the components of the politico-economic regime require the prior formation of consensus and *collective* action. These processes are not value-neutral but closely linked to values and interests.

From this follows the aforementioned lack of coincidence of the two processes, even if the intention exists to bring them together. The time lag of the politico-economic regime is the result of two factors:

(1) The extent to which both processes are intentionally linked to each other;

(2) The rate of the process of consensus-building, i.e., the rate at which collective decisions can be taken.

The first factor refers to the relationship between the economy and the state, which has varied historically as well as between societies. Despite of the new role of the interventionist state after 1932 (see below) the United States preserved a more liberal view of the relationship between the economy and the state. Thus, notwithstanding notable successes during the formation phase of the new regime (1933-45) this hampered the unfolding of the regime after 1945. The second factor relates to the political order and its mechanisms of collective decision-making. We assume that the time lag grows longer under more democratic decision-making processes. Authoritarian systems can more quickly adopt the regime to the style, but they do not reach as durable a level of basic consensus as democracies do.

These considerations about different time lags will be taken up again later. First, however, we must make certain simplifying assumptions central to our model. We are assuming a displacement of one-quarter of a phase, whereby the formation phase (1) of the regime and the crystallization phase (2) of the style are linked to each other. The new technological style starts before its crystallization as new elements have begun to unfold significantly earlier. In the crystallization phase all elements are present and linked but not homogeneously distributed over all enterprises.

In figure 7.1 both processes—problem-solving capacity (regime) and homogenization (style)—are depicted with a phase displacement of one-quarter. The development of these processes over time can be represented as two phase-displaced sine waves. The full unfolding of the regime only takes place after the technological style has reached its maximum homogenization.

FIGURE 7.1 Phase-displaced Cycles of the Diffusion of the Technological Style and of the Problem-solving Capacity of the Politico-economic Regime and the Ensuing Probability of Economic Expansion.

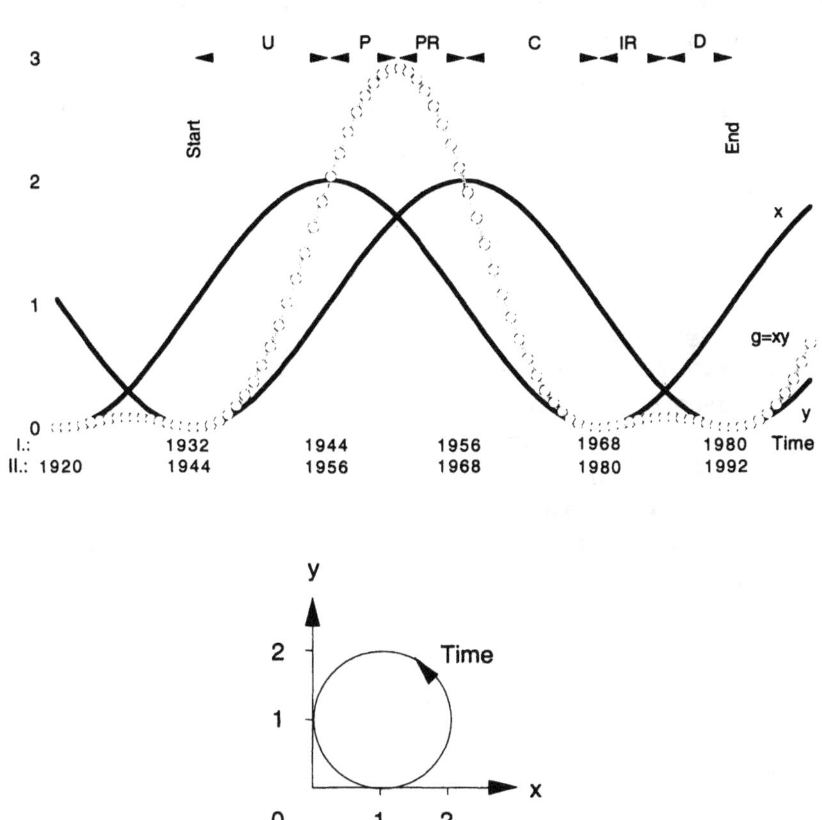

Legend:
I: Periodization
II: Adjusted periodization. Due to World War II the formation phase for large parts of the core—excluding the United States—was delayed (new beginning after the war). The new beginning is dated to 1944/1945 when the new world order of the post-war era was created (Bretton Woods, Yalta).

U (upswing), P (prosperity), PR (prosperity/recession), C (crisis), IR (interim recovery), D (depression, renewed crisis): structural phases of the long economic wave, see also p. 85f.

g: Ensuing probability of economic expansion
x: Diffusion (homogenization) of the technological style
y: Problem-solving capacity of the politico-economic regime

ECONOMIC EXPANSION

Following this formal treatment we suggest that economic expansion is a function of the extent of the diffusion of the style and the problem-solving capacity of the regime. In this perspective, the economic cycle becomes *endogenous* to the model.

The probability of economic expansion is—among other factors—a function of the diffusion of the technological style *and* the unfolding of the politico-economic regime. In other words: it follows that it accelerates the wider the diffusion of the style and the more advanced the unfolding of the regime. Here, we are confronted with a multiplier relationship. The hypothesis is formalized in figure 7.1 . To this end, the phases of the style and of the regime are multiplied by each other. The result is the expected economic expansion. Thus, our hypothesis predicts an economic peak and an interim recovery for each societal model. The peak is localized near the intersection of the unfolding of the style and of the regime, whereas the interim recovery occurs at the intersection of the unfolding of elements of a new technological style and the decay of an old regime. The model predicts a low level of growth during interim recovery. Independent of these differences in levels, the social processes underlying the peak and interim recovery phases are radically different. This point will be taken up again later.

Can this formalized model actually explain reality? We shall examine this question on the basis of the expansion of world industrial production. In chapter 4 (figure 4.1) and in connection with our discussion of long waves, we have suggested a structural formula of subsequent phases of industrial production for three waves: U—P—PR—C—IR—D. This structural formula can be explained on the basis of our model in figure 7.1.

The *upswing* phase (U) is mainly based on the diffusion of the new technological style. This powerful process, setting in after the crystallization of the style, is characterized by high, yet erratic growth rates. It can begin after a new regime has been formed as a supporting pillar. *Prosperity* (P) is a function of the style, the diffusion of which has lost some momentum but still has not ended, and of the unfolding of a regime whose problem-solving capacity increases substantially. *Prosperity-recession* (PR) is characterized by saturation in the diffusion of the style and a new heterogenization as a result of the emergence of elements of a new style. Growth during this phase results mainly from regime dynamics. In the past model this was the phase of intensive growth policy, creation of purchasing power and infrastructural investments in the framework of a still unfolding regime.

The *crisis* phase (C) begins after the regime has encountered the limits of its problem-solving capacity—at a time when the initial transition of the technological style causes an increased need for problem solving. Both style and regime move "downward." A good illustrative example from the latest societal model is the inability of Keynesian economic policy from 1970 onwards to cope with both recession and inflation resulting in stagflation (Bornschier 1976: 270-283). The crisis phase extends over a comparatively long period, during which certain events, like the oil crisis of the 1970s, usually lead to a general "crisis awareness."

Interim recovery (IR) is founded on the transition of the technological style. Although the new technological style has not yet fully crystallized, some of its elements are developing forcefully. But the old regime does *not* support the new style. Rather, it decays further because of its inadequate problem-solving capacity. During the career of the past model, there was a reversal in regime around 1980, characterized by tendencies towards cutting down the welfare state, a transition from Keynesian to monetarist policies (attempted control of the economy through the money supply) and supply-oriented economic strategy (deregulation in order to stimulate entrepreneurial initiative).

During *depression* (D) the regime reaches the low point of its problem-solving capacity; it becomes "ragged" and no longer coherent. Consequently, economic policy is politically challenged. At the same time the new technological style creates growing problems. During the interim recovery phase there is a wave of economic rationalization which, however, is not yet supported by a new variety of products and an upswing in consumption. With this, the cycle closes. Only the crystallization of the technological style (renewed variety of products) *and* the formation of a new social contract with the restoration of problem-solving capacity can bring about a stable, long-term upswing.

According to our model in figure 7.1, the probability of growth during the economic interim recovery is comparatively remote. Yet, this observation only applies to general or average growth. Overall, growth rates differ substantially as between firms, sectors and countries during this phase. Ascending industrial powers have the highest growth rates during interim recovery because there the style succeeds faster. Such new industrial powers were the United States and Germany during the period 1866-1872, the United States between 1920-1929, and Japan from 1982 onwards (see data in van Duijn 1983: 152f.). A group of large enterprises which accepts the new style particularly fast can create a boom for some years. This was the case in the United States during the 1920s. But the interim recovery phase is also the time of *speculative* fever in corporate take-overs, financial transactions, and in the stock market which, however, does not lead to real aggregate growth.

Thus, during the interim recovery phase there is a potential for higher growth rates than predicted by the model because the crisis leads to investment restraints in the face of worsening prospects. Investment intentions therefore accumulate and are only released when an obvious recovery (interim recovery) enhances prospect for profit. Such an accumulation of investment intentions can be accentuated by replacements made necessary by war damages. This was the case after World War I during the 1920s. As a result, France, with its enormous war damages, exhibited particularly high growth rates of industrial production.[1]

THE HISTORICAL-COMPARATIVE PERSPECTIVE

What has hitherto been discussed at the aggregate level must now be supplemented with more substantial observations referring to the neocorporatist, Keynesian societal model. These also serve to illustrate the use of the complicated model advanced above in explaining cases which do not seem to fit the general picture.[2]

There were two common elements in the new politico-economic regime of this century. The first concerned the role of the state in economy and society, i.e., interventionist Keynesianism and the redistributive welfare state. The second element concerned the social pact between capital and labor which would have seemed impossible to many during the 1920s.

Both elements were linked to each other in the sense that states either enforced the social pact between capital and labor (enforced corporatism) or initiated and monitored it as a referee and fiduciary (liberal corporatism). In all core countries these two elements arose and were linked to each other over the period 1932-1942. But there were some particularities (see also Weir and Skocpol 1985). In Great Britain, a successful pact of capital and labor was lacking, in the United States the unfolding of the new regime came to a halt after the victory of 1945 and later (from 1961 onwards) did not reach the level of refinement typical for the other countries.

The solutions adopted at the outset of the 1930s can be divided into an *enforced corporatist* and a *liberal or neocorporatist* variant. The first was promoted by national socialism and fascism. It is important to note that both variants were ways of coping with the problem of a decaying society after the dissolution of the old societal model. Authoritarian corporatism included an enforced alliance of capital with labor along with the loss of the trade unions' freedom of action. The authoritarian state either made essential economic decisions despite the fact that firms were under private control (as was the case in the Nazi economy), or made most of the decisions because enterprises were mostly state-owned (as with authoritarian-bureaucratic socialism (Stalinism), which made the Soviet Union the counter-core). Liberal corporatism moved from confrontation to continuous negotiations between capital and labor under the auspices of the state. Not force but "mutual accommodation" was the typical feature of this variant.

Underlying the new definition of the state's role in the economy and society were four elements of normative theory:[3]

(1) That market processes do not automatically create equilibrium, growth, and full employment;

(2) That market processes do not automatically create social justice and that therefore public authorities must provide social security and a redistribution of income in favor of those falling victim to the market process;

(3) That the social distribution system preceding the market, i.e.; the educational system, must offer more equal opportunities;

(4) That progress, i.e. , a new view of society in which everybody can enjoy material welfare through mass consumption of special goods like the automobile, can be used for social integration. A mass consumption society is accompanied by a leisure society. Spare time was seen as a condition for mass consumption, but also as a period of release from work constraints, which had become more intensive in the wake of the new technological style. While the liberal variant exploits leisure commercially (leisure industries) but otherwise leaves it unstructured, totalitarian regimes appropriate it for propaganda and mass mobilization purposes (see Lamprecht and Stamm 1994).

The "liberal" foundation of state interventionism had its intellectual roots in the "revolt" against neoclassical economic theory. John Maynard Keynes, the revolt's main champion, started his publicity campaign as early as 1924. In 1926 he published "The End of Laissez-Faire." and ten years later his "General Theory of Employment, Interest and Money" appeared (see Robinson 1962). In economic policy, Keynesianism became influential as early as 1933 in the United States (the New Deal) and Sweden. Things moved more slowly in its country of origin, Great Britain (see Weir and Skocpol 1985).

The core of the revolt consisted in Keynes's assumption that the economy by itself cannot reach equilibrium and a new upswing following the crisis. Accompanying public measures are needed to emerge from depression. This idea inspired economic planning. By 1945 at the latest, all kinds of short-term stabilization policies throughout the West were inspired by Keynes's ideas. Thus, the revolt against neoclassicism generated a new conception of capitalism that was naturally very broad. It reached from the moderate interventionism of neocapitalism (particularly in the United States, but also in Switzerland) to reformist socialism (early in Sweden) and labor politics in Great Britain.

These two main forms—neocapitalism and reformist socialism—have been called "commercial Keynesianism" and "social Keynesianism" by Margaret Weir and Theda Skocpol (1985: 133). Both notions emerged almost simultaneously but in very different locations: moderate interventionism (neocapitalism) in 1933 in the United States, social democracy in Sweden in 1932. In the Swedish variant the state intervenes less directly in economic processes and state enterprises are untypical. A variant of this model is the joint management by workers and trade unions of plants (for example, in Germany and Norway). A third variant that was not successful in historical perspective, even though it had its spectacular moments in political landslides, was labor politics. When the left won elections, nationalizations were carried out; these, however, were partially reversed by reprivatizations after election victories of the right. The main example for this pattern is Great Britain, but France can also be cited. Germany and Italy, too, have large sectors of state-owned enterprises, mainly due to the legacies of fascist public enterprises. After the war, the politics of nationalization were not prominent in these countries.

Historically, the moderate interventionism of neocapitalism coupled with a halt in the consolidation of the welfare state (United States), and labor's contradictory and discontinuous economic and social policies (Great Britain) were the least successful variants in the control of the economy, even though both countries adopted the Keynesian message quite early and eagerly (see Spahn 1976: 227).

BEFORE THE NEW BEGINNING: THE INSTITUTIONAL INNOVATORS

During the long downswing of the last wave (1903-1932), the important elements of the new technological style had already unfolded (see chapter 5). The new style asserted itself during the interim recovery of the 1920s, particularly in the United States. But Europe, too, witnessed a wave of rationalizations beginning in 1924. The new technological style included numerous other changes which still characterize industrial civilization, such as the distribution of goods. In 1923, for example, the first shopping centers opened in the United States. Thus, important elements of the new technological style were already present *before* the new beginning.

As is well known, the new technological style did not bring about an immediate recovery of economic stability, long-term growth and mass employment. On the contrary, the interim recovery which had been particularly strong in the United States ended abruptly with the crash in the autumn of 1929, paving the way for the world economic depression and horrendous mass unemployment.[4] This was the state of things before the transition of the politico-economic regime. As early as the 1920s important new developments could be discerned, but these were confined to conceptualizations. We have already mentioned Keynesianism, and to this we must add the fact that large segments of the socialist movement rejected ideas of proletarian revolution and thus made the reformist policies of social democracy possible.

During the years 1932-1933, conservative and restorative elements radically different from the innovators of the new beginning clearly dominated the interim recovery phase of the 1920s. In this light, pioneering developments within the Weimar Republic clearly constitute a special case. But from 1933 onwards, there was an historical change of course in the further evolution of the politico-economic regime: Hitler and his Nazi party assumed power in Germany while leadership in the formulation and formation of the new regime was assumed by Sweden and the United States.

Outside North America and Europe one should, however, not dismiss Australia and New Zealand from the list of democratic innovators, although their marginal position at the core limited at that time the impact of their new beginning. Both were consumer societies, fascinated by the new products before they really became affluent, and well in advance—notably of Britain—in providing social benefits. Their outstanding egalitarian self-definition and their "socialism without doctrine" enabled them to escape radical class confrontations (Lengyel 1990, and personal communications). By 1938 New Zealand's welfare state was probably the most comprehensive in the world.

Thus, the fact that fifteen dictatorships existed in the Europe of the 1930s and that the twelve democratic regimes became a minority by 1939 may blur the fact that this decade was also characterized by the impetus towards a new, *democratic* politico-economic regime that prevailed after World War II, eliminating the enforced corporatist variant. The new hegemonic power, the United States, became the main champion of the new model even if it did not itself complete it.

In the short time span of only one year the cornerstones for the institutional formation of two basic types of a new politico-economic regimes were laid. The years of 1932-1933 witnessed discontinuity and new beginnings. The innovators were Sweden, the United States and Germany.

In 1932, the Swedish social democrats under Per Albin Hansson assumed power for no less than forty-four years with their *folkhem* model, which in turn laid the basis for the Swedish welfare state. The first government was formed together with the farmers' party (Wilson 1979: 7f.; Weir and Skocpol 1985: 131). In the United States, Franklin D. Roosevelt of the Democrats advanced the *New Deal* in 1932 and was elected president with a vast majority, assuming power on March 4, 1933.

On January 30, 1933, Adolf Hitler was nominated chancellor of the Reich by President Hindenburg. Together with the German-National Peoples' Party, Hitler's National Socialist German Workers' Party formed (NSDAP) a government of "national concertation". In the following weeks, the NSDAP succeeded in side-lining the Reichstag (national parliament) and the state governments. A wave of open state terror began and culminated in the Enabling Act of March 23, 1933. Despite massive electoral terror, the NSDAP did not attain an absolute majority in the elections of March 5. But the Enabling Act paved the way for Hitler's dictatorship, central elements of which included forcing the population into line and rearmament. This totalitarian-populist variant of coping with unemployment, which lacked the element of basic consensus only survived for twelve years which were, however, most tragic for the world.

The basic type of the new democratic regime had a *social-liberal* and a *social-democratic* variant. The United States and Sweden constituted the two early poles between which most of the other countries later came to be situated. In Sweden, the social democrats succeeded in the elections with their populist *folkhem* model and the promise of creating a state pension system aimed at adequately supporting the elderly (Wilson 1979: 7). Similar plans also existed in other countries. In the United States, the Townsend Movement (from 1934 onwards) campaigned for an old age pension of two hundred dollars for all those over 60 years of age. In Switzerland though, an old-age pension law was rejected in 1931.

On the basis of the *folkhem* model, Sweden perfected the welfare state over the years and thus became—depending on ones perspective—the ideal or terrifying example of social bureaucracy. In retrospect the Swedish variant constituted a possible and comparatively durable solution at that time which created a high degree of legitimacy *and* of industrial development and made a high standard of living possible for decades.

After 1933, the United States make good progress in the formation of the new regime with its New Deal—i.e., a new social contract. Against the background of the dominant politico-economic philosophy and in view of the lack of a strong political left, this may seem surprising. Until Roosevelt's death in 1945, America changed radically, but after the war the improvement of the welfare state came to a standstill (Weir and Skocpol 1985: 147). For this reason, until the onset of the world economic crisis of 1975, the United States fell far behind not only in terms of the building of the welfare state but also in terms of economic success. Thus, from a historical perspective one cannot say that the welfare state whose development was arrested, namely neocapitalism in the United States, was the more successful variant: the contrary has been the case.

The remaining democratic countries of the 1930s—except for Australia and New Zealand (see above)—implemented the social innovations of the pioneers only hesitatingly and in "packages." However, the threat of Nazism and fascism together with the danger of war accelerated the process. The same was true for the communist threat. What was going on in the Soviet Union under Stalin accelerated the acceptance of Keynesianism as an alternative to revolution, even in the United States. In Europe broad coalitions emerged which finally advanced elements of the new regime. Although they lacked success before the war, one should not dismiss attempts at the European version of the New Deal (Telò 1988). In Belgium the "union sacrée" (Christian-Socialists, Liberals and Socialists) in the mid-1930s, led by Paul van Zeeland and Henri de Man, can be mentioned in this light. In France the Popular Front government of Léon Blum (1936-1938) had little lasting success, and soon there was a retrenchment of the reforms owing to resistance of the bourgeois right and groups of the extreme right.

Switzerland experienced more continuous albeit incremental development. A "crisis initiative" aimed at a planned fight against the economic crisis and at income guarantees for endangered groups was rejected in 1935. But the years 1934-5 also witnessed the important reorientation within the Swiss Social Democratic Party away from class struggle and towards the struggle against mass unemployment (Eisner 1991). With the first "peace agreement" of 1937 an initial institutional element was formed: metal workers and entrepreneurs agreed upon a system of arbitration. The grand coalition became a fact in 1943: The first social democrat, Ernst Nobs, became a member of the government. The second attempt at implementing—for the time very generous—old-age pensions was a vast success in 1947 with 80 percent voting in favor of the new law. But similar to the state of things in the United States, an initiative aimed at the "right to work" was opposed and rejected in 1946. Under the influence of the Keynesian theory of economic policy that was already in place in Sweden and the United States, the Swiss accepted economic legislating in 1947 that obliged the government to adopt measures to improve the welfare of the people and to provide economic security for its citizens. Despite occuring incrementally—although like Sweden, it was a process uninterrupted by the war—Switzerland also qualifies for the group of democratic pioneers of the 1930s.

What about Britain, where the emerging new doctrine of Keynesianism originated? Even though social security made early legislative progress, politics in Great Britain displayed great reserve concerning the new ideas in economic and social policy. Margaret Weir and Theda Skocpol (1985: 128) suspect that resistance was central in stimulating Keynes' work: "Ironically, it seems to have been after this frustrating experience that Keynes decided that a new, grand theoretical synthesis would be needed to overthrow the hold of 'economic orthodoxy.' Without the impermeability of the British polity to specific new economic policy recommendations, *The General Theory* might not have been written." But a coherent formulation of new societal elements mobilized by the innovators was lacking during the 1930s. Only confrontation with the Axis powers during the war led to a change in the situation. From May 10, 1940 until July 26, 1945, Great Britain was ruled by a grand war coalition under the charismatic prime ministership of Winston Churchill. In 1944, the government published a White Book in which it assumed responsibility for the maintenance of a "high and stable" level of employment. This White Book is the first official acknowledgement of the victory of the Keynesian revolution in Great Britain (Robinson 1962).

Britain after the war emerged as a prototypical welfare state, casting its influence throughout its Empire and in Europe (e.g., the Netherlands, France). The National Health Service was a pioneering model and full employment a chief aim. Yet the war coalition did not survive during peacetime and this laid the foundation for discontinuous Labour intervention, resulting in a stop-and-go policy. Under the Labour government of Attlee (1945-51) there were a great many nationalizations (in particular the Bank of England, coal mines, and transport and steel industries). Social policy followed the wartime Beveridge plan ("Social Insurance and Allied Services", 1942) which aimed at the control of demand. Compulsory insurance was introduced, but from 1951 to 1955 the Conservative government under Churchill returned and from 1952 onwards partial reprivatizations came into effect. Thus: "The concept of nationalization has been used (. . .) by Labour and Tory governments with varying intensity and in contradictory ways" (Spahn 1976: 226). The frequent alternation of leftist and rightist governments was facilitated by the British system of absolute majority election and led to an incoherent formation of the welfare state. And, at the level of the politico-economic regime, the second element of basic consensus between capital and labor remained weak.

THE ECONOMIC GROWTH CURVE IN THE CORE, 1932-1992

We have already pointed out that enforced corporatism may initially be faster in forming a new regime, but does not attain sufficient levels of domestic legitimacy and thus has to direct unresolved internal conflicts externally as well as towards domestic "enemies." For that reason, it may provoke international conflicts and wars during the upswing phase.

TABLE 7.1 Annual Growth Rates of Industrial Production, 1929-1993

*	United States	Europe **	Japan	World ***
1929-32	-16.6%	-9.0%	...	-13.0%
1932-38	7.9%	9.0%	11.1%	7.8%
1938-48	7.8%	-0.3%	-8.1%	3.3%
1948-58	3.3%	6.6%	16.7%	5.1%
1958-67	6.2%	5.4%	14.7%	6.3%
1967-71	1.7%	6.3%	11.8%	5.2%
1971-75	1.4%	1.9%	1.7%	2.8%
1975-82	2.2%	2.0%	4.8%	2.5%
1982-91	3.3%	1.5%	4.5%	2.5%
1991-93	1.9%	-2.3%	-5.1%	-1.0%

Notes:
*) Between the index values for the given years; from 1932 onwards, calculated from low point to low point.
**) European market economies (without Bulgaria, Czechoslovakia, Hungary, Poland, Romania, the German Democratic Republic and the Soviet Union).
***) Market economies of the world.
Sources: United Nations Statistical Yearbooks and Monthly Bulletins of Statistics, various years.

The general upswing of the period 1933-1938 also shown in table 7.1 was interrupted by the war in Europe and Japan. This interruption was particularly drastic in Japan, Germany, Italy, and Austria. Only from 1945 onwards is there a fresh start in Europe and Japan. Thus, World War II caused a "time lag" shown in table 7.1 between the United States, on the one hand, and Europe and Japan, on the other. Uninterrupted development in the United States resulted in a lead of a dozen years. After 1953 this lead decreases, however, but until the 1960s it remains clearly visible in the unfolding of the model. The United States entered the recession phase as early as 1967, Europe and Japan followed after 1971. For the time period 1958-1967 it is possible to detect a clear-cut peak of growth in the Western core as well as in the capitalist world economy as a whole. After 1971 the general downswing of growth rates sets in. Compared to the high growth rates of the previous thirty or forty years, the slowing down of growth since 1971 earned the label of crisis and stagnation.

The empirical evidence fits our theory which states that the interlinkage of style crystallization and regime formation results in an economic upswing. In addition, our model sees further growth as dependent on *both*: the *diffusion* of the style and the *unfolding* of the regime. From this follows a further empirical prediction: if the unfolding of the regime is delayed, a *bimodal* distribution of economic growth rates is to be expected. If the unfolding process is not only delayed but also incomplete we may assume that the second growth peak will be considerably lower than the first. We have argued that the consolidation of the regime in the United States was delayed in connection with victory in World War II and the reach for hegemony. A hegemonic position tempts elites to neglect domestic legitimacy on which initial success on their way to the top rested. Even the delayed unfolding of the regime during the Kennedy-Johnson era (1961 - March 1969) remained incomplete—at least compared to what had already been achieved in most of the other countries of the Western core.

The expectation of a bimodal distribution of growth rates with a lower second peak is confirmed for the United States (table 7.1), but the aggregated growth pattern in Europe does not exhibit a bimodal pattern. The oscillations of annual growth rates in the three periods from 1948 to 1971 are very small. The singularity of the United States' growth pattern becomes even more evident if we compare it to the patterns for Sweden and Switzerland, the other two innovators within the democratic variant of the new beginning of the 1930s. This will be discussed more fully in chapter 11, where similarities and differences between core societies will be addressed.

LEGITIMACY AND CONFLICT CYCLES

Another component of our theoretical model concerns legitimacy and the course of conflict during the career of the societal model. In our perspective, conflict is a permanent feature of societal life. Still, the sources, intensity, levels, and forms of conflict articulation are subject to substantial variations during the career of a societal model. On the one hand, the legitimacy of an order increases with mobility opportunities arising from new occupational structures and with the widening distribution of a variety of new products that the new technological style affords. On the other hand, legitimacy is increased with the unfolding of the new politico-economic regime and its ability to generate stability and a social balance, i.e., egalitarian justice. The fascination with the new as well as stability and justice are sources of legitimacy which, with different weightings, are important for maintaining legitimacy over the whole career of the societal model.

However, the course of conflict cannot be derived as easily as the economic growth curve from the theoretical model. Basically, there are two types of conflict phases over the career of a societal model. These are differentiated not primarily by their intensity, but rather by the *sources of conflict* .

An initial, constant source of conflict stems from the distribution of power, and here not only with respect to unequal distributions. Even an equal distribution of power does not imply the absence of conflict. Rather, it is a basic condition for the probable result of conflictive interactions between actors. *Power conflict* is thus the result of actors' differing interests—it is a *distributional conflict.*

The second source of conflict is rooted in the incompatibility of value interpretations, that is, in the realm of normative theories. These are the possible but not binding interpretations which set priorities and offer ideas for the negotiation of interpretations: we call them *value conflicts.* Not as constant a source of conflict as power and distributional conflicts, these can be settled or mitigated for a certain time by a basic consensus.

The third source of conflict is precisely the result of the temporary mitigation of value conflicts. When this is the case, a discrepancy between a model and reality arises. The reality represents the historical distribution of power and opportunities for participation in society. The resulting social *inconsistency* leads to *realization conflicts*, which only occur when value conflicts have been settled, i.e., when society is not in disorder.

The career of a societal model can now be divided into two stages: the first phase is characterized by *social inconsistency*—i.e., discrepancy between the promises of the model and reality, leading to realization conflicts. The second phase is characterized by *social disorder.* This is the consequence of a decaying model that loses its binding force and thus leads to value conflicts and to unregulated conflicts of interest. The phase of social inconsistency lasts as long as the two subsystems, the technological style and the politico-economic regime, have not reached the limits of their capacity to realize the values of equality and efficiency for a large part of the population. During the consensus phase (formation and unfolding) the *intensity* of conflict depends upon the legitimacy of society in the eyes of its members. Conversely, during the dissenting phase (dissolution and decay) resources that actors command and situational factors become more important. Such resources include, for example, the opportunities for collective action through new social movements (Ramirez 1981; Jenkins 1983; Brand 1982). Situational factors, on the other hand, refer to the economic situation or regime sanctions against the opposition (state repression).

Emile Durkheim (1983) and Robert Merton (1949) originated a well-known strand of theory that links the articulation of conflict and deviant behavior to the general state of society, which may result in anomie, i.e., disharmony or disorderliness. Merton's version of anomie theory postulates that the discrepancy between societal goals and the opportunities to attain them in the social structure is the source of anomic conditions. Merton's theory is somewhat deficient in explaining under which conditions anomie as a societal state becomes relevant at the level of actors (groups or individuals).

Peter Heintz (1968) argued that unequal participation in societal values and wealth as expressed in social stratification is not necessarily a source of anomie. In his reformulation, structural tensions—i.e., unequal participation—lead either to revaluations in the sense that societal goals and aspirations are given up or reassessed, or to anomic tensions. But this reformulation neglects the societal regulation of structural tensions. The notion of a career of societal models offers such an explanation.

Starting from normative theories, a societal model offers a vision of how things should be in the future and thereby regulates structural tensions resulting from the unequal participation in societal wealth. Thus, the latest societal model was able to mobilize wide sectors of the population by promising democratization of wealth. Expectations rose because subcultural differentiation in the stratification system were reduced. The old barriers between workers and the middle class were increasingly dismantled and a new status of employee emerged.

In Merton's understanding this should lead to increase in anomie because the discrepancy between shared values in society and the opportunity to reach them has widened. Such a conclusion is wrong because, in its formative phase, the societal model only lays out promises for the future. Thus, one also has to consider temporal aspects. In addition, the latest societal model admitted new groups (for example the labor movement) into inner power circles. To the extent that this took place, counter-cultural groups were demobilized. The conflict between capital and labor was institutionalized within the social power structure. The result was a long-lasting economic upswing after the war, historically unparalleled in terms of growth rates. Yet, precisely this success of the societal model in its first phase created new problems of legitimacy.

INTENSITY, LEVELS, AND FORMS OF CONFLICT AND CONFLICT ARTICULATION

The long economic upswing during the past societal model resulted in a *general* increase of wealth but could not significantly level out *positional* wealth (see Hirsch 1976). The items of general wealth can be democratized. During the long upswing of the latest societal model a new variety of products and services emerged and social security benefits became available for ever broader segments of Western society's population. To the extent that this was achieved, the societal model fulfilled its promises to democratize wealth. The initially widening gap between expectations and opportunities thus did not create anomie but was itself narrowed instead. With respect to conflicts, we call this phase that of social inconsistency. Social inconsistency thus refers to the gap between promises and expectations, on the one hand, and to the progress in democratization of general wealth, on the other. According to our hypothesis, social conflict decreases at all levels or remains low during this phase, which, however, is by no means free of conflict. But such conflict is special, namely a *conflict of realization*.

The legitimacy of an order increases with the expected diffusion of the greater variety of products that are offered by the new technological style. In addition, legitimacy increases further with the unfolding of the politico-economic regime, i.e., its capacity to generate stability and social balance ("justice"). The "fascination with the new" and "justice" are the two sources of legitimacy; their relative importance for its creation varies during the career of the societal model. From these observations and the model presented above (figure 7.1) an assumption regarding the intensity of conflict during the diffusion phase of the style follows. When the style becomes saturated and the regime has not yet fully unfolded we expect an interim conflict peak that lies within the economic peak phase. After that, conflict decreases again with the full unfolding of the regime. Its decreasing problem solving capacity leads to a renewed increase in conflict, however.

In this phase, realization conflicts become value conflicts: it is the transition from social inconsistency to social disorder.

Not all goods and opportunities in society can be democratized in a fashion similar to those pertaining to general wealth. This is the case of *positional social goods*, which result in a positionally stratified distribution of wealth. In what Fred Hirsch (1976) calls the positional economy, positional goods are commodities, services, and locations in the work structure which (1) are scarce in a socially defined way or (2) lead to excess demand, devaluation or displacement if they are extended.

The success of the societal model in democratizing wealth leads to new problems in the form of changing tolerance for inequalities. Over time the products of general wealth become trivialized, i.e., democratized property. But whatever is available for all loses positional significance: thus the positional inequality of wealth becomes important. The far-reaching attainment of general wealth opens perspectives on positional inequality and increases the competition for positional goods. In the face of the inelasticity of positional goods—greater availability through growth does not change their unequal distribution—such competition becomes hopeless or frustrating as Hirsch (1976) points out. Not economic efficiency but greater equality becomes the dominant issue. To keep anomie, in the sense of means-ends tension, latent becomes a major problem to which groups of actors react differently.

In this connection one must distinguish between different *levels of conflict articulation*. Initially, conflict is experienced at the individual level. This does not mean that it is also articulated by individuals, however. If at all possible, individuals will deflect conflict to remain functional. A large number of established societal groups can convey the collective articulation of conflict: parties, associations, labor unions, and groups defending the interests of their members. By shifting conflict to social groups, articulation becomes political. Whether an individual can find a suitable organization to express problems depends on cultural differences, the availability of established channels of conflict deflection, and cost-benefit calculations. As already pointed out, social power involves considerable expense which must be counterbalanced by the perceived chances of success or by a high intensity of individual suffering.

During the formation and unfolding phase, realization conflicts can be articulated more easily through the established channels of collective conflict articulation (e.g., parties, support committees for parties, labor unions and associations). It is this political system, which had earlier subscribed to a renewed social contract, that must now be realized. Naturally, this involves some conflict because vested interests are involved, but such conflict can still be seen as regulated. Independent of the intensity of conflict articulation we thus expect collective rather than of individual conflict articulation during this phase.

Things are quite different during the dissolution and decay phases of the societal model. For most value conflicts, extensive institutional "receptacles" of articulation are lacking. The majority of the population reacts by "internal retreat," a solution of anomie through a kind of subcultural differentiation. The most frequent form of individual adaptation to anomic tensions that have become manifest is a partial retreat into what Robert K. Merton (1949) calls "ritualism." Particularly under good economic conditions—a low level of unemployment, a low degree of work place uncertainty and high real wages—the abandonment of values in combination with subcultural differentiation may be the most popular form of adaptation. Concentration is focussed on the "small happiness" within the family and the circle of friends who share the same hobbies in leisure consumption and social clubs. The totality of society, which had been characterized by a decidedly functional societal model, begins to dissolve into "provinces of meaning." A growing pluralization of lifestyles breaks up the encompassing societal ties and transforms society into "fine-grained privatized life spheres." (Beck 1983: 59)

This is a transformation of anomie from a means-ends tension to anomie in the sense of Durkheim's conception, i.e., loss of orientation by society as a whole. This loss of orientation means that formerly binding socially and morally guiding ideas, which gave action a socially binding meaning, have been undermined, resulting in a loss of the conflict management capabilities of the societal model. This in turn results in an increase of various manifestations of deviant behavior, for example, criminality or self-destructing behavior.

For certain groups, the very anomic situation that leads to an increase in deviant behavior and to a retreat within society does not simply imply subcultural differentiation but also *counter-cultural rebellion* rejecting mainstream societal values and practices and demanding new values and institutions. The emergence of such counter-cultural rebellion is based upon increased mobilization potential, itself the result of affluence and the concentration of its social bases. During the latest societal model, large sectors of the young intelligentsia were mobilized at universities. In the United States, the black population was mobilized, too, as a result of migration to the cities where it was severely discriminated against in the labor market.

With counter-cultural rebellion a new type of conflict emerges, characterized by confrontation between actors not integrated into the power circles of the societal model and representatives of societal, economic, and political power. These are primarily *value conflicts* that challenge the basic consensus of the societal model; power naturally plays a central role. But the issue at hand is not participation in established power structures but a different distribution of power. Such value conflicts lie at the heart of social movements, which articulate conflict at the collective level without being institutionalized.

It is important to note, however, that social movements have at least *two* aspects. The common base for both types is their marginality with respect to society's power center. This is their only similarity because movements are triggered by different social crises and recruit their members from quite different social origins.

First of all, certain "new" social movements spring from educated middle class radicalism, and are characterized by progressive attitudes, their core being normally composed of critical intellectuals. The actors possess high levels of education, i.e., achieved status, which confers high prestige and elevated societal claims. Their starting point is a critical stance towards the interpretation of claims to freedom and equality. Emancipation from traditional authorities and sympathy for the victims of social injustice in different spheres are their features. Theoretically, these social movements can be interpreted as an outcome of a means-ends anomie.

The second type of movement is distinguished by reactionary attitudes and delineating itself from the power elite as well as from groups who do not belong to it, which it sees as outsiders and foreigners. The base of this movement—although not necessarily its leadership—is made up of those deprived of socially defined claims for status achievement and upward mobility. These social movements are the result of a loss of orientation and of crisis, and can be called populist. They arise from diffuse protest and may even extend to radical nationalistic movements that engage in violence against foreigners.

Both types of movement make their appearance at quite different points in time. The first can be located in the saturation phase—i.e., the 1960s during the latest societal model, which contributed substantially to the dissolution of the model. Because of their origins we may also call these movements of affluence: they started during a phase unmarked by economic crisis. Things are entirely different for the second type of movement. They are phenomena of crisis and manifest themselves in the interval between two societal models, i.e., when the old model has dissolved and a new one does not yet provide orientation. Experienced threat to economic security activates these potentials, the latent origins of which can also be traced back to the saturation phase of the model, however.

Radicalized middle class protest movements are the expression of value conflicts in the second phase of the downswing of the societal model. Through emerging value conflicts the remains of the old societal interpretation of the world come under pressure and a general lack of orientation spreads. *The consensus phase finally transforms into the dissent phase of the model.* In the further course of the dissent phase important former pillars of the societal model may become its opponents. Examples of this transition are the neoconservative and neoliberal currents of the late 1970s.

During the phase of social disorder phenomena arise that are at first sight quite disparate but concern different groups of actors: there is the main form of a retreat from society into privacy, then, initially quite limited by comparison, deviant behavior at the level of the individual, and finally counter-cultural rebellion confined to special groups.

It is not only individuals who may deflect conflict to the outside, i.e., to groups. Governments are in a structurally similar position. Domestic conflict can be developed on the basis of a large national group, which then goes on to articulate the conflict within the state system. This represents an attempt to temper the conflict domestically and engenders substantial war risks.[5] Yet, the possibilities for such a devolution are connected to state resources and to the geopolitical situation. Only hegemonic powers and their challengers are in a position to effect such devolutions with some certainty regarding their assessment of the risks involved. Thus, like our argument concerning the deflection of individual conflicts to groups, we may expect a displacement of intergroup conflict to interstate conflict for the formation phase. As conflict in general decreases during this phase, however, only the beginning of the formation phase and later the dissolution phase exhibit a clear increase of interstate conflicts.

These different levels must be set against different *forms* of conflict articulation. Here, we distinguish between "formally peaceful" and "violent" conflict articulation. The former is said to be peaceful because the means used in the struggle are normally defined as peaceful, such as economic competition. The violent type of conflict articulation can be further divided into spontaneous and planned violence. Spontaneous violence results from special situations; it arises from the "heat of battle" but has not been planned. If planned violence is aimed at an order which regulates the relationship between groups in the form of a contractual relationship, this contract is formally broken. The actual interruption of peace and the use of violent means meet the conditions of war. If one of the parties in conflict is a state, we speak of "domestic war"—"terrorism" or "civil war" being other terms for this state of affairs.

During the consensus phase formally peaceful social and political conflicts are relatively frequent whereas violent conflict becomes much more prominent during the dissent phase, though mostly as domestic *war* in the last case. The distinction between what is formally peaceful and violent is not identical to the distinction between what is legal and illegal. An important interim form in political practice is civil disobedience, which represents neither formal politics nor is aimed at revolutionary change. It is a way of illegal but not criminal articulation of conflict which claims legitimation beyond the law.[6] This subtle notion is founded in the Anglo-Saxon conception of the State which considers citizens as the inalienable holders of sovereignty which cannot be usurped by the social contract and furthermore that guarantees them a *natural* right to resist by appeal to a morality beyond the law—a right to which even the State as the guarantor of the social contract remains bound. It is on this basis that the troublesome figure of the citizen arises within the continental European tradition, of the citizen who "does not choose to refrain from his principal loyalty to state institutions although he occasionally resists (lawful, democratic) state power" (Kohler 1986: 95, our translation).

During the dissent phase, when value conflicts become important and social movements emerge, such forms of civil disobedience become relatively more frequent. We only have limited data at hand to illustrate this for Western society as a whole (see below) but we can point to evidence concerning Switzerland in the period 1945-78. Acts of civil disobedience in connection with social movements—e.g.., against the war in Vietnam, against nuclear power, against environmental pollution, and against the stationing of missiles—are examples illustrative of the dissent phase for the period between the late 1970s and the early 1980s.

THE W-CURVE HYPOTHESIS

Expectations concerning the patterns of conflict over the career of the societal model can be represented as the W-curve hypothesis, according to which the overall level of conflict follows a W-shaped pattern. At the same time and along the overall degree of intensity the character of conflict changes, as shown in figure 7.2.

FIGURE 7.2 Expectations of Conflict During the Career of the Societal Model

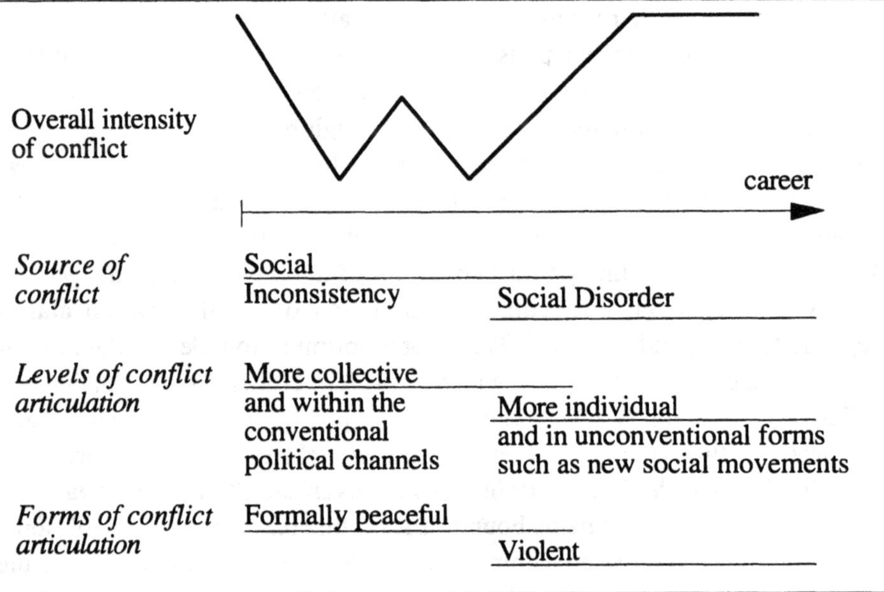

We have already pointed out that the legitimacy of an order increases on the basis of two processes, the importance of which changes over time: in connection with the fascination exercised by the diffusion of the novel products offered by the new technological style and in connection with the unfolding of the new politico-economic regime's capacity to create stability and social "justice." The transition from "fascination" to "justice and stability" during the prosperity phase is delicate because it assumes a change in orientations of the population.

Legitimacy on the basis of "fascination" can decrease as a result of saturation without being fully replaced by legitimacy on the basis of extended "justice." In other words, the wave of legitimacy connected with an extended variety of products and new lifestyles may ebb before the wave of legitimacy created on the basis of the unfolding of the politico-economic regime reaches its peak (see figure 7.1). In this trough between two waves economic expansion is greatest, but we must also expect an interim peak in dissent and collective forms of conflict articulation resulting from the transition in the principal legitimation strategy.

As the regime is still at the outset of its unfolding phase and its problem-solving capacity is not yet exhausted, it will react with social justice reforms to this interim conflict phase, its comparatively liberal reaction to conflict being expressed in sanctions which appear mild by comparison with the intensity of conflict articulation. During the latest societal model, reforms during the peak phase occurred in the following three spheres. The "integrated," i.e., the core status group of the economically active, was integrated even more fully by the automatization of the proportional distribution of growth. In addition, those who were *no longer* or *had not yet been* integrated into the distributional system, i.e., old and young people, were integrated on the basis of improved old-age pensions, educational grants, and the opening up of higher education. Finally, provisions to make men and women equal by law were part of these social justice reforms.

Apart from this interim peak of dissent and conflict we must expect a long phase of decreasing conflict levels in all realms of society during the formation and unfolding phase of the societal model. As soon as the problem-solving capacity of the regime is exhausted, however, we may expect a phase of increasing conflict of similar duration. With the decay of the model conflict becomes increasingly pointed, because the basic consensus crumbles and social peace is ever more broadly challenged. Consequently, governments react to conflict with greater repression.

Our formalization thus follows the phases in the career of the societal model depicted in figure 1.2 (chapter 1). While we have already adduced empirical evidence concerning economic expansion in the course of the long wave that fits our theory, an empirical test of the conflict cycle has yet to be presented. To test our hypotheses empirically for the Keynesian societal model we need long time series data, which narrows the gamut of conflict indicators. At the collective level (organizations and groups), we would have to distinguish between political, formally peaceful incidents (for example, political strikes and demonstrations with or without spontaneous violence) and violent ones (domestic war; armed attacks) as well as economic conflicts (strikes). The individual level can be measured on the basis of suicide rates, on the one hand, and murder rates, on the other. At the state level we would have to set off domestic state violence (sanctions by the government) against interstate conflict regulation (settlement of international disputes) and actual wars.

POLITICAL CONFLICT

Past research on political conflict is short on explanatory schemes. Ekkart Zimmermann, a recognized expert in the field, concludes in his comprehensive overview of the literature that "we know little about predictors of (violent) political conflict in Western European countries and the determinants of political stability" (Zimmermann, 1989: 192), which applies also to the whole OECD area (see Zimmermann, 1988: 67). Though explanations for the obvious country differences seem to be lacking, diachronic analyses have been rare despite variations that should have attracted more research.

Core countries, as democratic market economies, belong in many ways to a single type of society since they share many crucial institutional features. This would suggest the following methodology: to look first at the overall pattern of conflict in the aggregate and to explain differences between countries later (see chapter 11). But core countries are at the same time differentiated, a crucial aspect in the postwar era being the distance between the hegemon, the United States, and the other members of the core, which we here consider the seventeen stable democracies (Australia, Austria, Belgium, Canada, Denmark, Finland, France, Germany, Ireland, Italy, Japan, Netherlands, New Zealand, Norway, Sweden, Switzerland and the United Kingdom).

A hegemon enjoys means of conflict management not at the disposal of ordinary core members, which suggests that the hegemon should be treated separately. In greater detail this argument runs as follows. After World War II only the U.S. was able to externalize domestic conflicts (particularly those arising from race discrimination) by means of military involvement in the Third World (see Russett 1990), whereas the smaller European countries had to avert domestic insurgency through the provision of welfare. However, as the American Civil Rights Movement and anti-Vietnam War protest in the 1960s indicate, this "rallying 'round the flag" may fail in the long run if wars are not quickly concluded and victories clear.

The data on political conflict we use here are drawn from the *World Handbook of Political and Social Indicators* (Taylor 1985). The six indicators, covering thirty five years of systematic observation (1948-1982), were reduced by factor analysis. For the whole period the often replicated two-factor structure is apparent, which distinguishes between three indicators of moderate protest and three of high violence (see Hibbs 1973; Zimmermann 1980). Figures 7.3a and 7.3b show how the two additional indices of "collective protest" (annual number of riots, political strikes, protest demonstrations) and "domestic war" (annual number of armed attacks, political assassinations, political deaths) distribute over time. As argued above, we treat the hegemon separately and therefore present the trend patterns of conflict for the U.S. and the other seventeen core countries in two figures. In Figure 7.3a, the sum of these events, which can be classified as *internal war*, is divided by ten for the purpose of graphic representation.

FIGURE 7.3a Collective Protest and Domestic War Events in 17 Core Countries (aggregated), 1948-1982

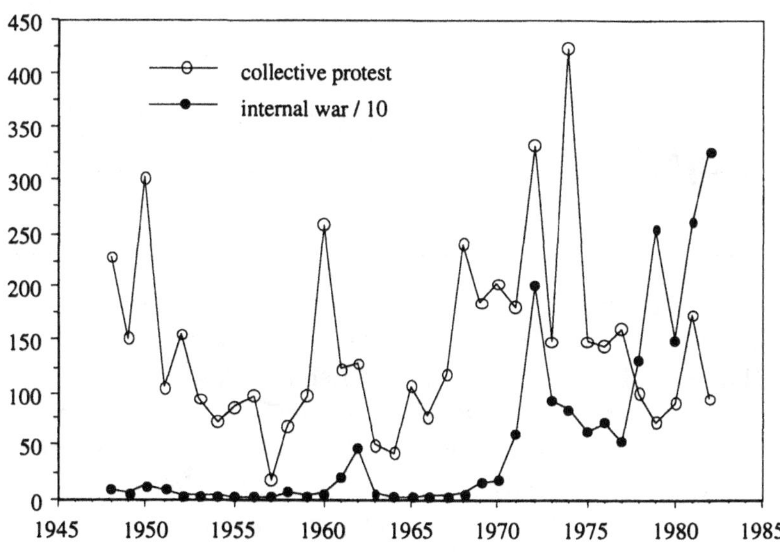

For the seventeen non-hegemonic countries, political conflict decreased markedly from the late 1940s until the late 1950s. Since the level again declined after a peak around 1960, we refer to the phase around 1960 as the interim peak. This description also makes sense in view of the renewed and marked rise of political conflict in the 1970s. The phase of rising and high conflict, which lasts until the beginning of the 1980s (the end of our data series), began with the student revolts in the late 1960s. After 1970 political conflict changed in character insofar as violent events became more frequent.

FIGURE 7.3b Collective Protest and Domestic War Events in the United States, 1948-1982

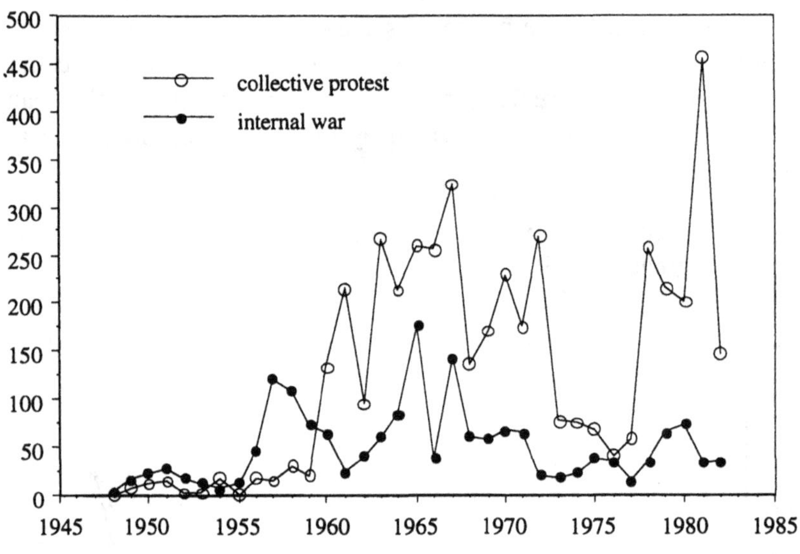

At first glance the pattern for the United States seems to be different (see figure 7.3b). This impression changes when we look at it as displaced in time. The lead of the United States—after the New Deal in the early 1930s—was, by contrast to most other core members, uninterrupted by the war. The earlier start of the new societal model of the Keynesian epoch offers an explanation. The dynamic of conflict in the United States should have run in advance of the other core countries and reached the first trough as early as the end of the 1940s (see Kerbo and Shaffer 1992). If this holds true, then—contrary to the aggregate of the seventeen core countries—the first descending line of the W-shaped pattern for the United States cannot, of course, appear in the data available starting in 1948.

This view is supported by the fact that the United States had already passed its peak of conflict at the time of the worldwide student revolts, which started there in the early 1960s. On the other hand, the level of conflict in the other core countries began to climb considerably only after 1968. We conclude that the patterns for the two groups are displaced in time with a lead of about a decade for the United States. Another difference becomes apparent: in the U.S. the number of collective protest events exceeds the number of violent ones, while in the other seventeen core countries—especially due to the inclusion of the United Kingdom, Ireland, France and Italy (see Nollert 1992: 253) domestic violence dominates by far. As an explanation we suggest that the hegemon was able to displace violent conflict into the interstate sphere (see Russett 1990).

According to both sets of figures, the level of political conflict at the core fluctuates considerably over the whole postwar era. Furthermore, both levels—collective protest and domestic war—appear to follow a W-shaped pattern, part of which is not observable in data for the United States. In line with the work of Tilly et al. (1975) on nineteenth century movements and Tarrow's (1989) study of trends of political and industrial conflict in postwar Italy we thus observe cycles in the magnitude of political conflict.

INDUSTRIAL CONFLICT

The deviant pattern of the U.S. both in trend and level of conflict is also evidenced in the course of industrial conflict. The statistics of the International Labour Organization (ILO) record the number of strikers and of working days lost as indicators of industrial conflict. Data on the years before 1948 and after 1982 are available, but we propose to compare trends and levels of industrial conflict with those of collective protest and domestic war. Numbers of strikers as an indicator has certain shortcomings since it does not control for their duration, hence figure 7.4 presents the time series on working days lost.

The severity of labor conflict declines between 1948 and the late 1950s, except for sporadic outlying years. In the early 1960s severity generally remained at a comparatively low level. From the second half of the 1960s on, a leap occurred in the level of working days lost. After 1968 the level of conflict was higher than in the 1950s and early 1960s. This leap was more pronounced in the aggregate of seventeen core countries than in the United

States. The data presented in figure 7.4 suggest that industrial conflict decreased until the middle of the 1960s and then began to rise again. This observation supports the argument elaborated by Pizzorno (1978) that conflict research should pay attention to cycles of social conflict (see also Tarrow 1988: 433).

FIGURE 7.4 Working Days Lost (in thousands) in 17 Core Countries (aggregated) and in the United States, 1948-1982

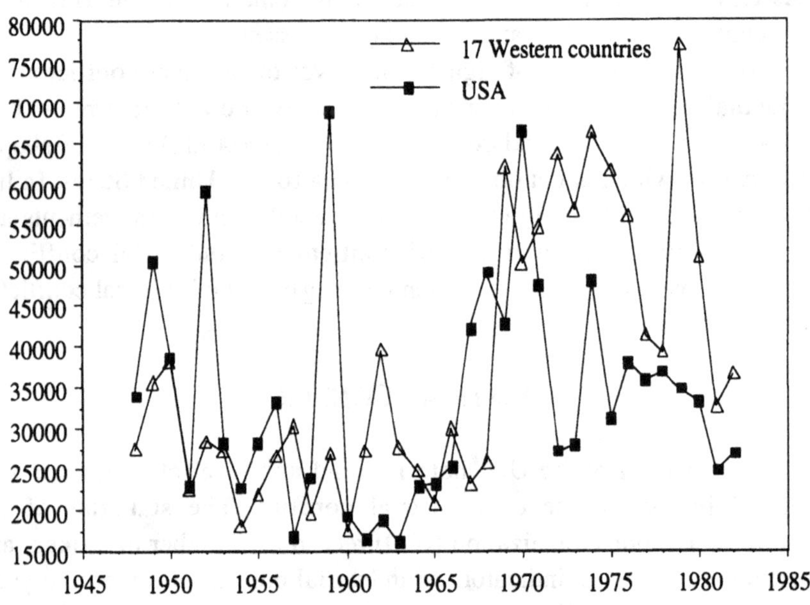

Concluding this portrayal of the trends in political and industrial conflict between 1948 and 1982 we stress the wide differences between countries in our sample. Indicators are presented in detail elsewhere (Korpi 1983; Paldam and Pedersen 1984; Zimmermann 1988, 1989; Nollert 1992) and remain very substantial when weighted. For political violence (domestic war) the differences are even more pronounced – in some cases due to exceptional constellations (like the conflict in Ulster). We will return to the explanation of these differences in chapter 11.

HOMICIDE AND SUICIDE

Contrary to common assumption, criminality and deviant behavior have not been increasing if we base our estimates on very long time series. The findings of Manuel Eisner (1992, 1994) and Ted R. Gurr (1981) show instead a decreasing secular trend, particularly with respect to violent forms of criminality. For the period after World War II the data bases provided by Archer and Gartner (1984) and by Gurr and Gurr (1983) initially reveal a decrease in the rates of delinquency for the highly developed countries. As the international comparability of criminality rates is rightly criticized, we shall only use homicide rates from the death records. We will be using homicide and suicide rates (per 100,000 population) as indicators of conflicts at the individual level which—following Emile Durkheim—were analyzed by Henry and Short as early as 1954.

A tendency towards a long-term decrease of violence against oneself and other persons can first be reconciled with Norbert Elias's (1987) thesis regarding self-control. But self-control can rest on various pillars. It can result from a strict internalization of norms, but it can also follow from insight. This control by insight can be linked to one of Immanuel Kant's ideas, which stresses the role played by reason. Such a conception appears idealistic at first sight, but the ways of our practical reason can also be linked to the mutual benefits of conforming behavior.

The mutual benefit of conformity may be entering a state of crisis, however, as a result of breaches of trust during socialization or in actual processes of exchange in society. If one feels that societal exchange is not satisfying or even unfair, the binding power of norms may break down. Thus, the effectiveness of self-control is also bound to the constitution of the societal model, which attempts to regulate human aspirations under the maxim of justice. With respect to feelings of bonds (e.g., the class pact or the contract between the generations) a working societal model arranges indirect internal controls. Indirect external controls are exercised by networks of intact social relationships generated by institutional regulations (occupations and job security; opportunities for upward mobility and access to education, jobs and income; fascination with attractive goods and services that can be purchased; and social safety nets providing security in case of a failure of aspirations).

The probability of violence at the individual level (homicide and suicide) increases during societal crisis phases, which start slowly with the saturation of the societal model and grow more serious until a renewed (implicit or explicit) social contract can be implemented. Apart from wide differences in some instances in homicide and suicide rates, the following patterns of change over time can be shown empirically.

In her study of the same eighteen core countries already mentioned above, Rosemary Gartner (1990: 98) reports the following results for the past few decades: "Homicide rates (averaged over nations) declined from the early 1950s to the early 1960s, then increased continuously to their highest levels by the 1980s (. . . .). Despite substantial changes in homicide rates over time, the relative ranking of nations remained quite stable from 1950 to 1980." The long-term homicide data for the United States and Switzerland presented below confirm this finding for two cases and show, furthermore, that for these two innovators of the democratic variant of the new model the decrease in the rates begins as early as 1933-1937 (see figures 7.6 and 7.7).

In the original German version of this book (Bornschier 1988: 180ff.) we presented more detailed data concerning suicide rates in eighteen core countries, which follow a pattern similar to the one for homicide rates. A large number of countries show a decreasing trend in suicide rates after 1948 and until the beginning of the 1960s. In some cases (Switzerland, Denmark, and to a lesser extent Austria) this decrease is very marked. For most countries the trend breaks off markedly at the beginning of the 1960s, when suicide rates reach a relative minimum, only to increase again later. Until the end of the 1960s they remain at relatively low levels. Only from the end of the 1960s onwards do the suicide rates increase to levels unusual for the postwar era. This increase continues through 1982. The data series concerning the United States and Switzerland presented below in figure 7.6 and in figure 7.7 show in an illustrative way that suicide rates can be regarded as also controlled by the renewal of the social contract and its ensuing career.

As already noted with regard to political and industrial conflict, cross-country differences in homicide and suicide rates are quite wide despite similar temporal patterns. For the eighteen core countries during the period 1948-1982 the average rate of suicides is 14.7 per 100,000 population. Continental Europe (16.5) and Japan (18.4) have substantially higher (average) rates whereas Britain (9.9) and the United States (11.1) are considerably below the average. These differences between countries will be discussed in chapter 11.

CHANGE OF CONFLICT PATTERNS AFTER THE RENEWAL OF THE SOCIAL CONTRACT

For the institutional innovators the emergence of a new politico-economic regime—the renewed social contract—can be dated quite precisely as a clear-cut break and a new beginning. In what follows we shall investigate somewhat more closely the three innovators of the democratic variant of the new beginning of the 1930s: Sweden, the United States and Switzerland. The *historical* phase of the 1930s has not been covered by the conflict data presented up to this point because the new Keynesian societal model was already in place before 1948—even in those countries that had to undergo another new beginning after the war. For the period following the new beginning, our theory implies a considerable change in the levels as well as in the intensity of conflict articulation. For this reason, empirical evidence for three particular cases must be discussed.

FIGURE 7.5 Number of Strikers in Sweden, 1918-1992

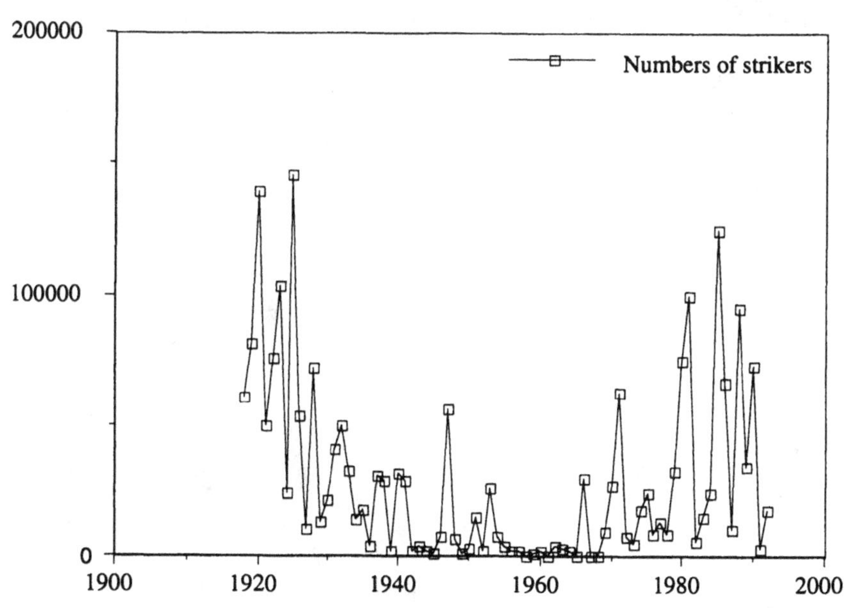

Sources: *Yearbook of Labour Statistics*, Geneva: ILO, various years.

A renewed social contract—if it rests on a neocorporatist arrangement of political interest mediation as was the case in the Keynesian societal model—includes the legitimization of collective but regime regulated and thus formally peaceful conflicts of interest. A case in point is Sweden, whose social democratic neocorporatist model of the regulation of industrial conflict resulted for decades in considerable industrial peace. Figure 7.5 shows that the Swedish new beginning of 1932 reduced the number of strikers substantially. Although the number of strikers again rose during the 1980s, this advantageous situation of moderated conflict remained more fully intact than in many other countries after the erosion of the societal model.

Illustrative cases for the regulation of conflict at the individual level—measured by homicide and suicide rates—are the United States and Switzerland. In a comparison with the other core countries, the United States is characterized by the highest homicide rates, whereas Switzerland can be found at the lower end of the ranking. Compared to its low homicide rates, suicide is very frequent in Switzerland whereas the opposite is the case in the United States. The homicide and suicide rates for the time between 1918 until the beginning of the 1990s are shown in figures 7.6 and 7.7.

FIGURE 7.6 Homicide and Suicide in the United States, 1918-1989

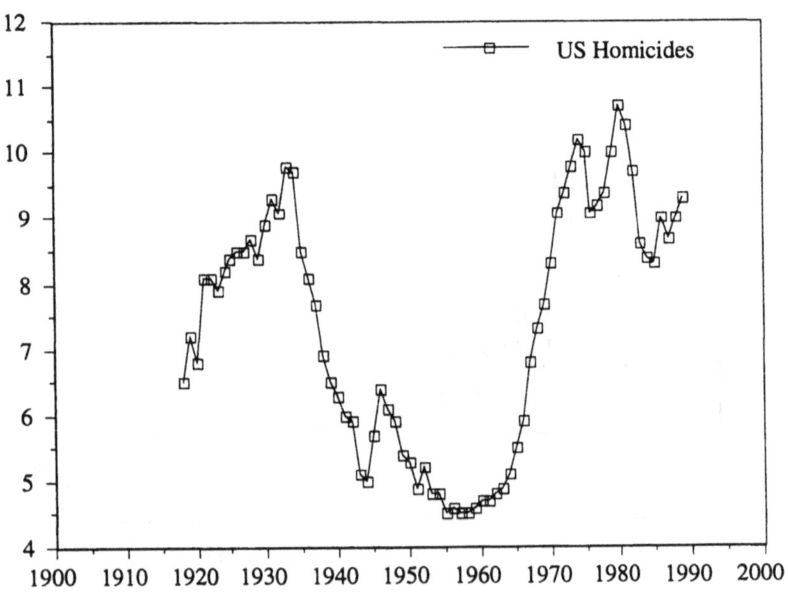

Homicide and suicide rates per 100,000 population.

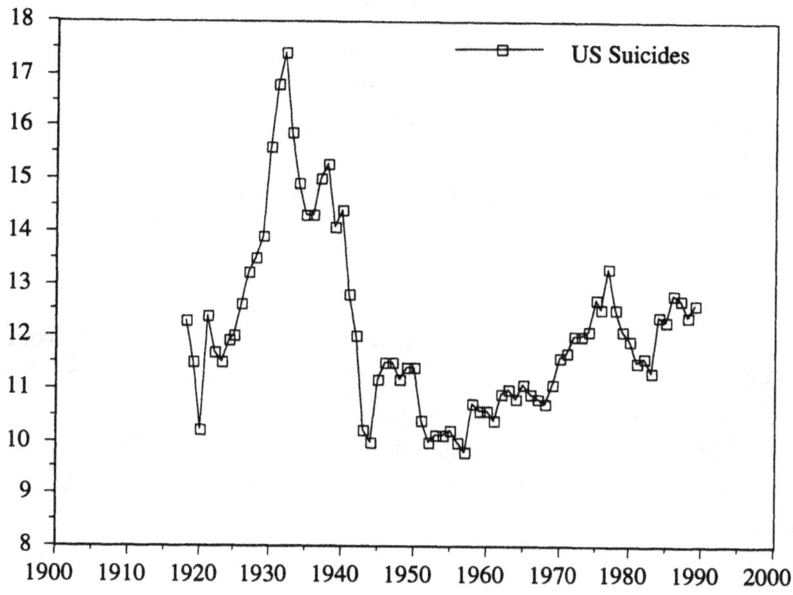

Source: Holinger (1987) and own updating from official sources.

In the United States, the new regime starts in 1933, in Switzerland somewhat later, where the first "peace agreement" of 1937 is the first important institutional element completed with the outset of the "grand coalition" in 1943. As our data also include the war, its effects must also be considered. We expect that the war causes a displacement of conflict as a result of solidarity within the nation which is either threatened (Switzerland) or challenged (United States). As the war did not cause any externally induced, lasting institutional changes in our examples we expect a delay in the articulation of contradictions. In other words: tension is only postponed but not resolved. War should thus cause a zigzag deviation from the overall trend in conflicts which is toward decreasing conflict during the formation phase. If war becomes probable, the level of conflict decreases more strongly than the general trend. If war is about to end, however, we expect conflict levels to increase substantially in the short run and a subsequent return back towards the trend later.

The marked turning points in the patterns of homicide and suicide are the years 1933 in the United States and 1937 in Switzerland. Thus they conform to our expectations. In the United States the suicide rates increase more or less continuously between 1918 and 1932, to decrease continuously after 1932 until they reach their low point in 1957. This decrease is only interrupted by the intermediate peak of the period 1945-1947 (or, 1950, at the latest). In the United States, the pattern of homicide rates follows that of the suicide rates very closely.

In Switzerland, suicide rates rise sharply between 1918 and 1938—in terms of a trend calculation from about 22 to 29 per 100,000 population. In 1937, the year of the peace agreement, which was characterized by the third highest unemployment rates of the 1930s, suicide rates begin to drop dramatically (1936: 28 per 100,000, 1937: 24 per 100,000). Apart from the intermediate peak years between 1944 and 1947, this decline continued until 1964, the low point of the data series. Thus, the data for Switzerland and the United States illustrate convincingly how social conflict is influenced by the renewal of the social contract and the subsequent phases of its career.

FIGURE 7.7 Suicide and Homicide in Switzerland, 1918-1992

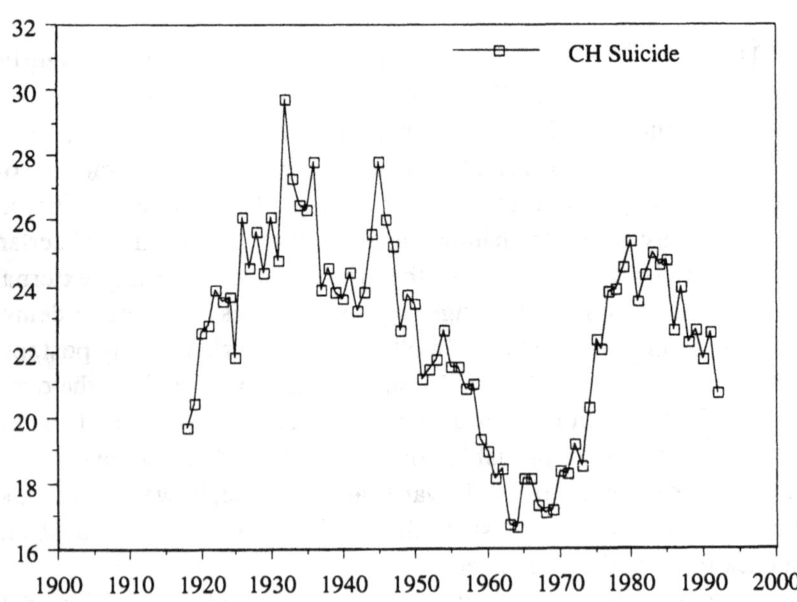

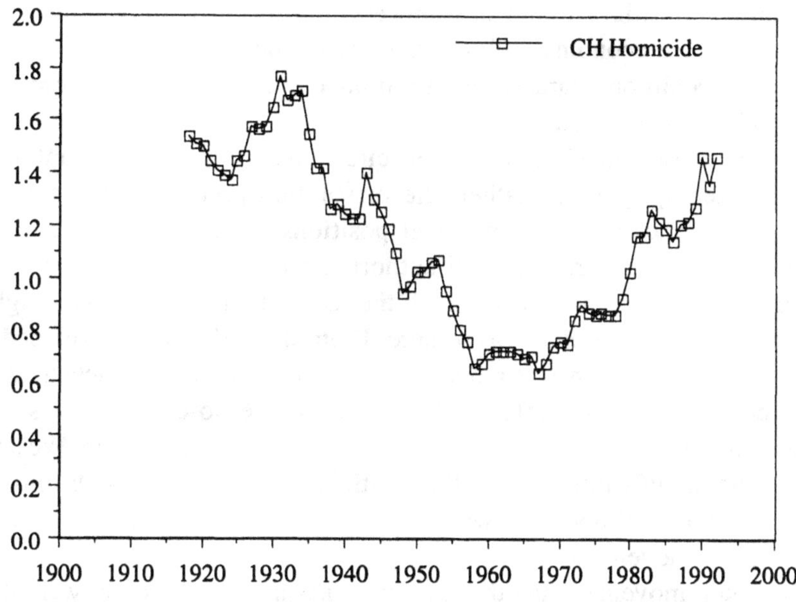

Suicides per 100,000 population; own computations from official sources.
Homicides per 100,000 population, moving averages; source: Eisner (1994) and own updating from official sources.

SOCIAL MOVEMENTS, DISSOLUTION OF THE SOCIETAL MODEL, AND SIGNPOSTS TO THE FUTURE

We have touched upon different manifestations of conflict, the patterns of which can be explained satisfactorily on the basis of the hypothesis concerning conflict regulation by the societal model. Social movements cannot be quantified as easily, although they are not only important forces in the dissolution of the societal model but also constitute signposts to the future by virtue of the themes they address.

Social integration under the neocorporatist Keynesian societal model ensured remarkable peace and limited the explosive force of political confrontations even under conditions of mass democracy. This was the case because, during the peak of the societal model, large organizations with conflictive potential, in particular organized labor, were bound firmly into a political-economic distributional alliance administered by the societal model. The crisis of the societal model produced an intensification of the intervention potential through an unprecedented concentration of power and alignment of the economy and the state. At the political level an actual or silent great coalition characterized by limited open political confrontation emerged in many countries.

Beyond those linked to the power circle there were no substantial or even threatening groups. Rather, the dissolution process of the societal model initially began from marginal positions. In the 1960s, the youth movement and its core, the anti-authoritarian student revolt, were the starting points, and in the case of the United States the civil rights movements must also be involved here. From these the base broadened in the 1970s through alternative movements, which increasingly reached out to the middle classes and offered the basis for the so-called new social movements. These movements became ever more important in Western society and significantly altered the political landscape until well into the 1980s. In what follows, we would like to sketch out this sequence of rebellion and movements.

The youth movement and the anti-authoritarian student revolt were thus the starting points. Despite spectacular peaks, particularly 1968, this intellectual counter-cultural rebellion—which, however, remained quite detached from everyday problems—failed because of the apathy of the broad population, state repression, the movement's somewhat naive strategy, and its self-isolation by the use of outdated Marxist rhetoric.

Against this background, the student mass movement ebbed after 1968 and certain small activist groups drifted off into criminality and terrorism. Yet, despite its failure the student protest movement resulted in a broadening process that became apparent in the 1970s in the alternative movement with its many different forms. Alternative lifestyles, which were increasingly practiced as islands within society, had already been matters for experimentation in the youth movement.

These counter-cultural currents in turn formed the basis for the new political movements which became an important feature of Western societies above and beyond youth, students and social class. They changed the political landscape and its themes into the 1980s, including the women's movement, the ecology movement, the anti-nuclear movement, the peace movement and those movements upholding solidarity with the Third World.

Once more, we would like to stress that social movements of this type—intellectual middle class radicalism (see Brand 1990)—emerge during the saturation phase of the societal model and contribute to its decay. These progressive movements must be distinguished from the reactionary movements of the crisis phase between succeeding societal models (see Kerbo 1982; Bornschier and Nollert 1994). The progressive social movements supplied Western society with ideas on which it could draw and which also contributed to its change. Initially, this learning process was bitter and very conflictive. Many were injured or arrested (i.e., criminalized) while protesting against what was later abandoned (for example, mid-range missiles or nuclear energy plants).

Since the nineteenth century, three such movements have been successful, in that they inspired the formulation of the subsequent societal model. The liberal movement led to free trade during the first societal model. In the second societal model, the democratic movements, with their many parallels to the anti-authoritarian movements, led to the extension of political rights and enfranchisement. Finally, the democratic variants of the socialist movement, ideologically led by middle class intellectuals with their universalistic value orientations, led to the extension and institutionalization of social rights and socioeconomic security in the third societal model. With the exceptions of the movements against nuclear power and for the Third World, the so-called new social movements of the progressive type (concerning women, environment, peace, alternative life styles, as well as an increase in autonomy and individual flexibility) have deep historical roots, but only managed to attract broad segments of the educated middle classes during the 1970s. The next societal model will most probably take up and institutionally shape a large proportion of the issues addressed by these movements. This is already clearly evident from the impact made by the women's, peace, and environmental movements.

CONCLUDING REMARKS

The theoretical ideas advanced at the beginning of this chapter concerning the relationship between the development of the technological style and the course of the politico-economic regime (summarized in figure 7.1) as well as the derivation of the forms and levels of conflict (summarized in figure 7.2) are very complex. Thus, one may ask if such a complicated model is necessary. A complex model must prove its value by its ability to explain different empirical findings within a single framework. Before we turn to such a test, we must introduce a further complication concerning the factors influencing the space for shaping a societal model. Against this even more complicated background, we can then go on to explain differences between countries. This analytical step will be taken up in part IV where we will address similarities and differences under the heading: "Convergence in the West?" First, however, we will examine more closely the various institutional orders, whose evolutionary patterns of which have been shaped by specific societal models.

NOTES

1 The average annual growth rate of industrial production in France was 8.1% during 1920-1929; in the USA it was only 4.8%, in Great Britain 2.8% and globally 5.1% (source as in chapter 3: van Duijn: 151ff.).

2 The historical events have been dated on the basis of various sources, including Gabillard (1967), Stavenhagen (1969), Bombach et al. (1976), and others cited in the text.

3 For the importance of normative theories compare also chapter 6. In his principal book, John M. Keynes (1964: 383) also stresses the importance of new ideas: "...the power of vested interests is vastly exaggerated compared with the gradual encroachment of ideas. ... The ideas of economists and political philosophers, both when they are right and when they are wrong, are more powerful than is commonly understood. Indeed the world is ruled by little else."

4 In 1933, unemployment rates reached their peak of 24.9% in the United States. Similar conditions prevailed in Great Britain (22.5% in 1932) and Germany (30% in 1932).

5 The hypothesis concerning the relationship between domestic cohesion and inter-systemic conflictivity has a long sociological tradition. William Sumner (1940: 12), for example, assumes that the consensus within the we-group is the higher the stronger the conflict with other-groups is. Still, international comparative studies have shown only little evidence for the relationship between domestic and external conflicts. Michael Stohl (1980: 325) summarizes: "First, there appears to be no single clear relationship between internal and external conflict that holds across time and space".

6 According to John Rawls (1979: 401) civil disobedience takes the form of public, non-violent, conscience-based, but politically illegal action which is usually aimed at a change of laws of government policy (see also Kohler 1977, 1986).

PART III

SHAPING INSTITUTIONAL ORDERS

Here we are concerned with institutional orders, not only in terms of the ruptures and cycles that occur during the careers of societal models, but also more broadly. The development paths of various institutional orders are explored, leading to a more extensive presentation of the forms of the Keynesian societal model. These themes are connected with a brief look at radical changes currently taking place. In chapter eight we analyze formal organizations. We first discuss the triumphant career of the 'artificial person' and then address changes in the division of labor implied by the evolution of formal organizations. How these organizational changes can be understood using our theory of discontinuous changes in societal models is also addressed. In connection with these themes, we concern ourselves in chapter nine with the function of legitimation, which is fulfilled in Western society by formal education. Chapter ten is concerned with the evolution of state forms. The processes at work in the conflict-laden conjoining of the development of the state and the unfolding of capitalism can be better understood if we place them in the context of the competitive and encompassing world order.

8
THE ARTIFICIAL PERSON AND STRUCTURES OF ECONOMIC POWER

THE TRIUMPHANT CAREER OF THE ARTIFICIAL PERSON

The person, the creative individual, has always been seen as the indispensable figure of economic action and civil society. Historical developments have shown that this is an exaggeration which does not hold for all phases to the same degree—particularly not for the peak phase of the technological style for which standard organizational solutions are typical. In chapter 2 we pointed out that there are sources of power whose origins and character are not rooted in the individual but are rather collective in nature. Apart from the social power of groups, the modern economic unit is a collectivity. John Kenneth Galbraith (1967) has argued that in the modern economy the person has been displaced by the successful creation of an artificial person (a so-called legal person, see Nobel 1978, 1980), by organizations which are much superior to natural persons for their specific purposes and have the added advantage of potential immortality.

In the modern corporation persons are interchangeable. Positions rather than persons are the organizational building blocks. Two parallel structures of social relationships thus coexist in society (Coleman 1974): those between natural persons, and those between positions as well as between corporations. Both structures are linked symbiotically because natural persons as role-actors are bound to the formal structures—but this linkage is neither complete nor durable.

The tension between person and position is a source of alienation, but there are also the liberties hidden within this structure. Natural persons are not completely bound to an encompassing order but act in an arena of both formal positions and personal relationships.

Formal organization is constituted by the contract between persons as the original sources and owners of power and the corporation as its user. Persons investing some of their resources in a corporation no longer fully control their use. As James Coleman (1974) stresses, this supposes an initial personal loss of power, but does not have to be a zero-sum game in which the organization gains what is lost by the person. The organization creates power that did not exist before: "Added value" is generated by a combination of personal, social and cultural power. Thus, the merger of natural persons is a source of power.

The new economic entity has far-reaching consequences for society:

(1) A delinking of power from persons (by the very process of organization building) and the coupling of power potentials with positions.

(2) The delinking of power from its particular sources (social, cultural and economic) by combining and blending them into something new.

(3) Further, a delinking of personal ownership, which becomes an entitlement by the corporation as a legal person.

(4) Finally, a collective increase of power, whose distribution and use is subject to potentially acute conflict.

In Western society this conflict is only partially played out by direct power competition between groups (workers vs. entrepreneurs, the competition among parties in politics). A substantial part of the conflict is managed by socially constructed criteria of distribution. These include legal entitlements guaranteed by the state, for example pensions, ownership certificates (particularly shares), as well as those attached to qualifications which are frequently endorsed by the state: certifications of formal education and occupational qualifications. Such criteria of distribution are not closely linked to their contribution to productivity but are rather socially constructed and can be based on a broad basic consensus for some time.

Though many questions arise in connection with the new economic entity, we will confine our argument to the following issues: How did these new entities emerge? Who disposes of the additional power and who are its beneficiaries? Which changes in the positional structure have been brought about by the new economic entity, and how is the tension between position and person being resolved?

THE RISE OF THE LEADING CORPORATIONS

The separation of person and firm is characterized by two steps: First, the delinking of the firm from the household, and second, the delinking of the firm from the natural person. Linkages of people by way of market transactions emerge in connection with the intensified production of goods. The traditional household economy, aimed at subsistence production, is split into the firm and into the modern household. Thus, production and consumption become separated, although they remain connected by persons who produce goods or sell labor in order to consume—even if they do not consume the very things they produce.

The delinking of the firm from the household implies three things for the businessperson: the firm becomes a *legal entity* (not a legal *person*) as well as an *accounting* and *credit* unit. Such separation took a long time but has been accomplished now for many decades. Even though the firm is differentiated from person and society, the businessperson as an individual remains the owner of his or her firm and its property. Apart from the informal sector, all firms have gone through this stage of differentiation, but only some of them have undergone the second stage of company development.

A business that had already become a continuous or durable undertaking with a more or less formalized organizational structure during the first stage of delinking turned into a new type of person—a *legal* person—during the second stage. As such, a corporation has legal powers and can also acquire property. It is the corporation which owns the business and not the natural persons who necessarily must act in its name. These persons no longer have material claims but only obligatory claims and the right to participate. The second phase of delinking makes possible an enormous differentiation of firms according to their economic power and control over economic resources.

Corporations are a relatively small group but they constitute the core around which the economic process and resources revolve. Owners of businesses are a much larger group, but most of them are quite marginal with respect to the economic core. This enormous differentiation of business enterprises can be illustrated for Switzerland: only about 50 corporations have sales of between 1 and 25 billion Swiss francs. In addition, there are about 50 larger banks and about 30 insurance companies with premium volumes between $ 75 million and $ 2 billion (Schweizerische Handelszeitung, and various publications of UBS). The comparatively small number of large corporations contrasts with a large number of smaller and very small businesses (about 320,000).

The economic importance of corporations is also shown by the fact that in the Western countries the 50 largest industrial corporations contribute from 30 to 55 percent of total industrial production (see for details, Bornschier 1976: 206).

The growth of the firm results in substantial structural change. Firm growth and technological development are two central processes derived from as well as intensifying the division of labor. The intensification of the division of labor and of the use of technology result in lowering organizational costs; they are closely intertwined with power concentration during the evolution of the capitalist economy.

In the economic literature, the *average scale* of firms in terms of employment, financial resources and turnover (i.e. net product) is called concentration in a general sense. Clear and strong concentration is shown by historical data (see Stockmann et al. 1983; Pryor 1973). Yet growth is uneven: the successful firms increasingly out-distance the large number of medium-sized and small ones. This centralization of firms can be called concentration in a strict sense, which implies the emergence of what is usually known as a segmented or dual economy. We will return to this below. It is undeniable that concentration in the strict sense has increased substantially over time and reached very high degrees at the end of the postwar model (see Bornschier 1988: table 8.2 and figure 8.1).

But whether increasing concentration is decisive for firm behavior and the functioning of markets (e.g., oligopolistic markets limit competition) is controversial. Our conclusion is that this process leads to an enhancing of the organizational steering of the economy *at the cost* of the market thus creating advantages which large and powerful corporations enjoy at the expense of other market participants. Organizational development, concentration and market structure have been discussed in more detail elsewhere (Bornschier 1976), here we will confine our following discussion to outlining only selected topics.

The firm as an organization and the market are mutually dependent yet contradictory elements of the capitalist economic system. The firm is an economic unit which makes plans and uses domination in order to carry them through. *Instruction* is the central element of the firm, whereas *invitation* is the basic concept of the market. The ability of the firm to attract purchasing power without sacrificing too much of its own also depends upon the structure of the market.

The fundamental logic of the firm's plans is quite simple. The firm buys goods, creates value by way of organization, and sells goods, the proceeds from which must exceed the cost of the material and organizational inputs *plus* the normal interest rate for the money used in the long run. Thus, entrepreneurs must economize their means. That is why they also try to save on wages, which points to *one* fundamental problem of the capitalist economy: firms pay minimal wages but at the same time they would like consumers to dispose of sufficient purchasing power to afford their products.

Let us look at the sales side. A firm's sales strategies are sanctioned by the market in which consumers use their purchasing power to buy the products of a given firm (positive sanction) or leave them on the shelves (negative sanction). Because of this sanctioning mechanism the plans of different firms become potentially conflictive—i.e., competition results. Competition is a special kind of social struggle perceived as "peaceful" (Weber [1921] 1972: 20). Weapons in this struggle include price, product quality, security of supply and after-sales service.

As a result of competition and the striving after profit, the strategies of firms cannot lead to market equilibrium and a fixed structure of markets and firms. Let us start from the ideal construct of a perfect market (atomistic demand and supply, homogenous goods). Each supplier will plan their production so that the cost of the last unit equals the market price; beyond that, each additional unit would reduce profit. Yet, the absence of complete market transparency will result in a period of trial and error that ultimately leads to an equilibrium in which the total quantity foreseen in the sales plans equals aggregate demand, which in turn depends to a certain degree on the prices.

In textbooks this celebrated equilibrium is most often seen as the end instead of the beginning of market-related firm behavior. Firms aiming at growing profitably face a situation which forces them to reduce costs to increase the profit span. Strategies to reach this goal are increased production (reduction of average cost because of fixed cost), cheaper inputs, or the introduction of new or improved production techniques. Firms following this road successfully are bound to grow, thereby reducing or even eliminating less successful ones. As a result, concentration and the average size of the firms increase. From a certain point, this leads to a qualitative change in firm behavior.

The additional number of firms also has its effect on prices. Prices and the level of profits become quantities that to a certain extent can be controlled by firms. However, in this case growth opportunities are fundamentally restricted by demand. Growth beyond an increase in demand can only be achieved at the cost of other firms (eliminating them from the market) or by *merger* and *acquisition*. Thus, successful and financially strong firms can expand beyond the growth of demand. Otherwise, an increase in supply by the leading firms results in lower prices and thus a reduction of profits. If, on the other hand, supply is restricted, other firms are bound to fill the gap. Thus, partial monopolies by large corporations result in monopolistic surplus profits which can no longer be used profitably for conventional economic activities.

The solutions for such situations are—once again, roughly speaking—predetermined. Products can be differentiated (e.g., brands) and advertising can be stepped up to increase the market share of a given firm. As successful as such strategies may be for a time, they are only temporary defenses against market saturation. For that reason, offensive strategies aim in two directions: product diversification and geographical diversification of the markets. Product diversification may imply the incorporation of known products, mostly by acquisition, as well as the development and marketing of new products (innovation). Geographical diversification may be achieved by either buying existing firms or establishing new affiliates.

This sequence of growth, concentration and monopolization, as well as product and geographical diversification, leads to the transnational corporation, typical among the largest firms both in their country of origin as well as in the so-called host countries. Thus, in the course of the evolution of the capitalist economy, concentration has led to a comparatively small group of corporations that is very different from local or regional firms. The financial power of these corporations is enormous; their organizational structure is very complex, characterized by steep hierarchies; and the framework for their planning is global (for more details see Bornschier 1976, Bornschier and Stamm 1990).

In small countries, the growth process described above encounters its national limits earlier than in large countries. Hence the leading firms of small countries are the first to go transnational, also because of early civil revolutions and industrialization in North Holland, England, and Switzerland. This trend can also be shown for the peak phase of the economic wave of the postwar era. In terms of transnationalization, Japan lagged during the 1960s, whereas Switzerland and the Netherlands held (and still hold) the top positions (see Bornschier 1976: 466, 468; Borner et al. 1983).

Still, American transnationals have been dominating global "big business" for a long time, even though these leading enterprises are not as "transnationalized" as those from certain smaller countries. A comparison of the world's largest enterprises according to their origin (Bergesen and Sahoo 1985; United Nations 1983, 1988: Informationen über Multinationale Konzerne, various issues) also shows that American industrial hegemony began to weaken during the 1960s while West European corporations started to reclaim their former position. Japanese corporations as well as some from newly industrializing countries only started to appear at the top during the 1970s.

THE SEGMENTATION OF THE ECONOMY

The uneven development process of firms leads to segmentation—a term we use as synonymous with "dual economy"—between the leading corporations, which constitute the core of the economy, and the numerous smaller firms, which lost out in the evolutionary process and now constitute the periphery of the system (see Bornschier 1976, 1982b, 1983a; Baron and Bielby 1984; Baron 1984). The distribution of employment between these two segments may vary among the highly developed core countries (the exact extent of such variation is not yet clear), but for all of them a split of employment into two large groups is typical. This is very different from the situation in the underdeveloped countries, where the core segment—which in most cases depends heavily on the external sphere—only absorbs a small minority of the employed (see Bornschier 1983b).

The core segment of the economy has great market power and dominates the peripheral segment, which is organized much more competitively. In many other respects the two segments are different, for example with respect to organizational structures, class composition, the functioning of labor markets, and the level and stability of profit opportunities. The two segments are differentiated in terms of material and organizational resources, and the functioning of the raw materials, sales and labor markets. The units of this stratification are enterprises rather than branches (Averitt 1968: 66). Because they are the most highly developed, transnational corporations are typically found in the core segment; they penetrate the centers of the economies of both core and peripheral countries.

A *secondary* consequence of this stratification of firms for the working population lies in the fact that the core segment offers different jobs, career opportunities and wages than the peripheral segment. And because of the *personal separation* of ownership and control in large corporations, the chances of entrepreneurs obtaining the three functional types of income—corporate earning, profit and interest on invested capital—are largely confined to the peripheral segment.

The *organizational structures* of the corporations of the core economic segment are complex and *bureaucratic*. Although they are part of a differentiated hierarchy, managers and experts have a great deal of power and control because of their position, and they also earn very high salaries. In comparison with the workers of the peripheral segment, workers and employees of the core segment also earn markedly higher salaries and wages. In addition, they form part of the large and powerful trade unions.

The wage difference between core and peripheral segment can be regarded as a robust empirical finding (Bornschier 1982b: 524-526; Lewin 1982). At first sight it seems paradoxical that there can be "income privileges" at all. In a narrow understanding of economic utility calculations, voluntary wage concessions by the employers are hard to imagine. Yet, even if income privileges are seen as part of the core's legitimation needs and its attempts at binding workers to its cause, economic utility calculations can still be applied.

Employers' ability to select is very important for the functioning of the dual labor market. A primary labor market is created by selection criteria which not only include efficiency but also conformity with organizational goals. Members of the primary labor market receive on-the-job training, protecting them against wage competition. The readiness of a worker to do a job in the core segment at lower wages does not automatically make the person more productive and thus cheaper than the person who already holds the job, who has both experience and the benefit of on-the-job training. The firm has already invested in an experienced worker and is willing to pay more for him or her. "Income privileges" in the core segment do not prevent economic utility calculations. They are functional in terms of the corporations' use of power, their legitimation, and the loyalty of their employees.

The core segment attempts to legitimize its economic and societal power on the basis of income privileges. These privileges, in turn, are linked to socially accepted elements of stratification, for example formal education, gender and ethnic origin or race, which are important for entering the permanent work force of the core segment. The peripheral segment thus becomes increasingly characterized by persons without "normal" biographies, people who are socially discriminated and—in the highly developed countries—by persons who do not wish to make a career and thus cannot or do not want to compete in the primary labor market. Thus, the economically founded separation of the two segments also has visible social features. Even a surplus supply of labor does not equalize the split in the dual structure.

The Separation of Ownership from Control

Firm growth and the innovation of the corporation as a legal person have brought about the separation of ownership from control (for more details see Bornschier 1983c, for a first statement, see Berle and Means [1932] 1967). Instead of the classical owner-entrepreneur, it is now bureaucrats who typically dominate the large corporations, even if they remain bound to the logic of the capitalist market. Of course, the bureaucratization of the economic elite depends on the scale of firms (see Biermann 1971: 61). In terms of their numbers, owner-entrepreneurs still dominate. But in the large firms making up the core segment of the economy, bureaucrats dominate the top positions. The rapid and long-term spread of bureaucratic rule has been demonstrated by Reinhard Bendix (1956: 229, 252) in one of his early studies on the composition of the American economic elite. He has also shown that formal education as legitimation becomes more important in connection with bureaucratic rule (Bendix 1956: 230; see also Bornschier 1976: 318f.). Here, the term "bureaucrats" is used as a general description of non-owners. We have already mentioned that—particularly after the saturation phase of the technological style—entrepreneurial skills are also very important for these bureaucrats.

Who controls the bureaucrats? First of all, they are obviously controlled by market processes, since even powerful firms cannot evade the capitalist logic of competition. In addition, interlocking directorates are important (Stockman et al. 1985). Economic leaders often cooperate in sitting on the boards of firms. Thus, the special group of leading managers is subject to a kind of internal self-control which in most cases works vertically, i.e., leading corporations or financial enterprises invade the boards of dependent firms and thus combine the control over blocks of shares with personal direction.

Normally it is assumed that the "owners" of large blocks of shares control bureaucratized enterprises. This is quite correct in the sense that even average shareholders have a substantial degree of sanctioning power. If they are not content with "their" firm they can sell their shares. This can be very inconvenient for management because competing corporations often wait for the opportunity to buy at low prices to assume control of a given firm, a situation most leading managers try to avoid. If, however, one defines control by the big shareholders as their ability to determine real business policy, one must admit that it happens occasionally, but is not the rule. According to available data, most cases conform to the following pattern (see Bornschier 1983c; Pryor 1976): in the majority of large corporations no single group of shareholders (natural persons) holds at least 5 percent of the shares. This is usually described as "managerial control" in the literature. In this case, the bureaucrats are confronted with a diffuse mass of shareholders who have no influence on business policy but press for legitimation in the form of attractive dividends and stock options. An illustrative example can be found in Michael Patrick Allen's (1981) study concerning the 218 largest industrial firms in the United States. If one extrapolates his results, more than half the total industrial wealth of the United States is under bureaucratic rule.

Power and Ownership

The separation of ownership from control is rooted in the capitalist economy itself. The classical owner-entrepreneur already had more power than would have been possible on the mere basis of personal wealth due to two things: credit and free wage labor. The entrepreneur as an employer does not own labor, which is also a source of power. He or she rents labor in a contractual relationship and disposes of it, combines it with other sources of power (credit, knowledge, machines, etc.), and controls the productive process as well as the final product. The latter is important. For the owner-entrepreneur, the separation of ownership from control does not exist because of the unbroken institution of private property.

Generally speaking, organization combines *and* recreates power, this being its synergistic effect. There are no original property owners preceding the organization who could lay claim to the resulting increase in power. The gain is owned by the organization, legally anchored in the corporation to which surplus power accrues.

Thus, one can say that because of modern society's formal organization, the quantity of power is greater than quantity of the property of all natural persons. The result is the powerlessness felt by many a natural person. At the same time, a minority—the holders of the top organizational positions—enjoys a substantial power surplus which, however, can be reduced by countervailing powers (the state, trade unions, the media, religion or science). In this case, we can speak of a pluralistic power elite in society whose basis is no longer simply property but organization, spread over different functional spheres: politics, administration, economy and culture. The three typical patterns of the separation of personal ownership and control of organizational power are depicted in figure 8.1.

To summarize, the process of change implies a dissolution of the civil ideas of property and ownership, in which having the law on one's side was equal to having power. Classical property rights are split up into possessing power (to control something), on the one hand, and limited rights of usufruct (to make use of something), on the other. As rights to participate are limited by formal organization and the "iron law of oligarchy" (Robert Michels [1911] 1949: 401), the shift of the distribution of rights towards usufruct (income) is of central importance for the legitimation of modern society.

For that reason we expect power distribution in Western society to be more unevenly distributed than wealth and income (see Bornschier 1988: table 8.4 for details concerning the United States). One conclusion to be drawn from our discussion is that property is no longer *the* central and determining category of Western society. Rather it is power—not personal power, but organizational power wielded by a comparatively small number of managers. The central locations of this power are the top positions in very formal organizations. Society as a whole is divided into a number of *functional spheres*—economy (firms, business associations, trade unions), politics (government, administration, parties, military/police) and culture (science, religion, mass media, publishers)—all characterized by formal organizations whose power bases are different.

If power has become the central category, does it also determine social classes? Are the holders of top positions in organizations becoming the ruling or dominant class? In a formal sense, yes. If classes are defined by their relative positions, then dominance in organizations effectively creates classes

(Bornschier 1983a, 1984). In a contextual sense, i.e., in the sense of a social position that influences the whole life of an active subject, the dominant class is not homogenous, however. In addition, it is divided into several fractions and also open to access by children from the middle classes to some degree.

FIGURE 8.1 Typical Patterns of the Separation of Personal Ownership from Control of Organizational Power

1. Power surplus

Command over power > *Ownership as a person*

Examples:
- Non-owners and partial owners of shares as organizers
- Leading bureaucrats in private associations and public administration

2. Power deficit (small)

Ownership as a person > *Command over power*

Examples:
- Classical rentiers
- Financial rentiers (securities)
- Land rentiers (land titles)

3. Power deficit (large)

*Quasi-ownership as a person** > *Command over power*

Examples:
- Majority of the population (including retirees)

*) Formal rights to control one's own destiny.
Formal rights to participate in collective decisions (politics).
Rights to participate in the outcomes of organizational power (educational certifications, pensions, participation in labor agreements).

If one also considers the *external* power of organizations, one must substitute power elite for ruling class. Power elite includes those who exercise a great deal of absolute power in society (Bornschier 1991).This elite is comparatively heterogenously recruited and diverse in its power bases, loyalties and political views, but it usually remains in power only for a relatively short time (see Bolte and Hradil 1984: 184-190).

Hence, despite comparable power sources (organizational power), Western society's power elite is not a homogenous bloc, which is why, even though all its parts are not equally powerful, a pluralistic elite model is necessary. This feature of the power elite can be viewed as a kind of compensation because it makes the power surplus in society created by formal organization more tolerable. Another compensation is the comparatively generous distribution of material rights to participate. Compared to power differences, income differences are smaller, and this satisfaction of basic needs is often provided by the welfare state.

THE CHANGE IN THE DIVISION OF LABOR

The development and growth of firms also brought about radical organizational changes. The *division of labor* has intensified and transformed, and *hierarchy* has been lengthened and thereby changed. *Technique*, i.e., applied knowledge and material aids (tools, machines), has been undergoing marked metamorphosis. In what follows we will briefly explain the roots of division of labor, hierarchy and applied technology. This discussion is also of practical relevance in that one may enquire what room for action exists within the structure of the division of labor, hierarchy and applied technology. Indeed, such room for action may be quite substantial. Yet, it is regularly limited during certain phases characterized by *coherent technological* styles, which are *social* phenomena rather than being caused by technology in the strict sense.

In what follows we will discuss organizational patterns during the past technological styles (see also chapter 5). Current transitions will be mentioned at the end. We propose to first discuss the division of labor in a general way and then focus on hierarchy. Figure 8.2 summarizes the three important factors interacting in the crystallization of a technological style: the danger of a loss of control, acceptance, and technology in terms of machines and knowledge.

Mediated by the production of goods and market competition, efficiency results in hierarchy, the shape of which can vary. Hierarchy and markets are conditional upon each other and result in the danger of a *loss of organizational control* to be discussed later. Acceptance emerges out of the claim to equality. Participation in the results of the striving after efficiency may temper a lack of legitimacy through tolerance, so that conflict and the refusal to work, which detract from legitimacy, vanish. Whereas acceptance was precarious during the technological style of the founding era and conflicts between capital and labor were very frequent, the current problems of acceptance are much more obscured and often perceived as tensions between persons and positions.

The significance of *technology* (tools, machines, knowledge) depends upon the achieved level of economic development. Enhanced labor productivity makes possible a *displacement of work* towards the means of production and knowledge.

FIGURE 8.2 Important Factors Interacting in the Crystallization of the Technological Style

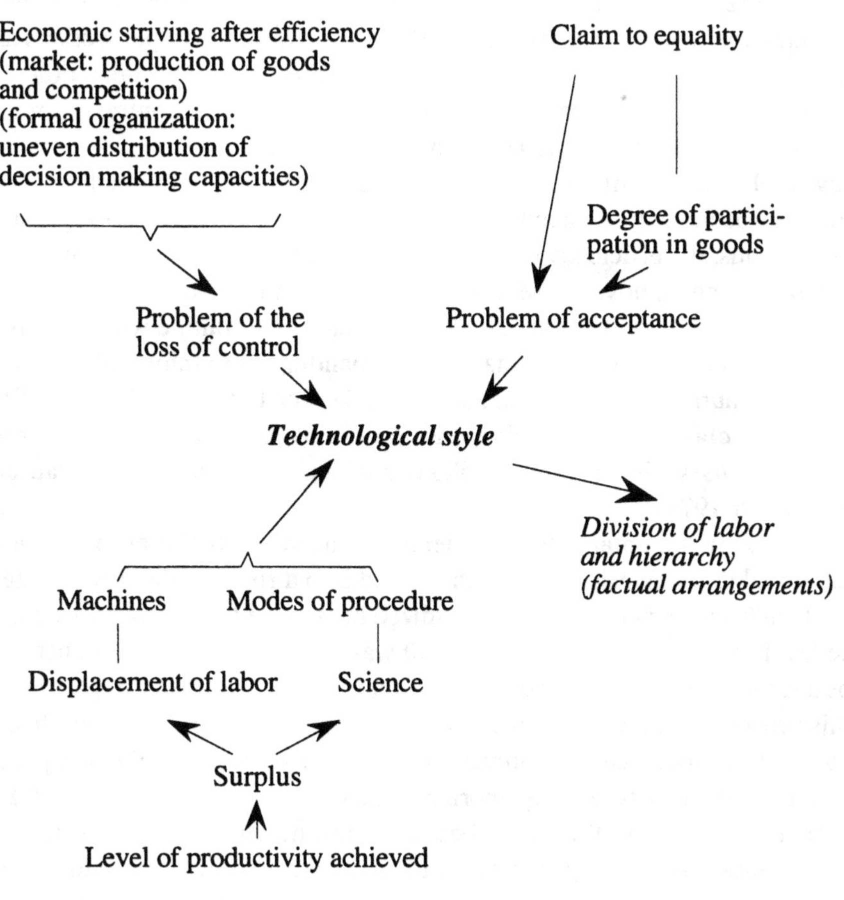

DYNAMICS AND EQUILIBRIUM

The division of labor in organizational expansion implies an increasing threefold bifurcation of labor that constitutes a systemic whole (for more details see Bornschier 1977, 1981, 1983a). This is shown in figure 8.3. The first class of labor is the work of command and control (dominant class); the second routine work (working class), and the third specialized work (expert class). Routinization and specialization are two entirely different ways of splitting up labor and each follows a different logic (see Blau 1974).

Routinization atomizes and simplifies tasks, which leads to increased operational efficiency already identified by Adam Smith: cheaper workers and enhanced labor productivity due to repetitive processes. Specialization also splits up tasks, but does not simplify work: quite the contrary, greater expertise is called for in the new tasks. At the level of the organization this may imply that existing functions are deepened or that new functions arise because specialization encourages the unfolding of capacities not possible earlier. Thus, the efficiency of specialization does not lie in cheaper work but in improved and innovative results; labor becomes more expensive.

The efficiency of the division of labor means that routine work results in savings, which are used to finance an expanding hierarchy and to put an increasing number of highly paid experts and specialists at the disposal of the dominant class to help solve the problems of ever more complex organizations within a polymorphous societal framework (see Blau and Schoenherr 1971).

Two complementary developments occurred: with the elimination of traditional craftsmanship, work was turned into a routine, the discrete steps of which became increasingly standardized because of task decomposition. At the level of the whole system, the result was an increasing cleavage between routine work, expert knowledge and specialist work (see also Simmel 1890). This process included an increasing impoverishment of the skills applied in work, of competence and power, resulting in growing social inequality within as well as between the laboring classes.

In the course of this split between routinization or deskilling and specialization or skilling, the tasks of planning, coordination and control became more important. The result is a threefold bifurcation of labor and a correspondingly complex positional structure that accompanies a shift from human capital to power.

FIGURE 8.3 Basic Dynamics of the Organized Division of Labor

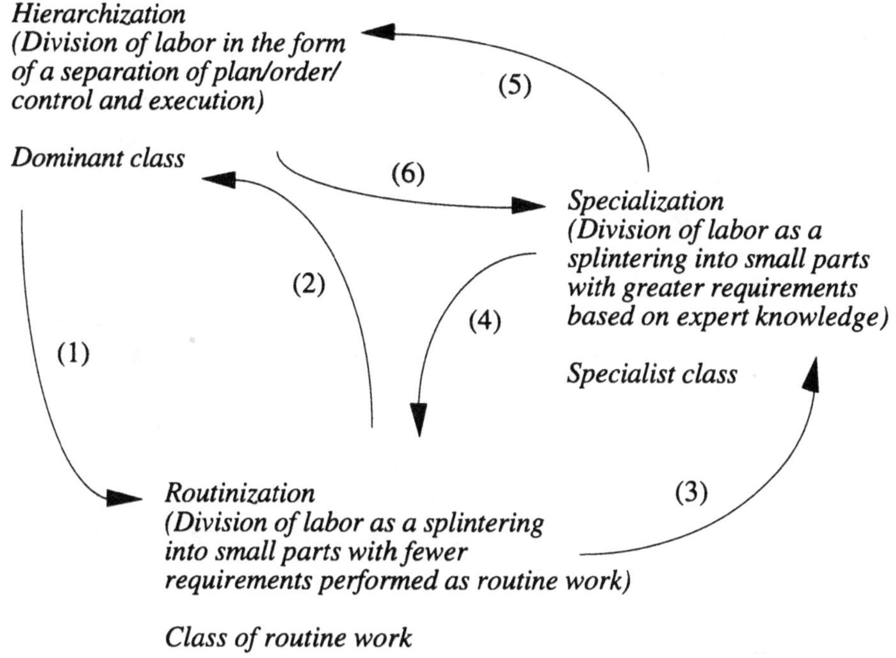

(1) Separation of plan/order/control and execution is seen as the basis for all complex forms of division of labor (see also Rueschemeyer 1977).
(2) The greatest advantages of the splintering of labor (gains in efficiency) is earned by hierarchy and expert knowledge (arrows 3 and 4). By way of accumulation and growth, these advantages lead to organizational growth resulting, in turn, in further hierarchization to avoid the threat of a loss of control resulting from the growing need to supervise.
(3) As a result of the splintering of labor, the workers experience a loss of skills as well as a loss of an overview of the work process. This is compensated for by specialist positions resulting in increasing specialization at the level of the organization.
(4) To the degree that certain jobs become more specialized, jobs suited to routine work can be separated, thus leading to an increase in routinization. This also makes possible a deepening of expert knowledge in the remaining tasks.
(5) The growing number of specialists and their actions have to be planned, coordinated and supervised. This increases control work and hierarchization.
(6) The growth of hierarchy and administration itself requires specialists to solve problems in planning, coordination and control.

We can thus conclude that—assuming a constant state of technology—the elevated class status of commanding and specialist labor is based on the exploitation of the routine laboring majority in organizations. At the same time, however, this also facilitates structural mobility from routine to expert and then to directive work.

The lack of satisfaction from routine work and this working class sector's small share of the gains of an intensified division of labor—both resulting in considerable suffering at work—is the basis for the (latent) conflict between the routine working class and the other two classes, particularly the hierarchically structured dominant class. Suffering at the workplace can be expressed by manifestations of discontent, such as absenteeism, slowdowns, strikes and sabotage.

The process of the division of labor described thus far would tend to some kind of "equilibrium" if *technology* and *market scale* were constant and *acceptance* were given (see Bornschier 1977). The threefold bifurcation of labor and the displacement of some employment to the expert and dominant class could first be expected to even out and finally cease when the costs of control, communication, and the higher salaries of the experts and organizers equal the savings from routinization. *Discontinuous* technological progress, the growth of the world economy, and the legitimation problems arising from the claim to equality, however, keep the system in a dynamic state. On this basis, further capital accumulation, technological progress, and an institutionalization of innovation and therefore a further bifurcation of labor become possible.

Under conditions of technological progress, enhanced productivity and consequently the possibility of a further expansion of the dominant and expert classes are no longer exclusively derived from the economic gains of routinization. In sociogenesis, such gains brought about the differentiated hierarchical structure and the organizational integration of experts and scientific procedures, and also accelerated capital accumulation. In a technical sense too the standardization and the splintering of complex work processes into simple ones—both consequences of routinization—were decisive steps towards mechanization and later automation. Thus, one can conclude that progress in productivity through automation is increasingly an alternative to the gains of routinization.

Empirical findings (see Kern and Schumann 1970, 1984; Blau and Schoenherr 1971) show that technological progress has in part displaced routine work, yet the latter has so far not become redundant. Indeed, technology adds elements to routine work, creating limited spheres of action and monotony at the workplace, which may well fuel the latent class conflict, in turn motivating further automation. Quantitatively, however, the relative share of routine work decreases in the later phases of technological progress; the number of routine workers decreases while the dominant and expert classes expand.

Shifts in the Job System

Our dynamics include a change in job structure, which can be conceptualized in three stages. We must distinguish between two processes: positional and distributive inequality, which are shown schematically in figure 8.4. During the transition from the first to the second stage, positional inequality increases without distributive inequality decreasing. The latter decreases only during the transition from stage II to stage III. Organizational development strengthens routinization, the relative extent of which does not decrease between stages I and II, but later and most markedly between stages II and III. Specialization is reinforced and demands more laborpower; the same is true for hierarchization. During the transition to stage III, on the other hand, a considerable number of workers are set free, which is not the case during the transition from stage I to stage II.

The diffusion of this technological style, which reached saturation shortly after the turn of the century, included a transition from stage I to stage II. The latest technological style, whose saturation phase took place in the 1960s, was characterized by the transition from stage II to stage III. The transition from stage I to stage II was accompanied by a drastic reduction in the share of the self-employed (see also chapter 5). At the same time, the share of non-manual workers increased by 10 percent during the transition from stage I to stage II, and by 20 to 25 percent during the transition from stage II to stage III. At the end of this process, non-manual workers held a typical share of about 50 percent in employment throughout Western society (see Gagliani 1985: 198).

During the transition from stage II to stage III the average level of job skills increases, but at the same time the "stretchi " of the skill hierarchy and the polarization of jobs into skilled and unskilleo increases. In the 1960s the transformation of the organized division of labor in the traditional technological style encountered its limits. The economic advantages of the division of labor and the increased productivity resulting from the new technological and organizational procedures were counteracted by the additional costs of specialists, communication and administration. In other words, this feedback served to limit the extent of organizational differentiation under the conventional technological style (see also Blau 1970, Huijgen 1983).

FIGURE 8.4 Shifts in Positional Structure During Different Stages of Organizational Development

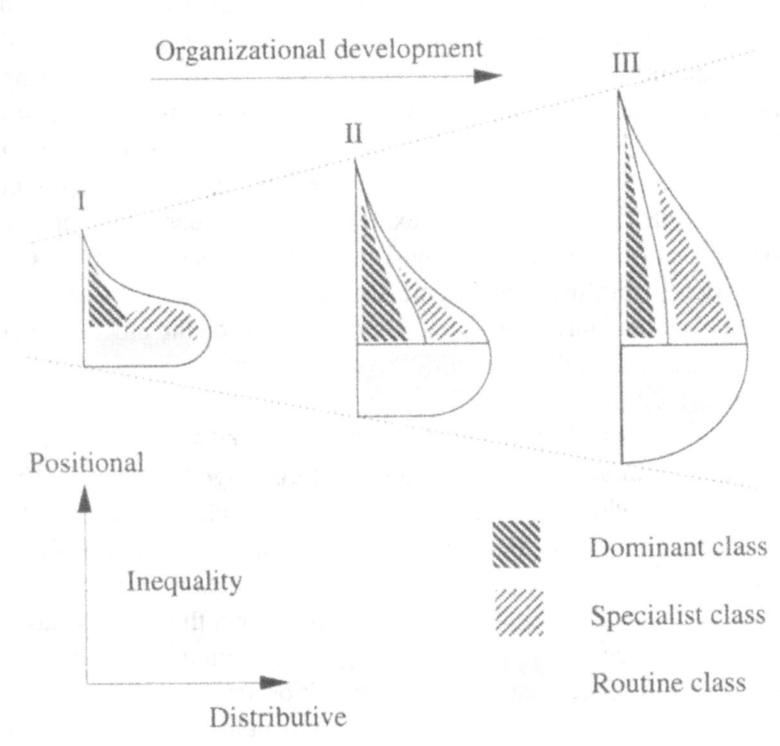

The economic decline of the 1970s brought about a surge in rationalization through the use of microprocessors, partial automation of production processes and wide-ranging office automation. These were similar in their radical effects to the spread of Taylorism fifty years earlier. The rationalization of the 1970s was accompanied by widespread layoffs and coincided as well with high levels of cyclical unemployment, which together added up to 35 million registered unemployed in the OECD area at the outset of the 1980s—i.e., a level comparable to that prevailing at the beginning of the 1930s.

Qualification and De-qualification

In the dynamics of the division of labor, skilling and deskilling exist side by side, resulting in a polarization of job profiles. The aggregate *net effect* is higher skills, however, which may be particularly marked during the socially regulated upswing of the new technological style. After the saturation phase, during the transition from the old to the new technological style, a special kind of polarization occurs. Secure jobs on balance undergo a process of further skilling, while an increase in insecure jobs and open unemployment also takes place. This scenario contradicts Harry Braverman's (1974) thesis of continuous deskilling of work during the twentieth century. It also modifies Horst Kern's and Michael Schumann's (1970) original polarization thesis, which did not pay enough attention to surges in the change of technological styles that primarily affect routine jobs.

Thus, from our model of the development of the division of labor we can deduce that, due to the current surges of rationalization, there will be another increase in the average skill level of jobs in the core segment of the Western economy, because ongoing automation also rationalizes away routine jobs. Our perspective is not as mechanistically optimistic as other skill theses, as for example the one advanced by Daniel Bell (1976). At least during the transition phase, the intensification in skills at the core go hand in hand with a multitude of insecure or unavailable jobs. Without a consensual societal model, this transition does not lead to a new upswing which would spread the technological style and thus generalize the higher skilling of jobs. Like Carlota Perez (1983), we are suggesting that the change of the technological style starts during the late peak phase of the long economic cycle instead of during the crisis and depression phases, the latter being reinforced by the onset of a new technological style (see also chapter 5).

Hierarchization and Other Control Devices

To date, the development of formal organization has been marked by an increasing hierarchization of positions. Even if the character of the hierarchy is to change in the future—as has also been the case in the past—hierarchy basically remains inevitable in the striving after efficiency . The basic reason for its necessity (which, however, does not determine its shape) lies neither in the logic of modern production technology nor in the desire of corporate heads to control their workers directly. Technology is not deterministic.

While it shapes the character of hierarchy, technology is not its fundamental cause.

The inevitability of a differentiated hierarchy arises because the particular interests of firms in a society integrated by the market cannot be fully reconciled and are only partially motivating for the work force. Generalized motivation is conveyed by utilitarian linkage with salaries and wages, but remains external, and results in a certain indifference without bringing about an internalization of goals. For that reason, loss of control at the dominant core of the organization emerges, hierarchization being one of the important strategies to avoid it (for more details on this and the following see Bornschier 1988: chapter 9).

However, hierarchization is not the only way to avoid a loss of control during the expansion process. Bureaucratization, with its central features of *formalization* and *standardization* makes closer supervision at the same level of efficient control possible. And the *professionalization* of the experts unburdens the supervisors, on the one hand, and introduces a new mechanism of control (expertise and practical constraint), on the other. *Bureaucratization* was put at the center of the analysis of modern structures of dominance by Max Weber ([1921] 1972). It impersonalizes power and, by way of rationalization, results in an increasingly closely administered world. "Rationalization always implies a process in the course of which things that were not analyzed previously and happened without planning and spontaneously are subjected to rules and controlled by them" (Kohler 1981: 13; our translation). Bureaucratic centralization on the one hand results in gains in efficiency because of the improved administration of problems, and, on the other hand, results in a reduction of any kind of independence beyond the core (Gorz 1980: 51). The power is part of the organizational plan, "it belongs to no particular subject but to the function, or position which an individual holds in the organizational plan of a firm, an institution or the state" (Gorz 1980: 43; our translation).

Thus, large organizations work in such a way that reliable performances become partially independent of direct interventions by top management. For that reason, hierarchy can—paradoxically—be extended; a comparatively *decentralized structure* can evolve in which the ultimate authority—i.e., the boss—stays in control.

The decentralization of decision making is also stressed in business administration research (see Witte and Bronner 1974: 10-15). By the decentralization of control, which may go as far as to include certain kinds of self-management, the directors' and senior managers' supervision can be decreased without incurring a loss of control. Decentralization thus prevents an excessive and expensive hierarchization; it does not make hierarchy obsolete, but rather keeps its growth in line with costs.

Control by bureaucratic and professional authority is supplemented by the *mechanization* of work. All three elements of control are formalized and impersonal mechanisms which appeal in a universalistic way to practical constraints and dictates of efficiency make *decentralization* possible. This impersonal control, which lies at the heart of staff professionalization, unburdens management. The mechanization of work makes direct supervision unnecessary. Both are fundamental for efficiency and for the maintenance of structural coherence in large corporations.

At its core, authority is centralized, but at the same time it is also decentralized to some degree, since impersonal standards and controls guarantee adherence to the organizational plan. Control is diffused within the organization in an impersonal way, which may give rise to conflicts within *people* who seek to pursue autonomous careers.

THE PROBLEM OF ACCEPTANCE

The tension between the rights of persons, their subjective need for autonomy, and the way work is allocated is a source of *latent alienation* and *suffering*, which can only be mitigated to a limited degree according to the criteria of efficiency prevalent in large organizations. Instead, the *separation of different life spheres* is one solution. For the maintenance of organizational goals of growth and profit as well as control, such a separation is only acceptable so long as it can effectively limit the potential risks of the organization of workers' refusal to work.

A system-stabilizing separation of life spheres must achieve two things at the same time: compensate individuals for their suffering and secure the firms' existence and growth by promoting consumption. Hence, separation is based on material compensation, which displaces the striving after a good life to consumption during leisure time. This, however, implies binding the claim to an autonomous life to the workplace, which is perceived by the individual as externally determined. This is problematic, since individual autonomy cannot be restricted only to simple consumption or mere distraction and recreational needs.

As long as material goods are attractive because of their scarcity, such compensation bound to the logic of the core segment may well create a functional linkage. The needs of the core segment are met and, at the same time, the tension between goals and controls at the personal level of the person is resolved. Loyalty to the economic system involves generous material compensations in the core segment, which is how large corporations attempt to legitimize themselves in the eyes of their actual and potential members. Such a legitimizing strategy works quite well for some time. The coercion exercised by scarcity of basic material goods is only a theoretical and not a practical alternative, because low compensation is not in the interest of the core segment, the growth of which depends upon mass consumption and the progressive commercialization of spheres of life.

Income saturation limits the legitimation function of loyalties, and thus work-related suffering can become manifest. Given the many modest incomes, the formulation "income saturation" may seem surprising. But the theoretical process underlying our notion is somewhat more complex because it not only embraces the numerical level of material compensation but also the discrepancy between material compensation and a lack of satisfaction at work (intrinsic satisfaction), noted in Heinrich Gossen's (1854) theory of suffering at work. Obtaining material goods leads to a depreciation of their value because of the problems arising from them. As Gossen (according to Stavenhagen 1969: 234) put it: Compensation can only be successful as long as one is in a position to increase the sum of pleasures by work and as long therefore as "the pleasure derived from work is greater than the suffering it causes."

New Forms of Conflict

During the technological style prevailing at the turn of the century, the class conflict between capital and labor was central to the unresolved acceptance of the existing order. For today's fading technological style, the problem lies in cultural conflict arising from the tension between person and position. This new source of alienation and suffering originated from the tension between the claims of persons and their work in large organizations with impersonal mechanisms of control, resulting in a refusal to perform and cultural conflicts that contributed to undermining the technological style from within and forced a change of style. As the line of tension runs through the individual, individualized strategies for its resolution, wide-spread individualism, and low levels of collective protest are probable. We thus expect the tension also to be reflected in widespread psychological troubles and the consumption of drugs.

The lack of satisfaction at work which resulted from the restrictive technical and social organization during the former technological style called for increasing material, yet in the final analysis external, compensations. In the course of this process, meaning derived from the work context decreased while materialism became inflated, resulting in reduced performance and conflicts. As André Gorz (1980: 74) once put it, the "essence of life," which is an end in itself, cannot be displaced into a hunger for surrogates.

FINAL CONSIDERATIONS REGARDING CONTEMPORARY CHANGES

For formal organizations acceptance is a big challenge. But since earlier changes occurred when growth limits were met, we can assume that they will also meet the challenge in a new round of organizational development. The direction of change in the technological style could not be clearly assessed by the mid-1980s, because the crystallization of innovations and the corresponding organizational changes still lay in the future. Today, organizational mutations triggered by a change of paradigm in management philosophy are clearly visible.

It is astonishing how management practices that held sway for so long have rapidly become obsolete. Those organizations that were managed according to entirely different practices until a very short time ago are facing an enormous challenge to "re-program their organizational software" so as to be able to face the new competitive style by adopting lean management first introduced in Japan. The new management philosophy is characterized by a flattening of the hierarchical pyramid, the mutual interpenetration of departments (which used to be functionally strictly separated) and by new forms of linkage with other firms—be they suppliers or customers. A new approach to the creative capacities of workers not only responds to the alienation in the traditional framework, it also reflects the recent insight that the intensified mechanization of the 1980s does not bring about expected rationalizations if the human factor is neglected.

9
Schools and the Myth of Equal Opportunity

Formal Education as a Pillar of Equality

The reasons for discussing formal education under the heading "pillar of equality" are not immediately obvious. After all, it can well be argued that the graded schooling system actually *generates* inequality. But the modern school system is also an attempt to institutionalize the principle of equal opportunity, just as democracy attempts to do the same in the political sphere. Right from the start, when all primary school pupils start in the same grade, individual performance alone is supposed to decide one's progress and final position in the educational hierarchy. Because formal education is functionally linked to society's positional structure, the educational system contributes to the acceptance of an uneven positional structure created by formal organizations.

Although individual capacities and performance are *supposed* to exclusively guide educational progress, reality of course always limps behind this idealistic claim. In addition, the legitimizing role of the educational system remains linked to uneven positional structures during a given historical phase, being conditional upon the current technological style. The number of pupils reaching the various grades cannot depend merely upon individual will and performance, for educational capital is also bequeathed. The children of parents with higher schooling have "natural" advantages that can only partially be democratized; hence the tendency of educational stratification to be reproduced over generations.

The overall outcome is a contradictory dynamic. If one attempts to preserve the legitimating function of education, access to it must be opened up and democratized to counteract those forces tending towards unequal opportunities. The result is educational expansion. On the one hand, the duration of compulsory schooling increases, and on the other, the proportion of a given age cohort with access to middle and higher schooling increases, which however, makes the legitimating linkage between educational certificates and societal positions highly problematic. The inflation of education devaluates its instrumental value. It becomes necessary to acquire ever more education to reach the *same* relative positions in society. In addition, legitimate claims acquired in the educational system cannot be fully redeemed and thus the instrumental character of educational capital is partially destroyed; this points to the limits of societal legitimation on the basis of education during certain historical phases.

THE STRUCTURAL PERSPECTIVE: FUNCTIONS OF FORMAL EDUCATION

The traditional perspective on the role of schooling stresses its *socialization function* (see Meyer 1977; Fend 1981; Hurrelmann 1975): the school as an agent of secondary socialization generates in those attending the capacities needed in modern society. Thus, the school is seen as the *"great socializer."* Another traditional perspective stresses the *allocation function* of education. The schooling system, with its differenting grades, distributes the chances of adults: position in society depends upon the duration and kind of schooling obtained. In this perspective, the school is seen as the *"great sorter."* Both perspectives are correct to some extent, but they are also incomplete because the role of the school as a social institution is neglected.

The institutional perspective perceives education as a system, i.e., a set of rules at the collective societal level, as convincingly shown by John W. Meyer (1977; see also Bornschier and Heintz 1977). The educational institution creates and administers a view of the world, a manner of interpreting it and coping with it. In this sense, education can even be called a secular religion, i.e., a system for interpreting the world rationally and pragmatically. The institution pursues the clearing up of mysteries and transcendental secrets: knowledge, ordered and increased, is supposed to help control uncertainty.

Basically, the modern educational system is directed toward progress. The realm of the unknown is to be circumscribed and, at the same time, knowledge has to be furthered, which is why new areas of knowledge and disciplines emerge permanently. The emergence of new areas of knowledge implies that mysteries are deciphered and brought under control by a social organization. Thus, at a societal level the unknown, which tends to arouse fears, is reduced by new disciplines and schooling; control is embedded in certainty according to the norms of modern science by an institution (Meyer 1977).

As John Meyer stresses, the authority of education is founded precisely on its ability to interpret the world, i.e., to transform traditional knowledge into rationally founded knowledge for use in addressing real problems. Further, the educational system is one of ceremonies and rites, particularly rites of passage from kindergarten up to post-graduate studies, the main stages being: pre-school, primary school, secondary school and higher education, creating a pyramid of societal positions. The most widespread right to participate in education is in the framework of compulsory schooling, which points to the close historical connection between mass schooling and the definition of citizenship, i.e., the interrelation between school and state, which we discuss below and which is shown by the fact that the educational system is administered by the state all over the world today (Inkeles and Sirowy 1983).

On this basis of compulsory participation, the institution creates the complementary roles of the educated and the uneducated. Even though the shaping and graduation of these complementary roles may vary, the core inequality remains intact: *positional goods* are created by certifying knowledge (see Hirsch 1976; Ultee 1980). Because it is impossible for everybody to take part in the full-time production and administration of knowledge, experts become necessary. New areas of knowledge also create new positions in society, both specialized experts and new clients—the public, groups, or other institutions—requiring specialized knowledge.

Education as an institution thus creates status as a positional good and certifies it to become marketable independently of the actual knowledge of the certificate holder. Thus, our perspective of interpreting education as an institution is much broader than the traditional socialization and allocation theories, for it creates a system for interpreting the world *and* a positional graduation of knowledge, thus helping to reveal rites which socially define *the* academic, *the* high school graduate and so on. Further, it can be shown that the institution of knowledge about the world is a modern construct. As John Meyer puts it: "If education is a myth in modern society it is a powerful one. The effects of myths inhere, not in the fact that individuals believe them, but in the fact that they 'know' everyone else does, and thus that 'for all practical purposes' the myths are true. We may all gossip privately about the uselessness of education, but in hiring and promoting, in consulting the various magi of our time, and in ordering our lives around contemporary rationality, we carry out our parts in a drama in which education is the authority (1977: 75f.)."

EDUCATION AS A SOURCE OF LEGITIMATION

The legitimizing content of education is based on its ability to integrate society by the functioning of it as an institution. We thus have to concentrate on the *integrational function* of education, which to become effective must meet two conditions:

(1) The model of interpreting the world in which the educational system is anchored must accord with the dominant culture in other domains of society, which are ordered around rationality and progress .

(2) The distribution of status in the educational system must be legitimized by conforming to the two central principles of striving after efficiency and equality.

Formal education fulfills these two conditions like no other institution, which is why it belongs to those very important key systems absolutely essential for the integration of modern society. The myth of progress runs through both science and economics and essentially reflects the desire to control nature and to limit insecurity. Thus, euphoria as well as periodic skepticism and animosity towards science and growth go hand in hand.

The system of rules of institutionalized education attracts broad assent because the principles of efficiency and equality appear to be very thoroughly embedded in it. The "social magic" of the school derives from symbolic equality, as each person starts their educational career at the same level. Later, performance measured in grades, i.e., personal achievement, is central to advancement within the system. No doubt it is a myth that only talent and performance count and a myth that neglects the inheritance of educational status resulting from differing cultural capital endowments and class-specific differences in aspirations.

Further, the legitimating power of the school is based on the fact that graduates at the highest educational levels have also gone through the same lower levels. By such linkage of different levels, school is legitimized by principles only really relevant at the very top, i.e., in the universities: autonomy, critical ability and the reign of reason. Mass education, on the other hand, remains confined to the teaching of obvious cultural elements and standard knowledge. The "comprehensive school" thus obscures the fact that the school system determines the number of pupils at different levels by selectivity. Reforms that favor a stronger anchoring of equal opportunity aim at loosening the ties between educational opportunities and social origin, and at a greater permeability between the different levels. Both measures would result in a democratization of education.

Various studies have critically pointed to the absence of equal opportunities in the acquisition of education (see Bourdieu and Passeron 1970). The importance of origins—particularly parental education—is empirically very clear. Thus, it is very easy to destroy the myth of equal opportunity—as easy as measuring the real economic structures against the ideal model of perfect competition. Such an exercise, however, is not very useful in determining the direction and speed of societal change.

In the sequence of societal models, Western society has achieved a higher degree of equal opportunity. The democratization of access to schooling was particularly important during the Keynesian societal model. On the basis of OECD data, Alex Inkeles and Larry Sirowy (1983: 325) have pointed to results according to which the relevance of origin with respect to educational success is seen to decrease markedly between 1960 and 1970. But the short time span, as well as the fact that parental education and not occupation is the single most important variable to explain educational success, calls for more evidence in order to point to an increase in equal opportunity.

Shifts in Educational Attainment

On the basis of representative material for eight Western countries in the mid-1970s (Federal Republic of Germany, Finland, the United Kingdom, Italy, the Netherlands, Austria, Switzerland and the United States) we have conducted a comparison of birth cohorts spanning from the beginning to the middle of this century, which allows us to make certain observations regarding changes in intergenerational educational mobility as well as the changing distribution of educational levels in Western society during most of this century.

The pooled representative samples from these eight countries represent two thirds of the total population of Western society after World War II. The basic data are taken from the eight-nation study titled *Political Action* (Zentralarchiv 1979: Study-No. 765). The common five-step scale used to make the educational levels comparable across the countries was developed by Martin Graf and Markus Lamprecht (1984; see also Lamprecht 1988, 1991: 137). Table 9.1 presents the distribution of the highest educational level obtained according to age cohorts for men and women; table 9.2 lists various measures of intergenerational educational mobility. The latter are not listed for women, first because it would be necessary to include mother's education, information we lack for the respondents in several countries in the pooled sample; and second because previous research has shown that the effect of father's education on respondent's level of education is clearly more important for sons than for daughters (see Bornschier 1986: 810f.). Without controls for mother's education, using these measures would overestimate the openness of education for women.

Table 9.1 evidences the remarkable shifts from basic to secondary and tertiary education levels when we compare the age cohort: 79.4 percent of the men born around 1875 obtained only basic education, whereas this figure drops to 21.5 percent for the age cohort born between 1940-1949. On the other hand, educational certificates at the highest two levels increased from 5.9 percent to 20.6 percent in the pooled sample of Western countries. Furthermore, the table 9.1 reveals the well-known gender differences in educational attainment but shows at the same time that they were reduced over time.

We come back to this aspect of educational expansion—indicated by increasing relative frequencies of certificates from middle and higher educational levels—when we address the forces behind the waves of educational expansion. Here we look at the evidence for the question of equal opportunity for which we so far have had only limited information. From table 9.2 we can conclude that inheritance of educational status indeed weakened over the whole century, but less than the enormous change in educational distribution would suggest. Later in this chapter we suggest status competition for educational certificates as a theoretical explanation for this persistent pattern of intergenerational educational reproduction.

TABLE 9.1 Distribution of Highest Educational Degree Attained for Five Age Cohorts. Pooled sample of Eight Countries, 1973-75: Austria, Federal Republic of Germany, Finland, Italy, Netherlands, Switzerland, United Kingdom and United States

		Age of respondents in 1973-75					Previous
		25-34	35-44	45-54	55-64	65+	Generation[1]
		Male respondents (percentage)					
1	Degree of university or college or equivalent	9.0	6.9	6.0	4.4	4.7	2.2
2	Degree that gives access to level 1	11.6	8.9	7.5	5.4	4.4	3.7
3	Secondary level degree[2]	20.6	17.3	12.0	12.9	9.1	3.0
4	Extended basic education[3]	37.2	33.7	29.8	25.7	21.6	11.7
5	Basic education at primary level	21.5	33.2	44.7	51.6	60.1	79.4
	Total:	99.9	100	100	100	99.9	100
	Number of observations:	1042	901	883	704	592	592
		Female respondents (percentage)					
1	Degree of university or college equivalent	5.2	2.6	2.2	1.2	1.1	2.9
2	Degree that gives access to level 1	10.0	5.9	4.8	5.5	5.0	3.7
3	Secondary level degree[2]	22.1	13.2	13.8	12.1	11.4	4.6
4	Extended basic education[3]	35.9	32.4	25.4	22.3	14.7	12.8
5	Basic education at primary level	26.8	46.0	53.9	59.0	67.9	76.0
	Total:	100	100.1	100.1	101.1	100.1	100
	Number of observations:	1102	972	1051	860	757	757

Source: Our computations from Zentralarchiv (1979: Study-No 765)
1. Fathers of those over 64 years of age, born about 1875.
2. Degree does not permit access to level 1.
3. Vocational training.

Comparing the different cohorts of men represented in table 9.2 we can make the following observations: educational mobility has increased from 32.3 percent to 58.6 percent since the beginning of this century. Of the men aged between 25 and 34 in 1973-1975, about six out of ten achieved a different educational level than their fathers. In addition, by 1973-1975 educational mobility of two or more levels, which is quite substantial, has more than doubled. What is remarkable is that during this period educational mobility is most cases upward. Thus, in the course of this century, a growing part of the (male) population has attained higher educational levels than their fathers. This illustrates how nicely the educational system fits the myth of progress which, as we have seen, is central to the Western societal model.

In general, intergenerational educational inheritance during the period studied clearly decreased from the older to the younger age cohorts but nevertheless remained considerable (see Somer's D, which drops from 0.63 to 0.48). The same is true for differential opportunities in obtaining degrees at the highest level (university or equivalent) as well, but the openness quite clearly increased during the Keynesian societal model (see the drop in the index of association for the last age cohort).

Educational mobility, it may be argued, is mostly fuelled by structural changes. This can be determined by separating total educational mobility into two components: "structural mobility," resulting from the change in the educational distribution between fathers and their children, and "exchange mobility," which is the net effect of total mobility minus structural mobility. Our results show that for all male cohorts structural mobility was always somewhat more important than exchange mobility. Thus, we may conclude from this that the increase in educational mobility was to a large extent the result of improved access to higher levels of schooling. Below we will show that this kind of *opening up of the schools* is the only way to substantially mitigate origin-related differences in educational opportunities.

The results of this study may be more precisely summarized in the following manner. Since the end of the last century it is possible to observe a considerable change in the distribution of age cohorts over various hierarchical education levels. Middle and higher certificates have become much more frequent. Although this aspect of educational expansion holds true for all Western countries, the fact that differences between countries have always existed must not be overlooked (see Lamprecht 1991: 138; Bornschier and Aebi 1992: 552; Heidenheimer 1981, 1993; Kaelble 1981: 245ff.; and chapter 12 below on Japan).

TABLE 9.2 Intergenerational Educational Mobility for Five Age Cohorts. Pooled sample of Eight Countries, 1973-75: Austria, Federal Republic of Germany, Finland, Italy, Netherlands, Switzerland, United Kingdom and United States

Male Respondents Compared to Their Fathers

Mobility Measures[1]	Age of the respondents 1973-75 25-34	35-44	45-54	55-64	65+
Intergenerational mobility (percentage)	58.6	52.8	44.7	38.9	32.3
upwardly mobile	50.7	46.4	39.2	35.2	26.9
downwardly mobile	7.9	6.4	5.5	3.7	5.4
Mobility at least over two levels of the education scale (percentage)					
upwardly mobile	21.2	17.8	15.1	13.4	10.1
downwardly mobile	1.3	2.0	1.5	1.7	1.7
Mobility due to structural change[2]					
percent structurally mobile	32.1	32.2	26.8	25.6	19.3
(in % of their total mobility)	(55)	(61)	(60)	(66)	(60)
Index of association for level 1, i.e., university/college[3]	4.7	8.4	10.0	9.1	13.0
Measure of association for the total mobility matrix					
Somer's D	0.48	0.52	0.56	0.60	0.63
Number of observations	1042	901	883	704	592

Source: Our computations from Zentralarchiv (1979: Study-No 765)

1. Measures based on a five-step intergenerational mobility matrix (see table 9.1 for definitions of the five steps).
2. Sum of row and column frequencies devided by the double number of observations.
3. Observed frequency at level 1 (see table 9.1, fathers and sons with university/college or equivalent degree) divided by the expected frequency (i.e., row times column sum divided by the total number of observations).

There is a decrease in unequal opportunity even though substantial inequalities persist. The family background effect decreases, but again differences between Western countries have to be stressed. At the peak of the Keynesian societal model the background effect was comparatively lower in the United States (Bornschier 1986: 815-819; Lamprecht 1991: 145) and in Japan (see chapter 12) as compared to Western European countries. Although such differences are of great interest in comparative research, we will not detail them here. In conclusion, we note that the educational career of children still greatly depends on their parents' education. Still, the myth of all starting together became a reality for an ever increasing number of people in Western society during this century, a fact that must be stressed when describing societal change.

Educational status is linked to other societal status dimensions, particularly in the occupational system. Thus, the legitimacy of the educational system, bestowed by its broadly accepted authority, is transferred to other spheres of society where education is not the most important passport to positions (for more details see Bornschier and Heintz 1977; Bornschier 1982a). Legitimation is the result of a transformation of instruction into graded institutionalized formal education, in turn objectivizing personal cultural power by way of certificates, diplomas and degrees, which then become marketable and are commonly linked to other forms of societal power according to certain rates of exchange.

FORMAL EDUCATION IN SOCIAL STRATIFICATION

The increased significance of formal education and "exchange rates" between educational titles and other status positions in society at first sight contradict the observation that there is also a high degree of *status inconsistency* in the social stratification of the Keynesian societal model. In terms of the coefficient of variation (CV), the distribution of formal authority at the workplace (CV=1.61) is ten times more unequal than the distribution of formal education (CV=0.16).[1] The inevitable result of these discrepancies is status inconsistency. The partially horizontal openness of the stratification system of the Keynesian societal model thus also leads to a weak linkage between the different status distributions in stratification (Bornschier 1986).[2]

Status Inconsistency as a Feature of Stratification

Privileges under the Keynesian societal model, which are—at least for formal authority—determined by the technological style, are problematic in the context of the claim to equality. Formal authority can hardly be reconciled with equal opportunity. If actually only one third can reach the target at all, and if formal authority itself is enormously differentiated for that third, not everybody has the same chances. If opportunities were closely linked to educational status, the educational distribution would have to be as unequal as the distribution of formal authority, thus precluding an opening up of schools, while advantages on the basis of qualifications *and* formal authority would regularly accumulate.

Making opportunities radically independent of the qualification and privilege components in stratification is a solution contributing to a partial opening-up of society and thus to more equality of opportunities within the whole social structure. At a higher level, this independence of opportunities can be balanced by assigning the same income-generating power to different status distributions, i.e., differences in status over each particular status distribution result in comparable income differences if the features of the other status distributions remain the same, as can also be shown empirically (Bornschier 1988, 1991).

An important side-effect of such legitimation of total inequality by a partial opening-up is the necessary emergence of status inconsistencies: rather than being exceptions, they become the rule. Status inconsistencies are thus an expression of the striving for legitimation in the whole structure, and thus have an *integrative* function, which substantially modifies the traditional notion that status inconsistencies result in conflict (see Bornschier and Heintz; 1977, Strasser and Hodge 1986). In our perspective, conflicts arising from a violation of norms governing equal valorization can only emerge if exchange rates between particular status dimensions and the income both deviate from the pattern for society as a whole.

Linkage Despite Status Inconsistency?

Widespread status inconsistency throughout Western society does not mean that rules of status linkage are lacking. But if rules exist, why is the observed degree of status linkage so low? We will discuss this question with reference to the linkages between educational status, position in job hierarchy and income (see Bornschier 1982a).

The two central themes of education research—those of change and of reproduction (see Haller 1980: 22ff.)—must be broached with some skepticism. Both postulate a high degree of correspondence between educational and other status dimensions in society and thus contradict the empirical findings. Theodor Hanf (1975) summarizes the theme of change in the following way: the educational system influences the distribution of status and income in the labor structure and thus the social structure in a decisive way. The human capital approach in the economics of education formulated this most completely and attempted to confirm it with numerous empirical studies (see Bornschier 1982a). According to this approach, aggregate income distribution equals the total time value of educational capital accumulated by individuals: thus, the distribution of educational capital influences income distribution directly. Education is the independent variable, whereas income distribution is one of its consequences. The reproduction approach argues exactly the opposite way: education is not an independent variable but is rather determined by social structure and only serves to legitimize and reproduce existing differences (Hanf 1975, see also Bourdieu and Passeron 1970). As opposites, these two approaches may seem in one respect paradoxically similar: both claim that educational level, position, and income in the labor structure correlate highly, which the empirical evidence for Western society dramatically contradicts.

A first step towards a realistic assessment of the linkage between educational and occupational status, income and formal authority has been taken by the legitimation approach to education (Meyer 1977; Bornschier and Heintz 1977), according to which the distribution of education also follows its own institutional logic, whereby the values of equal opportunities are more deeply anchored than in other spheres of society. This may explain why the educational system opened up in the course of this century. According to this approach, the transfer of the greater legitimacy of education to other spheres of society is attempted by creating equivalents for other status claims on the basis of educational certifications, i.e., "exchange rates" for other status dimensions are established. But, the transfer of status claims from a less unequally distributed to a more unequally and thus less legitimate status distribution cannot lead to a perfect correlation in the aggregate.

If legitimacy is to be transferred, the distribution of education must represent more equal opportunities than the status distributions of occupation and income being legitimized. If differences in opportunities are also reflected in an unequal distribution of a given status system, status linkage can never be perfect. Thus, in theory and as a norm, the correlation between education, occupational status and income can never be perfect even under conditions of optimal status linkage.

Still, pure legitimation leaves several important questions unanswered. The behavior of employers and professional associations is very important for the mechanism of status linkage, hence they must be incorporated into the theory. In addition, it remains unclear why positional distribution in the occupational system is more unequal and thus in need of additional legitimation. Finally, legitimation theory argues that the educational system creates status that of necessity must not correlate highly with what is known in the world of work as productivity. Yet it remains important to explain why employers continue to use education as a criterion for hiring personnel.

Elsewhere we have discussed two versions of selection approaches to education which supplement legitimation theory (Bornschier 1982a). For those arguing from the division of labor approach (see chapter 8), the structure of wages arises from developments in the course of organizational evolution and not from the educational levels of the workers. Accordingly, formal education and income are linked in the following way: the potential aspirants to higher, privileged positions in the occupational structure are more numerous than effective demand on the part of employers, so they may select among different applicants. Formal education is only one criterion among others in this selection process—a universal criterion helping selection, which also takes other legitimate claims into account and has the additional advantage of being more or less free of charge as a basis for decision-making. But more particular criteria are also important when people are selected by external recruiting or when they get promoted.

Thus, external recruitment at each level is not based only upon formal education, but also upon other criteria (conformity with organizational goals, etc.) which applicants awarded a job meet. The rest must apply at a lower level or remain in their jobs. Further, promotions are no longer based on formal education as an important criterion because this criterion was already applied for the initial hiring at different levels of external recruitment. At the initial level from which employees get promoted, they have similar levels of educational attainment.

The result is a weak correlation between formal education and wages, or, in other words, a substantial span of incomes at the same level of formal education. This aggregate outcome occurs even though education is important on the labor market and despite the fact that employers are interested in a correspondence between education and position in the work hierarchy. An interesting version of the selection theory of education that totally rejects any contextual linkage between formal education and job qualification has been advanced by Lester Thurow in his indicator theory of education, which claims that formal education is only of indicative value for the expected on-the-job training costs to the employer (for details see Bornschier 1982a).

Thus, a version of legitimation theory supplemented by selection theories of education gives a satisfactory explanation for the weak linkage between formal education and position in the work hierarchy as well as between formal education and income. This theory also shows that status inconsistency is a result of such processes and not an indicator of a lack of social regulation.

THE HISTORICAL PERSPECTIVE: ORIGINS OF MASS EDUCATION AND WAVES OF EDUCATIONAL EXPANSION

The school is not really a modern institution. Earlier types of schools sought to interpret the world, and modern schools still do the same. It is true that such interpretations of the world were frequently of a religious nature, although this was not always the case. For example, the Tao schools in ancient China educated "literati," i.e., the bureaucratic elite of the Mandarins. Schools played a role in the recruitment of elites, as in China and the monastic schools during the European Middle Ages. Long ago certain groups already attended schools administering final exams, e.g., the literati in China and the samurai, the mounted warrior elite in Tokugawa Japan.

However, schools did not always serve the purpose of elite recruitment. The philosophy schools in ancient Greece trained a small wealthy elite and certain talented individuals in the contemplative interpretation of the world, which also increased their social prestige; their societal position was not the result of their education. Attempts at changing this were not successful. Nor is secularization an exclusive feature of modern schooling. Ancient Greece already had secular education and in Europe secularization of knowledge began as early as the twelfth century during the Renaissance of the sciences without, however, establishing schools in the modern sense. Historically, several elements of the modern school were already present in rich variety during earlier epochs. Even simple societies adopt prototypical elements of schooling in their initiation rites, which are normally preceded by a prolonged separation from the group for "instruction."

What then is really new in modern schooling? Mass education is important but refers only to basic education. Yet the whole schooling system is built on this common basis, i.e., everybody has to go through the same basic levels. Thus, modern schooling also serves to spread the base of equality, an early agent of *social* democratization, which often preceded political democratization in Europe and the origins of which can be traced back to the Reformation.

Universal compulsory school attendance at certain ages is also new, and represents a noteworthy contrast with political democratization in terms of civil liberties. Compulsory mass education thus is not a right but rather a civil duty, which points to the historic importance of the origins of modern schooling, mostly dispensed from "above" and not the result of a struggle from "below." School attendance as a civil duty also points to the homogenization of citizens, the state's ability to mobilize and control citizens being the main impulse behind the emergence of modern schooling in Europe. Through common schooling, children become true state citizens who partake of the culture of the new, larger group, the nation, and who can also be mobilized in its cause. Universal compulsory school attendance helped to establish national identities, being a feature of state power-building during emergent nationalism at the end of the eighteenth and during the nineteenth century.

At the end of the eighteenth century, controllable mass loyalty which meant more equality, on the one hand, and more control from above, on the other, became an important resource along with naval power and industry in the economically motivated competition of European states for *world* power, and industry. Yet, it was not the leaders in world power, industry and capitalist development who were to become the innovators of compulsory mass education. Since schooling gives access to knowledge and because secularized knowledge through the power of thinking can always become the source of opposition, one must expect a great deal of resistance by secular and religious elites to mass education in public schools. Two factors helped to overcome this resistance: the will to move upwards from marginal positions in the state system, and the loss of position in the longstanding competition between states. Lost or bloody wars, for example, Prussia during the Seven Year War, blocked opportunities for upward mobility and made the loss of position obvious.

Such national crises helped to advance compulsory schooling against resistance; mass education thus became an element of societal reconstruction and renewal. Consequently, the outriders or innovators in this context were those countries experiencing national crises rather than those countries which might have been expected to assume that position for the obvious reason that mass education is a functional necessity for industrialization. Neither England nor France, the two big rivals of the eighteenth and early nineteenth century—one of them a naval and world power, the other the continental hegemon—were the innovators. Nor was it the early European leaders in capitalist and industrial development on the Continent (Netherlands, Belgium and Switzerland) which took the lead. Rather, the institutional innovators of universal compulsory school attendance were the marginal powers wanting to move upwards (Prussia) or threatened by downward mobility (Sweden, Denmark and Austria) as already suggested by John Boli-Bennett et al. (1985; Boli-Bennett and Ramirez 1985). They were mainly Protestant (including Norway, not listed in the group of innovators because it was not independent at that time) and had strong central state bureaucracies to which Arnold Heidenheimer (1981) and Reinhart Schneider (1982) point. The Lutheran-absolutist state with threatened ambitions in the interstate system is the obvious combination. Catholic-absolutist Austria—threatened too—is ambiguous: only the law of 1869 actually enforced the principle of compulsory education, which had been *de jure* but hardly *de facto* introduced much earlier (Schneider 1982: 211). Table 9.3 shows the years of introduction of laws at the national level according to Reinhart Schneider's (1982: 212) compilation.

Once the innovation was established, the other countries were forced to follow; they did not want to lose that source of mass mobilization through national allegiance and citizenship created by the legitimizing content of mass education. What is called 'latecomer' in table 9.3 is indeed the bulk of other countries which made primary education compulsory mainly between 1870 and 1880. The countries outside Western Europe (the United States, the British colonies in Australia and Canada, and Japan) also fit this pattern of followers. By 1870 the innovators no longer had a lead in terms of primary enrolment (Schneider 1982: 213; Heidenheimer 1981: 296, 298). The institutional innovation of mass education triggered subsequent waves of educational expansion which we will now discuss.

TABLE 9.3 The Introduction of Compulsory School Attendance in Western Europe. Dates of Laws at the National Level

In Europe, the spread of compulsory mass education starts from marginal positions in the following way: the middle powers wanting to move upwards but which see their aspirations blocked, and the powers threatened by downward mobility.

	Prussia	1763, 1817-25
Institutional innovators	Austria	1774, 1869
	Denmark	1814
	Sweden	1842 (under discussion since 1810)

The centers of early capitalist development and of early industrial breakthrough are not leaders but rather followers. France, the leading military power on the continent, is late too.

	Scotland	1872
Latecomers	England	1880
	France	1882
	Switzerland	1874
	Netherlands	1900

The remaining states passed the relevant laws in the following years:

Norway[1]	1848
Italy[2]	1877
Ireland[3]	1882
Finland[4]	1921

Notes: 1. Passes from Denmark to Sweden in 1809; Sweden, in turn, looses Finland to Russia. 2. Kingdom of Italy founded in 1869. 3. Until 1919 de facto and until 1922 nominally under British rule. 4. Becomes independent in 1918.
Source: Schneider (1982).

WAVES OF EDUCATIONAL EXPANSION

Around the turn of the century the diffusion of compulsory mass schooling was largely terminated and new educational dynamics began, characterized by two further processes of educational expansion: 1) extension of compulsory schooling, evidenced by an increasing trend throughout Western Europe after the turn of the century (Flora et al. 1983: 553-633); and 2) educational expansion by the increasing relative frequencies of pupils at the middle and higher levels (Schneider 1982, Heidenheimer 1981: 296, 298; Bornschier and Aebi 1992: 552)—a trend we have also demonstrated with our age cohort analyses in table 9.1. Both processes are linked to each other. Due to the split into different levels education loses certain of its legitimizing power, which the prolongation of compulsory schooling mitigates somewhat: basic education, which is the same for everybody is increased, i.e., education is somewhat more democratized despite differentiation.

We suggest the competition for status as a theoretical explanation for educational expansion, the exponential character of which is obvious. In this connection we must remember that formal education is a positional good, i.e., relative position is decisive for its exchange. Prior to the introduction of mass education, the ability to write, read and calculate constituted the important line of demarcation between the lower and the middle classes. The university only served to recruit a small elite for public administration, armed forces officers, the church hierarchy, or certain liberal professions. With the increase in the general level of educational equality, the differentiation into levels of education (i.e., the allocation function of education) becomes important. This dialectical process of equalization and differentiation is ongoing.

That education is a positional good has a paradoxical consequence: as a result of competition for status, education is not just a means for upward social mobility, but also increasingly becomes a protection against downward social mobility. This spiral of prolonged education to improve and conserve the position of one's children is without doubt the main reason for educational expansion in this century. Keener competition for the positional good of "formal education," responsible for the exponential evaluation of schooling at the middle and higher levels, can be divided into two phases characterized by technological styles and their corresponding occupational structures as well as their specific location in status competition. Educational expansion was first the result of narrow competition in the middle classes during the first half of this century. Later, extended competition of the middle classes under the technological style that began during the 1930s was generalized from 1945 onwards and unfolded fully during the 1950s and early 1960s.

Narrow Competition of the Middle Classes

Under the class-polarized societal model (1880-1932) the composition of workers, on the one hand, and employees and the self-employed, on the other, remained relatively stable, but the composition of the middle class was subject to enormous changes. Economic concentration during the wave of electrification around the turn of the century resulted in a marginalization of the self-employed. The complement of the decrease in the self-employed is the process of concentration, i.e., the emergence of large firms and corresponding bureaucratization. Expanding hierarchies posed problems of legitimate and efficient filling of positions. To secure status a certain matching of educational and hierarchic levels to legitimize power distribution in society became generalized.

Relative to the aggregate work force, the number of the self-employed decreased substantially while that of employees increased. Both processes—the fall of the self-employed middle class and the rise of the new middle class—were more or less balanced in their relative shares of the aggregate work force from the 1880s until the 1930s (see for example Kleber 1983).

The middle class as a whole (self-employed, employees and public officials) remained remarkably constant in its relative size, but within it there was intense status competition. While middle and higher education became a means for upward social mobility (in the case of employees and public officials), it compensated for the threatening loss of status for the old bourgeois middle class (self-employed) because, on the basis of formal education, they found access to the power hierarchies in formal organization. A contemporary observer, Max Weber described the new role of education as follows: "If we see a desire for the introduction of ordered educational careers and special exams in all spheres, the reason is, of course, not the sudden awakening of a 'striving for education' but rather the attempt to limit the supply for positions and their monopolization to the benefit of holders of educational status" ([1921] 1972: 577).

These processes occurred within the middle class, whose relative size remained constant. It is well known from various studies that it was primarily bourgeois children and children from the new middle class of employees who entered higher schooling, while workers' children did not enjoy such access (see for example Lundgreen 1981; Hoby 1975).

Extended Competition of the Middle Classes

The extension of competition among middle classes is rooted in the features of the new technological style since the 1930s. Two new features resulted from this competition. First, the relative size of the middle class, which had remained remarkably constant between the 1880s and the 1930s, expanded substantially. Second, manual work, which had remained quite homogenous during the preceding technological style, was increasingly divided into skilled and unskilled work. Formal education beyond compulsory schooling thus became the important demarcation line for ascent or descent in the recomposition of the division of labor among routine, expert and control types of work.

For that reason, the lower classes increasingly entered the status competition that had earlier been the domain of the middle classes, as is obvious in the markedly expanding access opportunities of workers' children to the university (see Bolte and Hradil 1984). This extended competition for status only became visible during the 1960s at the level of the universities, but, of course, the "decisions" for educational careers also open to the lower classes date back to the formation phase of the Keynesian societal model.

COMPETITION FOR STATUS AND EDUCATIONAL EXPANSION

Our perspective suggests that the two waves of increased competition for status are the reason for educational expansion. The question is, how does the competition for status experienced by the parents get transformed into educational success for their children? In this process the starting positions are unequal, because the parents with higher schooling have greater motivation to promote the education of their children. Their first aim is merely to ensure that their children reach the *same* educational level they themselves attained earlier, which does not spell ascent but merely status preservation. From this it follows that the differences in motivation resulting from the actual distribution of education are a strong force in reproducing educational stratification over generations.

To estimate the extent of these consequences we start from the assumption that the educational system only selects according to universalistic criteria, i.e., performance at school. Only the best out of a lower educational level gain access to the next higher level. In such a situation only cognitive capabilities appear to play a substantial role in educational success. Yet, in light of empirical findings this assumption does not hold (see Sauer and Gattringer 1985). Empirical findings support instead the notion of status competition by showing that parents' aspirations concerning the education of their children have a strong influence on performance at school—directly as well as indirectly, mediated by the fact that these aspirations promote the development of intelligence and decrease the fear of failure. If the school system indeed selects for better performance, then parents' aspirations for status preservation are important as well as cognitive capabilities.

The higher the educational levels reached by the parents, the higher their aspirations to preserve status. Thus, the higher levels of the educational system can only be kept open through equal opportunities that link educational success solely to cognitive capabilities if the number of students at the topmost levels increases. This has been the case since the beginning of this century and particularly during its second half. For the enlargement of frequencies at the higher educational levels collective, i.e., public decisions, are needed. Thus the state, which attempts to institutionalize the value of equal opportunities through education policy, must meet the mobility aspirations of the lower classes. At the same time, aspirations of the educated to preserve status operate in a quite universalistic way: by educational success. Thus, schools can only be kept open if they expand.

The competition for educational status cannot be separated from the increasing need of employers for certified and legitimate differences in qualification, which constitute a first selection criterion for job applicants. Societal expectations are the outcome of the normative strengthening of rules correspondence between educational status, job position and income. These expectations are necessary prerequisites for educational status competition—i.e., the pressure for upward movement as well as, for some, for the preservation of status. Yet, it is only possible to legitimize the social differentiation of occupations if educational access routes remain open and are not conditional upon social origin, which in turn means a policy of educational expansion that threatens the value of educational levels as criteria for recruitment.

Frustrating Competition?

Better personal formal education is only an advantage as long as others do not follow, otherwise additional educational investments are needed to keep the advantage, as Fred Hirsch points out, "If everyone stands on tiptoe, no one sees better" (1976: 5). The rapidly increasing population of graduates with higher education has thus had a paradoxical result. Under the pressure of competition, formal education has been converted from a means of ascent into a necessary defence against social decline, which has also decisively affected the climate within educational institutions. They increasingly become arenas of selection prior to entry into the labor market, characterized by performance pressure and "frustration." Many take an interest in the institution because of its ability to secure status and not because of its content.

According to the assessment of many observers, the educational expansion of this century has neither fulfilled the wish to preserve status nor the exaggerated hope for fundamental change in social opportunities. Ulrich Beck et al. address the resulting frustrations: "During the 1960s there was great hope that educational expansion would bring about societal changes in the direction of diminishing social inequalities. This optimism was followed by disillusion during the 1970s and is about to change into indifference and resignation at the beginning of the 1980s" (1980: 7). If this assessment is true as an empirical observation resignation is not what results.

It is true that euphoria about education collapsed at the peak of the recent wave and that it has been succeeded by a certain resignation ever since. Heiner Meulemann (1983: 781) has illustrated the change of mood in Germany with time series data. The question: "Does everybody in our country nowadays have a chance to be educated according to their talents and abilities?", was answered in an affirmative way by 68 percent of the population in 1958. Until 1963, the peak of the previous societal model, affirmative answers increased to 74 percent. However, during the downswing phase of the societal model they dropped to 59 percent in 1979. This marked decrease in popular assent of 15 percent between 1963 and 1979 occurred despite the fact that the chances of attending higher schools or universities doubled and tripled, respectively, between the mid-1960s and the mid-1970s respectively (Meulemann 1983).

With respect to education, Fred Hirsch's use of the catch-phrase "If everyone stands on tiptoe, no one sees better" is inappropriate because it is one-sided. If everyone has one additional year of schooling, nobody may reap an advantage in an instrumental sense, yet without doubt, the base of equal opportunities has been extended. Thus, education can also help toward understanding the world (enlightenment) and towards self-fulfillment, particularly if schools are not simply and closely directed towards the general status and occupational systems. Education as enlightenment and enjoyment, as a source of fulfillment, as a key to more sophisticated cultural and spiritual satisfactions and as the basis for the ability to criticize may not be its fundamental function but is still an important outcome of educational expansion. The demand for education (as a consumer good) depends upon society's material level and was originally confined to a small and wealthy elite. The enormous growth of wealth has democratized education extensively, and the public financing of schools and universities is also a true welfare-state function.

INTERNATIONAL COMPETITION

Today the instrumental role of education in international competition has again become more obvious. The new countries challenging the established economic positions of the old core countries have a well-educated labor force. Among the established core countries considerable differences still persist, a fact we omitted in our discussion of the overall patterns that characterized the waves of educational expansion following compulsory mass education. Specific structures as well as institutions have shaped the character and speed of educational expansion in the past; since public decisions are involved this also made for differences in outcome (see Lamprecht 1991: 138; Bornschier and Aebi 1992: 552; Heidenheimer 1981, 1993; Kaelble 1981: 245ff.; Kohl 1981; and our chapter on Japan). How will such differences develop? We suggest that they will be narrowed in the course of time (see also chapter 11).

Similar to compulsory mass schooling which spread during the nineteenth century through competition among nation-states, today technological competition fosters an equalization of the still considerable differences among the Western countries in terms of quality as well as access to academic education. While the United States performs well in sheer size of enrolment at higher levels, there is a growing concern about the quality of many schools. Japan seems to perform well with respect to numbers at the level of higher education as well as quality of schools (see also chapter 12), while Western Europe lags. The growing concern about this competitive weakness is evidenced by the diagnosis given in the 1993 White Paper of the European Union. One of the major weaknesses mentioned

> is the *relatively low level of training in the Community, and especially the fact that too many young people leave school without essential basic training*. In the Community, the proportion of people of normal school-leaving age who leave the educational system with a secondary qualification is 42%, against 75% in the United States of America and 90% in Japan. The proportion of young people [in the corresponding age bracket] who are in higher education in the Community is, on the average, 30%, as compared to 70% in the USA and 50% in Japan. (White Paper 1993: 118)

The technological and educational competition in the world political economy is likely to produce efforts that will level off the current country differences at the core. Yet, the expansion of education in conventional ways will sooner or later be subject to ceiling effects. At the same time the revaluation of human resources in the emerging technological style triggers a demand for more education. Already we witness the beginning of a new round of educational expansion, which is probably the most important social innovation in the field since compulsory mass schooling.

CONTINUING EDUCATION AND TRAINING AS A NEW WAVE OF EDUCATIONAL EXPANSION

From pre-school to university—for about a quarter of a century—schools shape the life of an increasing number of those between 5 to 25 years of age. We have discussed the dynamic of educational expansion which has led to this outcome. Schooling in the traditional framework can only expand to a very limited degree in the future. The new wave of educational expansion will instead concern continuing education and training (Bornschier and Aebi 1992; Aebi 1995). The central notion here is life-long learning and permanent training, which implies a fundamentally new orientation since the former division of life phases—by education, work and retirement—is moderated by life-long learning. The demarcation between school and work is disappearing and a learning society is increasingly evolving.

A further broadening of continuing education and training is needed to cope with the challenges of the new technological style. The revolution in microelectronics powerfully invades all reaches of society and threatens to split it. Because of an increasing cleavage in knowledge the majority is in danger of losing access to the emerging technological style which is going to characterize information society in but a few years.

Supply-side measures—deregulation and technological quasi-corporatism to stimulate technological change—are not enough to solve this problem of knowledge and of the corresponding lack of integrational power of the new technological style. Rather, in addition demand-oriented measures are today becoming increasingly important. If such measures included the redistribution of incomes and state-stimulated demand under the Keynesian societal model, they must now be aimed at reducing the widening knowledge gap observable in the new societal model; only on this basis can the circle of demand and supply be closed by a broader inclusion of the population. That is why educational policy—and particularly policies concerning continuing training—is very important today. The new concept of education paves the way toward the new societal model by creating conditions for the use of new technologies and corresponding life-styles (both inside and outside the sphere of work) by the broad population. Thus, responding to the limitations of traditional education implies addressing continuing education and training. We will discuss institutional frameworks accompanying these measures in chapter 15, which focusses on the cornerstones of the new societal model.

NOTES

1 For this analysis we have worked with a pooled sample of six countries from the Political Action study (the Federal Republic of Germany, Finland, the Netherlands, Austria, Switzerland and the United States), see Zentralarchiv 1979: Study-No 765; for the construction of variables, see Bornschier 1986. The coefficients of variation for occupational prestige and income amount to 0.31 and 0.57, respectively (see Bornschier 1988: 258).

2 In an analysis of the relationships between the aforementioned status dimensions one finds the following common variances (squared correlations): Formal education/ occupational prestige: 0.35; formal education/income: 0.17; occupational prestige/ income: 0.19; formal education/formal authority: 0.05; occupational prestige/formal authority: 0.11 (Bornschier 1988: 258; 1991: 53). A perfect relationship would result in a statistic of 1.0; independence would lead to a value of 0. Sources as given in note 1.

10
The Tortuous Paths of Capitalist and State Evolution

Functions in Social Structure

Few institutions have made as startling a career during modernity as the state. Along with the state, transnational corporations and, of course, schools must also be mentioned. Everywhere, however, the latter are organized by the state and thus form an important aspect of modern state evolution. Why did the state so enormously expand its functions, its power, and the resources it controls?

The modern state has achieved a remarkable consolidation of its sovereignty. The state claims ultimate rule over its territory and has a near monopoly of organized violence (civil and military). In addition, it claims to be the bearer of all rights and the independent creator of laws: state expansion was accompanied by an expansion of the legal system. The state has penetrated ever further reaches of social relationships, as demonstrated by the spread of bureaucracy and administration, resulting in a rationalization of ever greater parts of our lives. The financial reach of the state has grown out of all proportion: it has even taken over money ("bank note" still refers to the originally private issue of paper) until today, about every second franc, dollar, or pound in the Western world goes through the hands of the state, which has created a new, larger grouping—the nation.

In historical perspective, contemporary state functions are not universal: nothing like *the* state has always existed. Max Weber ([1921] 1972: 815) introduced his sociology of the state with the contention that "the state in the sense of a rational unit has only existed in the Western world." Originally there were very different notions of the state. Weber also emphasized the bureaucratic structure of the public administration apparatus and thus neglected somewhat the aspect of the state as a special kind of social power, a point we discussed in chapter 2.

The extension of the group as a source of collective, i.e., social, power has found persuasive expression in the modern state. Functionally, the enlargement of the group to a "state people" supposes the delegation of collective action to an administrative apparatus. The homogenization of a state people and the creation of an in-group-feeling are the basis for the full unfolding of social power. Historically, however, the nation-building process worked in exactly the opposite way: from centers of power towards the gradual integration of the base, i.e., the state people. The modern functions of the state, which mobilize and open up the sources of social power, were not intended by the early nation-builders. They were a long-term and unintended consequence of their particular power interests. Nation-building was a conflictive process that began in Europe with the decay of the medieval social system, a system that was more encompassing than any individual state.

In the course of its conflictive evolution the state was forced by a system that was always more extensive than any particular state, however powerful it may have been, to assume a number of functions. We are referring to the extensive system of economic and economically motivated competition carried out on a cultural basis, whose central dimensions (the striving after efficiency and equality) have already been described. Through this system a similar behavioral logic was externally forced upon both firm and state—the two enterprises of modernity. Thus, the firm and the state were linked to each other in a conflictive symbiosis based on a division of labor typical for the West, whereas in the state capitalist subformation firm and state were brought together in an enormous fusion.

Our perspective differs from most conventional theories of the modern state, regardless of their orientation. Jens Alber (1982: 76f.) has compiled a helpful overview of the theories of the development of the welfare state, based on a cross-tabulation of functionalist and group-conflict models, with pluralist and Marxist models. Common to the functionalist variants—Marxist or pluralist—is their emphasis on systemic necessities without adequately describing the system's expansion and basic structure. In group-conflict models, the structure of the state is either a reaction to democratization and the organization of workers or to the absence of legitimation of political elites. In our view, the general impact of these factors is not supported by historical data, particularly the central role of class struggles in the Marxist sense of the term. Conversely, there is no mention of conflict among groups organized as states (see also Hintze [1929] 1964; Tilly 1985).

Conflict theory becomes more convincing as soon as the actors and the social frame of reference are correctly specified. Interestingly enough, these conflicts and the struggles that accompanied them have led to a marked convergence in the form taken by the Western state. This fact seems to lend support to functionalist theory, but this is only correct in a superficial sense because the modern state is the conflictive result of a certain historical system in which competition is carried out by economic and politico-military means. This conflict can be discerned behind the apparently smooth structural surface of the modern state, which is characterized by its contradictions.

From the beginning, two contradictory forces have faced each other in modern times: the principle of territoriality, established on the basis of social groups within a certain area, on the one hand, and the capitalist logic of the free use of economic opportunities in markets, which are fundamentally trans-territorial, on the other. The tension between these shaped the specific forms of capitalist development and states. The final product of these processes is the various forms of convergence that can be empirically observed. These forms were not, however, the result of a logic arising from the development of individual countries, but rather of the fusion of two different logics in the context of competition fought out by economic and political means.

Historically, nationalism and liberalism have been the two contradictory ideologies in which these two forces have clothed themselves. In the course of its evolution, nationalism, having emerged from the principle of territoriality, led to the creation of a kind of abstract national community. Community and market are neither peaceful in themselves nor conflict-free in relation to each other. The state as the promoter of greater equality in the national arena exacerbated nationalism and conflicts between states in the international arena. In addition, state action helps to maintain differences in wealth along national boundaries and particularly between the core and the periphery; these differences are not merely the result of market processes.

Arguably, the strongest influence on state policy has always come from forces beyond its territory, i.e., in the external system. To be sure, domestic forces, contradictions, and group as well as class conflicts have also been influential. But because of the state's monopoly over violence, however, domestic forces which challenge the status quo have frequently been easier to control than external ones, which is why we still expect the shaping of the state to depend more upon a territory's place in the world system than on constellations of internal political forces.

In this century, the Western state has increasingly specialized in guaranteeing extended equality as this has become a necessary condition for social peace and thus, more significantly, a competitive resource which cannot be sufficiently generated by the market and capitalist firms without state intervention. In other words, citizenship is the dimension along which status is equalized, whereas markets and firms tend to make status more unequal. The modern welfare state therefore differs from its immediate predecessors in two ways: in the substantial extension of security and equality functions and in the guiding role it assumes in the economy.

Equality implies equal opportunities in the sense of equal points of departure, which includes guaranteeing the functioning of the market, formal education, and infrastructure (traffic and communications). In the welfare state, equality means more than this; it refers to equality in the result, which is brought about by social safety nets provided through social security and the redistribution of opportunity (income). These security and redistributive measures are no longer confined to charity but become instead a universal citizenship claim (Alber 1982). Citizenship in turn becomes a central tie binding citizens and state together in a relationship of mutual rights and obligation.

Security created by state policy concerns not only the guarantee and the protection of property rights (including quasi-property rights in the form of social insurance to which citizens are entitled) but the concept of security is also broader than this. The state provides security or protection as a public good—protection not only against external but also internal aggression as an important element of social management. The point must not be overlooked that this kind of "law and order" is the central requirement of any social arrangement, which can be produced either by coercion, i.e., state violence, or legitimately—in other words by the agreement of the citizens to an order guaranteed by the state. This is what characterizes the present evolutionary stage of the Western state when it is compared to its predecessors: sheer coercion and state violence have been increasingly replaced by order based upon legitimacy.

THE CONTRADICTIONS OF THE MODERN STATE

Conflicts of interest are permanent accompaniments of the social process; in any politico-economic regime they are moderated for a time, yet they are never finally settled. The intensity and degree of conflict oscillates sharply between the different phases of the societal model. Even the quite coherent institutions of a regime at the peak of its unfolding phase remain contradictory.

Depending on its function and behavior, the modern state is simultaneously the big equalizer and the big unequalizer. It guarantees the market and thus the point of departure for inequality in the result. With increasing outlays the state manages the educational system which mitigates unequal points of departure but in the end also results in inequality in educational certifications. The state leaves the big, transnational corporations alone. Through their formal organization and division of labor, these corporations create marked inequality while at the same time they generate wealth that is subject to taxation and thus provides an important part of the state's financial power. By redistribution through the provision of collective goods and social safety nets, the state then moderates the inequality it has made possible or failed to prevent in the first place.

Thus, the modern state is full of tension. Its policy imperatives and conflicts cannot be adequately described by reference to the current domestic left-right political spectrum, because the state's point of reference for its actions is a social system beyond its reach.[1] The result is a conflictive configuration of political potentials as shown in figure 10.1. The state must convert contradictions into a compromise if it is to fulfill its function successfully over the long term. Its status in the world system is not only determined by military and political strength, but also by originality and competitiveness in the world market.

If the world system's influence on state action is primarily understood in terms of the interstate system or the world market, then certain difficulties arise in explaining important historical facts. It was not the big political and military powers of early modernity (namely Habsburg Spain and later France) with their ambition of territorial expansion, which took the leading role in capitalist development and successful long-term state development. Rather, this role was played by the centers of world economic expansion, namely Venice, North Holland, and later England. The modern state owes much more to the latter line of development (orientation towards the world market) than to the former (territorial expansion); and it owes much more to it than is currently admitted in history books.

The diagram in figure 10.1 also clarifies "strange" and seemingly paradoxical connections, which run counter to our thinking because research usually addresses the state as if there were only a single kind of state. By their contribution to the solidarity of the nation, certain elements of the political left, for example, in expressing their claim to greater distributive justice (equality in the result), tend towards nationalism, which is conventionally seen as being a platform of the political right.

Because of competition for efficiency on a world scale and of the permanent danger of sliding back in the international race, the state is forced to generate two contradictory collective production factors as prerequisites for economic efficiency and national solidarity. In doing so it faces two claims to equality which cannot be fully reconciled: equal opportunities and equal results.

FIGURE 10.1 The Conflictive Configuration of Political Potentials

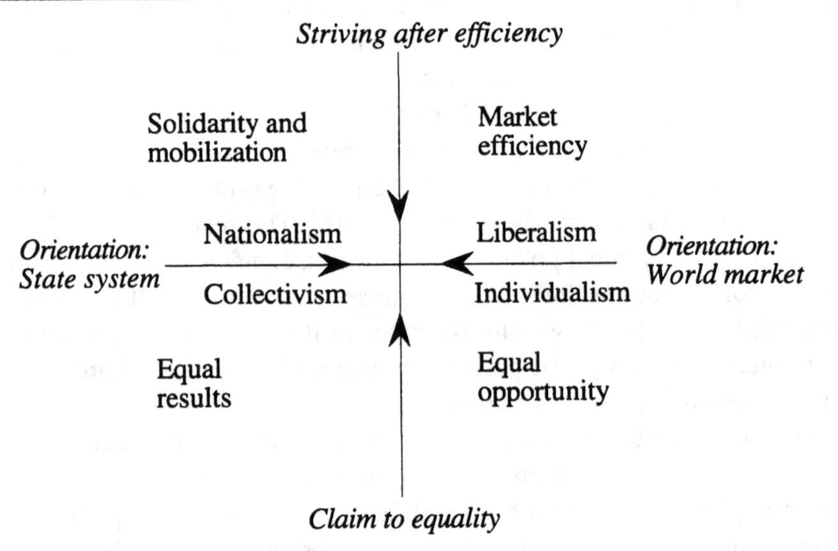

The more the state fosters economic efficiency and the more it consequently spends on the necessary infrastructure, the more it must also invest—if it wants to stay in the race for long-term success—in citizen welfare to strengthen the solidarity of the nation as a player. The need for economic

efficiency being more pronounced at the level of the world economy, the more a given national economy is integrated with the world economy, the more the state must invest in infrastructure while, at the same time, also guaranteeing its citizens equal results. That is why the state's reach expands together with the expansion of the world economy, a result of a systemic imperative and not primarily a result of domestic political dynamics.

From our perspective on the functions of the modern state, persuasive hypotheses regarding the development of state action can be derived. First, the quantitative expansion of the state's role is a function of the expansion of the world market. Second, the level of integration into the world economy of a given state determines the expansion of state action more than any other single factor—even more than domestic political constellation at any given juncture. In addition, this quantitative expansion is to a large degree used to enhance the legitimacy of a given society. Finally, we expect convergence between the states of Western society in the extent and the features of state action; a test of this hypothesis will be presented in a later chapter. The other hypotheses, however, will be scrutinized here.

Quantitative indicators of the expansion of state action clearly show an upward trend during this century. The resources controlled by states—or more precisely: state revenues as a percentage of gross domestic product, the relative size of the public sector—increased from an average of 12 percent to about 25 percent between 1910 and 1970 (Boli-Bennett 1980: 78). For countries belonging to Western core society, the average size of the public sector is even larger: in 1950 it already reached 26 percent, in 1960 29 percent, in 1970 35 percent and 39 percent in 1975 (Bornschier and Heintz 1979; Schmidt 1982: 135). Until 1982, the average size of the public sector in terms of revenues increased to 43.5 percent and the corresponding figure for expenditures is even higher: about 50 percent on average (OECD 1985: 29; see also Nutter, 1978; Kohl 1985).

Parallel to the considerable increase of the relative size of the public sector between 1910 and 1970, world trade grew enormously: during the same period from 79 billion to 373 billion dollars (in constant 1947-49 U.S. dollars). In relation to all sovereign states, world trade of particular countries—exports and imports in relation to gross domestic product, the so-called relative share of foreign trade—is subject to more marked cyclical fluctuations. Only in 1970 do average foreign trade shares reach values existing at the beginning of this century (see Bornschier and Heintz 1978; Boli-Bennett 1980: 99), when there were only about two dozen sovereign states, whereas in 1973 110 countries were included in the calculation. Once again, the foreign trade shares of the Western countries are much higher than the average for all sovereign countries.

From these data it is not obvious whether countries integrated strongly into the world economy (measured by foreign trade as a percentage share of gross domestic product) are also characterized by relatively large public sectors. Empirical research has clearly shown that this is true, however (see Boli-Bennett 1980; Schmidt 1982; Cameron 1978). How exactly does the domestic economic and political adaptation to the world market work? From studies conducted by Guy Peters (1985: 93), we know that the Western countries devote on average about 50 percent of their public expenditures to health, education and income policies, while a study by Swank and Hicks (1985) shows that state intervention usually has a marked and balancing effect on the distribution of household incomes. As a result, distribution (secondary distribution) becomes less uneven than was the case before state interventions (primary distribution). Interestingly, in 1970 the differences in primary income distribution were somewhat smaller than those found after taxes and public transfers for the 13 countries analyzed by the authors. Thus, state impact on the personal distribution of household incomes differs between countries. According to our hypothesis, balancing incomes would have to be a consequence of world market integration, mediated by a greater relative size of the public sector. That this is indeed the case can also be shown empirically (see Bornschier 1988: 286). The redistributive function was not equally important during all phases in the career of the latest societal model. To some degree, growth and redistribution are substitutes in the quest for legitimacy. During the long economic upswing, the creation of legitimacy by way of growth is not difficult, so that redistribution can to a degree be less pronounced. When the model and economic expansion become saturated, however, and particularly when the model enters its crisis phase, redistribution becomes more important (see Bornschier 1988: 309f.).

Thus, the quantitative expansion of states and the expansion of the world economy have occurred simultaneously during this century. Western states, with their orientation towards foreign trade (which must allow for competition in efficiency dictated by the world market) not only had relatively large public sectors during the postwar era, they also used greater shares of their resources to enhance national solidarity as measured by the redistribution of incomes. Thus, an important conclusion from the conflictive configuration of political potentials (see figure 10.1) can also be substantiated by empirical data, and we are able to explain a finding that is well documented in the literature but not the least bit self-evident.

ORIGINS AND CONFLICTS OF MODERN STATE-BUILDING IN EUROPE

Recent research on European state-building has linked political and historical sociology (see Thomas and Meyer 1984; Tilly 1975; Evans et al. 1985; Anderson 1986). According to Charles Tilly (1975: 27), the political project which became dominant after 1500 in Europe consisted of territorial orientation, centralization, demarcation from other social organizations, and a strengthening of the claim to a monopoly over organized physical violence (see also Elias 1969). Tilly summarizes the general conditions facilitating the survival of this special kind of political organization in Europe and its later transformation into nation-states in the following terms: the ample availability of taxable resources, the comparatively protected position of Western Europe in space and time (see also Bloch 1982), a continuous supply of political entrepreneurs, success in war (one would also have to add the impossibility of founding a world empire), the given or created homogeneity of populations, and a strong coalition between central power with the landed elite. Additional features of the state-building process included the enormous costs of and close linkage between warfare, the constitution of armies, and the extension, continuity, and monopolization of taxation (Tilly 1975: 632f.; Elias 1969; van Dülmen 1982: 321ff.).

The process of state-building is normally divided into phases. A frequently cited model was suggested by Stein Rokkan (Tilly 1975: 66ff.; Rokkan 1975) according to whom the fully mature nation-state can be recognized by four features: *central power, standardized culture, political mass participation* and *extensive redistributive policies.* In a developmental perspective, Rokkan identifies the following phases: penetration (the extension of central control over a territory and a population), standardization (the homogenization of administration through the creation of a bureaucracy, and of the population through the creation of the nation), participation (increasing political participation of expanding groups leading to mass participation), and redistribution (the elaboration and coordination of redistributive policies by the welfare state). These phases can be of varying duration or even run together in different state-building projects; development does not have to be linear. Charles Tilly (1975: 37) criticized the old liberal notion of European history as the gradual creation and extension of political rights, with liberty broadening from precedent to precedent. Even before the emergence of the modern nation-state, a multitude of representative political institutions existed, and the original state-builders were not among those who extended or supported these institutions. Quite the contrary: they struggled against such traditional rights. The state did not create representative political institutions, it only channelled and centralized them in a novel way.

Development from Two Entirely Different Origins

In contrast to such developmental theoretical approaches, we advance here a different formulation. We see the modern state as the outcome of a multitude of conflicts, which it still reflects today. These are expressed, for example, by the tension between the state as a community striving for equality and as a power center. The modern state did not develop along a single linear trajectory, here faster, there slower, according to local conditions. The modern state is a hybrid, a mix of different elements which originally emerged at different places in the decentralized European social structure. The apparently unproblematic legitimacy creation is thereby shown up as simplistic.

Economic and economically motivated competition in the European and later the expanding world system was the starting point and attendant circumstance of this conflictive process. Max Weber (1923: 288f.; [1921] 1972: 815) already recognized as much although he did not elaborate on it. For Weber, states and capitalism are interrelated, and the condition of their conflictive dynamic, which promoted state-building as well as the unfolding of capitalism, is the decentralized state system, i.e., the absence of a world state. This conflict selects ever more efficient forms of the state and the capitalist economy. But Weber lays too much stress on the identification of state logic with the interests of national bourgeoisie. The more efficient forms of capitalist development did not appear in places where this identification was strongest, for the most dynamic capitalism was never and is still not national (e.g., transnational corporations). Weber ([1921] 1972: 819f.) saw that mercantilism was more than a mere pact between the state and capital: it was the application of the capitalist mode of operating to politics. Yet this kind of fusion under the aegis of the principle of state territoriality was not to become the historically most successful variant—whether it took the form of the trade-monopolistic mercantilism of the early cities, national mercantilism (France), or state capitalism of this century. National mercantilism was neither the starting point nor the successful model of capitalist development. The starting point lies *before* mercantilism, and capitalist success came despite it. England was not the first capitalist success story, but rather Venice, the Hanseatic League and the provinces of North Holland.

Dissolution and Reformation

The starting point for the formation of the modern state in Western Europe was the dissolution of the medieval order in culture, politics and economics which can be dated to the eleventh and the twelfth centuries.

The cultural expression of dissolution of consensus in the interpretation of the world was the various "heretical" religious movements (Mühlestein 1957) that perceived each person as the responsible bearer of an "inner light," able to illuminate the world by him or herself. Such a conception of the autonomy of the individual put man and woman at the center of the universe and countered the absolutist claims of Rome and the Catholic hierarchy. Hans Mühlestein (1957: 384) stresses that for centuries the impetus behind the growth of the emerging burgher class was the impressive number of radical sects. The rifts within Catholicism also became embodied in the counter-popes: religious rifts thereby already became intermingled with political struggles for predominance. The abandonment of the idea of a devine empire, which—through God's representative on earth—legitimized the notion of a world empire, began long before the challenge that Protestantism presented to Rome.[2]

Political dissolution became manifest when it was realized that the establishment of a world empire was not feasible beyond the European core area. And even there, the struggle between pope and emperor delegitimized this idea and strengthened the autonomous republics of Italy. Empire suffered an early and possibly decisive defeat at the hands of the city as the new unit of political power through the successful revolt of heretical cities in Lombardy, Emilia, Tuscany, Umbria, and particularly Milan against Emperor Barbarossa (Mühlestein 1957).

Economically, such dissolution became apparent in the industrial revolution of the Middle Ages between the eleventh and the thirteenth century when the expanding milling system (the "firms" of the time) opened up unprecedented technological possibilities (see Gimpel 1975; Braudel 1979). The resulting improvement in productivity was in some instances as substantial as the leaps made in our century (see chapter 5). The "original" industrial revolution created whole new sources of wealth not derived from land but based on the use of natural energy sources and processes based on engineering rather than craftsmanship.

These discontinuities left a decentralized social system of old and new elements which had grown out of a common cultural framework but were no longer culturally unified by a central political, economic, and moral authority. It was a decentralized social system with no particular ethic, conducive to the unfolding of that ubiquitous social force, the striving for power. Unfettered by ethics, uninhibited competition for power could begin (see also the state theory of Hobbes [1651] 1962 as well as Elias 1969). In this unregulated environment, two movements surfaced, these being the two big social innovations of modernity in the conquest of power: the capitalist economy and the novel concept of political power, the absolute state (see Anderson 1974). These were not only in opposition to the old social order but also to each other. Their mutual antagonism was based on the fact that the two were based on entirely different justifications for action: individual freedom, on the one hand, and the absolute sovereignty of the state, on the other (see also Coleman 1974).

To this day, these two opposing principles have been the basis for and the permanent accompanying features of modern state-building, their interplay shaping the modern state. Nonetheless, the unfolding of the state project did not take place in only one location: rather, the opposition of these principles and the originally very differently shaped states adopted a zigzag course. Nationalism and liberalism, too, are seen as different expressions of this tension, and became an important source for the shaping of the state in Europe as well as in North America (see also Solo 1985: 75-78).

Modernity is characterized by the rise of political and economic entrepreneurs.[3] The latter were originally long-distance traders in cities which they dominated socially as well as politically. They were motivated by new economic opportunities not dependent on land, i.e., long-distance trade and industry growing out of milling. The political entrepreneurs usually originated from the high nobility or royal dynasties, interested in land and people as sources of their accumulation of power. The land kept people bound to the soil itself or to its owners; the city freed people as is expressed in a proverb from the late Middle Ages: "City air makes you free" (Stadtluft macht frei).

Basically, both groups of "modern" entrepreneurs wanted very similar things: wealth or an empire. Those seeking wealth were not territorial; those seeking empires were. The city, dominated by upper-class burghers, and aristocratic territorial rule were antipodes in a conflictive relationship. Out of these contradictions, two distinct forms of organization arose. The countryside was the origin of the absolutist state, while the city, with all its possibilities of extended political participation, was always characterized by a broader distribution of power, even though there were substantial differences in the development of these differences across space and time. The cities frequently coalesced in decentralized confederations, as was the case for the Hanseatic League. In the long run, territoriality was more successful and able to absorb many—but not *all*—cities. Particularly in marginal regions, economically important cities such as, for example, the Hanseatic members or the Italian cities (in the end only Venice) were able to remain sovereign through alliances. But they remained dependent upon long-distance trade, via the seas, which for reasons of cost were the most important route for world trade. According to Fernand Braudel (1979: chapter 8), capitalism and cities were basically the same in Europe, to which we must add that this was true only for the early stages of capitalist development. The polarity also influenced the debate on economic theory in the second half of the eighteenth century: the French physiocrats saw the land as the unique source of real wealth, whereas the Scot Adam Smith identified the division of labor in manufacture as the more important factor contributing to the "wealth of nations."

It is usually assumed that state-building in Europe started at the periphery rather than the "dorsal spine of Europe" with its broad corridor of urbanization reaching from central Italy to the North Sea (Tilly 1975; Rokkan 1975). This only holds true for the extensive territorial states, though it would be wrong to look for the roots of the modern state only in these countries. Europe also engendered the city-states, the original autonomy of which can be traced back to the corporate sovereignty they obtained by opposing the emperor, which made them only formally and symbolically beholden to a sovereign. The fact that survival became difficult for the cities on the verge of modernity must not be misinterpreted to mean that their tradition was unimportant for understanding the rise of the modern state. As a societal reality this tradition survived until the amalgamation of both principles: for example, the first remarkably early declaration of human rights on the basis of natural rights was promulgated by the city-state of Florence in 1289.

At first, state-building in Europe implied a vast concentration of political power on the basis of an extension of territorial rule, which subjugated small rulers and many cities in a merger wave of great scope. Around 1500, Europe consisted of about five hundred more or less independent political entities: in 1900 there were only about twenty-five of them left (Tilly 1975: 15). As a means for achieving, preserving, or extending territorial rule, war was a permanent feature. Thus, state-building and war went hand in hand. Between 1500 and the Congress of Vienna in 1815, only a few years passed without major wars in Europe (see Bergesen 1985: 320; Levy 1983; Goldstein 1985).

Gerhard Ritter (1967), an authority on the reordering of Europe in the sixteenth century, describes the unfettering of the striving for power in the ethically unregulated system in the following suggestive way. As early as 1500, Europe had entered a completely new situation that had nothing in common with the Christian community of states of the high Middle Ages. "A multitude of very self-conscious states which stressed their sovereignty entered the stage of history. Each of them tried to extend its power as far as possible—by any means, good or bad, without ethical considerations. Europe's foreign policy at the verge of modernity was dominated by Machiavellianism long before the great Florentine even wrote his famous *Il Principe*. At all times the big powers extensively outwitted and deceived their adversaries. The naive and unscrupulous way in which the emerging big powers of the 16th century cheated each other has always aroused much astonishment (Ritter 1967: 21)."

With the Peace of Westphalia in 1648, which followed the Thirty Year's War (actually the first 'world war') the European power structure experienced some peace in the form of the mutual recognition of territories. Continuous testing of mutual power relationships had resulted in a precarious "European balance of power," although it would not last. By this time, the city-states had already lost many of their political and economic advantages. With the exception of Venice, which remained independent but itself became "territorialized" by spreading to Northern Italy, the Italian cities came under territorial rule, like most of the German cities, which were either destroyed or lost their sovereignty.

Only one city area on former imperial territory was strengthened during the Thirty Year's War and no longer had to accept any superior sovereign: the provinces of North Holland. They continued the tradition of the Italian and Hanseatic trading republics. Within only a few decades, between the 1560s and 1609 (the beginning of the twelve-year truce with Habsburg Spain), the

Dutch, who rebelled against the project of the absolutist state, became the leading economic, seafaring and world power (Anderson 1986). It would be wrong to see Dutch leadership only as a result of its "petty spirit." Immanuel Wallerstein (1980) has already compiled evidence of Holland's industrial leadership, which encompassed agriculture, the textile industry, fishing (including processing and conservation), sugar, paper (including printing) and ship-building, one of the most important capital goods industries of that time. Like the earlier seafaring republic of Venice (Lane 1973), Holland combined a number of mutually supporting elements: dominance at sea, a politico-economic regime that promoted domestic capitalism and protected it against the outside, and advantages in industrial production which—by the standards of that time—could be described as mass production.

In the provinces of North Holland, the most fully urbanized area at that time, civilian rule had for the first time in European history created a state structure which was also able to dominate its territory, and become the home of civil liberalism (Ritter 1967). Intellectual and artistic influence was extensive; one need only recall Erasmus of Rotterdam, Hugo de Groot (Grotius), and the Dutch school of painters. Holland became an important haven for refugees, particularly for Sephardic Jews and the Huguenots. In addition, the great spirits of the time were attracted to Holland. René Descartes, the great French philosopher, lived a part of his life in Holland (1629-1649) and wrote all of his works there. Together with Baruch de Spinoza (also resident in Holland) and Gottfried W. Leibniz, Descartes was one of the founders of modern philosophy. Galileo Galilei, one of the founding fathers of modern science, subject to an ecclesiastical interdict for his ideas and later under house arrest in Italy, smuggled page after page of his main work out of confinement to be printed in Holland (Mühlestein 1957: 68). The ancestors of David Ricardo fled from Portugal to settle in Holland. After emigrating to England for economic reasons, Ricardo wrote his path-breaking theory of comparative advantage that advanced free trade. Still, it would be wrong to idealize this first civil state. It was subject to class rule by patricians and was not democratic in the modern sense. Similar to the later "glorious" English revolution, there was hardly any mass mobilization: the Dutch state was mainly defended by mercenaries (Anderson 1986).

In Holland, constitution and state were clearly dominated by civilian elements, despite class rule by patricians. By comparison to the absolutist central state of circa 1600, the decentralization of political power was an absolute novelty: a loose war-time alliance that also lasted during peace time, a kind of organized anarchy rather than a closed state structure—Gerhard Ritter (1967) calls it an oligarchy with two thousand sovereigns. It is true that the princes of the House of Orange represented monarçhy in the republic, but real power was clearly not in the hands of the nobility. Thus, a new form of rule was born in a (small) territorial state: "not a regime of self-confident, inconsiderate dynamics as was the case in the monarchist-absolutist states, but a regime of permanent compromises, of an ever new balance of powers (Ritter 1967: 354)."

Holland as a model modern state is not given proper attention in the literature; instead, interest is centered on absolutism and its sudden end—thereby neglecting two centuries of European state formation. Yet Holland, with its enormous wealth and liberalism had a great and lasting influence on state-building. Even though North Holland did not rule over a large territory, it was *the* world power for about a century, and attracted the attention of the intellectuals of the time as has been shown by Werner Gollwitzer (1972). Holland set standards for Europe, not only because of its monumental economic, intellectual and artistic achievements, but also because it could not be defeated by territorial rulers, i.e., the centers of the absolutism, Habsburg Spain and later France. Here is an important moment. Because of the overwhelming power of Habsburg Spain, everything could have turned out differently: modern state-building and the unfolding of capitalism would then have been set back for centuries and thus there probably would not have been any European advantage at the global level.[4]

Absolutist Europe had to face the burgher's accumulation of power and it responded with mercantilism: only later was a successful, organic compromise found in England, where a new element in capitalist development emerged in agriculture (see Moore 1974 as well as the description in Morus's *Utopia*). In England, capitalism was emancipated from its origins in the urban bourgeoisie.

In its territorial imitators, the Dutch success impelled the marriage between monied aristocracy and the landed aristocracy, which was by no means a generally smooth functioning and fruitful partnership. On the continent, it became barren under the authoritarian leadership of absolutism, national economic development being the mercantilist orthodoxy of the time. The unfolding of capitalism remained constrained because it took place within the enforced framework of a territorially oriented elite whose values rejected trade, industrial activities, and marriages with the bourgeoisie, so that the latter remained a junior partner without political weight. Under mercantilism of the monarchs, fiscal exploitation of economic opportunities and monopolies aimed at bolstering power were the order of the day.

Consequently, the monied aristocracy was strengthened in the cities. Wealth derived from trade, finance and industry was increasingly invested in land. Like the traditional aristocracy, the bourgeoisie began drawing land rents, particularly because big international business, also stimulated by the progressive enlargement of industrial infrastructure, was first monopolized by the Dutch and later the English. Only in England, where agricultural capitalism advanced through a linkage between the ownership of land and money, was the development process different. (See Cain and Hopkins 1986, regarding the role of the aristocracy.)

Whereas the Dutch revolution was mainly an urban phenomenon bestowing increasing weight on trade, financial, and industrial capital, England's revolution—civil war, Cromwell's dictatorship (1642-58) and the ensuing Glorious Revolution, ending with the Bill of Rights of 1689—was the road to power for agrarian capital. Politically, the landowners of the lower aristocracy (gentry) became the dominant class, as shown in detail by Perry Anderson (1986; see also Cain and Hopkins 1986: 503f.). Even though the representatives of trade and finance capital (Whigs) were only the junior partners of the aristocratic land owners (Tories) in parliament, there was a true amalgamation of the two groups—even by recurrent marriages. This linkage of countryside and city—i.e., the remarkable industrial activity in the countryside characterized by a flexible enterprise structure and few legal and customary constraints to capitalist-oriented industry and commerce has also been stressed by David Landes (1969). In our view, this development was substantially aided by the right of primogeniture because this resulted in many children deprived of land or titles amongst the numerous gentry, who were finally to become important in the expansion of the British empire.

The English revolution introduced a new element, the parliament, as the highest constitutional authority. The aristocracy and the bourgeoisie rejected attempts at establishing an absolutist monarchy and created a parliamentary system—during the ultimate phase with some military help from Holland. The victorious, middle-class English parliamentarianism was indeed revolutionary because the notion of individual freedom prevailed over the idea of the absolutist power of the state for the first time in a modern large state. In English philosophy, the state was interpreted as the product of a contract between completely free people (the main theoreticians having been Thomas Hobbes and John Locke). John Locke's (1632-1704) contribution was particularly novel (Locke [1690] 1967), since he perceived the state as something quite pragmatic, an explicit or implicit contract which must bend to the will of the majority (see also Skinner 1978: 18, 41). Even though the law making (legislative) power is supreme, it does not exercise absolute power because it depends on a rational basic consensus.

The theory of the constitutional state developed by John Locke was in line with the legality accepted after the Glorious Revolution, which set out citizen sovereignty as well as the contractual origin and limitations of the King's powers. Law was even superior to the King and Parliament, who agreed upon its inviolability by contract. The idea of the state contract sprang from the roots of this Anglo-Saxon tradition, though England's progressive constitution did not usher in democracy in the modern sense. However, it facilitated the struggle around the extent of the state contract.

At the beginning of the seventeenth century, England probably had about 5 million inhabitants, whereas France, the biggest European country at the time and the center of absolutism, had about 20 million. At the end of the century, England's population was still well under 10 million, whereas France's population had risen to close to 30 million. English leadership would most likely not have been so important for the further development of the state had it not equally represented the center of capitalist development. Superior competitive position in the world economy turned the new state into a model that absolutist-mercantilism of the time had to deal with. In many states, the antithetical ideologies of nationalism and liberalism were embroiled in struggle. The answer to English advantage came from France, namely a radical version of revolution, the groundwork for which had already been prepared by the English example.

Not only did leadership in capitalist development and hegemony in the world system shift from Holland to England, there were also certain important links in political and economic spheres. William III of Orange, the governor of the provinces of North Holland, mounted the English throne in the Glorious Revolution (1688). On the invitation of Parliament he landed in England to promote "Protestant freedom and a free parliament." Capital, too, was pooled to some degree. Dutch capital derived from the large joint-stock companies of the time—the Vereenigde Oost-Indische Compagnie and Westindische Compagnie, in their new forms since 1602 and 1621, respectively—financed similar trading companies in England (Schneeloch 1982). In the wake of William III, the Dutch introduced new financial institutions. From the beginning, Dutch investors were important shareholders in the Bank of England (founded in 1694), and there were intense links between the capital markets of Amsterdam and London (Neal 1987). The Dutch-English mergers have survived up to the present day, for example the shares of two transnational corporations—Royal Dutch Shell and Unilever—are still the common property of the British and the Dutch, a unique situation.

In the history of political thought, it can be established that the opposition to absolutism moved from the Italian cities to Holland and on to England, from whence it spread to the North American colonies returning again to the Continent in the form of the constitution of the French Republic. During the Dutch Enlightenment, Hugo de Groot (Grotius, 1583-1645) referred to the pacifist tradition of the Dutch humanist, Erasmus of Rotterdam, who in turn had been influenced by the Italian humanistic tradition, which had peaked with Francesco Petracco of Arezzo (Petrarca, 1307-1374). For Grotius, the law was superior to the state. He was thus one of John Locke's precursors and a clear antagonist of Machiavellian "realism." According to Grotius, along with Divine Will, a natural law also existed which was not only binding on all individuals but also on states as well as states at war and at peace. This made Grotius the founder of modern international law (ius gentium). In the tradition of Grotius, John Locke introduced these ideas during the English Enlightenment. Toward the end of the turmoil of the English Revolution, Locke moved to Holland because of political persecution (1683-1688). Later on, he followed William III of Orange, who ended the revolution in England. Locke's ideas were taken up in the subsequent constitution.

The disputes between France and England during the eighteenth century concern not only political economy, but also ideas. Hans Joachim Störig (1961: 411f.) writes: "The *discovery of England* by the French can be seen as the decisive event of European intellectual history of the early eighteenth century. (. . .) French enlightenment (. . .) mainly differs from English enlightenment in one point: in its greater radicalism" (our translation).

DIGRESSION: EXTERNAL EXPANSION

So far, we have not addressed Europe's overseas expansion (colonialism), and its significance for state-building and the unfolding of capitalism. What role did colonialism play? We suggest an answer which probably differs from many other assessments: generally, colonialism delayed these processes.

Wealth and luxuries created by revenues derived from dominance have never accelerated capitalism and industry, though they may well have promoted high culture, nobility or aristocratic ideals. The latter are based on consumption and landed property rather than industry, which is why they support the development of a state that does not welcome capitalism. The special case of England will be discussed below.

Since the High Middle Ages and the crusades of the eleventh to thirteenth centuries, the European social system expanded, accelerated by the discovery of the New World and the passage to India. Such expansion was mainly geographical and did not at first concern the populations in the colonies. Wealth flowing from the colonies to Europe is usually seen as the central or at least as an important contribution to the unfolding of capitalism, its importance for primary accumulation being stressed (see Johnston 1981; Korn Liss 1983; Elsenhans 1984). Such a perspective needs some correction. It is true that colonial expansion was of some importance in *one* case of state transformation compatible with capitalist development, but the linkage usually assumed in a simple causal chain is not correct. Rather, a complex process appears to be at work. Here it is important to note that we are referring to the relevance of colonialism for the core and not for the development of the periphery.

To begin with, colonization in terms of dominated populations was comparatively restricted until 1750 despite the large territories that came under European control. Relative to the European population, the population in the colonies only amounted to about 11 percent in 1700 and to about 14 percent in 1750 (Bairoch 1986: 197). Later, there was a sharp increase, which continued until the first half of our century, when the colonial population amounted to 100-200 percent (including the semi-colony of China) of the European population including Russia. Despite decolonization in North and South America, this proportion rose after 1800 because such populous regions as India had been newly integrated. Thus, the significance of European colonization measured in terms of populations did not precede the Industrial Revolution but accompanied it until the present century.

Still, is it not possible that early, albeit restricted colonization facilitated the industrial revolution? There is some evidence against this. Had colonization really been *the* dynamizing factor, one would have expected the Industrial Revolution to have begun on the Iberian peninsula, not in England. In terms of population, the colonial empire of the Portuguese and the Spanish was about ten times the size of the British empire at the beginning of the eighteenth century. In 1720, about a million people lived in the British colonial empire, whereas over 10 million lived in the Portuguese and the Spanish empire (Bairoch 1986: 212). Of the British colonial population, about half were free settlers in North America.

So, why did industrialization and colonialism develop together such that the later world empire of the British would overtake the Spanish and the Portuguese? The answer appears to lie in the two originally contradictory logics of capitalism and the state, whose historical merger brought about the peaks of colonial expansion. Contrary to French experience, this trajectory was not revolutionary.

The founding of a world empire, promoted by the "logic of tribute," is central to state-building in modern Europe. The ruling class of the world empire project, typically aristocrats, was interested in tribute (skimming off), and also in jobs in public administration and the military. Conversely, pure capitalist logic takes an interest in markets and profits ("the logic of profit"). At most there is also an interest in securing and controlling the mechanisms of world trade (oceans, strategic straits, protection of markets in central places and control of piracy). But the control of entire territories and populations is foreign to this logic for reasons of cost.

In fact, colonialization oriented towards territories either aristocratized capitalist centers, as was the case with Venice (at the end with its reach for terra ferma), or strengthened the aristocratic elements of metropolitan centers and thus hampered the unfolding of the capitalist logic, as was the case in Spain and Portugal, where colonial expansion was an initiative of the monarchy. In the long run, industrial and trade capital were neither economically nor politically strengthened thereby. At least in the beginning, Holland's colonial expansion, on the other hand, was not primarily oriented toward territories but rather toward dominance of the seas, the highways of world commerce. Colonial exploitation strengthened the bourgeoisie, who had already taken over power and who were engaged in an almost permanent struggle with the large absolutist territorial states of Europe. It is possible that this capitalist ruling class would have become more aristocratized later. Holland's power base was too narrow to defend overseas territories and hold its military position on the continent, so to a degree the Dutch bourgeoisie merged with the emerging new world power, England.

In another way, however, England demonstrates the importance of colonial expansion for capitalist development and the revolutionary transformation of the state structure supporting capitalism (see Johnston

1981; Korn Liss 1983; Cain and Hopkins 1986: 510ff.). In our opinion, this importance is due to a lesser degree than usually supposed to the effect of accelerated accumulation. England's colonial expansion made possible cooperation between bourgeois capital and the part of the gentry oriented toward agrarian capitalism. The alliance between these two blocs was the basis of the English state following the Glorious Revolution characterized by oligarchic parliamentarianism (Anderson 1986). As a junior partner at home, bourgeois capital was able to concentrate on expanding opportunities in the sea-based world empire. Further, we must not forget that the wealth flowing from the colonies to England did not result in aristocratization—which would have hampered the capitalist logic—because agriculture had already been organized in a capitalist way before. Finally, English capital oriented toward the world economy also had a solid territorial basis in the English state, which guaranteed the protection of economic opportunities against the main contender, France.

To be sure, England's colonial expansion also had a substantial territorial component, and was not confined to control of the oceans and selected central trading posts. After the *first empire* was lost in the American War of Independence, the territorial component grew stronger during the second empire (with India as the new centerpiece), despite the policy of "indirect rule." The importance of the territorial, tributary component is particularly evident in the booming slave trade at the end of the eighteenth century. The rise of Liverpool as the biggest harbor in the world is characteristic of this boom—a rise that came to an end in 1833 when the slave trade was abolished and gave way to a decline which has continued to the present. It is hardly a coincidence that the English Industrial Revolution accelerated during the transition from the first to the second empire.

Since 1750, at the latest, the logic of capital begins to prevail, but a further dual unfolding is still required. On the one hand, the tribute paid in the form of taxes by capitalists must be reduced, and on the other, the state must use taxes primarily for investments. Structurally, the result is a loss of power of the old aristocrats whose incomes were mainly derived from tributes or who worked in the bureaucracy administering large territories. Colonial expansion increased the mass of tribute while taxes could be kept low at the center. Thus, expansion favored a comparatively harmonious, non-revolutionary transition of power from the old to the new elite (see also Cain and Hopkins 1986: 515)—at the cost of politico-economically weak world regions, however. In short: colonialism can be interpreted as the historically functional accompaniment to the victory of the capitalist logic at the center. This hypothesis stresses the importance of colonialism for *political* development rather than *economic* development as is usually assumed.

Tribute from the extension of the colonial empire created a situation in which the old elite did not strongly resist the emerging new economic logic at the center. Resistance was weakest in England and the forces of the opposition were further weakened once the most important colony was lost in the American War of Independence. England's first colonial crisis (1776) may well have accelerated its later industrial revolution, a connection which has not yet received enough attention. Agrarian capitalism had created a capitalist labor market as well as a remarkably liberal and integrated national market in England. Colonial expansion had strengthened the bourgeoisie and increased financial resources. The societal elites were related by marriage and, if they were aristocratic, mostly capitalist. In short, the situation was ready for the new strategy: the capitalization of formerly artisan production on the basis of new energy sources and power machines.

THE RIVAL OF ALBION AND THE SPREAD OF THE TERRITORIAL STRATEGY

While the industrial revolution was in full swing in England, Napoleon was so occupied with his territorial strategy that France definitively lost its links with its much-hated rival, Albion. France, the perfect embodiment of the modern territorial principle (national mercantilism), had never managed to build capitalist leadership because capitalist logic is not territorial and because few alliances of state and capitalist logic are competitive. Thus, despite its formal program, mercantilism never brought about a homogenous domestic market (Anderson 1986).

France was the prototype of the nationalist element in the European state-building process—the bureaucratic, directed model as the most perfected version of the absolutist state. Yet France was unable to catch up with much less overtake England in economic and military rivalry. Because of England's island location, France was unable to prove its military superiority in land wars. Napoleon's continental blockade once again directed all energy into the territorial project.

Contrary to traditional historic assessments, the French Revolution is more the result of France's losing the competition with England than it is the beginning of modern state development. The French Revolution introduced a novelty in the development of the European state: equal rights for all men (although not for women). Even though elements were drawn from America, the republican constitution of France set forth the English idea of a state contract. Thomas Paine, for example, co-authored the American Bill of Rights as well as the French Declaration of Human Rights. Thomas Jefferson, the drafter of the Virginia Bill of Rights and of the Declaration of Independence (1776), surely felt flattered when he recognized his ideas in the constitution of the French Republic.

The explosive mixture resulting from the absorption of French nationalism into further state-building manifested itself in mass mobilization, which had not characterized the earlier Dutch and English revolutions. This mass mobilization surprised Europe and demonstrated its power first in defense of the revolution and shortly thereafter when the populist dictatorship of Napoleon overran the continent. Mass mobilization as a power source spearheaded state development during the nineteenth century. The old European contradictions synthesized into a new whole, whose two principal components were liberalism and nationalism (see O'Brien and Keyder 1978).

The next-to-last element of this synthesis was the provision of the free market in the territorial states and the gradual participation of all citizens with equal rights —though these would still be confined to men for a long time. In Western Europe free trade was practically universal by 1860, thus diffusing an important element of the modern central state. In England, free trade originally arose out of common law and only became more formalized in 1813 (see Alber 1982: 39).

During the second half of the nineteenth century, further elements for the institutionalization of mass mobilization followed, including the right to associate, the founding of trade union confederations and labor parties, decisive extensions of the franchise (Flora et al. 1983), compulsory schooling (see chapter 9) and expanded accountability of the executive branch to the legislative branch of government.

Certainly, these democratizations were in a large part the result of struggles from below. But such pressures, if necessary, were not sufficient. Equally important was the fact that the French Revolution set up a competitive pressure which made such domestic struggles look promising. The fear on the part of national elites that they might slip back in the international competition encouraged them to make concessions. Not only the unfolding of capital but also the labor movement and the unfolding of mass democracy finally profited from this basic competition.

TOWARD THE WELFARE STATE

The final version of the modern state, the redistributive welfare state and state intervention, did not evolve directly from democratization in the nineteenth century (see Ashford 1986). As with compulsory mass schooling, the countries setting norms were not the same as those which had introduced political democracy the earliest or where democratization had advanced furthest. Towards the end of the nineteenth century, political rights of citizenship and welfare provisions were to some extent *substitutes* in the state's quest for legitimacy. It was the German empire which pioneered social insurance with Bismarck's laws (1883, 1884 and 1889) during a decade when, in other places, there was typically a broadening of political mass participation, compared to which political participation and parliamentary accountability remained incomplete in Germany until the Weimar Republic in 1919.

The leaders with respect to political participation of men and/or parliamentary government were countries such as England, Switzerland, France, the Netherlands and Belgium, which introduced social insurance systems comparable to the ones of the innovators only at the beginning of this century or even later (Alber 1982: 28, 39). German standards and extended political participation elsewhere soon obliged the others to follow suit; they already had made up much of the gap by World War I (Alber 1982: 197).

Between the wars, impelled by the political situation, the welfare state became consolidated. According to research findings by Jens Alber, social security systems advanced most rapidly in countries where leftist parties attracted most votes. During the 1920s and the 1930s the welfare state received important additional support from Keynesian management principles for the macro-economy (see chapter 6).

Later, Germany gave its already long-standing advance a new label in the Weimar constitution: the technocratic concept of social insurance was succeeded by the term "welfare state," which only became generally accepted from the 1940s onwards, starting in England (Flora and Heidenheimer 1981: 18f.). The new state function of this century was described quite adequately by Winston Churchill in 1906, when, referring to the social security system of the German empire, he spoke of the need for an "averaging machinery" (Flora and Heidenheimer 1981: 18). After World War II, there was a rapid expansion of the welfare state throughout Western core society, regardless of the strength of labor parties. The late-comers caught up, and the differences between Western European countries investigated by Jens Alber averaged out, "whereby, apart from workers, the unoccupied and marginal groups were increasingly covered. Almost everywhere, subsidized voluntarism vanished in favor of compulsory programs, which frequently encompassed the whole of the population, providing citizen security" (Alber 1982: 197, our translation). As measured by diminishing differences in expenditures for the most important social security measures between 1930 and 1970, the convergence of welfare programs was remarkable. Based on Alber's (1982: 60) data, the coefficient of variation for the differences between thirteen Western European countries decreased from CV=0.75 in 1930 to CV=0.19 in 1970. This does not imply, of course, that differences disappeared (see Flora 1986, 1993).

By the mid-1970s, the countries of Western Europe were allocating on average almost 25 percent of their national resources to public social expenditures, and North America had surpassed the 20 percent level (Flora and Heidenheimer 1981: 5). While the United States was the second country after Sweden to adopt Keynesian management in the 1930s, it became a laggard in the welfare state era after the war. Large-scale, publicly financed welfare programs became a specific West European characteristic in the Keynesian societal model, while Japan managed to obtain remarkable social cohesion for long without much public financing (see chapter 12 on Japan).

Since the dissolution of the last social model began in the 1970s, quantitative as well as qualitative differences in the welfare regimes of Western countries have persisted. Research reveals at least three types of regimes: a conservative, a liberal, and a socio-democratic one (Esping-Andersen 1990). These three arrangements are related to political forces and possess deeper historical roots; they intervene in specific ways in structures of inequality (Esping-Andersen 1990). If differences remain in the shape of these arrangements, we nonetheless underline the remarkable degree of historical convergence of the Western state forms, including the legitimizing functions of welfare. Rearranging but not abandoning this evolutionary outcome is one of the tasks in shaping the next societal model (see chapter 15).

CONCLUDING REMARKS

The tortuous paths of state evolution and of the development of capitalism clearly demonstrate that the modern state originated from diverse roots, but that competition between models enforced convergence. In the encompassing framework of the world political economy it is of little use trying to assign primacy to the political logic of economic action or the economic logic of political action. It seems obvious that the market and economic competition are politically motivated and founded on rules of the game expressing political will (Kohler 1994). As collective goods of this kind cannot be produced by the market, the *political* logic of economic action naturally applies. At the same time, the economic logic of state policy also applies, because collective goods as prior conditions for markets—provided and regulated by the state—compete with each other and have to meet this test (see chapter 3). It is no surprise that such interrelationships resulted in the welfare state, since claims to basic goods and equal opportunity cannot be adequately met by economic dynamics alone (Kohler 1994; Dahrendorf 1992). Unless it meets such claims, capitalism may not last.

Solutions to the problem of creating legitimacy are not without their contradictions, however. Redistribution by the state not only benefits the socially disadvantaged, since market interventions also help certain other groups. Interventions favoring highly motivated small groups can hardly be avoided if the victims constitute a large group, among whom the damage is widely diffused. For members of the large group the impact may only be of limited concern and thus not influence voting behavior. Even under mass democracy the state is not only the big equalizer and guarantor of the "free" market; it also creates inequality precisely because it protects the market, on the one hand, and because of its market interventions in favor of the few and at the cost of the many, on the other. Social welfare—according to Stein Rokkan the final stage of the fully mature Western state—will be rearranged in the future and is not the final Western European innovation. In the European Union, the European state is once again forced out of its national boundaries.

NOTES

1 Other theoretical perspectives put the importance of the traditional left-right-dimension into perspective. It is argued that class cleavage is only one, though in some phases and places the dominating line of conflict. On the other hand, the modern state is also subject to ethnic, religious and ecological lines of conflict (see Lipset 1981; Parkin 1979; Brand 1982; Inglehart 1983).

2 This line of reasoning suggests that "Protestant" orientations among the burghers as one of the impulses for European capitalism were present earlier than the well-known Weberian thesis of Protestant ethic and the spirit of capitalism (see Weber [1920] 1965) would suggest.

3 For these two types of entrepreneurs, see also chapter 3 and Otto Hintze ([1929] 1964). For earlier statements on the driving forces of capitalism and the character of the state, see Werner Sombart (1928).

4 An alternative explanation has been advanced by William H. McNeill (1982: 118f.). He assumes a strong relationship between economic and military efficiency and argues that the complete rationalization of the army (drill and efficient handling of weapons) was an important reason for the success of the Dutch against Spain's superior manpower.

PART IV

CONVERGENCE IN THE WEST?

Our theory predicts a narrow tolerance for variations among Western countries because at the global level a model can only be successful in a given historical situation if it optimizes legitimacy and thus delineates the bounds within which conflicting principles of an epoch will be incorporated into institutional frameworks. For this reason, a process of convergence is postulated, one that is supposed to become more pronounced with each new societal model. In chapter 11 we conduct a systematic examination of similarities within the Keynesian societal model. Different aspects of the institutional orders and of social inequality already discussed will be taken up again in a comparative perspective. However, the theory does not merely predict similarities. By extending our model we are able to explain persisting differences. Japan, the first non-Western country to become a member of the core, is discussed separately in chapter 12. Postwar Japan is a strong test of our theory, which states that Japan's spectacular success was the result of a comparatively higher level of internal legitimacy, which in turn was founded on a more complete anchoring of principles in social structure. Following the chapter on Japan, chapter 13 offers a comparative analysis for longer historical periods and for different societal models. Whereas the historical materials are mainly descriptive, the test of our theory for eighteen Western countries during the postwar era is quantitative.

11
CONVERGENCE AND PERSISTING DIFFERENCES

ARGUMENTS FOR CONVERGENCE

Convergence implies a lot more than mere similarity: it refers to a movement from different positions towards homogeneity (Inkeles 1981). It is not evident why there should be convergence at the global level despite historical, cultural, and political differences. But we do not base our expectations of convergence outside the cultural and political realms. The culture of a societal model, as manifested in its institutions, limits social variation on the condition that the *legitimacy* of an order is a competitive advantage in the encompassing multi-state world system. Legitimacy, in turn, depends upon the compatibility of the distribution of power with the values of striving after efficiency (self-fulfillment, freedom and economic efficiency) and the claim to equality.

Nevertheless, the framework within which this convergence process, which is mediated by conflict, unfolds must be clearly elaborated. The social form of the world system, a specific interrelation between the world economy and the system of states, was already discussed in chapter 3 and will be taken up again in chapter 13. The expectation of convergence must be precisely circumscribed in space and time. Differences *between* subformations of the world social structure persist over time, i.e., between the liberal Western core, the mercantilist-authoritarian counter-core, the dependent societies of the partially Western semiperiphery, and the periphery. This limits social convergence at the global level.

Within Western core society, however, convergence in the direction of very similar arrangements of social structure is to be expected. Yet, in historical perspective Western societies differ substantially as a result of the sequence of societal models which have been discussed in Part II.

Arguments for convergence that proceed independently of cultural and political forces include a Marxist and a pluralist version. According to Karl Marx's argument in "*Critique of Political Economy*" ([1859| 1974) the shaping of social institutions depends on the economic structure. Culture and politics are not autonomous. The pluralist version stresses the "logic" of industrialization (see Kerr et al. 1960; Goldthorpe 1967), according to which modern technology and a differentiated economy lead to standardization, culture and politics again not being autonomous.

Both approaches fail to describe the social system within which economic development takes place. This system is not inaccurately but insufficiently described as "capitalism." The particular historical pattern that took shape in the Europe of modern times is a world environment of economic and economically motivated competition with a decentralized distribution of power. Although the world environment is not subject to direct cultural regulation, the striving after efficiency and the claim to equality are two powerful cultural fundamentals which are rooted in individualism, universalism, rationalism, and pragmatism, i.e., the cultural pattern of modernity.

Despite their substantial differences, Marxism as well as the non-Marxist "logic of industrialism" form part of the encompassing theoretical perspective of modernization theory, which argued most powerfully in favor of social convergence and flowered during the 1950s and 1960s. Yet, modernization theory also allows for other formulations. It suggests a dimension along which all societies can be ranged. Societies at one point of the continuum tend towards similar social and cultural patterns. Convergence is the result of a process of catching up, i.e., of "Westernization." Modernization research thus focusses on such processes of catching up in the world system of the postwar era.

The framework of societal development is inadequately addressed by this theoretical perspective. While cultural aspects do not necessarily have to be neglected, the distinction between *development* as an economic process and *modernization* as a social process remains unclear and thus problematic. On the one hand, one could argue that economic development is the condition for social modernization and thus arrive at the same conclusion as the "logic of industrialism."

On the other hand, modernity can be seen as an autonomous phenomenon. The social ferment of "modernized" actors might create institutions which precede economic development rather than being adjusted to it. But one question still remains unanswered: what is "modernity"? Is it historically accidental, i.e., the diffusion of cultural patterns which emerged in certain centers of *successful* development, or is it the basic goal and reason of history, the logical aim of societal development?

Earlier we derived the elements of "modernity" from basic anthropological constants. The unfolding of these elements would have to be bound to the organization of society, however. Societies which have more fully integrated these anthropologically founded basic values would then become spontaneous models. They would thus be points of reference in a specific historical epoch.

Arguing in this manner poses a problem. Only those societies that not only survive in global competition but are successful can become models in specific historical phases. This, however, would mean that the anthropologically rooted basic values constitute a competitive advantage. Thus we return to our starting hypothesis, according to which the legitimacy of a social order is a competitive resource in the evolutionary process. Such a perspective is open to criticism, which may sometimes be substantiated by robust evidence. But it has the advantage of being able to explain certain phenomena of social evolution which can hardly be elucidated by other approaches.

SIMILARITIES IN INSTITUTIONAL FRAMEWORKS

On the basis of empirical findings regarding various aspects of social structure we will have to examine whether similarities or differences in the West are predominant. In doing this we will, in the sense of a general summary of the evidence presented in earlier chapters, discuss various aspects of the Keynesian societal model and particularly the period of the early 1970s when the model fully unfolded. We will first turn to an examination of social institutions and then go on to discuss the stratification and mobility regime. Finally, the results will be summarized and briefly assessed.

The State

Social security. The consolidation of social security was a cornerstone in the construction of the modern welfare state. Social security was the *differentia specifica* of the past societal model. We have already referred to Jens Alber's (1982: 60) data on the expansion of social security in Western Europe. As measured by expenditure for social security as well as its coverage, convergence is plain enough. The share of the gross domestic product assigned to old-age pensions, health, accident, and unemployment insurance by the thirteen Western European countries not only grew but also converged between 1930 and 1950. We use the coefficient of variation (CV) which is computed as the relation of the standard deviations of different countries to the overall average as a measure of convergence. This coefficient was reduced by more than half from 0.75 (1930) to 0.31 (1950). A similar process of rapid assimilation can be seen in the expansion of coverage of widening segments of the population by social security networks during the same period (CV falls from 0.44 to 0.26).

After 1950 there is continuing convergence in the consolidation of as well as in the expenditures for social security. The aggregation of expenditures reaches its peak in 1965 (CV=0.17) when the societal model also peaks, and remains at this level until 1974 when our data series end (CV=0.19). The coverage of the working population by social security also reaches maximum similarity after 1965 (1965: CV=0.08, 1975: CV=0.07). In thirteen Western European countries, an average of more than four-fifths of the population was covered by social security networks by 1975.

Duane Swank and Alexander Hicks (1985) have sampled similar data for our eighteen Western countries. These data concern public transfer expenditures for pensions, unemployment benefits, accidents and illness, family allowances, social welfare and similar expenditures. In 1960, these eighteen countries allocated an average of 8.2 percent of their gross domestic (GDP) product for these purposes. This increased to 11.6 percent in 1973 and to 15.3 percent in 1980. The corresponding coefficients of variation are 0.32, 0.36, and 0.35, which suggests that differences in the West as a whole are more pronounced than in Western Europe alone. One of the reasons lies in the fact that the public sector differs more widely over all Western countries than within Europe.

If we compare the social expenditures of the state (health, education and income security) with its total expenditures great similarities become obvious.

For 1981, B. Guy Peters (1985) has sampled social expenditures as a share of total public expenditures for nineteen Western countries. They amount to an average of 56 percent and the coefficient of variation has a very low value of 0.11, which implies a high degree of similarity between countries.

Size and expansion of the public sector. In the following we apply a broad understanding of the public sector which includes all statutory charges, i.e., taxes and social security payments. The relative size of the public sector measures all statutory charges as percent of the gross domestic product (GDP). In this century we observe a trend towards increasing state outlays (see also Boli-Bennett 1980; Kohl 1992). Up to 1920 this increase was very steep; between 1920 and 1938 it stagnated, increasing thereafter until 1970. In the OECD area the average state share (i.e., current receipts of government as a percentage of GDP) rose to 38.8 percent in 1975 and to 43.7 percent in 1985 (OECD 1985, 1989).

The data regarding state shares for the time between 1950 and 1975 collected by Manfred Schmidt (1982) can be examined for convergence. From 1950 to 1960 we have computed a decrease in the coefficient of variation from 0.19 to 0.13. By 1975 it had increased again to 0.21 and remained there until 1985 (see OECD 1989). The growing differences between countries since 1960 are a result of imperatives induced by interlinkage in the world market. David Cameron (1978) has already pointed to world market interlinkage as a central explanation for the expansion of the relative size of the public sector. Manfred Schmidt, too, has confirmed the central role played by this externally induced expansion of the public sector. For that reason, the diverging trajectory of state shares points to the need to secure legitimacy by redistribution in the later phases of the societal model—all the more, if a country is strongly linked to world trade.

Similarities in the shaping of the state must not blur the fact that there was much room for variation in the patterning of politico-economic regimes in the West during the latest societal model, ranging from social-democratic consensus to Keynesian class compromise. Typical institutions were not set up with equal success everywhere, as demonstrated by labour politics. In all Western countries the politico-economic regime was confronted with an initial process of dissolution from the 1960s to the 1970s. Yet, true decay was not experienced everywhere, even though it was in the United Kingdom and the United States, both of which adopted monetarism and "Reaganomics." Rather, during the long downswing—the phase before the new beginning—there was greater divergence in development. Divergence, however, is limited to this special phase in the career of models and must not be misunderstood as a general symptom.

In the years ahead we expect renewed convergence, which can already be seen in fresh data. In 1991, the European Community had a state share (all taxes and social security payments as percent of GDP) of 40.1 percent, Japan of 30.9 percent and the United States of 29.8 percent. The corresponding figures for 1970 were: 34.4 percent, 19.7 percent and 29.2 percent (Commission of the European Communities 1993: 136).

Legal enactments. In a discussion of state development mention must be made of juridical reform, since the state claims superior authority over the process of legal enactment As an example we can take the reform of marital law because it shows very clearly the broader mooring of the fundamental principles of social structure. In almost all Western European states marital law was revised during the early 1970s. Such reforms at the end of the unfolding phase of the model we have called legislative reform during the peak phase. In addition to the fact, that from an international perspective such reforms were not isolated, the similarity of principles and their legal expression are remarkable (Stoffel 1985)

Educational Institutions

Convergent educational developments have been scrutinized by Alex Inkeles and Larry Sirowy (1983). They do not distinguish between subformations in our sense but examine all countries. Their arguments concerning "rich countries," "advanced countries," or "Western Europe" can be applied to an assessment of all of Western core society. They use very sophisticated criteria and present data on the ideal, legal, and structural frameworks of the educational system, including educational expenditures, schooling rates at different grade levels, average size of classes, educational opportunities for both sexes, and the relationship between access to higher schooling and social origins.

In all these spheres there was progress, the principles of modern social structure being increasingly moored in the educational system. Here, we shall not address the question of how far this progress went in particular spheres. Our interest is in convergence within Western society. Inkeles and Sirowy also use the coefficient of variation as a measure to assess convergence. Their central conclusion from extensive material is that "the overwhelming weight of evidence, both quantitative and qualitative, indicates that the tendency for national educational systems to converge on common structures and practices is pervasive, deep, and often accelerating. Such convergence is manifested at all levels of the educational system, and it affects virtually every major aspect of that system" (Inkeles and Sirowy 1983: 303).

Formal Organization

Formal organizations can be found in all spheres of modern society—in public administration, in associations, and, naturally, in economic enterprises, the latter being no doubt the most pervasive. In view of the millions of firms in Western countries, one is, at first sight, not inclined to make generalizations about their structure. But their large number is misleading, since economic activity is largely concentrated within a comparatively small number of corporations. At a rough estimate one might say that some 1,500 corporations produce about half the total value added in Western countries. Cross-national studies on firms are not as frequent as the comparatively small number of leading firms might suggest. Still, a systematic attempt at comparison exists in the works of Cornelius Lammers and David Hickson (1979) and David Hickson et al. (1974).

Organizational structures. An important paradigm of comparative organizations research takes context or situational factors as a starting point. The relevant research has been summarized by Michael Wollnik (1980) and Herbert Kubicek and Alfred Kieser (1980). In many studies structural features such as the number of hierarchical levels, specialization between functional spheres and work roles, standardization of work procedures, and decentralization of decision-making have been identified as depending closely on situational factors. In this connection, scale (measured by the number of employees) and technology (for example, degree of integration and automation of work procedures) play the central and determining role. In all systematic cross-national comparisons organizational structures proved to be very similar (Hickson et al. 1974). Alleged differences seem to result from limited comparability of samples (see for example Child and Kieser 1979).

Control in organizations. On the basis of a subjective method of determining the distribution of control in organizations—the so-called control graph method by Arnold Tannenbaum—several comparative studies have been conducted (Tannenbaum and Cooke 1979). They can be summarized as follows: the distribution of control in organizations follows a universal pattern of hierarchical grading. The control graph method distinguishes between the overall volume of control in organizations, the steepness of the decrease of control from the top to the bottom, and the discrepancy between ideal and actual distribution of control.

The more participatory an organization, the more even is the distribution of control, although gradation still exists. The ideal and actual distribution of control are always remote from each other, since hierarchy always creates problems of legitimation. Further, criteria measuring the efficiency of organizations (satisfaction, morale or loyalty of employees, productivity, efficiency and profitability) are often positively associated with the *overall volume* of control. Conversely, there is no general relationship between steepness in the distribution of control and efficiency (Tannenbaum and Cooke 1979). Formal organization as an instrument of efficiency thus implies an increase in control but not necessarily a specific distribution of such control.

Technological styles. Cross-national studies of formal organizations must take into account the diffusion of the technological style and its specific features in various branches of the economy. The technological style generates a particular pattern of hierarchy, division of labor, and decentralization, which while universal also depends on scale. Yet, between different technological styles, these scale-specific patterns differ: the relation of the scale-specific administrative component (clerical and technical employees) to production workers differs substantially between measurings for the periods 1907 to 1933 and 1950 to 1970 (see figure 5.1). Due to the change of technological style in this century the overall exercise of control in organizations has increased, but the control curve has become less steep.

For comparative organizations research this implies that empirically measured cross-national differences must not be attributed hastily to the specifics of national cultures. First of all, one must control for the technological style, since some countries are pioneers and others followers with regard to the style's diffusion. In addition, one has to control for the scale and branch composition in comparisons, because the features of technological styles vary according to scale and branch. Finally, the question of whether the enterprises are independent or part of an overarching corporation must be addressed. Studies which control rigorously for these dimensions are lacking. Still, the numerous comparative studies concerning structural features of organizations have shown a multitude of patterns which must be considered as universal within the West's technological style. Our conclusion on the basis of existing research is thus that similarities in the shaping of formal organizations are indeed extensive.

Stratification and Mobility

The basis for the prominence of stratification and intergenerational mobility research lies in the legitimation problems created by social inequalities. Investigations of this topic can be interpreted as testing whether the ideological claim of Western society regarding the distribution of social opportunities has really been met (Bornschier 1986, 1991). They address, on the one hand, the degree of inequality of the positional structure (stratification research) and, on the other, equal opportunities in the filling of these positions over generations (vertical mobility).

Studies on mass mobility over generations usually concern occupational mobility. From the beginning a problem presented itself: how to distinguish changes in the occupational structure and the "actual" openness of society. All observed mobility between the occupational classifications of children and their parents is usually broken down into two components: "pure" mobility (also called circulatory or exchange mobility or social fluidity) and structural mobility. The latter is the result of differing distributions of parents and children in the occupational classifications observed. In this connection, structural mobility is often also called "enforced" mobility—a somewhat unfortunate term if one tries to interpret mobility as a source of legitimacy, because an increase in equal opportunities can also result from a multiplication of opportunities.

Unfortunately, such structural mobility as can be derived from intergenerational mobility matrices does *not* represent the modification of the occupational structure. The latter influences structural mobility but does not represent it. In an attempt to overcome this unsolvable problem, research has often ignored structural or enforced mobility in the matrices of intergenerational transition to study only "pure" mobility. Of course, this implies some lack of realism in the research question: how unequal *would* the distribution of opportunities be if there *had not been* any structural mobility?

Change of occupational structure is an important source of overall mobility opportunities, however, even if we cannot study it adequately with current techniques. This is of particular importance, because change of occupational structure does not occur continuously over time and does not reach countries simultaneously (Bornschier 1983a). On the one hand, change depends upon the discontinuous spread of the technological style. On the other hand, the pioneers in the spread of the technological style are affected much earlier than most of the followers, who are still experiencing change when it has already ended elsewhere. Thus, the extent of intergenerational mobility becomes a much more discontinuous variable than would be expected on the basis of measures of "pure" mobility. This is important for the creation of legitimacy of the social structure, and would still be relevant even if "pure" mobility were constant. The industrial pioneers initially have advantages, which they subsequently lose, while the followers are still enjoying this additional source of legitimacy when it has long stopped working elsewhere.

The empirical findings concerning occupational mobility show that Western society was "open" in the sense that a majority of its populations were intergenerationally mobile during the peak phase of the Keynesian model (at the beginning of the 1970s). The differences between countries are small (Bornschier 1986). Of course, mobility over short social distances is much more frequent than mobility over long ones.

Occupational mobility in the lower and middle reaches of social strata may be very similar in different countries, but there could be differences in the intergenerational access to the upper strata. In fact, it can be shown that openness in the upper reaches of Western society is much less pronounced than is suggested by the findings concerning broad mass mobility: this is a well known general feature of Western society. What at first sight are dramatic differences between countries can be traced back to certain general regularities. To claim substantial differences would mean basing the assessment on methodological artifacts. The recruitment (in the narrow sense of the word) of the elite in Western society is also characterized by an opening up for the middle and lower strata (see Bolte and Hradil 1984; Wildenmann et al. 1982; Heath 1981). Even if the relative opportunities of children from lower social origins are poor, recruitment of the elite from the middle and lower strata has important consequences for the way the elite perceives itself: the majority does not originate from the upper strata.

Apart from processes of mobility, research has always been focussed on actual stratification structures. Elsewhere we have studied the stratification patterns for a merged sample of Western societies during the peak of the Keynesian societal model in detail (Bornschier 1986, 1991). The sample included six countries (Austria, Finland, Germany, Netherlands, Switzerland and the United States), and for some analyses data on Italy was also used. It thus covered 60 percent of the population of Western core society.

For Western society during the period 1973-75 a picture of only loosely structured social stratification emerged, although certain status distributions exhibited a high degree of inequality. The generally weak "inheritance" of social positions is particularly noticeable. One must of course draw different conclusions for other parts of the stratification, but here we are only interested in the basic tendency of the general stratification system. Tests for country-specific differences in the stratification and mobility regime revealed only minor differences (Bornschier 1986, 1991)

By and large, the differences revealed in stratification between the six countries are not substantial enough to advocate treating them individually. On the contrary, one can conclude that there is a single underlying basic regime of stratification, despite local differences in culture and history. The country-specific effects estimated in the pooled sample, albeit significant in some cases, add only modestly to an explanation of the data (Bornschier 1986, 1988: 329-343).

EXPLAINING PERSISTING DIFFERENCES

This overview of different institutional frameworks and processes of convergence emphasized similarities. Of course, Western countries do not become identical nor are their noteworthy differences absent. A case in point is the level of political and industrial conflict, which is, despite similar patterns over time, quite different for Western societies (see Bornschier and Nollert 1994). Our theory not only allows us to predict convergence but also persisting differences. In order to demonstrate this we must discuss factors which influence and modify the mechanisms which we have discussed so far. This will lead to an extension of the explanatory model. Several cases will then be discussed in order to illustrate that what seems to be a deviant case finds an explanation within the extended model.

Factors that Produce Differences

Three groups of variables in particular seem to shape the societal model: the influences of the world system; those which we place under the heading "institutional legacy;" and, finally, particularities related to the other two factors which also possess historical components, i.e., historical framework.

In the world political economy markets, power and state action interact. Under more or less functional world economic institutions (the exceptions are the years after 1929 until Bretton Woods, 1944) the world economy acts as a transmission belt for economic cycles which affect all market economies. With reference to the influences of the world system, two concepts are of importance: dependence and dominance. Dependence upon the world political economy results in external pressure "to close ranks" to face world competition. Dominance in the world political economy is reflected in the ability to set rules and to apply force. Hegemony is a special case of such dominance. To summarize we can say that hegemony, at least in our perspective, is dominance that is felt to be legitimate. Hegemonic positions induce the hegemons to neglect the internal legitimacy on which their original advantages, and thus their way to the top, rested. The U.S. dollar as world currency partially facilitates a life on credit for the United States, which can pay for surplus consumption in its own currency. Further, a hegemonic power can deflect internal conflicts by diverting them to the international system.

Apart from the world system, the "institutional legacy" as a limiting condition affects the shaping of the societal model. By listing such factors we are by no means offering an ad hoc explanation for differences which must be taken into account because of their discernible influence.

A first point is the pioneering or follower role in the development of the technological style. As in the first societal model during which Britain was the clear pioneer, there was an evident leadership role for the United States during the third societal model. The formulation of a new technological style occurred much earlier in the United States, and during the interim recovery phase of the 1920s this process had already diffused more broadly than elsewhere in the West. The discrepancy between the requirements of the new style and the lagging response in the form of a new regime may have been one of the reasons for the particularly severe economic crash of 1929 in the United States. A second complex refers to the consequences of war. In comparing the core countries we observe huge differences in the disruption of societal development caused by World War II, which favored a closer coupling of style and regime formation in societies which were severely affected (Germany, Japan). In addition, status as a colonial power, or entanglement in colonial wars (in Indochina and Algeria) was of particular importance for France.

Finally, one must address cultural and constitutional particularities which affect the shaping of politico-economic regimes. Thus the power distribution between parliament, government, and head of state varies greatly amongst Western societies (for this and the following see Schmidt 1983, 1992; Hartmann 1983), which influences the formation of a coherent and stable politico-economic regime.

There are two basic forms of parliamentary democracy: the parliamentary system, which originated in Britain, and the presidential system founded in the United States. France's Fifth Republic is a mix of both types—a parliamentary-presidential hermaphrodite, since the president can appoint and dismiss the prime minister and the party affiliation of the president does not have to coincide with the majority in the parliament. In addition, there is consociational democracy (Lehmbruch 1992: 206ff.) which is found in Switzerland, Austria, the Netherlands and Belgium. In the political system of Switzerland, which basically belongs to the presidential type, the Bundesrat (Council of Ministers) is a comprehensive body, i.e., the head of state, government, and head of government all in one. The majority principle is not the central-decision making mechanism, but rather techniques of compromise and mutual accommodation. The participation of important minorities in government as well as proportionality in appointments to public offices is typical of Switzerland.

Consociational democracy and neocorporatism are not identical. It is true that consociational democratic systems are more or less neocorporatist by the recruitment of organizations into politics, but the neocorporatist systems of Scandinavia are not consociational democracies. Rather, their political culture is characterized by a deep distrust of broad coalitions, which leads to favoring minority cabinets. Neocorporatist and consociational democratic systems prevent the fragmentation of political culture and thus favor continuity in the shaping of the societal model. However, these systems limit the access of groups with weak electoral support to the power circle. Issues which have not been put on the agenda by the governing groups (the political power bloc) thus lead to political opposition outside established party channels. For that reason and despite the prevalence of neocorporatist and consensual democratic elements the increase in political protest and violence in Switzerland has been comparatively sharp because leftist parties, which take up similar issues in other countries, for example in Sweden, are only marginally integrated into the power circle. Apart from this and due to its particularities, the Swiss "committee system" is very suited to guarantee the continuity of the political structure and thus the consolidation of the societal model.

In the United States there is a separation of powers because executive power and Congress are independently elected. In the legislation process, however, executive power and Congress must work together. The Congress can and does introduce legislation on many issues quite independently of the president. In such cases the President must endorse or veto. Also the president may propose legislation, but has to introduce it via members of Congress. Yet, the Congress does not endorse all of the President's propositions. In parliamentary systems the government would be overthrown in a comparable situation. In the United States, the search for compromises and negotiation between president and Congress—itself bicameral, composed of the House of Representatives and the Senate—are necessary. Both chambers have similar rights in legislation (except that the House has sole power to introduce legislation to raise revenue for government, Section 7 of the Constitution). Furthermore, the difference between US and European parties has to be mentioned, i.e., the absence of party programs in a European sense, and the complete absence of party discipline in terms of voting or positions on issues. The aforementioned elements of the political system can easily lead to blockages but also to abrupt changes if charismatic presidents take office. The outset of the past societal model, Roosevelt's New Deal (1932), is a case in point. Eisenhower in 1953, Kennedy in 1961 and Reagan in 1980 are examples of later abrupt changes. Apart from the assumption of the hegemonic position in 1945, this seems to have been of considerable importance for the continuous but later also less complete unfolding of the regime in the United States.

A further important institutional influence originates from the administration. In the United States, for example, the federal administration includes "(...) a conglomerate of various agencies which, in part, are structured by departments (equivalent to the ministries in parliamentary systems) and, in part, enjoy independence." (Hartmann 1983: 186) In addition, the American administration is not staffed by a higher civil service. About 800 political officials are appointed by the President, among them the Secretaries (ministers). These appointments have to be agreed by the Senate, which is normally done. A further 2000 political officials are appointed by the Secretaries, i.e. indirectly by the President. Contrary to Western Europe and particularly Japan, the body of senior officials does not lead to continuity because it changes with each new President. In Europe, on the other hand, tenured civil servants staff the ministries and in Japan one may even say that the legislative and governmental process is dominated by an elite senior civil service which cooperates closely with economic bodies.

Finally, election procedures must be discussed (Nohlen 1992: 519f.). In most of the Western industrial countries (15 out of 23) elections are held on a proportional basis. Thus, parliamentary representation mirrors more or less voting patterns. The less frequent majority rule, on the other hand, is aimed at producing strong governments and thus tolerates a disproportion between votes and deputies. Such a disproportion may be even more substantial in case of relative majority rule in single-candidate constituencies (United Kingdom, Canada, New Zealand and the United States).

One can thus observe much variation in the political structure of Western society. As Jürgen Hartmann (1983) puts it: "Western Europe, the United States and Japan are variants of democratic-capitalist industrial societies," but these variants are by no means neutral with reference to the shaping of the societal model and thus for the economic and conflict cycle.

The Extended Model

Figure 11.1 summarizes the interaction of these factors with the societal model and the ensuing consequences: the aforementioned frameworks influence the societal model—characterized by normative elements, technological style and politico-economic regime—which in turn has effects on the economic situation and the kind and level of social conflict. These influences depend on the career of the societal model. During the formation and unfolding phases basic consensus predominates but there is also inconsistency between what is and what should be, i.e. conflict of ends. Under a functioning societal model, the economic situation improves despite short-term economic fluctuations. Peaceful conflicts decreasing over time predominate. During the saturation and dissolution phases dissent and growing social disorder arise. As a result of the limits and dissolution of the model and beyond short-term cycles the economy is adversely affected and conflicts (which increasingly include value conflicts) not only increase but also become more violent.

Our discussion has led to a further complication of our earlier explanatory model summarized in figures 7.1 and 7.2. The complicating factors are shown and summarized in figure 11.1. In the world political economy, the world market and state action interact as mentioned above. In figure 11.1 this relationship is indicated by arrow 1.

FIGURE 11.1 The Extended Model

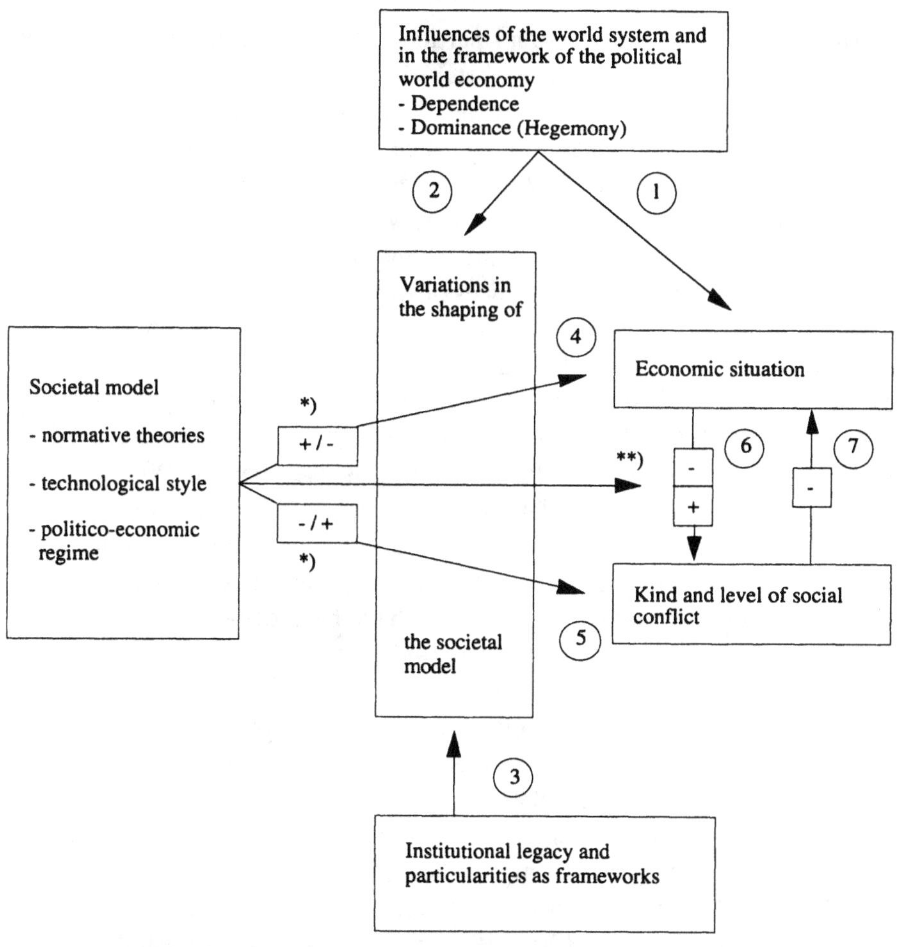

*) Depending on the phase in the career of the societal model
**) Depending on the character of the societal model

In the influences of the world system two variables already mentioned are of importance: dependence and dominance (arrow 2). Dependence upon the political world economy results in external pressure to close ranks in order to compete. Dominance, on the other hand, is reflected in the ability to set rules and exert power. Hegemony is a special case of dominance. Examples of studies which examine arrow 2 include research which correlates the degree of external trade interlacing with characteristics of the political structure as, for example, neocorporatism. This case has been exposed for some time in the literature (Cameron 1978: 1260, Schmidt 1982: 93, Katzenstein 1985, Nollert 1992).

How institutional legacies and particularities affect the shaping of the societal model has already been sketched out. In figure 11.1 these effects correspond to arrow 3. The power distribution between parliament, government and head of state, for example, varies substantially in Western societies. Such institutional differences affect the formation of a coherent and stable politico-economic regime. Further, we have mentioned the leadership or follower role with reference to the technological style and the status as a colonial power as well a consequences of war.

The influences on the shaping of the societal model in turn affect the economic situation and social conflict. Arrow 4 points to the fact that different elements of the societal model have their effects on economic growth. In the neocorporatist, Keynesian societal model the expenditures for social security would be an important variable. For the post-war period, Walter Korpi (1985) has shown a positive relationship between social security expenditures and the growth of per capita wealth as well as productivity. Relationships between neocorporatism, low rate of unemployment, low rates of inflation and high real growth rate of the economy have been demonstrated by Kerry Schott (1984: 55) and Michael Nollert (1992).

Different shapings of the societal model thus subdue social conflict to varying degrees (arrow 5). We observe inversely proportional relationships between political conflict and neocorporatist forms of interest mediation, different regulations of labor relations, the extent of income redistribution and the degree of social openness as measured by differing attainments of equal opportunities in intergenerational occupational mobility (Bornschier 1989: 228; Nollert 1992). In a comparison of highly industrialized countries during the post-war era, Douglas Hibbs (1987: 67) finds that state expenditures for civil purposes and participation of the political left in government reduce strikes. Michael Nollert (1992) shows that neocorporatist countries were able substantially to limit the increase in conflict at the peak of the societal model (see also Bornschier and Nollert 1994).

Finally, we propose to discuss the relationship between the economic situation and the kind and level of social conflicts (arrow 6). Without exception, cross-national as well as time-series studies for countries report negative relationships between economic growth rates and indicators of social conflict (see Hibbs 1973: 38, Zimmermann 1988: 67, 1989: 188 and Jagodzinski 1983: 36). Jagodzinski (1983) summarizes: "Economic growth does not increase the risk of internal political conflicts. On the contrary, it has a weak negative effect on collective protest which, however, was not very robust." Our own studies of Switzerland also show negative relationships. Years of strong economic growth are years of below-average political conflict. This is also true for conflicts at the individual level like suicide rates.

Does economic growth have destabilizing consequences over the long run? Manuel Eisner (1991) observes that individual conflict increases late in the economic upswing phase. His empirical material suggests that the beginning of the neocorporatist, Keynesian societal model reduced the long-term destabilizing effect of economic growth. The middle arrow in figure 11.1 (**), which originates in the societal box can thus be understood as follows: depending on the integrational power and social compensations, a functioning societal model is able to reduce, or at least delay, the long-term conflict-enforcing effect of economic growth induced, for example, by destabilization and growing social disparities as a result of growth surges. Conditions for this were most probably only present during the neocorporatist, Keynesian societal model.

The negative feedback of social conflict on the economic situation (arrow 7) will be discussed in more detail in chapter 13. There exists a fairly broad body of evidence from cross-sectional studies that the level of social conflict is negatively related to measures of economic growth. Less frequently has the causal hypothesis that the level of social conflict reduces subsequent economic growth been tested. Such a causal effect, however, has been established for eighteen core countries by employing the method of lagged cross-panel regressions (see Bornschier 1989).

Illustrations from Deviant Cases

In what follows we will briefly turn to some case studies the particularities of which we attempt to explain with the model. We will first treat the United States' deviations from the growth pattern of other innovators of the latest societal model which we explain through its reach for hegemony and one institutional particularity. We then go on to contrast neocorporatist countries with others by reference to conflict management. Further, the example of The Netherlands shows that changes in external pressure induced by early participation in the Western European integration process demobilized Dutch neocorporatism and thus also affected the chances of conflict limitation. Following this, we will point to particularities resulting from the consequences of war, examples including Germany and Italy. Finally, we will briefly discuss an institutional explanation of Great Britain's stop-and-go policy.

The Example of the United States: The Reach for Hegemony

Let us first take another look at figure 7.1 in chapter 7. If the unfolding of the politico-economic regime is checked and later perhaps continued, but the regime remains comparatively incomplete, we may expect a bi-modal distribution of economic growth rates (apart from the interim recovery phase). The case in point for the period after 1933 is the United States whose growth pattern can be compared to that of the other two democratic pioneers of the 1930s, Switzerland and Sweden.

In figure 11.2 the typical uni-modal distributions of growth rates for Switzerland and Sweden with peaks around the mid-1960s can be observed. The pattern for the United States is quite different. During the 1930s and the 1940s, the United States had very high growth rates which were clearly supported by the new technological style and institutionally flanked by the New Deal. Growth diminishes markedly during the 1950s and reaches a new, although less pronounced peak, around 1960. Other data show that the first growth peak cannot be attributed to war production alone. As early as 1932 and until 1941, when the United States was caught off-guard at Pearl Harbour by Japan and thus entered the war, industrial production increased substantially (Bornschier 1988: 161).

We have already outlined our explanation: hegemonial position favors a comparatively weak internal unfolding of the politico-economic regime. If, during the career of the societal model there is—as in the case of the United States—a hegemonial break-through, then the original path is depleted. The renewal of New Deal policies in Kennedy's New Frontier program and in Johnson's Great Society came late and remained weak if compared to the welfare state oriented societal model in the European countries. In the case of the United States there was another factor already mentioned under the heading of "institutional legacy." The presidential system is not so useful for guaranteeing the continuity of the political structure and thus for the formation of the societal model.

FIGURE 11.2 Growth Patterns of the Innovators Sweden, United States and Switzerland, 1933-1979

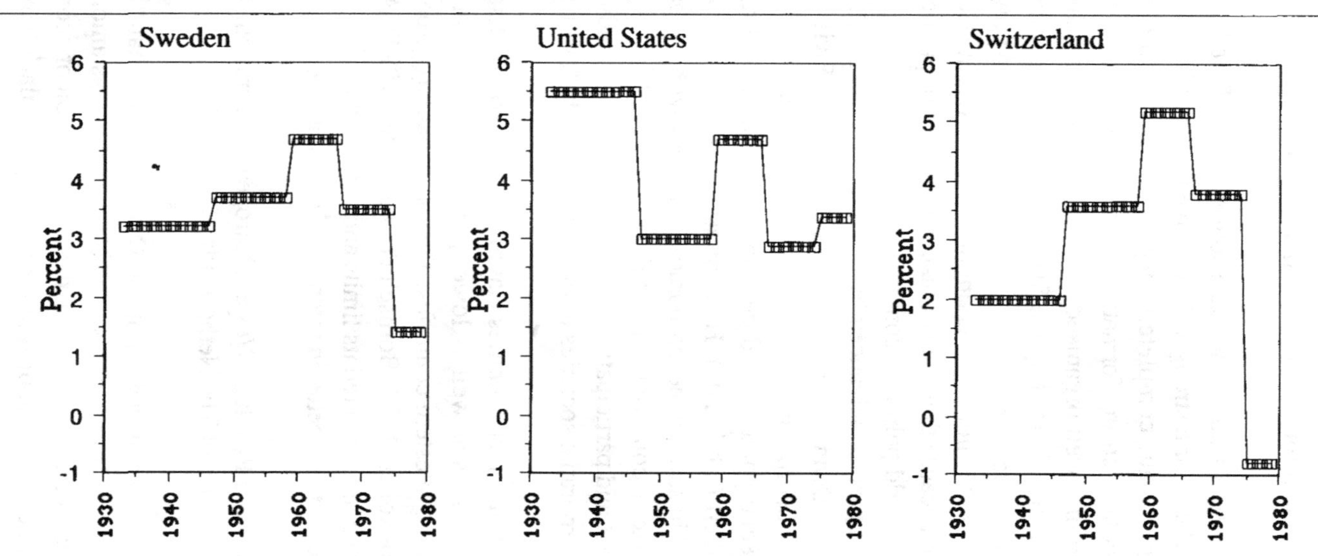

Note: Average yearly compound growth rate of the real gross domestic product in the following periods: 1933-46, 1947-58, 1959-66, 1967-74, 1975-79. The source of the basic data is Maddison (1982).

The Case of the Strongly Neocorporatist Countries

A high degree of integration into the world economy (e.g. Sweden, The Netherlands and Switzerland) or a strong will to move upwards in the world political economy (e.g. Japan, completely dependent on imported raw materials) favor a particularly strong formation of the societal model which is—inter alia—reflected in a well organised mediation of interests through associations, initiated and coordinated by the State, called neocorporatism in the literature. Small core societies which belong neither to a powerful politico-military pact (NATO) nor to an economic treaty system (EC) are under particular pressure because they cannot take part as "junior partners" in the power of blocs in the world political economy.

According to the classification advanced by Michael Nollert (1992: 201), Austria, Sweden, Norway, Denmark, The Netherlands, but also Switzerland and Japan are strongly neocorporatist. There is a close, yet scarcely known relationship between neocorporatism and dependence on the world market again confirmed by Nollert (1992: 206). He contrasts the course of conflict for the period 1948-1982 in strongly neocorporatist countries with the pattern for the remaining Western countries. As indicators of conflict he uses collective political protest and participation in labor disputes: both indicators show the strongly neocorporatist societies to have substantially lower levels of conflict.

Figure 11.3 demonstrates that countries classified as neocorporatist have lower collective protest values as well as lower participation rates in labor conflict than the remaining Western countries. This is particularly true from the mid-1960s (see also Nollert 1992; Bornschier and Nollert 1994). As the societal model increasingly encountered its limits and entered the crisis phase, the neocorporatist countries fared better in internal conflict management.

Change of Corporatism as a Result of Western European Integration: The Case of The Netherlands

Let us now turn to a closer examination of the Dutch case. Gerhard Ritter (1989: 168) states that "apart from Austria, The Netherlands was among the countries in which neocorporatist elements in the determination of economic and social policy and integrative labor relations were particularly strongly institutionalized" (our translation).

FIGURE 11.3 A Comparison of Political and Labor Conflict in Strongly Neocorporatist and Other Core Countries, 1948-1982

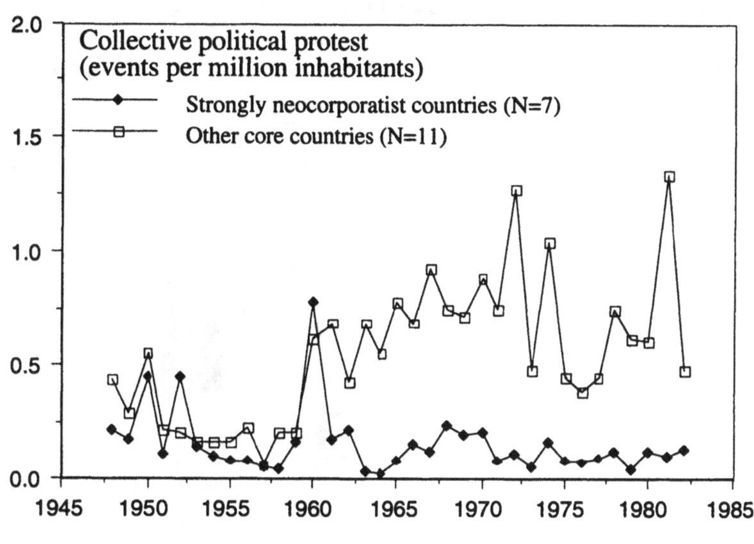

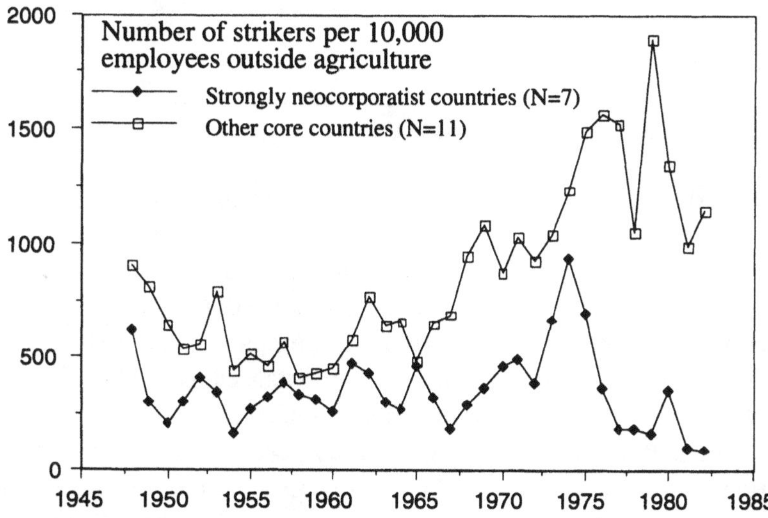

Notes: The classification of countries is taken from Nollert (1992: 201). As strongly neocorporatist are classified: Austria, Sweden, Norway, Denmark, Netherlands, Switzerland and Japan. They are contrasted to Finland, Belgium, Germany, Ireland, France, Britain, Italy, USA, Canada, Australia and New Zealand. Data for collective political protest are from Taylor (1985), for strikers they were collected by Michael Nollert from International Labour Office sources. Procedures: the figures for strongly neocorporatist countries are pooled and then related to the pooled weight (population 1965 in million or employees in 10,000). The same was done for the contrast sample of other core countries.

The Netherlands' temporal pattern of political mass protest and political violence is shown in figure 11.4. It differs substantially from the pattern found for all neocorporatist countries in figure 11.3.

FIGURE 11.4 Incidence of Political Mass Protest and Political Violence in The Netherlands, 1948-1982

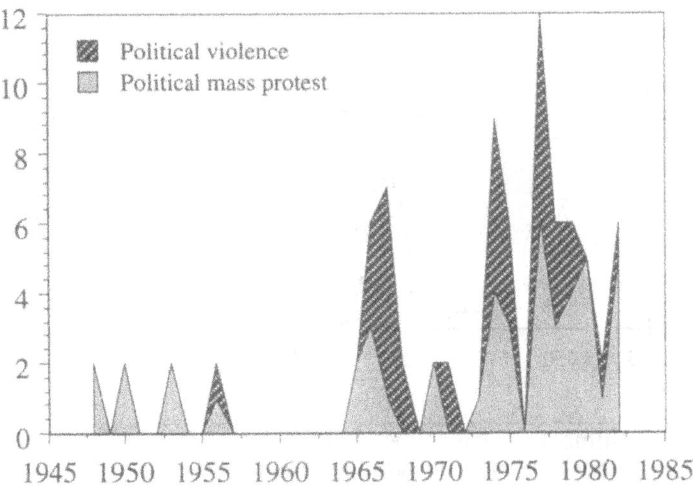

Note: The source of the basic data is Taylor (1985).

The Netherlands was one of the founding members of the European Community (1957). Due to the European integration process and the shift of power from the capitals to the institutions in Brussels, Luxembourg and Strasbourg the relevance of the national framework diminished for economic actors. Over time, the parent organizations of employers and workers which had been guided by national economic policy distanced themselves from them progressively to join the European parent organizations with their European goals. The result was a dismantling of neocorporatist and social partnership institutions, applying primarily to The Netherlands because the other strongly neocorporatist countries are to date not members of the EC or became members long after The Netherlands (Denmark in 1974).

The consequences for Dutch conflict management have been observed by Gerhard Ritter (1989: 169) who, however, does not mention EC integration as an explanation: "In central institutions in which employers' and the employee bodies were represented either alone or together with persons designated by the government, legislation regarding government economic and social policy was substantially influenced and in 1964 a central wage policy was agreed upon. Then, and particularly since the wave of unofficial strikes in September 1970, the system of labor relations in The Netherlands has changed toward a withdrawal of the state from wage policy and a more pronounced polarization of the relationships between employers and labor unions. Thus, the Dutch system more closely came to resemble those of most Western and Central European countries." (our translation)

The Consequences of War: The Case of the Federal Republic of Germany

Substantially different dislocation of their societal evolution by World War II occurred in core countries which favored a more pronounced coupling of the formation of the new style and the regime in those severely affected by the war.

Figure 11.5 shows data referring to political mass protest events and political violence in Italy which exhibits the frequent conflict pattern with an intermediate peak around 1960. Some European countries—Germany, Sweden and The Netherlands—do not experience such an intermediate peak.

FIGURE 11.5 Political Mass Protest Events and Political Violence in Italy, 1948-1982

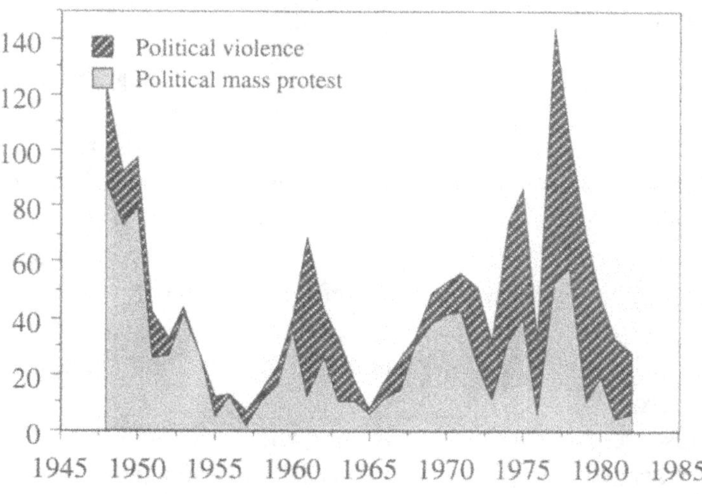

Note: The source of the basic data is Taylor (1985).

The data for political mass protest events and political violence in Germany are shown in figure 11.6. As the countries compared have about the same populations the data have not been weighted. Both countries are not classified as strongly neocorporatist, yet the conflict level in Germany is markedly lower than in Italy and does not exhibit an intermediate peak.

FIGURE 11.6 Political Mass Protest Events and Political Violence in the Federal Republic of Germany, 1948-1982

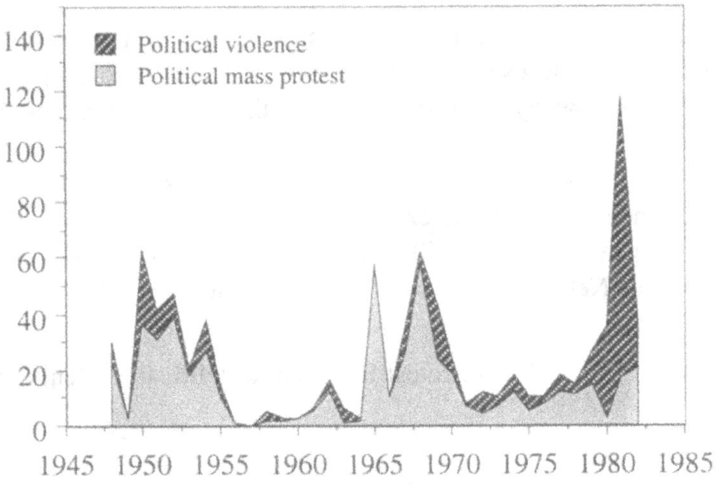

Note: The source of the basic data is Taylor (1985). For reasons of presentation the figure for political violence for 1981 was recoded to 100 (observed: 435).

The differences between Italy and Germany can easily be explained. Our theory suggests that an accelerated formation of the politico-economic regime after 1945 avoided or at least hampered the intermediate conflict peak around 1960. As a good indicator of the unfolding of the regime we can use measures of redistributive justice. In table 11.1, Germany and Italy are contrasted with each other, and the table also shows the average values for Western Europe.

We observe that Germany was well ahead of the Western European average of social security expenditures as early as 1955 and even more clearly in 1960. Italy later caught up so that by the mid-1970s the differences became less pronounced. We thus conclude that an early consolidation of the politico-economic regime in the direction of redistributive justice can prevent violent political conflict for a long time. In the case of Germany, the new beginning after the war resulted in a strong coupling of technological style and politico-economic regime which can only be observed in neocorporatist countries. Sweden, The Netherlands and Switzerland also have a low level of conflict without an intermediate peak around 1960.

TABLE 11.1 Social Security Outlays in Percent of the Gross Domestic Product in the Early Phase of the Societal Model. Figures for Italy, Germany and 13 Western European Countries

All figures are in percent

	1955	1960	Difference 1955-60	Difference 1960-65	1974
Italy	4.5	6.1	1.6	3.2	13.9
Germany	7.9	10.0	2.1	1.0	14.9
Average*)	5.8	6.9	1.1	1.7	13.0

*) 13 countries of Western Europe, including Italy and Germany. Source of the basic data is Jens Alber (1982: 60).

Germany's early coupling of economic development and redistributive justice is described by Gerhard Ritter: "In contrast to the new British system of social security marked by the deprivations of the post-war period, the rent reform of 1957—the most important law in the construction of social security in the Federal Republic of Germany—was already linked to the economic upswing. (...) The reform of 1957 which involved an immediate and drastic increase in the average pensions of workers by 65.3% and of employees by 71.9% broke the vicious circle of poverty and old age, achieved balance between generations, while through closely linking pensions to earlier contributions, a stimulus to increased performance was given. Together with the long economic upswing and the successful integration of refugees the rent reform contributed significantly to the legitimation of the new state." (Ritter 1989: 156f., our translation)

Stop-and-go in the United Kingdom

Over the course of the societal model, some countries are characterized by violent fluctuations which harmed coherence in the realization of the societal model. One explanation is voting patterns. In the majority of Western countries elections are held on a proportional basis. But—as mentioned above—there are exceptions. Even if there are only slight changes in voter preferences, the majority vote in single-candidate constituencies where candidates are elected according to relative majorities, as practiced in the United Kingdom, may result in landslide changes in the configuration of parliaments.

No country has therefore experienced comparable seesaw policies like the United Kingdom during the post-war era. Sven Steinmo 1989: 534, citing Michael Stewart, concludes: "Both Labour and Conservative parties, while in opposition, have succumbed to the temptation to condemn a large proportion of the government's policies and have promised to reverse many of these policies when they themselves took office. *The result has been a fatal lack of continuity.*"

Concluding Remarks

In our overview of different areas of social structure we were able to show remarkable similarities in different Western countries. Political and cultural variations undoubtedly exist but the limited room for action makes the similarities stand out even more clearly. On the basis of his extensive material, Hartmut Kaelble (1987) arrives at the same conclusion. But we have also discussed several differences. Our extended explanatory model summarized in figure 11.1 includes different variables which influence the room for manoeuvre and thus are able to explain cross-national differences.

An assessment of similarities and differences always depends on what play is allowed for something to be called similar. There are of course differences in the West and later we will see what consequences they had for development during the post-war era. But compared to the substantial differences between successive societal models and the wide available range of responses to the decay of a societal model, variations within one and the same model must be put into perspective.

Despite persisting differences between West European societies on the one hand, and between West European and North American on the other, the similarities are nevertheless significant. However, the presence of such similarities in the Atlantic West does not constitute sufficient evidence of convergence. To provide such evidence, our model must be capable of accounting for the modernization of Japan and its unprecedented ascent after 1945.

12
JAPAN: ANY LESSONS FOR THE WEST?

IS JAPAN A SPECIAL CASE?

Whether Japan is a special case is important for our theory, because so far it is the only non-Western society to have achieved core status. In addition, the question is of practical political relevance for the future of Western society since Japan did not become the post-war economic "wonder child" by neglecting the claim to equality in its social structure.

Thus, one has to ask whether Japan managed the compromise between power, efficiency, and equality differently from the old West during the postwar model. We are suggesting both "no" and "yes" as an answer. Overall, the claim to equality may have been more thoroughly institutionalized in Japanese postwar social structure than in the Atlantic West. Japan used this as a source of additional legitimacy, while it caught up with the rest of the West in economic terms (and may well surpass it in the future).

Even though in general the institutionalization of modern principles in social structure does not differ, there are particularities in the actual arrangements. From this perspective, Japan is a variant in the shaping of Western principles. Neither the ideal nor the final point of Western development, the Japanese variant is one that made possible a comparatively high degree of legitimation of Japanese society during the postwar era. Therein lay its success.

It is sometimes said that Japan should be regarded as pertaining to the far West rather than to the Far East because it has so many common features with the West (Ishida 1971). Still, as its cultural origin lies in the Orient, one has to consider the influence of "traditional" culture. The fact that certain institutional arrangements are compatible with existing cultural strands must not be misinterpreted to imply that these arrangements were "traditional" or "preindustrial." Correspondence and causality are not the same thing. Important reasons for the present institutional arrangements can be found in modern Japan; these are the result of deliberate efforts and were not determined by cultural premises alone (Alston 1983: 344). Generally, the emphasis on cultural continuity in many sources seems to underestimate the radical transformation of Japanese society as a result of the lost war.

The seniority principle and the system of life-long employment are often mentioned as examples of cultural continuity. Takeyoshi Kawashima (1983) relates the seniority principle to the traditional family system influenced by Confucianism. Yet, at an intercultural level it is so common a principle that this genealogy does not help much in the explanation why seniority principles are so important in modern Japan.

A good example of the fact that correlations do not necessarily imply causality can be found in the social arrangement of lifelong employment as practiced by large corporations in modern Japan. James Abegglen's (1958) well-known study suggested interpreting this practice as a continuity with traditional social relationships. Recent research has become more skeptical. Chie Nakane ([1970] 1985), for example, mentions the strong structural and ideological linkage of the employment system with the organizational structure of traditional households, but also points to the fact that the trend toward lifelong employment during the interwar period was promoted by the bureaucratic structure of large corporations. The household-like functions of firms emerged at the direction of the state in the context of the war economy. This development was to be completed later in the postwar period through practices originally introduced essentially by management through the trade union movement, which mostly consisted of company unions.

Robert Cole (1980) has also shown in his detailed study that lifelong employment is by no means a result of traditional social conditions but rather a practice that emerged during this century brought on by the attempt of large corporations to reduce the rate of mobility of their personnel. Traditionally, this rate was quite high, as has been shown by Koji Taira

(1962). At the beginning of this century the rate of job-hopping between firms amounted to ten percent per month. During the interwar period, this rate was reduced to five percent and it declined to about two percent during the 1950s (Taira 1962: 160).

Although the basic pattern of job security for permanent employees can be found in all large corporations (Bornschier 1976) it is more common in Japan. This is also due to a higher degree of dualism, i.e., the cleavage between the mass of small firms and the economically important large enterprises, a subject to which we shall return. But references to the role played by the "traditional" work ethic as a reason for Japan's economic success should be regarded as mere myth. Robert Cole (1980) goes even further, arguing that reference to diligence at work is more a sign of ignorance than a mode of explanation. Progress in productivity is brought about by the complicated interaction of technology, labor, management, work organization and social structure. The orientation towards work in modern Japan is a specific product of modern Japanese society and by no means originates in preindustrial Japanese society. Thus, the labor relations system described by Gerhard Ritter (1989) in his comparative study of the welfare state in Japan is the result of a prolonged process of struggle and compromise between management, workers' representatives and state bodies:

"There emerged a special kind of labor relations in Japan which has attracted a lot of attention because of the country's development into one of the leading economic powers. Permanent employment is characteristic for the large enterprises, which recruit their staff primarily from schools and universities and keep them until retirement age. Also characteristic are payment according to seniority, mobility of workers and managers within the enterprises, generous corporate social benefits, and the central role played by the firms' unions, next to which associations across particular branches are only of limited importance. A large proportion of social security benefits—as for example unemployment compensation or pension funds—is paid entirely by the enterprises" (Ritter 1989: 190, our translation)

This system of labor relations has the advantage of facilitating technological change, a fact also mentioned by Ritter (1989: 170). When new technologies are introduced, employees are not disqualified or fired but rather retrained. Due to permanent employment, firms are able to invest more in continuing education, which in turn positively influences labor morale and the quality of personnel.

THE BREAK FOLLOWING THE OCCUPATION OF JAPAN

It is difficult to imagine the severity of the discontinuity in Japanese history created by Japan's defeat in Asia and its subsequent occupation by the Allied powers from 1945-1951 under General Douglas MacArthur (see Williams 1979). Tadashi Fukutake (1982) describes the defeat of 1945 as a watershed in the societal development of Japan. This break may well have been as consequential for Japan as the French Revolution was for large parts of the Atlantic West. Whereas in the case of the French Revolution the United States exerted only indirect influence (in the form of Jefferson's influence on the revolutionary constitution), in Japan the United States as occupation power radically changed society. It established a democratic system based on Anglo-Saxon models; in 1947 a new constitution was introduced and in 1948 Japanese civil law was revised.

The secularization of society imposed by the occupation forces was definitive. In Japan, Buddhism (originating from China and enriched by Confucianist and Taoist elements) and Shintoism had been blended. While Buddhism is a universal world religion, Shintoism features a particular myth of creation of the Japanese people, who enter history by way of tracing the Tenno (emperor) genealogically back to divine origins.

The influence of Shintoism had two consequences for Japanese culture. On the one hand, it brought about a worldly and pragmatic orientation lacking in Buddhism's spiritualism (Ishida 1971). On the other hand, and contrary to Buddhism, which does not recognize any transcendental deity, Shintoism introduced a personification of God in the person of the Tenno. This religious fusion of the Japanese people and the state, represented by the Tenno, led to a true state cult which elevated the worship of ancestors and patriotism in an ideological and racist way.

After World War II the separation of Shinto and state was affected by order of the Allies. The most important point of the new Anglo-Saxon inspired constitution is the transformation of the quasi-theocratic absolutist monarchy into a constitutional monarchy. Under pressure from the Americans, the Tenno (Emperor Hirohito) announced the central element of the new constitution in his New Year's speech of 1946: henceforth, the

Japanese emperor would cease to be of divine nature. According to the new constitution, the emperor is only the symbol of the state and of unity of the people; his position derives from the will of the people, in whom sovereign power is vested (Williams 1979: 20; Harenberg 1984: 975). For many Japanese a world collapsed after this declaration. Up to then, religion, society and state had been inseparable. The whole conception of the world began to crumble (Harenberg 1984, see also Tsurumi 1970: 183ff.), and a wave of suicides followed and in fact accompanied the whole postwar transition until its peak around 1955 (Bornschier 1988: 184).

Apart from this secularization, enforced by the occupation force and the new democratic constitution, Japan underwent far-reaching purge of the army and industry between 1945 and 1951, the end of the occupation period. War criminals were convicted, large corporations of the prewar period were dismantled, and agrarian reform aimed at a more equitable distribution of land was enacted. Like Germany, Japan faced a zero hour beset by huge economic problems: 1.8 million war victims, enormous war damage, and a nearly completely destroyed industry were the heritage of the war. In addition, 6 million returnees needed to be re integrated into Japanese society.

POWER DISTRIBUTION

Kazuko Tsurumi (1970: 195-197) examines the change in the distribution of power brought about by this rupture by discussing its impact on three exclusive elites. The *gunbatsu* (military elite) was dissolved by the occupation army and theoretically abolished by the new constitution. The *zaibatsu* (financial elite), too, was dissolved by the occupation force by way of a number of anti-monopoly laws. According to Tsurumi, the "new zaibatsu" of the postwar period differs in various ways from the old one, in which the family ties of the controlling clans kept the corporations together on the basis of closed, particularistic criteria. The "new zaibatsu" is characterized by the separation of ownership from control. Management is chosen on the basis of ability rather than family ties. True holding corporations have ceased to exist and the shares have been spread comparatively broadly among the public. Instead of the holding companies of the old zaibatsu, banks assume the financing of corporations of "new zaibatsu." The *gakubatsu* (academic elite) at first survived the societal transition following the war, but the enormous growth of higher education and increased equality of opportunities in access to higher education during the postwar period resulted in a growing democratization of this elite.

Partly due to agrarian reform, partly because of the disintegration of the old zaibatsu, the changes in Japanese society resulted in a radical redistribution of wealth. Through strong progressive taxation and comparatively heavy inheritance taxes the concentration of wealth in private hands was restricted (Tominaga and Tomoeda 1986; Kerbo and McKinstry 1986; Ishida 1971; Kerbo 1991).

The comparatively low concentration of economic power in private hands stands in sharp contrast to the concentration of power at the level of the corporations, as is quite common throughout Western society (see chapter 8). Yet, it appears that the gap between the comparatively low levels of personal power and high levels of corporate power is bigger in Japan than it is in the old West. The concentration of power at the personal level in Japan may be lesser, whereas the concentration at the corporate level is greater.

According to Tadashi Fukutake (1974: 81f.) more than 80 percent of the money market is controlled by the ten largest financial corporations and in several basic industries over half the business is controlled by only three corporations. Yet, such conditions are not exceptional in the West. More interesting is a point by Harold Kerbo and John McKinstry (1986: 6, see also Kerbo 1991), who observe that about 70 percent of corporate stock is in the hands of institutions, mostly banks, the rest being spread broadly throughout the public. In the United States only 45 percent of stock is held by institutional investors, but the remainder in private hands is more concentrated than in Japan (Kerbo 1991).

Surely one of the outstanding features of Japan is the marked stratification of power at the level of organizations. The core area of the economy, i.e., the corporate segment, includes about 30 percent of all employees. Here, and only here, does Japan's well-known social principle of lifetime employment prevail. But such a markedly dualistic structure is also to be found in the West, where the segmentation of the economy according to power and the quality of jobs is also important. This is especially true of the United States, where the extent of segmentation is similar to that found in Japan (Bornschier 1976: 307, 1982b; Boltho 1975: 26-28; Fukutake 1982: 82f.). The particularity of Japan lies in the fact that the dualistic structure does not have adverse effects on income distribution as it does in the United States.

That economic enterprises in Japan are vastly stratified in terms of power, influence, and resources while at the same time there is a lesser degree of income inequality than, for example, in the United States, seems paradoxical at first sight. But this paradox leads us to the heart of the special functional logic of Japanese social structure. The key to understanding it lies in a different linkage between social rank and material rewards.

STRIVING FOR EFFICIENCY

One of the particularities of Japan is the social embeddedness of the striving for efficiency. The tradition of individualism—freedom in the sense of self-designed life itineraries (Ishida 1971: 15)—is weak compared to orientation towards the group. According to Takeshi Ishida (1971: 71), the term "freedom" cannot be translated exactly into Japanese because the corresponding conception is lacking in the culture. However, groups are not formed on the basis of ascribed characteristics. Rather, group formation in Japan is in "basic contradiction to groups which rely exclusively on the principle of descent and kinship" (Nakane [1970] 1985: 20). By way of such instrumental groups, to which firms also belong and through which firms compete with each other, group membership becomes more important than individual status within the group.

In Japan, striving for efficiency resides in the group rather than the individual. The prosperity of the group is seen as a guarantee for individual success. The orientation towards the community and the marked striving for harmony within groups, characterized by numerous rituals to enhance solidarity, are the vehicles for the striving for efficiency (Smith 1983: 49f.). Voting within groups is typically repeated until there is a result that can be accepted by each and every group member without losing face. Despite intense competition between groups, this results in a low level of social conflict that has surprised many observers (Krauss et al. 1984: 377ff.).

The Japanese make a remarkable investment in social power, i.e., networks of mutual relationships to which the group member can have recourse (see chapter 2). An important example of such group processes, which take place outside the sphere of work but remain bound to it, is "tsukiai"—the informal free-time network of colleagues that also includes superiors (Smith 1983: 63f.; Cole 1980: 231). The special form of the striving for efficiency, i.e., the emphasis on social power even during leisure (the group as insurance) has positive effects for the work process, as the strong feeling of solidarity can be used there to bolster the corporate identity of the firm.

The transformation of the striving for efficiency into group processes in which individuals work together and the ensuing harmony can also be found at the societal level in legal proceedings. According to Robert Smith (1983: 40) reconciliation is the central notion and procedure frequently used by Japanese courts; they are less concerned with who is right and who wrong than with the reconciliation of the parties.

STRIVING FOR EQUALITY

In all societies there is some correspondence between social rank, in the sense of esteem, and material rewards. Such correspondence does not preclude different weightings of ranks and differences in material rewards in the structure of inequality, however. Against the background of the powerful claim to equality in modern society, difference of either rank or material reward can be levelled out in the social structure. To a certain degree, one can be substituted for the other. They are functional equivalents and accommodate the claim to equality while also allowing for the human striving for differentiation in society. We find differences between the old West and Japan with respect to the role of such functional equivalents in the social structure, particularly with respect to the value of equality. In Japan, there is a clear and accepted hierarchy of social rank, and thus differences in material rewards can be smaller.

In the old West, and particularly in the United States, differences in social rank (in the sense of privileges) are rejected on cultural grounds. To compensate, differences in material rewards are much wider. The rejection of social rank at the symbolic-cultural level is particularly evident in everyday American culture, in which the emphasis on equality is very strong. At the workplace it is also common for managers and employees to call each other by first names, even if this is somewhat of a sham, since the boss keeps on being the boss and the subordinate the subordinate.

The functional equivalence of rank and material differentiation, i.e., comparable accommodation of the claim to equality each provides, would suggest that legitimation remains about the same in both cases. The particularity of Japanese social structure and its advantage in the creation of legitimacy lies in the fact that differentiation according to rank remains very open, i.e., it is not strictly ascribed. For that reason the Japanese guarantee of the claim to equality is not simply of the same value but is even superior to that found throughout Western society.

Rank in Japan. According to observers, the emphasis and omnipresence of social rank is much more marked than it is in the West (Nakane [1970] 1985: 43-62; Smith 1983: 77-83; see also Kerbo 1991). This emphasis on status is also reflected in the Japanese language, with its special forms of addressing those of higher, equal, or lower rank (Nakane [1970] 1985; Smith 1983; Kerbo and Sha 1987; Kerbo 1991). Discussion partners in Japan feel most uncomfortable until their ranks have been clarified, which is why the exchange of business cards is of great importance, as they make possible a comparison of relative and societal ranking (Nakane [1970] 1985: 49f.).

Everything is clearly structured according to rank: universities, public bodies, corporations, occupations, and, of course, hierarchical positions at work. Rank stratification according to age (seniority) is particularly marked for organizations as well as for individuals. Seniority as a ranking criterion provides legitimate access to societal rewards (Nakane [1970] 1985: 29; Alston 1983: 344f.; Tominaga and Tomoeda 1986). Such an emphasis on ranking differences is rejected in the dominant Western culture because it is regarded as a feature of traditional society that contradicts the claim to equality.

However, the particular feature of the Japanese ranking system is that it is not associated with "aristocratic" criteria and remains compatible with the claim to equality in a special way. Legitimation thus becomes possible despite the existence of marked rank differentiation. The emphasis on rank unites the principle of individual accomplishment (meritocracy) with an ascribed feature, age, in a remarkable way. Further, age as a basis for ranking can be regarded as comparatively just because everybody gets older and thus attains status. Thus, by linking privileges to age, Japanese society has a surprisingly simple and efficient source of legitimation: equal opportunity, guaranteed in a temporal sense.

Individual accomplishment is guided by educational success and becomes particularly important at two points in the career of any Japanese. The first is access to carefully ranked schools and universities. With about

800 institutions of higher education, Japan has a comparatively large number of universities per capita. A single country-wide set of entrance examinations to public high schools (in which only academic accomplishments determine admittance) also indirectly affects entrance to the universities later on. Those who score best in the examinations will enter the highest ranking schools and later the best universities, which, in turn, give access to the top jobs. This process influences one's chances at the second point in the selection process. Only the best schools and universities give access to the best jobs in large corporations or in public administration. These employers also use selective entrance examinations to choose their employees, who will be rewarded with lifetime employment.

There are many references, particularly in the press, to the strains and stresses of the "examination hell" caused by this competitive educational system in which selectivity often begins as early as preschool and has the effect of forcing the parents of potentially good students to pay for private lessons (Ishida 1971: 44f.). It must be remarked, however, that it is not true that Japanese society is characterized by a continuous dynamic of meritocratic status attainment, because the greater part of careers in educational and business institutions is not characterized by unremitting competition, but rather by collective solidarity according to age cohorts once the selective process has been completed.

Furthermore, once a pupil has been admitted to a certain high school, he or she more or less automatically passes the final exam, i.e., almost everyone reaches the goal. According to Ulrich Teichler (1975: 198), the rate of success in Japanese high schools is about 90 percent. From the time one has succeeded in entering an organi zation, one's career path then rigidly follows the seniority principle. As a rule, promotions therefore occur together with one's age cohort. For this reason, it is uncommon for someone to have a superior who is of the same age, and almost unheard of to have one who is younger. Thus, rank on the basis of seniority and relative position in the job hierarchy only collide on rare occasions. Retirement age is normally reached by the age of fifty-five. Only a few employees are selected by top management to fill the highest positions as senior managers. Even at these top levels the rule that superiors not only occupy a higher position in the job hierarchy but also, being older, a generally accepted higher social rank, remains unbroken. In this way, age stratification in Japanese society provides an additional source of legitimation for hierarchy that does not exist in Western societies.

THE STRUCTURE OF REAL INEQUALITIES

In the first edition of this book our comparison of Japan and the large Western countries proceeded in more detail (Bornschier 1988: 357ff.), because at that time Japan was not yet a prominent subject in the social science literature. This has changed and so we can be brief here. We do not need to demonstrate the accelerated process of economic catching up in any detail. We need only remember that income per capita in Japan was only about 23 percent of the Western average in 1950; by the 1990s, Japan had advanced to the top of the scale. Corrected for purchasing power, income per capita in Japan is now similar to that in the United States, Switzerland, Canada and Germany (World Economic Forum and IMD 1992: 285).

In 1990, Japan's export ratio (exports of goods and services as a percentage of total value added) of 15.2 percent was only slightly higher than that of the United States (1990: 12.0 percent), but much lower than the average for the Western European countries (1990 average for 16 countries 39 percent) (World Economic Forum and IMD 1992: 336). This shows that Japan's economic success was less the result of external growth effects than was the case in Western Europe. With respect to the relative size of the public sector (i.e., all taxes and legally mandated social security payments) as a share of the gross national product, Japan was always at the bottom end of the scale during the postwar era compared to other Western countries. In 1970, the corresponding figures amounted to 19.9 percent in Japan, 29.2 percent in the United States, and 34.4 percent in the European Community. In 1991 the figures were 30.9 percent (Japan), 29.8 percent (United States) and 39.6 percent (EC) (Commission of the EC 1993: 136). These figures should not be misunderstood, since during the postwar era the Japanese state played only a subordinate role in quantitative terms if not in planning and moderation.

The intergenerational openness of Japanese society is comparatively great, by reference to occupational mobility as well as educational opportunities (Bornschier 1988: 358, table 13.2). Measured in terms of occupational mobility, Japan has a comparatively low degree of intergenerational ascription of social position. Recent findings by Hiroshi Ishida (1993) reduce this assessment somewhat but still show a higher degree of openness of the Japanese stratification regime in comparison to the United Kingdom and the United States. Further, the data for 1970 show that Japan has the least unequal income distribution in Western society, even when "egalitarian" Sweden (where inequality of income distribution is only reduced through massive public intervention) is included in the comparison.

Educational inequality is comparatively narrow, and the average educational level is high (Bornschier 1988: 358, table 13.2). Access to higher education is quite independent of social antecedents in postwar Japan, being more meritocratic than in the Atlantic West. According to OECD data (1975: 168), the relative chances of children with a working-class background attending a university were somewhat better in 1960 than the Western average.[1]

Even elite universities exhibit a remarkable degree of openness for children from lower strata. The highest ranking university, Tokyo University, is a prime example. According to Harold Kerbo and John McKinstry (1986, citing Vogel 1979), during the 1970s about 35 percent of its students were from families belonging to the highest income quintile, whereas 14 percent originated from the lowest quintile (see also Kerbo 1991). Kerbo and McKinstry argue that such a low level of association between enrolment and social background cannot be found for Harvard. Yet, William Cummings' (1980: 226) data for private universities shows a less favorable association, because there tuition fees are higher. In general, however, private universities do not rank among the best universities in Japan (Teichler 1975: 177). Although Cummings' data also indicate that the chances of children from lower income strata entering public universities have declined somewhat between 1961 and 1976, even in 1976 the comparatively low level of recruitment according to social origins is remarkable.

In his detailed study of university and society in Japan, Ulrich Teichler (1975) reaches the conclusion that the Japanese educational system was rebuilt after the war to reduce the inequality of opportunities according to educational success: "In fact, the empirical data at hand show that there was a reduction in inequality. Today, the inequality of educational opportunities does not only seem to be substantially narrower than, for example, in Germany, but is also a lot less marked than in most other countries" (Teichler 1975: 200, our translation).

Income differences. The comparatively small income differences in Japan, which are discussed by Harold Kerbo (1991) in some detail, are remarkable. Statistical data concerning the income distribution are difficult to compare between countries and over time. However, even using different data, various researchers have reached the same conclusion: after World

War II, Japan had the most egalitarian income distribution of all industrial countries. (Boltho 1975: 165-167; Wada 1975: 149f.; Ono and Watanabe 1976; further sources can be found in Cummings 1980: 256f.) Our own compilation of data for the personal income distribution of households (1988: 358, table 13.2) also shows that Japan was among the least unequal Western societies in 1970. This holds for basic distribution measures (Gini-index) before and after redistributive measures by the public sector as well as for the relation of the richest to the poorest twenty percent of all households.

The comparatively low level of income inequality in Japanese society is not self-evident; on the contrary, it appears paradoxical at first sight. As noted above, there is a substantial stratification of economic enterprises in Japan, and also average incomes differ according to firm size. So how can overall inequality be so small? As an explanation we suggested a certain degree of substitution of rank for reward. It is true that average salaries differ between the core segment of large corporations and the mass of the other firms, but differences within firms are much smaller than in other Western countries. Top managers in the Japanese automobile industry, for example, only earn about seven times the salary of an average worker. The corresponding ratio for American automobile corporations is 36:1 (Kerbo and McKinstry 1986; see also Kerbo 1991).

The educational and income distribution in Japan are thus comparatively levelled out, and the intergenerational openness of the status structure is high. The remarkably weak correlation between education and other status indicators—despite the importance of education in Japanese society—is a result of the fact that the best jobs are distributed according to good diplomas, while financial rewards depend on the length of time spent in the firm, i.e., seniority. Yet, in all dimensions of social structure that show advantages for Japan, one thing is remarkable: compared to Western norms, women are worse off (Robins-Mowry 1983; Hielscher 1984; Kerbo 1991: 445ff.).

MORE LEGITIMACY AND LESS CONFLICT AND CRIMINALITY

Over the course of the postwar period, Japan's realization of the claim to equality must in certain respects be actualized as a leading one for the core countries. In all our comparisons—with the exception of the status of women—Japan fares better than the rest. The special aspect of the striving for efficiency—its orientation towards the group—furthermore strengthens firms. Against this background we can presume that the legitimacy of postwar Japanese society was higher than in the traditional West even without large-scale redistributive measures by the state. If, as proposed by our theory, legitimacy is a resource in world competition because it enhances the motivation of the population and reduces inefficient control costs, then collective efficiency should have been greater in Japan than in the traditional West. Without doubt this has indeed been the case.

This poses the question of whether there is also empirical evidence for the intermediate link in our argument: that legitimacy as a product of the realization of the claim to equality and the striving for efficiency results in a tempering of societal conflict, and this is associated with higher levels of motivation and reduced public control costs. Earlier (Bornschier 1988) we were able to show that Japan in fact exhibited lower levels of political conflict than other large Western countries during the postwar era (Taylor and Jodice 1983; Bornschier and Heintz 1979: 275ff.) Thus, measured in terms of levels of political conflict, the legitimacy of Japanese society during the postwar era can be considered comparatively high. However, different costs may be attached to this legitimation. In the postwar model the state generally skimmed off a substantial proportion of the social product in order to inter alia legitimate society by, for example, redistributive welfare spending and by covering the costs of the educational system. The extent of competitive advantage in the world system follows from the level of legitimation and the necessary public expenditures (in effect, funds withdrawn from alternative private uses) to reach this level. In this comparison, too, Japan has looked very good during the postwar era. Legitimacy in Japan has been high and public expenditures for most of the time have been among the lowest in the core. In Western Europe, legitimacy has also been high, but so have public expenses. In the United States, on the other hand, legitimacy has been lower since the late 1950s (Bornschier 1988: chapters 7 and 15). Even though public expenses were also once low, the United States has therefore been at a disadvantage when compared to Japan.

Not only are the low levels of political mass protest and political violence in Japan remarkable, but so too are the low levels of labor conflict and of criminality. This finding is illustrated in figure 12.1 in which we compare Japan with small and large countries of the Atlantic West. How can this result be explained within our theory?

TABLE 12.1 Extent of Criminality, Political and Labor Conflict: Japan in Comparison with Small and Large Countries of the Atlantic West

Type of interest mediation[1]		Rates of criminality[2]			Political Conflict[5]	Labor conflict[6]
		Murder and manslaughter[3]	Robbery	Fraud and similar offenses	Index for 1948-1982	Index for 1948-1977
	Large core countries					
pluralist	USA	8.4[4]	221	n.a.	31.7	26
pluralist	Canada	2.3[4]	94[4]	484[4]	16.3	18
sectoral	France	2.3	90[4]	1.016[4]	76.6	9
	Average	4.3	135	750	41.5	17
	Small core countries					
neocorporatist	Austria	1.0	38	252	16.7	0
neocorporatist	Denmark	1.5	41	240	13.0	3
neocorporatist	Switzerland	1.2	25	164	11.4	0
	Average	1.2	35	219	13.3	1
neocorporatist	Japan	0.6	1	44	7.6	1

Source: Bornschier 1992; Dörmann 1991: 38ff.; Bornschier 1988: 405.

Notes: 1) According to Nollert's typology (1992:201). 2) All figures refer to rates per 100.000 population in 1989, unless otherwise noted. Source is Dörmann (1991: 38ff.). 3) Attempted murder and manslaughter not included. 4) 1988 rate per 100,000 population. 5) Political conflict covers events of protest demonstrations, riots, political strikes and armed attacks, source is Taylor and Jodice (1983) and Taylor (1985) per million inhabitants in 1960. 6) Number of years with high losses of working days due to strikes between 1948 and 1977, source: Bornschier (1988: 405)

Comparing Japanese and European modernization, Yasusada Yawata (1994: 5) describes one European feature as follows: "One of the essential features of European modernization is 'individualism' as both an ideological and social principle, i.e., historical communities were dissolved or, at the very least, weakened during the modernization process in Western Europe." During European modernity, the claim to equality and individualism resulted in an increasing displacement of behavioral control to the willfully and autonomously acting individual. For the Atlantic West, this has been discussed by Norbert Elias (1969), who also addressed the long-term changes in the I-We balance (Elias 1987: chapter 3). According to Elias, the equilibrium between I- and We-identity changed over the centuries as a result of the transformed social structure of personal relationships. This also led to enhanced self-control. Conformity through external pressure was partially replaced by self-control. Elias's argument, however, is substantiated with wholly European material, and does not consider the fact that self-control can arise from a variety of sources. On the one hand, it can be the result of a strict internalization of group norms as in the case of Japan. On the other hand, it can be rooted in the autonomous ego as in the marked individualism in the Atlantic West. We will return to consequences of the different roots of self-control, but first we isolate and compare the functioning of structural factors (external pressure of the world system) and cultural factors (strong or weak individualism).

With regard to the rates of conflict and criminal behavior, Japan, a comparatively large country of the non-Atlantic West, could be expected to lie near other large countries in figure 12.1. Yet, exactly the opposite is the case: Japan has the lowest rates. Let us first address the structural factors. In estimating the influence of the world system, dependence and dominance are of relevance (see chapter 11). A high degree of economic interlinkage with the world economy (e.g., Switzerland and the Netherlands) or the will to move upwards in the political world economy (e.g., Japan) favor particularly strong societal integration, a syndrome that has been labelled neocorporatism or consociational democracy (even though the two forms of organization are not identical). As discussed in chapter 11, these arrangements prevent the fragmentation of political culture and favor consensus-oriented conflict management, particularly at the middle level of society (associations). For that reason, manifestations of conflict are comparatively less frequent in such societies. Thus, we find similarities between Japan and smaller core countries such as Switzerland, Sweden, the Netherlands and

Austria. In addition, the small countries are characterized by stronger group ties (and thus social controls) in the immediate societal sphere (neighborhoods, clubs etc.).

But Japan is not a small country. How then can we explain its higher degree of societal integration at the immediate level (e.g. firms, neighborhoods, clubs)? Stronger group ties may well be a result of de-emphasized individualism. Thus, the remarkably lower rates of criminality and conflict in Japan cannot simply be explained by corporatism at the intermediate level of society. They must also be linked to the greater degree of integration in this society at the immediate level. These distinctive group ties are the result of a cultural difference of a less-pronounced individualism.

Finally, we would like to turn to the different functions of self-control that are manifested in such a society. Self-control as we have said can be established on different bases: it can be the result of a strict internalization of group norms, or of insight mediated by the autonomous ego. An explanation of the guidance of self-control by insight can be connected to the ideas of Immanuel Kant which we have already mentioned in chapter 7. There we argued that the working of our practical reason can also be founded on mutual self-interest. No one would want everybody to steal, since this would also endanger one's own possessions. A culture emphasizing individuality and freedom must necessarily rely more on insight and mutual self-interest for achieving conformity to norms. Such a basis for self-control is more vulnerable, however, because conformity is anchored less mechanically in strict group norms. This vulnerability is also the result of the fact that the autonomous ego can weigh conformity against the personal advantages of non-conformity more often and, finally, because conformity remains tied to the faith that others will also behave according to the norms.

If the faith that others will also respect the norms is betrayed, the efficacy of normative ties is reduced (see chapter 7). As a result of less pronounced individualism in the sociocultural system of Japan, self-control is less vulnerable there, and thus higher degrees of conformity to norms can be expected. However, this only holds true as long as people are strongly bound within groups. If individuals transfer from one group to another—status passages in the life course—deviant behavior might also become rather frequent in Japan.

Will the cultural difference between Japan and the Atlantic West last? It is difficult to tell. Some observers believe that the westernization of the younger generation in Japan is progressing and that individualism is becoming more important. What consequences would follow from a cultural change in the direction of the pattern of the Atlantic West in Japan? If, during the modernization process, individualism and the value attached to personal freedom were to increase markedly, this could lead to problems, since Japanese culture is less experienced in managing conformity through self-control rooted in the autonomous ego. The societies of the Atlantic West have recently begun to learn from innovative Japanese organizational forms in the management of the new technological style (see chapter 5). In the management of individuality, Japan may well learn from the Atlantic West, where people show a remarkable degree of self-control despite heightened individuality and the importance of personal freedom: a large number of people respect the rules and do not become delinquents even under stressful conditions of urban life and in face of major societal problems.

FINAL REMARKS

We can conclude this case study by pointing to the fact that at a general level Japan is not a special case; the same structural principles are at work there as in the Atlantic West. Harold Kerbo arrives at the same conclusion: "Though modern Japan is an industrial nation with many important cultural differences compared to the United States and Europe, we find more similarities than differences in Japan's system of social stratification." (1991: 457) This holds true for various other societal characteristics as well as for Japanese capitalism as a whole. It is not true that everything is different. In the assessment of Henrik Schmiegelow, the particularities of the Japanese economy and society are "more Western than the West" in their particular mixture (1993: 509; see also Schmiegelow and Schmiegelow 1989: 155-177).[2]

It is true that Japanese social structure has some particularities as we have already mentioned: (1) a strong emphasis on the group at the cost of individuality; (2) a stronger emphasis on rank on the basis of seniority and educational achievements; and (3) a more marked dualistic structure of the economy with social benefits at the level of the large corporations. These differences generate patterns which are only variants within modern social structure, however. For our theory, the following is of importance: on the one hand, the particularities made more equality possible, and, on the other hand, have resulted in less conflict and criminality over the career of the Japanese societal model of the postwar period.

The case of Japan is also proof of the fact that a high degree of legitimacy can be achieved without an excessive quantitative role of the state. This is possible if the openness of society and primary equality are greater and if the social networks creating personal ties are more dense so that the state's "secondary repair attempts" can be held at a low level. Whether these advantages will continue to work in their present form is not at all certain.

Thus, it would be wrong to associate the enormous economic success of Japan during its modernization period directly with any leadership role in the future societal model. The problem of the creation of legitimacy is always posed anew at the end of a societal model. Thus, our case study of Japan primarily shows that success in the competitive world environment must be preceded by an optimization of legitimacy.

NOTES

1 Relative chances of children of managers and professionals attending university were compared to the chances of workers' children. The values for 1960 were 36 : 1 for the Western countries (average) and 30 : 1 for Japan.

2 More fundamental treatments of Japanese social structure and Japan's position in the world can be found in the works by Ulrich Menzel (1989, four volumes), Harold R. Kerbo and John A. McKinstry (1995) and Hanns W. Maull (1993). Further references regarding Japan have been included in other chapters, particularly that on the technological style.

13
LEGITIMACY AND COMPARATIVE ADVANTAGES

INTRODUCTION

The idea that legitimacy is a source of success in the competitive world environment is a central thesis of this book. In chapter 3 we advanced our theoretical perspective on the competition between social orders, i.e., the world market for protection, which functions as the central mechanism through which more legitimate orders are rewarded with success and less legitimate orders are punished and fall behind. This competition, based on the quality of order and decisive for economic success, is the central means of selection and supports convergence in the shaping of core societies. The rise and decline of nations thus each depend upon political decisions, which create societal models and their specific arrangements (cf. Olson 1982, and Kennedy 1987, for alternative explanations).

Societal models temper and regulate conflict. Success varies, however, as any comparison of societal models or of different outcomes at the level of different nation-states will show. Such variation has been discussed systematically in chapter 11. The definitions of conflict and legitimacy are closely linked to each other in our understanding. The degree of legitimacy attributed to a social order by its members depends upon the extent to which its conflicting social principles (see chapter 2) are reconciled with each other and on the extent of acceptance of its basic values by citizens.

If we relate the guarantee of basic values and conflict management (which together make possible societal organization and thus generate legitimacy) with the rise and fall of societies over the long term, or with relative success during any one epoch, an empirical test of our ideas becomes possible. For our theory, this test is most important.

In what follows we will first discuss long historical periods, which in turn will lead us to the beginning of the sequence of societal models that are the subject of this book. The question of economic success is briefly taken up for the first and the second societal models, although we do not claim to be able to vigorously test our theory with respect to these models. For the third societal model, the test becomes more stringent through the use of statistical methods made possible because the data for cross-national comparisons are a lot sounder for the postwar period than for preceding periods.

EVIDENCE FOR LONG HISTORICAL PERIODS

Long before modernity, two basically different societal projects struggled for predominance (Bornschier and Lengyel 1990). For millennia and until the present, the competing logics of their political and economic elites were of importance for societal development. In one societal type, the market assumes the central societal steering function and brings about less strongly hierarchical structures, which are linked to each other in a decentralized fashion through "world economies." The essential feature dominating societal dynamics of the other societal type is the hierarchical structure of political rule and the attempt at building "world empires" by politico-military means. Hybrid forms have also evolved. During its colonial phase, for example, the modern world system consisted of societies that integrated key features of both societal types within their colonial empires (Britain, for example; see chapter 10). But not all colonial empires were mixed types (e.g., Habsburg Spain, Russia).

The differences in the central societal steering mechanism—market versus hierarchy—refer not only to the formal dimension of both societal types but also to their inner logics and the predominant orientation of their elite: the logic of profit versus the logic of tribute (see chapter 3). This basic difference between the two predominant orientations of action is also stressed by several scholars.[1] For our argument, these contradictory orientations towards action are not used simply as analytical and classificatory categories; in their historical forms as opposing societal types, they were also historical actors and thus of importance for understanding the evolution of human society.

This leads to two related questions. Why did the profit logic only prevail relatively late at the core of the world system? How can we explain the fact that, up until the nineteenth century, the leaders of capitalist development were societies of the maritime type?

The breakdown of the socialist counter-core has once again highlighted the advantages of capitalist market societies. Yet, the historical origins of capitalism are subject to controversy. In contrast to Immanuel Wallerstein (1974), for example, who dates the origin of capitalism in the so-called long sixteenth century, Fernand Braudel ([1979] 1984) and also Frederic Lane (1979) point to the emergence of capitalism during the thirteenth century in Italy. If we go back even further, societies in which the market played a central role can be found during antiquity and even as early as the third millennium B.C. (Chase-Dunn 1992; Bornschier and Lengyel 1990).[2] In view of the fact that capitalist market society has recently proven to be so very successful, our first question becomes relevant: why did this societal type not become dominant much earlier?

Capital accumulation and trade in the early world economies were always threatened by the large early empires. Rulers were able to appropriate property or to capture the centers of the world economy, i.e., to block the trade routes. Thus, efficient protection of property rights became quite expensive, at least territorially. World economies were endangered for a long time and at risk of being captured and transformed into world empires, due to the politico-military advantages of tribute-seeking and thus rapacious states.

The politico-military struggle for predominance drove the world economies back to marginal regions, particularly islands and relatively inaccessible coastal areas. Until modernity, their maritime basis and their economic and innovative superiority remained basic features of world economies for millennia. Despite permanent threats originating from the large continental powers, there has been unbroken continuity in the niche occupied by maritime world economies.[3] In contrast to Gerhard and Jean Lenski (1987: chapter 8), who see maritime societies as evolutionary byways, we suggest viewing them as historical ancestors of the societal type that finally prevailed at the core.

An idealization of this societal type would be wrong, but at the same time we must acknowledge that maritime societies were originally characterized by freer institutions and a wider decentralization of political and economic power. This was due to the fact that they were not based on maintaining borders (Carneiro 1973) and because they were difficult to capture. The limits imposed on power hierarchies and the favoring of independent economic and military entities in the societal type were also a result of their transportation technology: ships. Ships not only offered maritime societies decisive advantages in maritime warfare (the battle of Salamis is a historical example) but were also the central capital good and the only profitable means of mass transportation. A very early maritime society has been described by William McNeill in *The Rise of the West* (1963). He stresses the following important features of the maritime society of the Minoans: wealth and power were founded on external trade and not on land rents nor on enforced labor in the form of slavery (1963: 111).

Starting from these maritime societies, the "world economy" was the cradle of the modern capitalist market economy. In the social sciences, however, too much energy has been spent on working out the typically Occidental features of modern capitalism (à la Max Weber) instead of viewing the long continuity of capitalist development within the framework of the evolution of social systems.

From this perspective, European capitalism stands within a long tradition of world economies that mainly linked city systems to each other. Examples in this historical sequence are: Southern Mesopotamia (Sumer from 3,500 B.C. onwards), the world economies of the Minoans, the Mycenaens, the pre-Hellenist Greeks, the Phoenicians, the Carthaginians, the Greeks, the Etruscans, the Venetians and the Genovese (as well as the remaining cities of Northern Italy), and the German Empire, particularly the Hanseatic League. Later, the city confederation of North Holland, and finally England.[4]

In world systems not transformed into world empires by way of conquest, the capitalist logic can become dominant if it proves to be conclusively superior in economic terms, as was the case of the English industrial revolution. Only then is there a massive transformation at the core of the state system. Tribute logic must be subordinated to capitalist logic and the capitalist state emerges. The latter must serve the logic of capital accumulation and the creation of legitimacy by integrating the population into the societal model, because efficiency and legitimacy are central resources in a competitive world system with an industrial base. There is no other way to attain or preserve core status in such a system.

Modernity in Europe has not been characterized by such dominant logic from the start, nor did profit logic and tribute logic first emerge in Europe. Rather, they intermingled under the sway of profit logic only after a prolonged phase of opposition—between absolutist states, on the one hand, and the leaders of the world economies, on the other hand: Venice, North Holland and England. This phase of opposition lasted until the English industrial revolution, when the world economy was finally wrested from its maritime base. Only then did the capitalist world economy become clearly superior to the territorial project of the world empires, and only since has it assumed core status in the world system, although counter-cores, for example the Soviet Union, challenged it until recently.

Both our questions can thus be answered. During most of societal evolution, rapacious and parasitic elites in centralized and militarized societies had military advantages over the decentralized, interlinked city systems of the world economy. These city systems, however, persisted in marginal maritime regions and finally stimulated the emergence of modern core societies much more decisively than did the monumental world empire project primarily founded on coercion. The English industrial revolution finally brought about a marked change. The territorial counter-cores in Europe were institutionally changed either by revolution (e.g., France) or by reform (e.g., Prussia) and integrated into the capitalist world economy. The wave of liberalization of the early nineteenth century signified a massive extension of the capitalist core. The world economy—seen not only as a form of exchange, but as a societal type—penetrated additional territories.

EVIDENCE FOR SUCCESS DURING THE FIRST TWO SOCIETAL MODELS SINCE THE NINETEENTH CENTURY

Success During the First Societal Model

From our perspective, societies which, after the liberal revolutions of the past century (1830, 1848) not only adopted freedom of trade but also extended political democracy, i.e., were characterized by a comparatively high degree of political participation or division of political power, should have been rewarded economically. In order to test this hypothesis, we compare contrasting groups of countries in table 13.1.

TABLE 13.1 Comparative Economic Success during the First Societal Model of Western Core Society

Contrast groups	Gross domestic product per capita (in 1970 US prices)			
	1820	1870	Absolute Increase	Percent Increase
A) Early economic liberalization *plus* relatively early democratization				
Netherlands	400	831	431	
United Kingdom	454	972	518	
United States	372	764	392	
Belgium	354	925	571	
Switzerland	333	786	453	
Average	383	856	473	+ 123%
B) Early economic liberalization but unsteady or delayed democratization				
France	377	627	250	
German Union	310	535	225	
Average	344	581	238	+ 69%
C) Delayed economic liberalization and delayed democratization				
Austria	400	573	173	
Denmark	363	572	209	
Norway	294	489	195	
Sweden	307	415	108	
Japan	251	251	0	
Average	323	460	137	+ 42%

Source: Gross domestic product per capita: Maddison (1982: 8)

The first group shown in table 13.1 is characterized by early liberalization and comparatively early democratization. The second group combines early economic liberalization with unsteady or delayed democratization (France and the German Union). The third group is composed of five additional countries representing delayed economic liberalization and delayed political democratization. Here, we are comparing economic performance per capita for the time period 1820-1870 according to data gathered by Angus Maddison (1982). The first group is characterized by the biggest absolute as well as relative increase in economic performance per capita. The second group exhibits clearly lower values which, however, still surpass those of the third group. Thus, our notion that legitimacy was also paying off in economic terms is empirically confirmed.[5]

Success During the Second Societal Model in the Imperialist Phase

The changes in the interstate system—often termed neo-mercantilism—were accompanied by a very limited capacity for internal reform (see chapter 6). Liberalism began to lose strength during the 1880s (Mommsen 1969). The cultural struggle with the Catholic Church, the absence of many Catholics from political life (particularly in Italy), and the fear of the political and unionist workers' movement created a crisis of political integration. The new nationalism after 1870 was an attempt at ideologically mending these societal ruptures without having to undertake more fundamental reforms (Mommsen 1969). Within a few years this development led to imperialism.

European imperialism from 1885 until the end of World War I can be seen as an extreme form of nationalist thinking. Wolfgang Mommsen (1969: 19) gives some examples: "Cecil Rhodes and Joseph Chamberlain in England or Friedrich Naumann in Germany, to mention just a few, preferred to justify their national imperialism with the thesis that only a forceful overseas policy could create a lasting and economically secure living for the labor force" (our translation). The social variant of such legitimation (social imperialism), in contrast to economic explanations—stresses the function of imperialism as a means of diverting attention from domestic problems, particularly the pressing social question in the class-polarized societal model of this era. The social variant of imperialism was tied to Social Darwinism—the survival of the fittest—and racist delusions of superiority and thus also attempted to bind the fate of the members of the lower strata to national expansion. As Mommsen points out, "In this, the idea that only those nations that became world empires would have a future in the world played a decisive role" (1969: 16, our translation).

Not only in the continental countries, but also under liberal imperialism in England led by Lord Rosebery, terrible racist formulations can be found, such as: "What is empire but the predominance of race?" and: "It is a part of our responsibility to see that the world, as far as it can still be shaped, assumes an Anglo-Saxon and not any other character." (Mommsen 1969: 20, citing Lord Rosebery's statements of 1893 and 1900) Cecil Rhodes, for example, referred to the Anglo-Saxons as the most noble race destined to reign over all other peoples (Harenberg 1984: 770). We are stressing the English sources, although the nationalist discourse in the other countries was by no means less pronounced, to show how imperialist ideology penetrated even where classical liberal ideology had strong roots. As against the liberal ideology as well as the internationalist, egalitarian socialist ideology, imperialism was without doubt a step backward in terms of the anchoring of the values of modernity in the basic conception of society.

Extreme nationalism, popular arrogance, and accompanying racism and xenophobia were reactions to an insufficient compromise in the class-polarized societal model, which became even more pronounced during its decay phase. Once again, during the 1920s and the 1930s, such attitudes can be observed in many core countries, and something similar, although much weaker, took place during the 1980s and the 1990s. By contrast to the decay phase of the latest societal model, during which such attitudes were primarily articulated by the losers in the societal transformation process, during the imperialist phase these ideologies were used by the elites to divert attention from domestic conflicts. In this respect Hitler's race hatred and lust for conquest are directly related to this imperialist phase.

The second societal model is the one under which dramatic changes in economic and political positions within Western core society became evident. By its end, Europe had lost its leadership position to the United States. How did the competitive world system sanction the strongest imperialist variants in the societal model? For an empirical comparison, we use status as a colonial power as an indicator of a lack of pressure to carry out domestic reforms. In addition, dominance over parts of the world favored the elites' tribute logic and hampered industrial development based on efficiency. Which of the competing societies were successful, which of

TABLE 13.2 Ascent and Decline of Great Powers during the Imperialist Phase (1870-1914) of the Second Societal Model (1883-1932)

	Percent Shares in World Production			Percent Shares in World Manufacturing		
	1872-82	*1907-13*	*Difference*	*1880*	*1913*	*Difference*
I. Great colonial powers						
Great Britain	19.0	14.6	- 4.4	22.9	13.6	- 9.3
France	16.1	10.1	- 6.1	7.8	6.1	-1.7
II. Lesser Colonial Powers						
German Empire	13.8	14.1	+ 0.3	8.5	14.8	+ 6.3
United States of America	22.7	33.6	+ 10.9	14.7	32.0	+ 17.3
III. Rest of the world	28.4	27.6	- 0.7			
IV. Remaining core countries				25.2	26.0	+0.8
V. Semiperiphery and periphery				20.9	7.5	-13.4

Sources: World production: Solomou (1986); world manufactures: Bairoch (1982).

them lost? According to the data presented in table 13.2, status as a colonial power was a long-term reason for the decline of world powers. More open and more democratic societies had an advantage. Of the two contenders to succeed British world dominance, the German Empire, with its attempt to counter-balance the lack of democracy with a paternalistic social policy (Bismarck's social legislation of 1883), was much less successful than the United States. Both countries were relatively insignificant colonial powers. Thus, in a comparative perspective, nationalist relapse and colonial expansion have been reasons for a loss of status during the second societal model. The more legitimate society of the United States, on the other hand, was on its way to the twentieth century. This is also visible in table 13.2, where we have compiled selected data concerning economic evolution during the second societal model.

EVIDENCE FOR SUCCESS DURING THE LAST SOCIETAL MODEL: A QUANTITATIVE TEST

If the basic argument of long-term competitive advantage is correct, we should also find empirical evidence for the working of such forces over a much shorter time-span. This is what we test in the following section by comparing eighteen core countries in the period between 1948 and 1983. Our empirical study tests the impact of effective social order as evidenced by the absence of mass political protest and includes only core countries, which are the topic of this book.[6] Other outcomes on the world market for protection in different subformations of the world system have briefly been discussed in chapter 3.

By restricting our analysis to core countries we introduce certain noteworthy conditions. The institutional framework under the rule of law—political democracy with civil rights permitting expression of dissent and opposition—drastically narrows the range of options between the use of force and measures that enhance legitimacy. Seen from the perspective of the history of state formation, governments in postwar core countries employed comparatively little overt force. In the postwar era the techniques used in Western countries to elicit popular legitimacy for a social order are those typical of the welfare state era. A cluster of such policies, which became very popular in several Western countries, consists of neo-corporatist arrangements of conflict resolution, strategies to help dampen class conflict, measures to redistribute income (including substantial social security benefits), measures to reduce inequality of opportunities in status allocation through the opening of the school system, and other interventions.

From the very characterization of the whole period under study as the welfare state era, it becomes obvious that government in general played a large role. Yet, more specifically, we expect that the extent to which government policies were successful in containing social conflict represented a valuable asset, i.e., legitimacy, which resulted in comparative national economic success. This does not imply that the sheer size of government matters. Quite the contrary: economic resources controlled by the state, but which are not channelled into political action to enhance legitimacy, should have an unfavorable impact on comparative economic success (being relics of the past or new forms of tribute logic).

In order to test the hypotheses of the comparative advantage of legitimacy, we rely in this study on the frequency of mass political protest events taken from Taylor and Jodice (1983, vol. 2), weighted by the number of citizens in millions. The inverse of this conflict measure we consider as an indicator of legitimacy. This approach is obviously not without problems. Frequent mass political protest is of course an indicator of limited legitimacy. But the absence of such protest does not necessarily indicate legitimacy, but may only mean mere tolerance of the social order or may be the result of government repression of mass political conflict. The latter objection we do not consider relevant in the context of core Western societies, but it seems of importance in other societies. Yet, the objection that the absence of protest may indicate either mere tolerance or legitimacy cannot be ruled out in this study, which is thus exploratory. The reader who is skeptical about our interpretation of the legitimacy indicator may simply interpret the empirical results more straightforwardly: absence of mass political protest.

In testing for the effect of legitimacy on comparative economic success we must control for measures of government size in order to show that economic advantage is not simply a correlate of government, but is politically created by a specific set of measures at the heart of the welfare state model. Although we do not analyze such measures in detail, we shall point to some empirical correlates of legitimacy as measured here.

There is no single plausible measure of the quantitative role of government, since it depends on one's perspective. In national terms, the resources which, for example, the Dutch state controls may be quite impressive (government expenditures of the Dutch state as compared to Dutch GDP), but in absolute terms, states in larger countries have much more impressive resources on hand. Thus, even if the relative share of government were the same among Western societies (which is, of course, not the case), the absolute size of government would still differ enormously. This is due to an important structural feature in the world system: large differences in power among states. Since absolute government size may provide a basis for influencing the world political economy, we have to consider such a measure as a control variable in our model.

Furthermore, if a certain level of absolute government size is necessary in the world political economy in order to protect national economic interests, the relative size of government in smaller countries will necessarily be larger than in bigger ones. Thus, we would not expect relative size per se to be unfavorable for economic success. Smaller countries are forced by the world political economy to reconcile the imperatives of the world economy and those of the national economy to a greater extent than larger countries. In order to be competitive within the core, they have to enhance state strength but use it in a way that increases domestic legitimacy. This is all the more the case if a small country is highly integrated into the world political economy (see chapter 11).

In earlier studies we employed an additional control variable with the following reasoning. Trade among the core countries was effectively regulated under the GATT rules (non-discrimination and liberalization) for only part of the period under study (1948-1983). The exercise of power in international trade relations became more important after 1971-73 (see Bornschier 1990). In addition, over the course of the period under study, new trading blocs emerged, like the European Community, while the (British) Commonwealth disintegrated. Commonwealth membership was included in earlier tests but did not produce significant effects in the test models we report here.

We must also highlight a variable which we consider to be very important for explaining comparative economic success: the catch-up or latecomer effect. The United States emerged from World War II as the consolidated economic and political hegemonic power. As compared to Japan and large parts of Europe which faced heavy economic disruption and destruction, the United States entered the postwar era strengthened: it initially took a clear lead in the new economic sectors providing the greatest dynamism to the postwar boom. Thus, in terms of industrial development, but also in terms of standards of living and the spread of mass consumption, the United States was far ahead; others lagged behind, although to quite different degrees. This is evidenced by the considerable range of GNP per capita in 1950, when the U.S. figure, the highest at that time, was ten times higher than the lowest figure, that for Japan. In the postwar period, however, the initially poorer countries caught up rapidly, that is, other things being equal, those with lower initial GNP per capita grew faster on the average. This catch-up effect, limited as it was to core countries, will be included in our quantitative test.

Finally, our concept of comparative economic success needs some comment. In order to test the impact of our explanatory variable legitimacy, we need to cover a long period, since we expect the effects to appear gradually but cumulatively. The frequently used measure of real growth rates of aggregate economic figures, like the GNP, have clear limitations since revaluations of currencies (especially under floating exchange rates in effect since the 1970s) have an impact on national economic wealth. This is of even greater importance if countries trade extensively across borders.

Therefore, we do not use real growth rates as our measure, but compare instead the relative positions of countries at the beginning and the end of the period under study. As the dimension of comparison we use a country's share of the total gross national product of the core converted to U.S. dollars.

TABLE 13.3 Indicators used in the Empirical Study

Economic success[1]

- GNP growth: the ratio of a country's share in total GNP of the core, 1980 and 1955: (GNP 1980/GNP 1955, times 100). The source is World Bank (1971, 1983).

Test variables

- Mass political protest, 1948-1977, per million inhabitants in 1965. This indicator includes all anti-government demonstrations, riots, and political strikes and relates them to the total population. The source is Taylor and Jodice (1983, II: 16ff.). The source reports for the years 1948 to 1977 a total of 7742 events for all 18 countries. Hibbs (1973) has demonstrated that the aforementioned conflict items load on one factor, which was confirmed by our own factor analysis.[2]
- Initial wealth as indicated by GNP per capita in 1950 (World Bank 1971).

Control variables

- Relative size of government over the 1948-1977 period, indicated by government expenditures as a share of GDP, average for the figures for 1950, 1960 and 1977. The sources are Schmidt (1982) and OECD (1985).
- Absolute size of government over the 1948-1977 period, indicated by government expenditures in U.S. dollars. This variable is constructed by multiplying the government share by total GDP.

Note: 1) Results for alternative measures of economic success are briefly mentioned in the text, for details see Bornschier (1989). 2) We interpret the inverse of political mass protest as an indicator of legitimacy.

In the following we report results of rigorous tests measuring whether the successful management of conflict in the welfare state era was a source of comparative economic success. The reader not too familiar with procedures of statistical inference may prefer to proceed to the discussion of our findings and to the concluding remarks on our empirical studies.

Design of the Test

We analyzed a large part of the postwar era, as the epoch in which the welfare state was institutionalized and expanded, and categorized the whole period from 1948 to 1977 using an indicator of mass political protest, which we interpret as relative lack of legitimacy. We do not consider changes in legitimacy over time (see chapter 7); instead we compare differences in solutions for moderating the ever-present social conflict over the whole epoch and relate them to comparative economic success among the core countries. Our causal hypothesis is difficult to test since we take a whole epoch as our unit of analysis. In order to include a causal ordering in our design, we estimate the lagged effect of legitimacy in the 1948-77 period on economic performance from the mid-1950s to beginning of the 1980s. The results we obtained with this method were checked by estimating lagged cross-panel regressions. The advantage of such a design is that we can rule out false causal inferences, but this is achieved at the expense of confining our observations of mass political conflict to shorter periods.

The model we apply proposes that our measure of comparative economic success is proportional to the inverse of mass political protest and the inverse of initial wealth. To this model we add control variables in a second step. The model is given in formula 1:

Formula 1: $$y' = \frac{a}{x \cdot z}$$

where: y' denotes the estimated growth ratio, a is a constant (which represents the unmeasured growth effects), x denotes mass political protest, and z represents initial wealth.

The model in formula 1 specifies non-linear relationships. In order to be able to apply linear regression methods we have to transform the model into linear relationships. This can be done by taking the natural logarithms of each of the variables.

Formula 2: $$\ln y' = \ln \mathrm{a} - \mathrm{b}_1 \cdot \ln x - \mathrm{b}_2 \cdot \ln z$$

The model specified in formula 2 can be estimated by ordinary-least-squares techniques (OLS). In order to show that such a log-linear model yields better results and thus corroborates our non-linear specification of effects, we also report the results for linear effects between the variables.

Results

Table 13.4 presents the results of regressing the ratio of GNP1980 / GNP1955 on mass political protest, on initial GNP per capita, and on the two control variables in log-linear form. Equation 1 includes only the two main predictors without any control variables. Initial GNP per capita has a significant and very substantial negative effect on comparative GNP growth. The same applies to mass political protest, which has a significant and substantial negative effect on the GNP growth ratio. Both predictors are virtually independent: the correlation between initial wealth and mass

TABLE 13.4 OLS Estimates of Comparative Economic Success as Measured by GNP Growth.

Predictors	Equation 1				Equation 2			
	b	beta	t	p	b	beta	t	p
Mass political protest	-.267	-.50	4.92	.0002	-.268	-.51	5.37	.0001
Initial wealth	-.558	-.80	7.78	.0001	-.540	-.77	8.12	.000
Relative size of government	not included				-.478	-.18	1.94	.073
Absolute size of government	not included				not significant			
Intercept	9.249				10.792			
R-square, corrected for degrees of freedom	.82				.85			

Note: The insignificant predictors in equation 2 were removed from the final regression.

political protest is r= -.06. Equation 2 tests whether our control variables (relative and absolute size of government expenditures) have an impact. Only for the measure of relative size of government do we obtain a negative effect, and its inclusion leaves the effects of initial wealth and mass political protest almost unchanged. Again, the correlations between the independent variables are practically zero (relative size of government with mass political protest: r= -.01; with initial wealth: r= .14). The effects of the other control variables are insignificant.

Robustness of the Results

The regression of the GNP growth ratio on initial wealth alone, on mass political protest alone, and on relative size of government alone are presented in figure 13.1. Removing outliers from the regressions still yields very significant results for initial wealth and mass political protest, whereas removing the outlier on relative size of government from the sample (i.e., Japan, with the lowest value on this variable and the highest value on GNP growth ratio) makes the effect of relative size of government expenditure drop to insignificance (t=.88).

FIGURE 13.1 Zero-order Regressions of the Variables in Equation 2 of Table 13.4

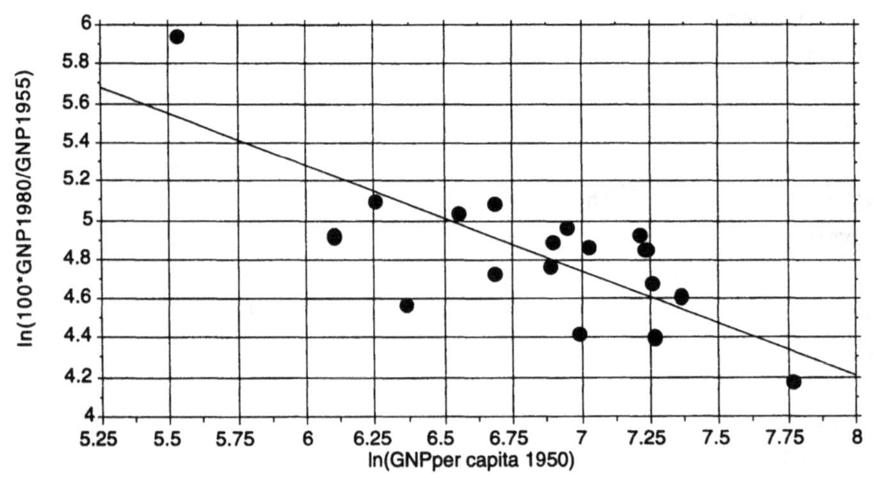

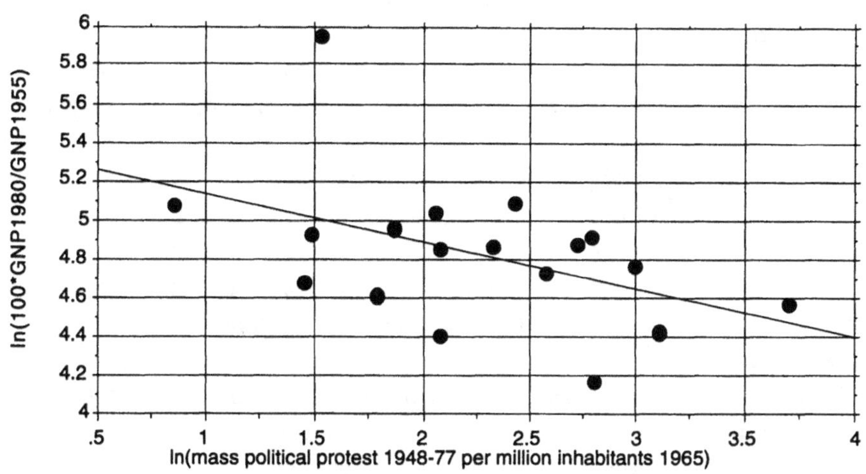

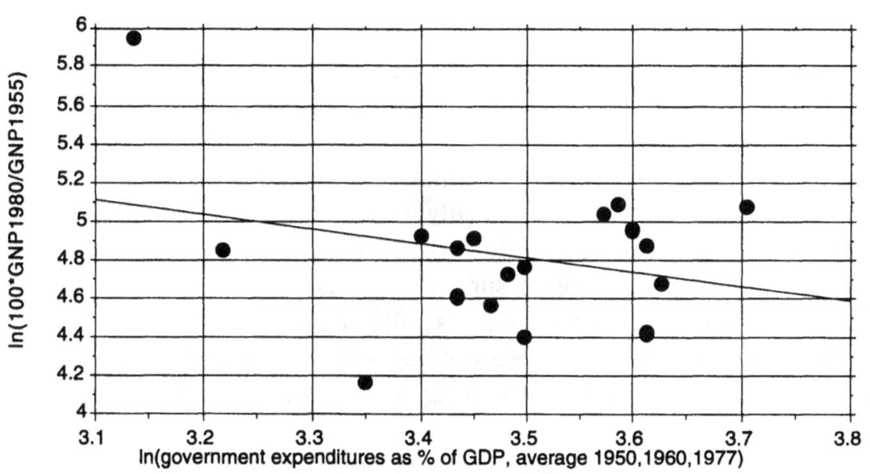

A further test for robustness pertains to the question: does only the log-linear specification produce the results? When we regress the GNP growth ratio on the predictors, both dependent and independent variables being now in un-logged form, we obtain the same structure of results as listed in table 13.4, albeit with a less significant total regression because non-linearities are now involved. But in this case both initial GNP per capita and mass political protest have significant negative effects on GNP growth, whereas the effect of the relative size of government expenditures is negative, but again not robust.

We thus find for eighteen core countries that mass political protest 1948-1977 per million inhabitants and initial GNP per capita 1950 have substantial negative effects on the growth of GNP between 1955 and 1980. The quantitative role of government has either no effect at all or a negative effect that is not robust because it rests solely on the impact of a single outlier. Since we interpret mass political protest as an indicator of relative lack of legitimacy, we can conclude that legitimacy has been an economic advantage, whereas the quantitative role of government as such had no impact on economic growth.

In additional tests not reported here in detail we checked whether this finding holds for other indicators of comparative economic success and whether our causal inferences were appropriate (see Bornschier 1989). GNP per capita growth ratio as the dependent variable was the first alternative measure of economic success. Also in this case mass political protest and initial GNP per capita were significant predictors. Relative scale of government expenditures has a significant negative effect which is, again, not robust once we remove only one outlier. Growth of the share in world export was the second alternative for the dependent variable. Again, both initial GNP per capita and mass political protest had significant negative effects on export share growth. Finally: was a sound economic performance helpful to keep social conflict low, or does causality also apply the other way round, as our hypothesis suggests? A lagged cross-panel regression model that included measures of mass political protest between 1948-67 and 1968-1982 was tested (see Bornschier 1989). The results support the contention that political protest reduces comparative economic success.

Discussion of the Findings

First we wish to highlight what we consider to be our main findings:

(1) Countries with lower initial wealth had an economic advantage over others. This catch-up effect among core societies proved to be very strong.

(2) Furthermore, countries with a lower level of mass political protest from 1948-1977 had more comparative economic success in the period between the mid-1950s and early 1980s. This holds for all three measures of economic success. This finding appears to be robust and additional tests suggest that our causal interpretation cannot be ruled out.

(3) We did not find the quantitative role of government over the 1948-1977 period to be substantially related to comparative economic success. The effect was either not robust or small.

We interpret our findings in the following way: legitimacy or effective social order has been a competitive advantage in the postwar era for Western core countries. It was therefore not government intervention as such that mattered, but intervention that enhanced legitimacy among the citizens. This appears to us to be an often neglected point in the debate about the welfare state.

How do the results of our tests compare with other findings? Negative associations between political protest and economic growth indicators are also reported in previous research (see Hibbs 1973: 38; Jagodzinski 1983: 36; Zimmermann 1988, 1989; and our chapter 11). In contrast to these earlier findings for world samples of countries, the effect revealed in our study appears remarkably robust and is more substantial. One likely reason is that we confined our analysis to core countries, employed controls and covered a long period. In a recent reanalysis Weede (1994) could replicate the findings reported in this chapter. He finds significant negative effects for political mass protest, of the relative size of government and a significant effect of initial wealth also when he introduces the 'age of democracy' as an additional predictor of growth (with a significant negative effect).

The empirical analysis in this chapter has concentrated on legitimacy itself while measures to achieve it were not analysed. There exists also empirical evidence that measures to achieve legitimacy are related to comparative economic success. Walter Korpi (1985) found measures of welfare spending significantly positively associated with growth of GDP per capita as well as growth of productivity in the period 1950 to 1973, as well as from 1973 to 1979, for seventeen OECD countries. His measure of welfare spending was social security expenditures related to GDP. Korpi (1985) had to exclude the case of Japan in order to obtain significant results, since a large proportion of welfare spending in Japan is firm-based (see Ritter 1989: 190) and thus does not enter Korpi's measure of public social security expenditures. Japan is thus not a deviant case, but one that partly uses different means to achieve legitimacy.

The relationship between various measures to achieve legitimacy and legitimacy itself needs further work. Outcomes of policies and socio-economic characteristics which covary with our measure of legitimacy were found already in earlier research. Redistribution of income through the state and the openness of society measured by overall intergenerational occupational mobility are both significantly related to legitimacy as we use it here (see Bornschier 1989: 228). Furthermore, we know from earlier findings that dependence on the world economy (export share of GDP) and internal characteristics of policy formulation and conflict resolution (neocorporatism) are significantly related to our measure of legitimacy (see Bornschier 1989: 228). Such findings suggest the following causal chain: countries which are highly exposed to the world market make more efforts to achieve legitimacy among the citizens and apply neocorporatist forms of conflict resolution. This is in line with prior work on world market links and internal characteristics (see Cameron, 1978; Schmidt, 1982, Nollert 1992) as well as with Lewis Coser's (1956) Proposition Nine derived from the work of Georg Simmel (1908), a body of research which we discussed earlier in chapter 11.

Concluding Remarks on Our Empirical Studies

We can summarize our results for the three societal models as follows. During the first societal model (1835-1883) those national variants were successful which not only established economic liberalism, but also guaranteed a comparatively high degree of political freedom. During the second societal model (1883-1932) status as a colonial power was a long-term reason for the decline of world powers and more open and democratic societies had an advantage. During the third, the neocorporatist-Keynesian societal model (1932-1992), those societies fared better which spent more on social security, as has already been demonstrated by Walter Korpi (1985). In general, societies good at tempering social conflict were more successful. In our empirical tests we could not reject the hypothesis that politically created effective social order matters for long-term economic success. Effective social order in which citizens invest legitimacy we found to be positively associated with various indicators of economic performance over a thirty-five-year period. There is no reason to accuse the welfare state of having been a "leaky bucket;" on the contrary, it was an indispensable "irrigation system,"[7] one of the bases for success. This statement applies to the qualitative role of government.

In a comparison of all three societal models, the second—the class-polarized societal model during its imperialist phase—was the weakest.

Correspondingly, it offered less stable overall conditions for economic success. This can be seen in a comparison of the economic growth of all three societal models (see chapter 4).

From a long historical perspective, we conclude that social arrangements which enjoyed high-quality protection had an edge over their competitors in the world system. To avoid falsifying history, we must acknowledge the following regularity: the "long run" in more successful social formations has always been characterized by protection options that favor legitimacy. This should be understood in comparative-historical terms, i.e., social formations as compared to their contemporary competitors. For this reason they were successful and, for a while, leaders in capitalist development. Freer arrangements of wage labor, more opportunities for larger parts of the population, and more liberal institutions were typical for all the industrial leaders of the modern world system. This also holds when one goes far back, beyond Venice and North Holland, which pioneered the world economy project in European modernity. Since the nineteenth century, this option, typical for ascending social formations, became even more urgent due to increasing levels of industrial complexity. Those who tried to "buck this trend" never reached the peaks of the world industrial pyramid.

The world market for protection thus seems to regulate the political undertakings in the long run through the differential economic success associated with differences in effective social order it provides. The mechanism of competing social orders may thus tell us something about why social structures, including the state, converged at the core of the world system. The sanctioning of that specific social system to which Max Weber (1923: 288) first drew our attention in a very short paragraph of his posthumous work seems to have been powerful. Social formations which did not conform could not attain or maintain core status in the industrial system.

CONCLUSIONS FOR EVOLUTION THEORY

Thus far our empirical analyses refer to the economically visible advantages of high-quality protection within the core. The long-term advantages of favorable economic protection find their empirically observable reflection in a higher degree of economic efficiency in world competition. This holds for the past as well as for the present. From this perspective, attempts at optimizing legitimacy against competitors yielded better results the more coercion was confined and the more investment was made in the tempering of conflict and the creation of legitimacy.

These results are of importance for evolutionary theory. For this reason, some clarifications are in order. Evolutionism, as influenced by Charles Darwin's descent and natural selection theory, entered the social scientific discussion under the label of "Social Darwinism" and has rightfully been discredited. Herbert Spencer ([1880] 1969), the theoretician of a deterministic, universal evolutionism, introduced Social Darwinism into sociology. The notion of "natural selection" ("the survival of the fittest and the elimination of the unfit") can also be found in attempts to substantiate race theories. The dominance of power and its glorification has also appeared in social philosophy, particularly in the works of Friedrich Nietzsche (see Wieland 1975: 226).

Social Darwinism completely neglects two particularities of human social life that cannot be biologically deduced nor compared to biological processes: Human freedom of choice and human social solidarity, which defines the different models of societal development. But within this typical societal framework, the problem of "selection" remains crucial for evolutionary theory (see also Giesen 1980; Davis 1961; Sanderson 1990). Thus, important questions attach to the meaning of "the fittest" and to how social selection proceeds.

If one sees the world as dominated by competition, it seems plausible to assume that the "strongest" will eventually prevail. Violence in the internal as well as the external sphere might seem to be the best survival strategy. Our perspective and our results contradict this idea. The history of the West cannot be adequately described on this basis because it leaves a number of questions open: why did the monumental absolutist states of modernity—Habsburg Spain and France—not prevail in the long run? Why was fascism not successful? Why is forced labor not the typical form of the organization of production? Why are our political orders not similar to the former South African apartheid regime? Many similar questions could be posed. Even if one accepts historicity as a part of events and developments and as an expression of free will—of persons as well as whole societies—the question as to why things happen must be asked.

The answer seems clear to us: "strength" in the sense of coercion and violence cannot have been a successful long-term survival resource in the competitive world milieu. Rather, it was strength founded on a higher degree of legitimacy that guided the more successful societies to the top. In this argument is hidden a convergence thesis regarding historical developments. Mediated by success in the external sphere, those arrangements of social structure advance which can claim more legitimacy, since they are more easily justified in terms of the leading values of modernity. Yet, the evolutionary process is not linear; models of social structure emerge and pass away. Change throughout the Western world cannot be described as a cycle—history as such is not repeated—but rather as a metamorphosis, which also includes elements of history in the true sense of the word, i.e., the choice between alternatives of action—individual as well as collective—without which there would be no human freedom. However, the basic driving forces behind events (the contradictory principles), the limiting condition (the world market for protection), and the cyclical processes of unfolding and decay (the career of societal models) are constant factors. Max Weber[8] noted earlier in this century: If the limiting condition changes, this particular type of society too will come to its historical end.

NOTES

1 Talcott Parsons (1964) refers to the two types of action when referring to the mobilization of resources through the market or, alternatively, through requisition by direct use of political power. In the so-called new political economy we find the same pair of opposites in the concepts of "profit seeking" and "rent seeking" (see for example Buchanan et al. 1980, or Tollison 1982). In the political economy advanced by Hartmut Elsenhans (1992) the difference between the "logic of profit" and the "logic of rent" is also of importance. Here, it is used to examine the change of the world system after the victory of the market over the planned economies. Already in earlier contributions, Elsenhans (1981) had suggested explaining the continuing underdevelopment of the Third World by the predominant rent logic of the corresponding state classes.

2 A great deal of inspiration in our treatment of the long-term evolution of social systems is due to Christopher Chase-Dunn, whose research has not yet been fully published. Some of his ideas can be found in Chase-Dunn (1981, 1989, 1992) and Chase-Dunn and Hall (forthcoming). Despite our lively exchange of ideas we have chosen different avenues for our conceptualization and have therefore also reached different assessments of long historical evolutions in some instances.

3 The neolithic revolution discussed by Jean-Jacques Rousseau ([1755] 1978) as important for the evolution of social systems—in the sense of a historical and not merely fictive hypothesis as advanced by Thomas Hobbes ([1641] 1962)—brought about not only one but three evolutionary avenues that became important for the conflictive sociogenesis of societal structure. These were the avenues of (1) agriculture

(horticulture at first); (2) cattle-breeding (nomadic, but still tied to the land); and (3) fishing, which historically branched off before the other two. These three development patterns were preceded by important innovations: the cultivation of plants, the domestication of sheep and dogs, the construction of boats, fishing-hooks, nets, and traps. From the first two patterns the land-bound territorial systems emerged whereas the third led to non-territorial maritime societies.

4 North Holland and England have been discussed in chapter 10. Earlier cases include: Sumer (Curtin 1984); Mesopotamia (Oppenheim 1967); the Minoans (McNeill 1963); the Phoenicians (Harden 1963; Moscati 1988). The Phoenicians and the Greeks are analyzed by Mann (1986), the Etruscans by Grant (1980), the Venetians by Lane (1973), and the Venetians and the Genovese by Braudel ([1979] 1984).

5 Similar relationships can be found if the per capita level of industrial production (Bairoch 1982) is taken for the years 1830 and 1880.

6 We rely in this section on our research published in the European Sociological Review (see Bornschier 1989). We include the same 18 countries as in other empirical investigations on the postwar societal model (see, for example chapter 11), i.e., Austria, Australia, Belgium, Canada, Denmark, Finland, France, German Fed. Rep., Great Britain, Ireland, Italy, Japan, Netherlands, New Zealand, Norway, Sweden, Switzerland, United States. We exclude those countries with very small populations (Iceland and Luxembourg) as well as one involved in quasi-continuous warfare (Israel).

7 The metaphors "leaky bucket" and "irrigation system" have been taken from Walter Korpi's (1985) work.

8 Max Weber (1923: 288f.): "Aber im Unterschied von damals [Antike] gerieten sie [die Städte] in die Gewalt konkurrierender Nationalstaaten, die in ständigem friedlichem und kriegerischem Kampf um die Macht lagen. Dieser Konkurrenzkampf schuf dem neuzeitlich-abendländischen Kapitalismus die grössten Chancen. Der einzelne Staat musste um das freizügige Kapital konkurrieren, das ihm die Bedingungen vorschrieb, unter denen es ihm zur Macht verhelfen wollte. Aus dem notgedrungenen Bündnis des Staates mit dem Kapital ging der nationale Bürgerstand hervor, die Bourgeoisie im modernen Sinn des Wortes. Der geschlossene nationale Staat also ist es, der dem Kapitalismus die Chancen des Fortbestehens gewährleistet; solange er nicht einem Weltreich Platz macht, wird also auch der Kapitalismus dauern."

PART V

PRESENT TRANSFORMATIONS AND FUTURE COMPETITIVE EDGES

This final section starts with a discussion of Western European integration as a model case of competition at the core. In chapter 14 the transition of Western Europe towards the political union is described and explained. For the first time in the sequence of societal models, a compromise between state sphere and market goes beyond international regimes and transcends the traditional framework of the nation-state. Chapter 15 addresses the probable features of a new societal model; it discusses the consolidation of market society and the new treatment of efficiency, security and equality. The European Union also changes the competitive situation at the core. Only now, and after the elimination of the Soviet Union, is it possible to speak of a triad of comparably powerful actors on the world stage. Yet, this constellation is not a mere transitory stage. Although a change in hegemonic practices is in sight, in the concluding chapter we argue that, contrary to the predictions of mechanistic cycle theories, the transformation will not end with the emergence of a new hegemonic power in the sense of the traditional key role of a single nation-state.

14
WESTERN EUROPEAN UNIFICATION AS A COMPETING MODEL IN THE TRIAD

THE REVITALIZATION OF WESTERN EUROPE

In a booklet distributed at Seville's 1992 Universal Exposition, the European Community (EC) presents itself to the world as follows:[1]

> Now an economic giant, the Community is striving to consolidate the Single Market into an economic and monetary union and to put in place political structures that will give it a *prime* role in helping define the post-Cold War world order (Commission of the EC 1992: 2, emphasis added).

This presentation admits that the European Community is only part of the so-called triad:

> The Community is one of the three pillars, along with the United States of America and Japan, on which the system of pluralist democracy and market economy is built (ibid.).

Yet, the European Community's claim to a *prime* role could also signal a bid for mastery in global affairs. Does this claim mean a striving for hegemony, or is it rather an admission of weakness?

The political Euro-entrepreneur Jacques Delors, who assumed the presidency of the EC Commission in Brussels on January 6, 1985, brought impetus to a Community paralyzed by lethargy and budgetary squabbling. Recently he declared in an interview: "Out of the dynamic economic and commercial power which we already are, a great political power must develop" (Delors, 1991: 20). He explains this by a "historical responsibility" and feels it would be sad if "the Europeans of the year 2010 (...) were to become mere spectators of history" (ibid.: 21). Anxiety about projecting European brilliance into the future appears in Jacques Delors' warning:

> We must move quickly otherwise Europe will become an archaeological excavation site, where Americans and Japanese seek for lost ideas and ways of life (Delors, 1991: 21).

In the following discussion, we will first address the emergence of the Single European Act. Because the project of Western European integration was characterized by marked cycles, we link the revitalization of Europe during the 1980s to the perspective of discontinuous social transition, i.e., the rise and decline of societal models, the subject of this book. This is why we emphasize the timing of events, the social forces behind the relaunch and its protagonists.

What effected the relaunch? Our explanation of the qualitative surge in the politico-economic development of Western Europe, which will be further elaborated, proposes that changes in the world political economy offer a starting point. The trigger was the challenge perceived by Europe's economic and political elites at the end of the 1970s: the dissolution of the Keynesian societal model, the relative decline of American hegemony and the economic crisis. Japan, the new Far Eastern industrial giant, set about pushing the European powers from second place, behind the United States, to third place. The institutional independence of the EC Commission was surely a prerequisite for initiative and political entrepreneurship on its part, but a serious explanation can only be put forward if we also introduce elements pertaining to the world market for protection, which concerns the supply and demand for public goods, i.e., state actions. In this framework, we will discuss the role of the transnational European economic elite. We advance our version of an elite pact as an explanation of the emergence of the Single European Act and discuss certain findings of our research to substantiate our thesis.

STATE-BUILDING IN EUROPE

Why do we stress the role of the Single European Act in the course of Western European integration, which has been proceeding for about thirty years? Because the Act is the decisive crossroads from European economic integration toward statehood. Under the banner bearing the magic inscription "Europe 92," Western Europe is preparing to transform itself economically and politically. How can this relaunch be viewed within the framework of the

European state-building process? Western European integration in the perspective of unification means in some respects a continuation, in other respects, however, an overcoming of previous features of the European state-building process. The continuation of the 500-year-old European state-building process refers to the concentration of politico-territorial rule (Elias [1969] 1977)—an implosion of originally 500 state-like structures to only two dozen (Tilly 1975: 15). On the other hand, the union exhibits features that point to an earlier successful yet untypical state project to be discussed at the end of this section.

Western European integration is a social innovation in various respects.

(1) The process will mean the end of a multistate balance of power in Europe. The problem of the distribution of power at the core of the world system was already posed anew after Western Europe lost its previous undisputed leadership earlier in this century. Thus, Western European integration by no means creates a concentration of power for the whole of the core, which will remain at least trilateral.

(2) The unification project does not conform to two crucial characteristics of state-building according to the Western European model (Rokkan 1975, 1981). As far as can be anticipated, the future union will not have a prominent central authority nor a standardized culture. Thus, the integration process will not continue the European nation-state-building tradition.

(3) During previous changes of the societal model, one constant was obvious: the articulation of the linkage between the political and economic realms, although it differed between societal models, always took place within the framework of nation-states. Via the Single European Act and continued by the political union, for the first time a supra-state linkage of the two realms is created that goes beyond loose international regimes. This is new, as is the extension of welfare state issues to the interstate determination of life chances.

(4) Finally, Western European integration is developing in the direction of a new state that exhibits certain similarities with an earlier European state project (see below) but, for the first time in European history, does not rely on military structures for the integration of such a huge and economically potent body, but rather on a legal and economic community which does not aim to deprive its members of their cultural specificities.

Legal and economic issues are the starting point for some remarks on statehood. A community as a type of political body is characterized by the rule of shared laws based on treaties. According to the dominant doctrine, communities are not (federal) states in the true sense (Nicolaysen 1991). From a social scientific perspective, such an exclusive distinction does not make much sense, however. In any case, communities are characterized by supranationality according to legal principles (Nicolaysen 1991). In sectors specified by treaties, sovereignty is assigned to the community and thus supra-nationality is created. In international law this remains dubious, however. To distinguish communities from states, constitutional law points to the fact that communities only cover limited goals, that is, communities are only a means of functional integration (Nicolaysen 1991). Yet, have Europe's goals really been as limited as this since the emergence of the Single European Act?

How communities can claim statehood could be determined on normative-theoretical grounds. Yet, for empirical sociology it is also useful to define statehood as a variable with threshold values in a descriptive, factual way. Whether statehood in this sense is reached not only depends on threshold values, however, but also on the societal type which circumscribes the role of the state. The characteristics of the societal type under discussion are the market economy and political democracy already discussed in chapter 1.

As economic actors, the people in the states of the Community have become fully integrated citizens of the European Community with the adoption of the Single European Act. With respect to citizenship, the new Community is only indirectly endowed with legitimacy by these economic actors by way of democratic elections of the heads of state and governments who negotiate and renew the treaties. This is true despite the fact that the European Parliament is directly elected and has been upgraded by the Single European Act. Its increased weight notwithstanding, the parliament's jurisdiction does not match the jurisdiction of national parliaments. If we measure these developments with reference to the criteria of the societal type, we must therefore conclude that statehood is being developed in a different way.

Yet, in the important sphere of the market economy statehood has already gone quite far. With reference to the market economy we can thus claim that a community assumes state character: 1) if important economic policies are set by the community; 2) if the community has its own financial jurisdiction and its own fiscal resources; 3) if it has monetary authority, and 4) if remaining central areas (policy, security) are at least coordinated between the member states and if the community is at least party to such coordination. According to such a list of criteria, the European Community can be said to have possessed proper statehood since the adoption of the 1986 Single European Act (ratified 1987)—and not just since the 1992 Maastricht treaty regarding the political union (ratified 1993).

In order to clarify, some points must be added. The significant change within the Community during the mid-1980s becomes evident in two events that find expression in two documents published by the Community—the Commission's White Paper (1985) for the European Council (heads of state and governments) regarding the completion of the internal market, and the Single European Act, adopted in December 1985 by the European Council and formally approved by the Council of Ministers (ministers of foreign affairs) on February 28, 1986. The White Paper was a political initiative of the Commission; as such it was not exceptional, because within the European Community the Commission is a supranational body, whose independence from the member states was already set out in the treaties of 1958. The Commission is at the same time a partner of and in opposition to the Council (Fusion Treaty, article 15). Because of the multitude of its functions the Commission plays a key role within the Community—it is its motor, has a right to make proposals in the legal process (which then are formally agreed upon by the Council) and is mandated to take initiatives. The plans, programs and memoranda of the Commission are believed to advance the development of the Community. All this was already agreed upon in the treaties in effect since 1958.

The White Paper had already been prepared when Jacques Delors assumed the presidency in spring 1985. As our own research shows, the first initiatives of the Commission to establish the internal market can be traced back at least to 1981 (see below and table 14.1). The internal market project was negotiated between the Commission and the European Round Table of Industrialists (ERT). The ERT is an informal panel founded at the initiative of Commissioners Etienne Davignon and François-Xavier Ortoli in April 1983; it was composed of seventeen top European industrialists, and was later expanded to include forty members. Wisse Dekker—head of Philips, already an influential figure in the ERT and later its president, who formulated the "Agenda for Action: Europe 1990"—and Lord Cockfield—then vice-president of the Commission, under whose auspices the White Paper "Europe 1992" was drafted—were bound together by more than common intentions. At least since April 1983, the informal panel of the ERT (informal because it is not a body within the institutional framework of the Community) linked the protagonists of the Commission and the transnational European economy together in a single organizational framework.

Naturally, formally and as foreseen by the constitution, the member states of the Community had to become active and renegotiate the original treaty for the Single European Act. According to our hypothesis, which has also been substantiated empirically, the initiative did not originate in the Council (representing the member states). The Council only transformed the new project into applicable law. The renewed treaty brought about a marked broadening and overstepping of the original EC treaties. The Single European Act marks the transition to proper statehood.

The Single European Act is called *single* exactly because it regulates European policy cooperation by treaty and changes existing treaties of the Community at the same time. Since its adoption the new superior body of the Community, the European Council (heads of state and governments of the member states), coordinates political and economic policies with the president of the Commission, who is a member of the European Council with equal rights.

The intentions of the new formulation of the treaty are evident. The Single European Act is explicitly understood as a step towards European union (see its preamble). The second part of the Single European Act (Part II) includes changes of the original European Economic Community treaty affected by the new one, and the third part (Part III) regulates political cooperation in Europe. In the first instance, the provisions regarding the establishment of the internal market by the end of 1992 are worth mentioning. These conceptions of "Europe 92" were the most prominent in the headlines at the time.

Further, the renewed treaty also involved substantial changes in the institutional frameworks. The procedure for enacting law changed as follows: the majority vote in the Council was extended. Now, for all decisions concerning the internal market, qualified majority votes are stipulated. In connection with the alignment of legal regulations either a qualified majority vote or the mutual recognition of the equivalence of regulations in the member states is called for. Further, the participation of the European Parliament in formulating legislation and its budgetary authority are expanded. Finally, the treaty broadens the role of the European Court of Justice by way of the coordination of courts of first instance.

In addition, the agreement concerning new and extensions of earlier authority of the European Community is worth mentioning. The section regarding the progress of economic and social cohesion (Part V) is new jurisdiction. Also new is the fact that environmental policy falls under the Community (Part VII). Further, the Community obtains the authority to support research and technological development to advance international competitiveness (Part VI). Earlier authority has also been significantly extended, for example, in connection with social policy (improvement of working conditions, minimum standards, dialogue between social partners) and economic policy (the creation of the European monetary system and its corresponding institutional changes).

These briefly described elements of the renewed treaty allow us to speak of the Community's statehood with respect to the sphere of the market economy. A supranational linkage of the political and the economic spheres going beyond loose international agreements is for the first time detached from the national framework. What consequences follow? A rearrangement of the state sphere, which is to be one issue of the future societal model, is very difficult (see chapter 15). For that reason, a rearrangement in the direction of a lean state may be easier in those instances where there was previously no or only limited jurisdiction at the highest level of public administration. In this connection, European integration towards a new political arrangement is of the highest interest.

The European Union remains a somewhat strange hermaphrodite, between a state confederation and a federal state. Is it not too early to speak of state-building in Europe? In many respects, the new form is a novelty, but it has at least one European antecedent which made history for a century. In chapter 10 we already pointed to the two very different roots of state-building in Europe. The theory of the social contract also distinguishes between these two poles: the "contract of association" and the "contract of domination" (Dahrendorf 1992: 47). In a social philosophical perspective, Immanuel Kant can be linked to the former variant, whereas the latter can be traced back to Thomas Hobbes. During the process of amalgamation described in chapter 10, the modern core state was influenced more strongly by the "trade and economic state" as a "contract of association" than by the colossal rapacious states founded on domination and military power. The European Union supports this process towards a lean state. Similarities with the Republic of the United Netherlands cannot be overlooked despite the centuries that lie between the two.

In *The Perspective of the World* (the third volume of *Civilization and Capitalism, 15th-18th Century*), Fernand Braudel ([1979] 1984, vol. 3) reports the boundless astonishment of contemporaries in the face of the vertiginous rise and unexpected power of such a small and in some respects entirely new country as North Holland. "Can the United Netherlands be called a 'state'?," Braudel (1984, 3: 193) asks and then explains that "the seven provinces considered themselves sovereign, and that they were moreover divided into tiny urban republics. It is also true that none of the central institutions—the Council of State or Raad van Staat (which was properly speaking the superintendent of all the Republic's affairs, a sort of executive or more accurately a Ministry of Finance) and the States-General which also sat in the Hague and was a permanent delegation of ambassadors from the provinces—had in theory any real power at all. Every important decision had to be referred to the provincial States and approved by them unanimously. Since the interests of the provinces diverged considerably—in particular those of the coastal from those of the inland provinces—this system was a perpetual source of conflict." Apart from the "vertiginous rise," it is possible today to detect many parallels with the European Union in this description by simply changing certain institutional designations.

EXPLANATIONS FOR THE EMERGENCE OF THE SINGLE EUROPEAN ACT

In recent years various books and articles have been published on the accelerated integration of Europe (Sandholtz and Zysman 1989; Moravcsik 1991; Cameron 1992; Bornschier [1992] 1994; George 1992a, 1993), which we have reviewed in detail elsewhere (see Bornschier and Fielder 1995). Here, we propose to mention the controversy between neofunctionalists and neorealists in the political science debates to clarify the particularities of our own approach.

Neofunctionalism and Neorealism

The analysis of Western European integration has revived the old controversy between neofunctionalists and neorealists (George 1992b: 21-24), while some recent contributions represent a combination of perspectives (George 1992a, 1993; Cameron 1992).

The central idea behind neofunctionalism is that of "spillover," distinguishing between "political spillover" and "functional spillover." Functional spillover pertains to the dynamics that occur when states decide to integrate certain economic sectors, forcing them to integrate further sectors in order for the integration of the first to succeed. These dynamics are seen as a result of the interdependence of economic sectors. Political spillover is the result of a new political reality in connection with the shift of political decisions from the national to the supranational level. As decisions are now made at the supranational level, relevant interest groups and other political actors shift their lobbying to the supranational level to influence the decision-making process. Those interest groups which benefit from integration then start pressuring their national governments into shifting ever more political functions to the supranational level. According to neofunctionalist theory, both spillover processes should be spontaneous and incremental because they result from the internal logic of integration. They not only occur in the lower realms of politics, but move from these technical areas to higher political fields of state sovereignty such as security and defense.

Neorealists, on the other hand, believe that because governments have been elected by the people, and therefore have legitimized power, they remain the truly significant actors in the integration process and defend national interests. Neorealists do not believe that a spillover from low to high politics will occur. Defense and security, which represent the essence of state sovereignty, will remain excluded from the integration process. Yet, the neorealists see the power structure in the overarching and global context as an important element reactively influencing states' decisions.

Neofunctionalist and neorealist explanations of this kind have various weaknesses, all of which stem from the fact that these perspectives regard nation-states as the only relevant actors. Further, neofunctionalism has too limited an understanding of transnational actors, while neorealism takes too narrow a view of government motives.

Transnational Corporations in Search of a Political Entrepreneur

The theoretical perspective on the world market for protection advanced in chapter 3 may overcome some of the theoretical limitations resulting from an approach centered on policy. As already discussed, two kinds of "enterprises" are introduced: states and firms. Thus, a framework is suggested that integrates supply of, and demand for, order. Together with the rise and decay of societal models, this approach seems promising, especially when we focus on questions of timing and of the protagonists behind the relaunch.

According to world market for protection arguments, states compete with each other not only in a politico-military sense—the classical form of their competition—but also in the framework of the world economy, essentially mediated by the production factor of social order guaranteed by the state. Thus, states also compete in a genuinely economic way, and in addition, they are forced to recreate, improve, or qualitatively reorganize interstate regulatory mechanisms in case they should break down or prove insufficient.

The idea of a world market for protection enriches the theoretical apparatus in one important respect. The economic motives of political undertakings—even more: the view thus implied that states are producers of economically valuable goods—become important. Such motives are added to the classic ones of security and power politics. In this our perspective differs from the neorealist approach. It also differs from neofunctionalism because the economic motives of state actors become predominant if the world economy is central to status distribution and if transnational corporations increasingly force states to compete with each other as sites of economic activity.

If we start from the competition of political entities supplying order and economic enterprises demanding order, it is easy to assume similar strategies for states as those pursued by economic enterprises. While competing they may cooperate, build strategic alliances or even merge; contrary to the neofunctionalist argument, such processes are not automatic results of internal spillovers; rather they are primarily generated by the competitive conditions of the world political economy. Such strategic alliances or even mergers are much more likely to happen—or maybe even possible only—if supranational institutional preconditions are met and available for political entrepreneurship. This was the case with the European Commission, whose independent role was stipulated at its inception in 1958.

Our theoretical perspective thus differs in important respects from the functionalist and realist theories of international relations. The argument from the theory of protection rent is as follows: European corporations asked the political entrepreneurs in Europe to provide them with the locational advantages their rivals were enjoying in the United States and Japan. This demand stimulated the negotiation of a new state project along the lines of a wide homogeneous market combined with strategic planning, particularly with regard to the ever more important production factor of technology.

This project was negotiated in the informal European Round Table of Industrialists (ERT). With his paper "Agenda for Action: Europe 1990," Wisse Dekker, a central figure in the ERT, created an important conceptual basis for the White Paper by the Commission's Lord Cockfield. The EC Commission acted as a political entrepreneur, launched and popularized the project, overcame the resistance of governments and submitted it to the Council for decision. The Commission's own motives and interests are discussed briefly below.

Sandholtz and Zysman (1989) have pointed to changes in the world economy as necessary for the relaunch of the European project. For decades Europe had not been the center of the world political economy. After the "civil war" of 1914-1918 the European powers had to relinquish this role to the United States, which actually only assumed it following the Second World War. The European powers took their place behind the United States after the Second World War and were startled when, due to the hegemonic decline of the United States, the previous stability of the world economic structure was no longer guaranteed and the impressive rise of Japan thrust Europe into third place in the world.

This perspective can be linked to the interests of the transnational corporations. The competitive disadvantages of Europe as an industrial site were first directly felt and articulated by the transnational corporations. After the economic crisis of the 1970s, the United States and particularly Japan recovered much more easily than a Europe immobilized by "Eurosclerosis"—a term coined by American observers. The United States, despite its loss of competitiveness, was able to take advantage of its own huge and rather homogeneous internal market; and Japan enjoyed the advantage of its elaborate strategic planning, which had already earlier been essential for Japan's extraordinary rise. It was the (certainly mild and flexible) "planned economy", tied indeed to capitalistically inspired business and oriented to long-term strategic goals that made Japan big, without being *laissez-faire*.

The second necessary condition for Europe's revival concerns the cyclical dynamics of societal models, a central theme of this book. The Western societal model disintegrated towards the end of the 1970s. Former hegemonic normative theories like Keynesianism were replaced by monetarist and supply-side oriented ones after the world summit in Bonn in 1978. In 1982 the new doctrine was anchored in the Organization for Economic Cooperation and Development (OECD) paradigm for a new economic policy of the Western world. The technological style, characterized by Fordist mass production, reached its limits, and the political shifts at the turn of the 1980s destroyed the unquestioned position of former politico-economic regimes in the postwar era. In terms of this approach, recasting the European

Community can be explained as a move towards a vision of a renewed social contract in Western Europe. Many statements by commissioners support such a view, for example: "Truly '1992' will mean a transformation of society. Mentalities and habits will change. Everywhere the key players in the economy realize that the future lies in the fullest sense in Europe" (Karel van Miert, Member of the European Commission, quoted in EC Commission 1992: 8). Recently, key EC publications can even be found using a central term of this book. The White Paper of December 1993 (p. 15) declares: "The renewal of the European societal model calls for less passive and more active solidarity."

The Decline of the Hegemon

The relaunch of the European Community must also be seen as an answer to contradictions inherent in the interventionist role of the state—a cornerstone of the neocorporatist-Keynesian societal model. Economic interventions are only free of major interstate conflicts if they are embedded in, and curbed by, international regimes.

One important pillar of this coordination was the U.S. dollar-gold exchange regime of Bretton Woods. In 1971 the United States, which once had established this system, was no longer in a position to defend the dollar. From an institutional viewpoint, the hegemonic power abdicated at the very time when the US gave up the exchange system it had itself created by "suspending" the obligation to maintain the U.S. dollar-gold parity. By 1973, as the European countries were forced to switch to floating rates, the system of fixed exchange rates broke apart completely, and the discipline of coordinating economic policies no longer existed. The important, even irreplaceable linkage had broken, because—as hegemonic stability theory would argue—no country was in a position or willing to guarantee the international exchange system. The relative decline of the United States and the disintegration of the societal model, which depended on interstate coordination of economic policy, are mutually linked. Both factors can be combined to explain the integrational momentum of the European Community.

We consider as a sufficient explanation the alliance of economic and political entrepreneurs to ensure protection rent. This answers the question: who were the actors, who gave the impulse for the relaunch? The fact that the EC Commission as a political entrepreneur has relative autonomy was certainly important since it could become innovative and make the merger of

FIGURE 14.1 The Genesis of the Single European Act

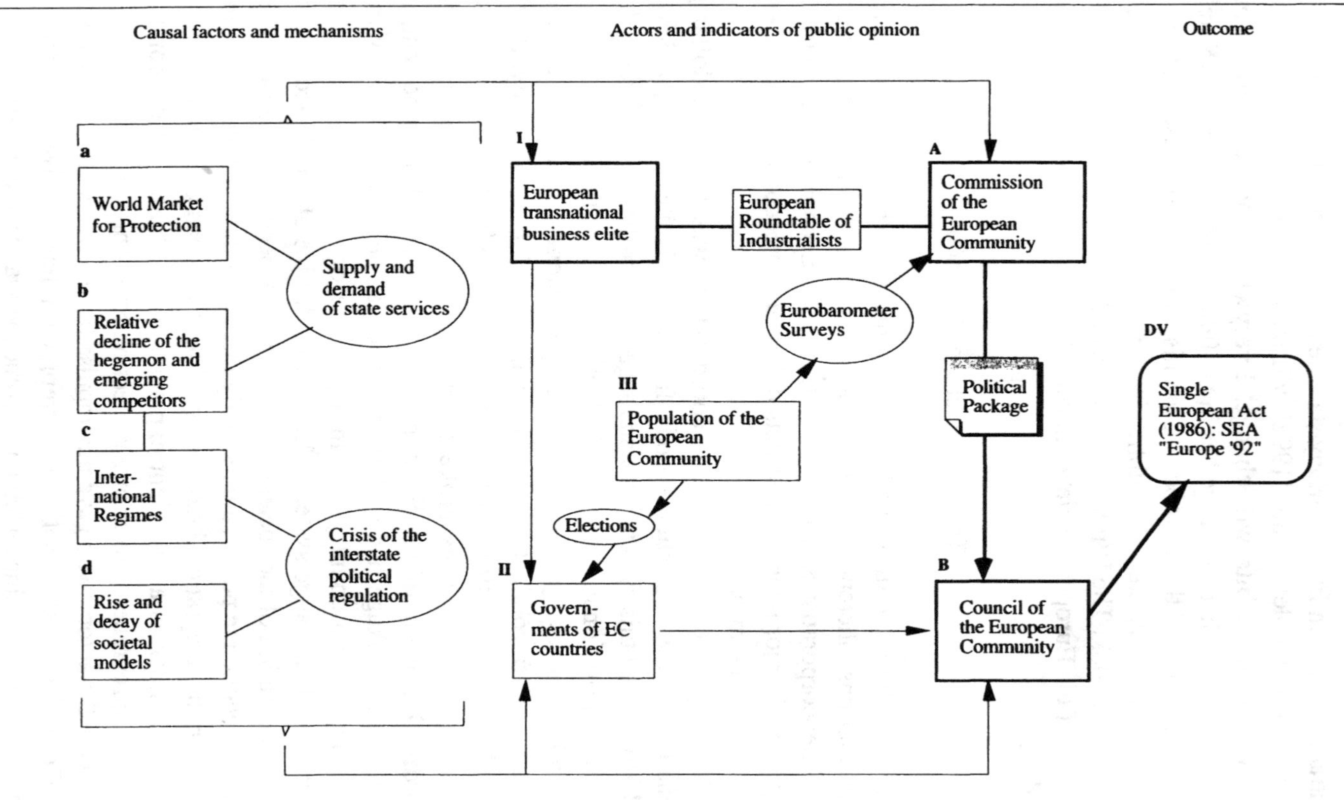

(FIGURE 14.1 continued)

Legend:

a,b,c,d	Causal factors and mechanisms
I, II, III	Social actors
A,B	Central institutions of the European Community along with the European Parliament and the European Court of Justice, as defined by the Treaties of 1957 and 1965.
DV	Dependent variable: the Single European Act (1986), a restructuring, deepening and widening of the European Community.

Comments:

1. According to EC law the final resolution on the Single European Act can only be passed by the Council. This is not a point of debate. It is the path to the final agreement on which the various authors differ.

• *Elite Bargain*	(a,b,c,d) -> I -> A -> B -> DV (Single European Act) "transnational networks & supranational institutionalism"
• *Alternative Elite Bargain*	II (mainly the "big three": F, GB, D) -> B -> DV (Single European Act) "intergovernmental institutionalism"

2. The population of the European Community (III) influences the process indirectly via the elections of the respective governments and through the Eurobarometer surveys (see below).

state services attractive to national governments. This institutional role was, however, not new in the 1980s; it has existed since the very beginning of the European Community.

Our emphasis is therefore on the timing of events and protagonists. At the turn of the 1980s certain constellations became apparent. The Western societal model had decayed during the 1970s, and the hegemon was no longer able to guarantee stability. Europe was confronted with Japan's success in mastering the world economic crisis on the one hand, and challenged by America's experiment under President Reagan to defend its world economic position on the other. At this juncture, the "demand" of transnational European business and the "supply" of the supranational EC Commission met and provided the impetus for a relaunch with a new politico-economic regime which would create the conditions for post-hegemonic competition in the world economy.

This explanation for the rebuilding of Western Europe is somewhat similar to the explanation advanced by Sandholtz and Zysman (1989) and can easily be brought into line with George's (1993) idea of the linkage of supranational and national levels. Of course, the European transnationals not only exerted influence on the Commission but were also mediated by national governments which were thus forced to take up the case of the Commission.

Our perspective is, however, in clear contradiction to Moravcsik's (1991) neorealist explanation. He claims that the Single European Act can be explained as the playing out of the national interests of the three big member states, Germany, France and Britain. Contrary to the somewhat less than clear position of Sandholtz and Zysman on this matter, Moravcsik offers a purely neorealist explanation. In what amounts to a sort of game theory explanation, the three big states are seen to have converged on the lowest common denominator of their national preferences. This view stresses that the heads of government and their direct representatives took the lead in the negotiations and produced the break-through which is represented by the Single European Act.

The substantial difference between these theoretical positions is thus whether the governments of the big countries took the lead via the EC Council of Ministers (intergovernmental institutionalism), or whether this role was played by the transnationals together with the EC Commission (transnational and supranational institutionalism). The latter is the competing hypothesis, and in figure 14.1 our arguments in support of it are summarized once again.

Evidence from Documents and Interviews of Witnesses

The results of our research to demonstrate empirically the differences between the two hypotheses have been documented in a special research report (see also Bornschier and Fielder, 1995).[2] Some methodological remarks are in order, however. At the level of the formal legislative process, it is impossible to decide between the competing hypotheses. Of course, the Council formally agreed upon creating the Single European Act. For constitutional reasons, this could not be otherwise. In order to glimpse the background—to detect and clarify the social forces at work and to see who were the important protagonists—we must analyze documents published before the decision. In order to substantiate our explanation, we have to verify these documents and to supplement them with interviews of protagonists and witnesses, necessary because our thesis stresses the informal relationships and negotiations between the representatives of different social forces which, precisely because of their informal character, are perhaps not clearly reflected in documents.

Our empirical research began with an analysis of documents starting from the Commission's 1985 White Paper, whose history in the interplay of Commission and Council was traced back to 1981. This White Paper was drafted in the EC Commission and then forwarded to the Council. Its exact title is: "Completing the Internal Market: White Paper of the Commission to the European Council." The secondary literature is quite clear that one of the most important authors of the White Paper was Lord Cockfield, then vice-president of the Commission and head of the Directorates General Internal Market (DGIII), Customs Union and Taxation (DGXXI), and Financial Institutions (DGXV). The steps towards the Single European Act reconstructed on the basis of documents are summarized in abbreviated form in table 14.1.

The documents only partially mentioned in table 14.1 show clearly how energetically the Commission pushed the internal market. The answers and documents supplied by the European Council, on the other hand, appear as automatic responses without any real content. As early as 1982 the Council declared: "The European Council [heads of governments and states] instructs the Council [of ministers] to agree on the preeminent measures aimed at strengthening the internal market advanced by the Commission before March 1993."[3] Following this declaration, very little was actually agreed upon. The

"Solemn Declaration of the European Union" of 1983 also stresses the importance of the internal market and the need to take steps towards the internal market—yet there were no concrete measures.

The analysis of the documents thus clearly shows the great importance of the EC Commission in the establishment of the internal market. The support provided by industry is also frequently mentioned. In addition, the documents show that the internal market project was from the beginning planned against the background of the competition of European enterprises within the Triad. A quote from a 1982 communication of the Commission to the Council can substantiate this

"European undertakings must be assured that their activities will be able to develop in an economic unit similar in size to the American market and distinctly bigger than the Japanese market (see table 14.1)"

TABLE 14.1 Steps towards the Single European Act (SEA)

• Communication of the Commission on the *State of the Internal Market* of June 17, 1981/COM (81) 313 final:
"The decline in confidence which threatens the internal market must immediately be halted by convincing political action" (p. 2)

Meeting of the Council of July 29-30, 1981
The Council took up the Commission's point, yet there was no effective improvement.

• Communication of the Commission on the *Re-Activation of the European internal market,* November 12, 1982/COM (82) 735 final:
"As the Commission has never ceased to affirm European undertakings must be assured that their activities will be able to develop in an economic unit similar in size to the American market and distinctly bigger than the Japanese market (...) To date, this has not been achieved. Although the problem issues have been clearly identified and fully discussed, the decisions have not yet been taken." (p. 1)

Meeting of the Council in Copenhagen, December 3-4, 1982
"The Heads of State and Governments at the European Council meeting in Copenhagen in 1982 pledged themselves to the completion of the internal market as a high priority." (Quoted from the White Paper 1985: 5)
Stuttgart Solemn Declaration of June 19, 1983

• *Consolidating the Internal Market,* Communication of the Commission to the Council of June 13, 1984/COM (84) 305 final:
"The Council's inaction cannot relieve the Commission of its obligation to take whatever measures are necessary to ensure the free movement of goods within the Community under conditions which are consistent with the aims of the treaty." (p. 14)
"The renewed drive will produce results only if the business community is again convinced that the European market is attractive." (p. 3)

Council meeting in Fontainebleau, June 25-26, 1984

"It [the European Council] asks the Council [of Ministers] and the member states to put in hand without delay a study of the measures which could be taken to bring about in the near future the abolition of all police and customs formalities for people crossing intra-Community frontiers" (Quoted from the White Paper, p. 3: "Declarations by the European Council Relating to the Internal Market")

Council meeting in Dublin, December 3-4, 1984

"The European Council agreed that the Council, in its appropriate formations: (...) should take steps to complete the internal market, including implementation of European standard." (Quoted from the White Paper, p. 3: "Declarations by the European Council Relating to the Internal Market")

"Programme of the Commission for 1985," presented to the Council on March 6, 1985:

"The Commission will be asking the European Council to pledge itself to completion of a fully unified internal market by 1992."

Council meeting in Brussels of March 29-30, 1985

"[The European Council] called upon the Commission to draw up a detailed programme with a specific timetable (relating to the completion of one single large market) before its next meeting." (Quoted from the White Paper, p. 3: "Declarations by the European Council Relating to the Internal Market")

• *Completing the Internal Market*, White Paper from the Commission to the European Council of June 1985

"Europe stands at the crossroads. We either go ahead—with resolution and determination—or we drop back into mediocrity. We can now either resolve to complete the integration of the economies of Europe; or, through lack of political will to face the immense problems involved, we can simply allow Europe to develop into no more than a free trade area." (p. 55)

Council meeting in Milan of June 1985

• *Single European Act*, 1986

"The Single European Act (. . .) is an expression of the political resolve voiced by the Heads of State or Government, notably at Fontainebleau in June 1984, then at Brussels in March 1985 and at Milan in June 1985, to transform the whole complex of relations between their states into a European Union, in line with the Stuttgart Solemn Declaration of 19 June 1983." (p. 27)

Source: Bornschier et al. (1993); see also endnote 2.

The similarity of this perspective with the one adopted by the European economic elite is evident from the first Policy Memorandum of the European Roundtable of Industrialists which had officially been handed over to the Commission in 1983:

> Despite the efforts of the European Community to liberalize trade, Europe remains divided into national markets with different industrial structures. This prevents many enterprises from reaching the size necessary to

withstand the pressure of competition from non-European concerns. But the European market must serve as a single "home base" so that European firms can develop into powerful competitors on world markets.

Our analyses of documents also served as background information for the interviews with experts that supplemented our research in order to substantiate the informal cooperation between the Commission and European leaders of the transnational economy. Of eight interviews, two were with informants who are experts on the subject of European integration and six were with actual witnesses to the integration process. The list in table 14.2 shows the institutional affiliations of our interviewees.

TABLE 14.2 Interview Partners

From the Commission

Lord Cockfield took office as British EC-Commissioner in Brussels in September 1984. During his term as Secretary of State for Trade he served as the British representative on the Internal Market Council, which was founded by the European Council in Copenhagen in December 1982. He was a vice-president of the Commission and was Commissioner responsible for the Directorates General Internal Market (DGIII), Customs Union and Taxation (DGXXI) and Financial Institutions (DGXV).

Vicomte Etienne Davignon was Commissioner for Belgium in the EC Commission and also served as its vice-president. From 1977 to 1981 he was head of the Directorate General Internal Market (DGIII) and from 1981 until 1987 he was the Commissioner responsible for Industry, Energy and Research. (See also below.)

Fernand Braun (from Luxembourg) worked in the European Commission from 1958 until 1990, finally holding the position of Director General. He worked with Lord Cockfield in the Directorate General Internal Market at the time of the White Paper.

From the European Roundtable of Industrialists

Prof. Dr. Wisse Dekker was President of Philips Electronics B.V. for many years including the early 1980s. He has recently become Chairman of the Supervisory Board of Philips. From 1988 until 1992 he was Chairman of the ERT and also influenced its establishment in 1983. Today he is still the Philips representative to the Roundtable. Under the leadership of Wisse Dekker, the Philips company actively supported the European integration process. In 1985, for instance, it submitted a report to the Commission entitled "Europe 1990: An Action Plan for Europe."

Vicomte Etienne Davignon heads the Société Générale de Belgique since 1987 and is its representative in the ERT.

Representatives of leading European economic associations

Dr. Hanns R. Glatz has been working in Brussels since 1970. He first worked for Ford Europe in the department of government affairs, i.e., the department dealing with the European Community. From 1979 he established the first permanent secretariat of the CLCA, the Comité de Liaison de la Construction des Automobiles, the umbrella association of automobile producers in the European Community. In 1989 he moved to Daimler-Benz and now heads the representative offices of the German corporation in Brussels.

Mrs. R. Verschueren has been working for UNICE (Confederation of European Industries of the EC) since it was established in 1958. Before that she worked for the Belgian Federation of Industries. When her immediate superior was nominated first Secretary General of UNICE, Mrs. Verschueren moved to Brussels with her and has since risen to the rank of Deputy Secretary General.

Experts

Mr. M. Rüte has been working as an assistant to Riccardo Perissich, Director General of the Directorate General Internal Market, since 1989. He has been in the Commission since 1986; earlier he was a lecturer at an English university.

Prof. Stephen George is a member of the Department of Political Science at the University of Sheffield in England; he is a specialist on the subject of Britain in the EC and has published books and articles on this subject.

Source: Bornschier et al., see endnote 2.

For the analysis, the oral interviews of an average duration of one and a half hours were transcribed. First results are documented in detail elsewhere (Bornschier and Fielder, 1995; Bornschier et al. 1993, see endnote 2). The findings once more confirm the central role of the EC Commission in connection with the Single European Act. In addition, they clearly show the tight cooperation between the ERT and the Commission which could only be suspected on the basis of the documentary analysis. The interviewees agreed on the central and influential persons. On the part of the Commission, Davignon and Cockfield were mentioned, whereas Dekker of Philips—who advanced a sketch of ideas with his paper "Europe 1990: An Action Plan for Europe," which surely influenced the White Paper—seems to have been the Roundtable's most important person.

In order to illustrate this basic tendency, we only propose two quotes from the interviews.

> I think [the influence of the European Roundtable of Industrialists on the Commission and the White Paper] was very strong, but not to the extent that industry could more or less dictate what they have to do, that of course was impossible, but there has been very, very fruitful cooperation between the Roundtable and the Commission (excerpt from an interview with one of the protagonists).

> ...it was mainly Wisse Dekker, then the head of Philips, who developed an initiative within the European Roundtable, which set totally parallel goals to the initiative that Lord Cockfield was developing in the Commission. So Commission and industry firmly stood together on the issue of finally creating a real internal market without frontiers (excerpt from an interview with one of the observers, our translation).

We can thus conclude that our research clearly contradicts the contention of Moravcsik (1991) that the initiative had been taken by the big three prevailing in the Council. Rather, our theoretical explanation of an elite pact between the European transnationals and the EC Commission is empirically substantiated by the documents as well as by our interviews of witnesses who confirm the tight cooperation between the Roundtable and the Commission in the negotiations.

The Interests of the Commission Itself and the Indirect Significance of the Citizens

So much for the origins of the elite pact. Apart from 'more market and strategic planning,' social compensations were a cornerstone of the new Single European Act from the beginning. The welfare state has been a specific Western European strength during the postwar era. How then can the disintegration of this old societal model explain the transfer of this strength to the EU level? Neither the Western European states nor the EU followed the socially regressive American deregulation model of Reagan and Bush.

We have argued that the Commission took up the demand by transnationals for a larger market and greater strategic planning, which may give rise to the false impression that the Commission was only acting as an overall agent for the European transnationals (as agent for the transnational European capitalist class) and has no interest itself in the launching of a project that included more than mere national deregulation and quasi-corporatist steps to advance technology. One explanation lies in the fact that political entities and their representatives must legitimize themselves. In this respect, the situation of the EC Commission is very precarious. Even if the European Parliament was somewhat strengthened by the Single European

Act, normal democratic legitimization is still only achieved indirectly through the democratically appointed and controlled representatives of the member states in the Council. This situation, even before the Single European Act, weakened the Commission as it simultaneously strengthened the Council. As a result, the political ambitions of the Commission were blocked. However, at an earlier point the Commission began, through opinion polls, to make direct contact with the citizens of the European Community to find out their views on political questions. Since 1972 under the auspices of the Commission, a biannual survey of the opinions of EU citizens has been conducted—the so-called Eurobarometer studies.

As an improvised substitute for the weak representation of the European population, this polling of opinions by way of the Eurobarometer has a considerable political function for the Commission insofar as it endeavours to legitimize its policies by reference to popular acceptance of the Community project. This can be illustrated with a quotation from a 1992 Commission brochure promoting a "Citizens' Europe:"

> More than half (53%) of the citizens of the 12 member states feel themselves to be at times or often Europeans. This comes from a 1991 Eurobarometer survey. The feeling of not only belonging to one country, but also of being European, is increasing in all of the member states of the EC." (Commission 1992, *Europa der Bürger)*

However, at the end of the 1970s and beginning of the 1980s support for the European Community sank to a long-term low and remained there until 1984. At the same time, differences between countries in the levels of support for the European Community decreased continuously, which represented a convergence of opinion across member states. These trends are illustrated in the graph in figure 14.2 which uses information from our EC project .

At the end of this period in which "Eurosclerosis" was reflected in the mood of the public, the Commission began to make the elite pact more palatable to citizens. This is why there are also elements in the political package of the Commission which cannot be explained solely in terms of the interests of transnationals. Rather, they express the Commission's need for legitimization.

In June 1984 the project "Citizen's Europe" was launched through an ad-hoc commission (formally set up by the Council), and already by 1985 an important symbol followed—the European passport. With the assumption by Jacques Delors (who had been the socialist Finance Minister under President Mitterrand) of the presidency of the Commission, the social dimension had arrived. Since then, Delors has made "Europe '92: The Social Community"

FIGURE 14.2 Changing Support for European Integration Among the Population of EC Member States

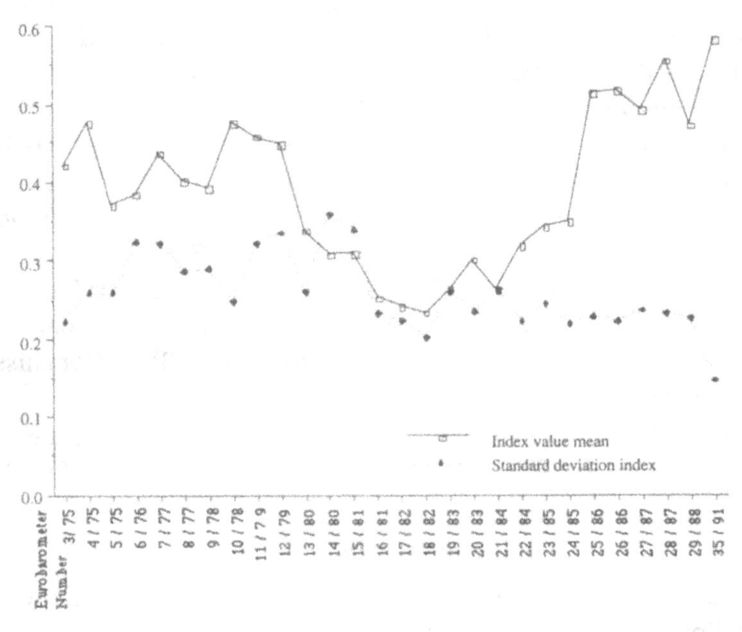

Note: The basis of this analysis corresponds to the conception of "diffuse" support for a political system developed by Easton (1965). Such support is established in all Eurobarometers. The exact question reads as follows: "Generally speaking, is the membership (of the country of the respondent) a good thing - a bad thing - neither good nor bad?" The responses were coded in four categories: 1) a good thing, 2) neither good nor bad, 3) a bad thing, and 0) do not know, no answer.
According to Niedermayer (1991) it is not appropriate only to analyze a single aspect of the question to measure popular support. Following his recommendations an index has been constructed that considers all responses, thereby assigning missing values the value of 2 (neither good nor bad). The index values are the result of the difference of positive and negative answers divided by the total of possible answers ([category 1 - category 3] / [category 1 + category 2 + category 3]). The index has a maximal span of -1 to +1. It takes on a value of -1 if all answers are negative. Conversely, in the case of positive responses only, it has a value of +1. A value of 0 means indifference. For each country and each point in time, this index was calculated on the basis of the Eurobarometer surveys and then submitted to a oneway analysis of variance with the index as the dependent variable and the time of measurement as the classification variable. The resulting values—means and standard deviations—can be interpreted as measures of the central tendency of the index values and their deviation (homogeneity of country differences).

his political platform: "More social equality in Europe—a lively and humane society, is what the EC is seeking for its 340 million members." (Commission of the EC 1992: 2)

After launching the political package, which not only included the interests of the European transnationals but also the Commission's quest for legitimacy—i.e., a larger market, strategic planning, *and* social compensation—and which was then formalized in the Single European Act, public support among the citizens of the Community increased sharply after 1985 as the poll results in figure 14.2 show. Our ongoing research is aimed at further clarification of the issues regarding strategic planning and the shaping of social policy. Without doubt, the social dimension is the weakest part in the new political package of the 1980s—partially due to the resistance of some member countries, particularly the United Kingdom. Against the background of earlier experience, the influence of declarations of intent and of guidelines of the treaties should not be underestimated. The law of the Community, with its unmediated effect, constitutes an autonomous legal system with its own jurisdiction. In this framework, the European Court of Justice has a substantial influence on the application and transformation of the treaties that must not be underestimated. In the sense of functionalist theory's spinoffs, the process of legal creation brings about other legal processes which have always worked towards an extension of the Community (Nicolaysen 1991).

CONTEMPORARY WEAKNESSES AND THE ATTEMPTED DEPARTURE OF THE UNION TOWARD A NEW EUROPEAN SOCIETAL MODEL

The shares of North America, Western Europe and Japan in world product and trade have developed very unevenly since the 1960s. Only Japan was able to increase its share considerably; the United States and, more markedly, Europe have lost shares since the downswing of the long boom of the world economy of the late 1960s. Despite this development, the aggregate economic weight of the European Community has increased, mainly due to the merger.

The aggregate European Community figures mask the weakness of several Western European countries in the world economy. Since the mid-1960s, each European Community country has lost shares in world product and industrial production. But, due to the waves of expanding European Community membership in 1973, 1981 and 1986, the European Community has been able to place itself ahead of Japan, at the same time reducing the gap with the United States.

Thus, the economic weaknesses of the earlier Community and today's European Union in comparison with the United States and Japan cannot be ignored (see also Seitz 1991). The aggregated economic data of the Community concerning welfare, industrial production and trade shares are quite misleading in forecasts regarding future competitive positions. In the 1980s the European Community lost ground in precisely those branches which advanced the new technological style. The new style is particularly characterized by pervasive information and communication technologies (IC technologies) and has begun to displace Fordist mass production. This is evidenced by figures compiled for a conference of the EC Commission in 1991 on information and communication technologies analyzed in detail elsewhere (Bornschier 1994; see also Freeman and Soete 1991; Gerstenberger 1991). Also in its latest White Paper (1993; see also Seitz 1991 for earlier records) the EC Commission points to the impending technological lag in comparison with the United States and Japan.

From our discussion it becomes evident that "recasting the European bargain" at the beginning of the 1980s was hardly a bid for mastery in terms of hegemony but rather a measure to prevent national decline and to remain a player at the core of the world system.

The inclusion of the strategic advantages of the two rivals—a larger market and more flexible planning—into a new political project that is supplemented with a Western European solution for the welfare state, may well be a long-term defensive measure on the part of the European Community to prevent its impending decline. But in the future the new beginning of the European Community may become a model for larger parts of world society: it is multinational and promises the end of the nation-state as the only organizational entity of social relations. In addition, it represents the first time that a kind of supranational social policy is being sought that is aimed at limiting the cross-national differences in welfare by way of suprastate political regulation.

Since the 1980s, the Community, which took one more step towards political union in 1992, has assumed the challenges resulting from its comparative economic weakness in the triad. Recently, it has also begun to advance more binding normative theories designed to facilitate the necessary institutional innovations (see White Paper 1993). In the United States, too, there has been an attempt at a new beginning under President Clinton and his Vice President Gore since 1993. And in the same year, the necessity of a new departure to handle a crisis that was much more fundamental than the marked economic recession became evident in Japan. We will return to these questions pertaining to the future structure of the core in chapter 16.

The thrust towards a new beginning in Western Europe with the European Union as the center of activity can clearly be shown in the White Paper of December 1993, largely influenced by the problem of unemployment. Whether the strength of European civilization is sufficient, and whether it will prove possible to break the inertia and the resistance of vested interests, is not yet certain. In any case, the latest White Paper with its subtitle "The Challenges and Ways Forward into the 21st Century" addresses nothing less than "The new model of European society" (1993: 15).

NOTES

1 The exhibition presented in the Community Pavilion was entitled: "From Renaissance Europe to the Renaissance of Europe". One main topic in the pavilion was "The European Community: A Great 20th Century Discovery"—the theme of Seville's 1992 Expo being *The Age of Discoveries.*

2 A first phase of this research "The Acceleration of Western European Integration as a Part of the Social Transition at the Core of World Society"—partially funded by the World Society Foundation whose contribution is gratefully acknowledged—was finished with a research report in July 1993 (Bornschier et al. 1993). In this research, Nicola Fielder investigated the genesis of the SEA, Felix Keller analyzed materials pertaining to people's perception of the integration process, and Michael Nollert addressed the role of European interest associations. The EC's policy on technology and education was treated by Irene Bloch and Doris Aebi. Funding for continued research on the "Genesis of the SEA" has been provided by the Swiss National Science Foundation for which we are grateful. In this research Patrick Ziltener and Simon Parker also participate investigating social policy and technology policy respectively.

3 From "Completing of the Internal Market: White Paper of the Commission to the European Council", June 1985, p. 3, under the heading "Declarations of the European Council concerning the Internal Market". According to Lord Cockfield, these declarations were made to "nail down" the government representatives (source: our interview with Lord Cockfield, July 1993 in London).

15
CORNERSTONES OF A NEW SOCIETAL MODEL

SOCIAL MOVEMENTS AS SIGNPOSTS TO THE FUTURE

Postmodernity is passé and a return to the future is indicated. History has not ended. This is shown by the many historical events of the 1980s. Despite spectacular discontinuities and fresh beginnings characterizing the sequence of societal models there is a remarkable persistence in the basic values efficiency (economic progress, freedom), equality and security in the project of modernity. At the same time, the securing of these basic values in the social structure has increased with each of the three societal models.

According to the predictions of our evolutionary conflict theory such enhancement must also hold true for the coming societal model. Evolution thus exhibits features of progress. Early signposts and social forces opening up the way can be found in the broad variety of social movements that make their appearance during the peak of the societal model. On the one hand, they help to slowly dissolve the normative closure of tradition; on the other hand, with their radical claims they open a perspective on the essentially utopian content of the basic values of Western society. The anti-authoritarian and autonomous movements started with radical claims to *freedom*. The critical discussion of allegedly "one-dimensional" economic progress was linked to the critique of consumerism and of inhuman work conditions. Equality was radically claimed by the Women's and Third World movements, whereas security was the issue advanced by the peace, environmental, and anti-nuclear power movements. Thus, various social movements can be linked to the basic values.

New Thinking about Environment, Development and Markets

Two far-reaching events of the 1980s must be discussed in somewhat more detail: awareness of the environmental crisis, on the one hand, and the victory of the market over its historical competitor, on the other.

During the years 1985 to 1987, popular perception of the ecological crisis reached a new level. During the second half of the 1980s, the hole in the ozone layer and global warming, the two most prominent environmental problems, became of global urgency. Unlike the loss of biological diversity, the destruction of forests, or the erosion of arable land, which may also become global problems if they occur on a large scale, a change in our fragile atmosphere directly affects the whole world.

In 1989, the world witnessed another historic and revolutionary year in the course of which existing orientations dissolved with incredible speed. The long-standing struggle of opposed systems ended with the victory of capitalist market society over its principal challenger since the industrial revolution. True, Western society, too, is in need of reforms. But the victory of this nevertheless open society—which up until then had not been able to prove its superiority beyond the core—is fundamental. In the time since its competitor has vanished no alternative has emerged that promises progress and an improvement of material wealth in a fundamentally different way.

It is true that the breakdown of communism as an effective alternative to the West and its world order did not at first bring about the widely expected peace. Nationalisms and fundamentalisms seem to blanket the globe with civil wars. While regrettable, this is hardly surprising during a phase when systems of thinking and power that created orientation are decaying.

The important question in connection with the future is whether the victorious market society of the West will be able to close the global gap in wealth and avert the threatening environmental collapse. Today, more than ever, populations and governments of the now approximately 200 sovereign states are forced to share in a community of fate by virtue of economic relations, the world-encompassing transport and communication networks, and, not least, the ecological crisis. Such a community is not automatically peaceful. It can only find peace if a new order for our presently fragmented world society emerges. No doubt, such an order involves politics and economics, power and its redistribution. The important prerequisite, however, is a change in thinking. Really significant new departures always begin by making suddenly reconcilable what was hitherto considered irreconcilable. Environment and development have become recognized as the two urgent challenges. What attitude is being taken to them after the "victory of the market"?

Since the first counter-cultural movements—the origin of which is said to lie in the events of 1968—environmental and development issues have been on the agenda of the new social and political opposition movements. These movements, which followed the anti-authoritarian youth protest of the 1960s, found support in broad sectors of the educated middle classes. Since the 1970s, they have increasingly shaped the political landscape, particularly in core countries, albeit winning only limited political representation. Within these opposition movements, whose exclusion from political responsibility and accountability promoted certain fundamentalist limitations, the market and environment on the one hand, and the market and development on the other have long stood in diametrical contradiction. Yet the increasingly wide acceptance of such diagnoses together with the manifest "victory of the market" altered the framework for further thinking. The counter-project to market societies has missed its historic opportunity, not least because, in its real incarnation, it could not guarantee human rights, perverted the idea of social equality through self-inflicted shortages that had to be shared by too many, and failed even more miserably than the market economies to grapple with environmental problems.

The dynamics of development, ecology and the market have been discussed elsewhere (Bornschier and Lengyel 1994). Here, we would only like to point to a result. The notion of sustainable development is a remarkable example of the new thinking, which is also supported by entrepreneurs (Schmidheiny et al. 1992). Ecology and development are fused together into sustainable development to be managed by market solutions, the central point being the internalization of environmental costs so that the prices of products and services accurately reflect their environmental costs. The broadening of the market, and not its restriction, and thus the old ideal of free trade—admittedly under new societal conditions—is seen to be the key to sustainable development.

If ecological and economic goals are no longer seen as opposites, if they are instead fused into a synthesis aimed at producing harmony between the members of society as well as between humankind and nature, this implies a revolution of economic doctrines that has only been paralleled by one other reorientation during this century: the Keynesian revolution, the path-breaking formulation to make social welfare, redistribution and stable growth compatible, an achievement which had earlier seemed to lie far beyond the potential of economics and which subsequently ideologically nourished the successful welfare state of the highly developed countries.

During 1992 United Nations Conference on Environment and Development (UNCED) in Rio de Janeiro the interests of the core and of the periphery were still diverging significantly, but within the two blocs there were also divergences. The "Rio Declaration," originally to be called the "Earth Charter," was planned to become a key statement like the Universal Declaration of Human Rights had been earlier. Yet, for the sake of consensus, many programs (e.g., Agenda 21) lost their teeth—particularly due to concessions to the United States and to Saudi Arabia as the leader of the oil producers. In the meantime, the United States has turned away from the doctrines of the 1980s under President Clinton and Vice President Gore.[1] A social-democratic and ecological transition has become visible in that country, one that is very important not only for its own sake but also because without the United States taking the lead, very little can be achieved in world politics.

The new thinking was not confined to the issues of world society addressed in Rio.[2] The state of diffusion of the new thinking as a guideline is evidenced by the White Paper of the EC Commission of December 1993, entitled "Growth, Competitiveness, Employment—The Challenges and Ways Forward into the 21st Century." This report (White Paper 1993: 150f.) calls for a new model of "sustainable development"

> It is important to develop a societal project for a higher quality of life in the Community, which can motivate people and hence can generate the required human energy:
>
> (a) The serious economic and social problems the Community currently faces are the result of some fundamental inefficiencies: an "underuse" of the quality and quantity of the labor force, combined with and "overuse" of natural and environmental resources. Both elements are at the heart of the economic development model followed by the Community during the past few decades.
>
> (b) The basic challenge of a new economic development model is to reverse the currently negative relationship between environmental conditions and the quality of life in general on the one hand, and economic prosperity on the other. In this respect, a widespread implementation of clean technology is a key aspect. It is to be stressed that much scientific

knowledge is already available but is waiting for insertion into the economic system.
(c) The transition towards a new "sustainable development" model requires the development of a consistent set of market incentives (. . .) that market prices have to incorporate all external effects.(. . .)

THE EXTENSION OF MARKET SOCIETY

At the beginning of any societal model, a new ordering of the political sphere and its linkage to the economy is required. Which features will this new model have? It will not completely renew society, but, will change it in important respects. The evolution of societal models exhibits features of accumulated progress in the sense that earlier features which have proven to have a high problem-solving capacity in one societal model are retained during the transition to the next. Market society and democracy are important examples.

Of course, the market remained quite restricted politically even in market societies. At the same time, however, the limitations of the market changed from one societal model to the next in a characteristic way. In this, there has been one remarkable constant regarding the character of the state: the articulation of the relationship between politics and the economy always took place within the framework of the nation-state. This changed for the first time with the accelerated integration of Western Europe.

The debate concerning the capacities and limits of the market did not end with the liberal movements at the beginning of the past century. Economic liberalism with its belief in the market always experienced ideological phases characterized by particular interests hidden behind the pretense of universalistic legitimations and by the glorification of the market as a means to attain justice. During the 1830s, economic liberalism set off with the zeal of a crusade, and laissez-faire became a truly militant creed (Polanyi 1978: 189, 192); according to Karl Polanyi it even became a "secular religion". One hundred and fifty years later, after liberal market society had been transformed into the social market economy by a multitude of state interventions and regulations—quite successfully in economic terms—the reaction of the neoliberals and monetarists constituted another thrust of this secular religion, which unhinged the societal model of the postwar era on the verge of the 1980s.

Market Failures

In sociological terms, the market is a useful institution because it discharges responsibility. Yet its advocates frequently forget that it is only a means and not an end in itself. For that reason, external effects must be considered, and the market's performance, as well as its failures, discussed against the background of the basic values of equality, liberty, and security.

Dysfunctional side effects of the market are results of failures, two of which we propose to mention. Those who cannot participate in the market because they (temporarily) do not dispose of marketable resources, cannot satisfy their basic needs through the market. This shortcoming must be met by market society unless it is to suffer a deficit of legitimacy.

Further, market failure with regard to public goods must be mentioned; here, for reasons of brevity, we shall only discuss environmental issues. The environment does not by itself emit market signals in the shape of prices and therefore remains beyond market calculations. For this reason, actual and estimated future costs to avoid and counter environmental damage inflicted by market society must be injected into the market from the outside. The market itself cannot do this because it is not a reflective system that can save itself from its own self-destructive tendencies.

The basic institutional regulation of market society was not challenged during the transition from earlier societal models. This will also be true for the next model, in which the market as a regulatory mechanism will in fact be upgraded.

Changes of the Market

A short look back may be helpful. The constitution of market society reconciled the difficult contradictions between freedom and equality by transforming the claim to equality into a question of justice. It became possible to delegate the legitimation for positional allocation to the market (see also chapter 2). However, the market did not remain constant over time. Rather, its function evolved through various historical stages. The decrease in the number of the self-employed during the second societal model made the educational system into a socially constructed criterion of distribution. To maintain legitimacy, access to higher education had to be opened up, particularly during the neocorporatist Keynesian societal model. Later, schooling lost much of its function as an allocational criterion, and the educational question once more became a political issue. As our society's rate of school enrolment can hardly be further improved on the basis of its traditional institutions, and because large numbers of a given age cohort enter the highest educational levels, the role of formal education as an allocational criterion is encountering its limits, continuing education and training is taking on increased significance (Bornschier and Aebi 1992). In the future, this will bring about a further differentiation of education.

The renewed politization of the educational issue could be mitigated by the provision of a large proportion of continuing education and training by private bodies (Aebi 1995). This would once again imply the delegation of an important question of justice to the market and, at the same time, partially disestablish education. However, this requires measures of social compensation, which will be treated in greater detail under the heading "equality" below. Institutional solutions could include educational tickets or vouchers for continuing education and training (Aebi 1995). Educational credits issued to every young person as a starting capital, which could be used for the acquisition and renewal of knowledge and qualifications during the course of their life, are another possible solution (White Paper 1993: 134). A certain degree of disestablishment of the educational system—particularly of continuing training—by no means implies a less important role for education. On the contrary, education will become a catalyst for societal change.

Power and Markets

Due to economic concentration, the informal merger of firms in the economy, and the ensuing powers of markets, price- and wage-fixing in the core countries have increasingly become a political issue. This had already started during the second societal model, and during the third model was evidenced by the integration of labor organizations and the assumption of conflict regulation under the aegis of the state.

But agreements between powerful organizations under the supervision of the state did not result in an income policy legitimized by the whole of society. It led to inflexible solutions, market distortions, and—from the viewpoint of justice—to questionable solutions, because powerful associations and economic organizations were able make their own interests prevail. The result was a loss of legitimacy for the state as the arbiter of the balance of interests.

Since the 1980s we have been living in an era of intensified global competition. The liberalization of national markets by opening them up to international competition has been a source of economic efficiency. The globalization of the economy could well become a counterweight to empowerment within national markets through firm concentration and interorganizational agreements. Still, it would be wrong to mystify the mechanism of competition in market society. In the future, too, competition will be limited—even though the limitations will be of a new kind. Globalization and deregulation by no means lead to unfettered competition. Rather, "coopetition" will be the feature of the new political economy. This new mixture of cooperation and competition is characteristic of evolving technological corporatism, i.e., the cooperation between politics, economics, and science. Japanese experience shows that intensive cooperation and intensive competition do not necessarily preclude each other. So-called strategic alliances between different firms will be featured in the new epoch.

Coordination of State Spheres

Globalization and the new economic policies of states also underline the need for the coordination of state spheres, a need by no means mitigated by supranational coordination at regional level. Without a regulated coordination of different supranational state spheres more problems will be created than are solved. Seen from the perspective of the world economy, Western European integration, which to date has culminated in the European Union, represents a potentially dangerous trade bloc. In response to this threat, a race to build additional blocs has begun. The European Union, the North American Free Trade Agreement (NAFTA), the Asean Free Trade Area (AFTA), and Asia-Pacific Economic Cooperation (APEC) have recently signalled the growing danger of increasing protectionism.

After years of pessimism in international trade circles, the conclusion of the GATT's 8th World Trade Round (Uruguay Round) is of particular importance. This ambitious and historically unprecedented package, aimed at liberalizing trade, was adopted against the expectations of many observers. Thus, the mistakes of the 1930s have up to now not been repeated.

The creation of a World Trade Organization (WTO) as an institutional framework for the existing GATT regulations and their extensions through the Uruguay Round—both agreed upon in mid-December of 1993—are leading to greater legal security in international economic relations and thus reduce the danger of future efficiency-reducing conflicts within the triad, formed by the United States, Western Europe, and East Asia. Contrary to the origin of the world economic regulatory systems that followed the Bretton Woods agreements (see Bornschier 1990: 37-40), the new beginning of mid-December 1993 was not sponsored by a hegemonic power, but negotiated by the actors of the three approximately equal powerful economic blocs of the triad.

In what follows, we shall briefly discuss the new kinds of managing the realization of basic values necessitated by this new situation. Our discourse is normative in nature and aims to further not only academic but also political debates.

A New Approach to Efficiency

In our understanding, efficiency includes the striving for autonomy and liberty, on the one hand, and economic progress, on the other (see chapter 2). One of the features of the new societal model is the upgrading of liberty, continuing the project of modernity. The greater desire of modern people to assume responsibility to organize their own lives is clearly evident. The demand is for a society of multiple choices that renders possible an individualized yet still socially embedded lifestyle. If, during the past societal model, the promise to democratize welfare by means of mass production and the welfare state was of central importance, the promise to democratize liberty will be of central interest in the future.

The new technological style with the key of "flexibility" can meet this desire. The movement towards the information society finally makes possible an increased number of choices, and future quantum leaps in productivity even guarantee a de facto basic income without achievement incentives becoming obsolete. Lean production creates much more flexibility, reduces costs, preserves the environment and conserves resources. It also offers workers remaining in the material production process increased responsibilities as well as more autonomy and therefore a more integrated field of action at the workplace. These new workplaces, characterized by flatter hierarchies, are increasingly attractive for the professionally ambitious.

The new organizational forms make it possible to reduce external constraints and dissatisfaction at work that block ideas and frustrate initiative. Quite apart from technical processes, team management is also taking the human factor into consideration. The "humanization of work" movement had already emerged in the 1970s to confront the dead-end of Taylorism, but it was the economic success of the Japanese that brought about a broader acceptance of the new group-centered organizational forms as the model for management.

Group-centered organizational structures may level out the huge intrafirm income differences caused by Taylorism. But new wage models for the remuneration of group labor have not yet been thought through. Here we refer, for example, to further decentralization of so-called profit centers to partially autonomous groups, which distribute part of the productivity gains to group members through a process of negotiation. Resistance to such an organizational structure can be expected from middle management, which will become partially obsolete. Neither income disparities between more and less productive groups nor those between people with and without a job will be removed by group centered systems of income determination, however. Measures of redistributive justice are necessary—particularly with reference to transitory unemployment which will increase enormously during the diffusion phase of the technological style. Thus, we will encounter problems similar to those at the outset of the 1930s.

Here we must add that market society's claim to self-realization can only be incompletely realized in the sphere of work for a majority of the population. The new societal model diminishes the problem of the linkage of the striving for freedom with market logic to a greater degree than the former model, but it does not eliminate it. Leisure, which makes possible a higher degree of autonomy, will assume increased significance in the solution of such contradictions. As a result of leaps in productivity, leisure time can once more be extended. Here, and despite the "social order of leisure" (Lamprecht and Stamm 1994), autonomy can be realized to a higher degree. Thus, to a certain extent the new claims to liberty can be brought into line by lean production in the information society and by the upgrading of leisure.

A New Approach to the Guarantee of Security

A broad and legitimacy-generating upgrading of freedom presupposes the solution of security problems. With respect to collective, military security there has been much progress since the end of the East-West conflict. At the end of the 1980s, the long-standing threat of a global atomic holocaust vanished overnight in a remarkable "silent revolution." In the short time between November 1989 (the fall of the Berlin Wall) and the end of 1991 (the dissolution of the Soviet empire), the East-West conflict which had dominated the postwar era, became history, thereby liberating humankind from the strategy—supposedly adopted for security reasons—of atomic overkill: MAD (Mutual Assured Destruction). This important advance has been forgotten by many in the face of ecological threats and the imponderabilities following from the break-up of the Soviet Union.

Nowadays, human wellbeing is threatened from another side. From the beginning, the market as the creator of wealth stood at the core of the legitimation of market society. In this respect there has indeed been progress—in the form of increased democratization of wealth in mass consumption society. It is certainly true that market societies depend on growth. But it would be wrong to suppose that growth always has to be quantitative in the sense of material resources. Growth can be qualitative as well as indicated by the increase in services.

For a long time, growing segments of the population have been fearing losses of wealth for themselves and their descendants as a result of environmental damage. We do not know exactly to what extent these fears are justified. But the degree of insecurity itself is politically relevant. As already mentioned, a responsible treatment of the environment is not incompatible with a significant role of the market mechanism.

As the 1993 White Paper of the European Union observes, scientific knowledge for a sustainable environmental policy is already abundantly available and only waiting to be incorporated into a new regulatory system for the economy. One of the reasons for this delay is that the market economy instruments for this purpose are not yet sufficiently well-known in the broad population. Apart from transparency and credibility, under democratic conditions the new legal measures that need to be adopted also require personal incentives for cooperation. The immediate advantages for every citizen must be sufficiently motivating. Further, since environmental damage is to be averted, measures must be preventive and work permanently. Whoever causes environmental damage must bear the costs; those who are already limiting environmental damage must be stimulated by incentives to decrease the environmental burden even further.

Two market economy instruments satisfying these criteria must briefly be mentioned: environmental directive charges and tradable environmental vouchers (see Meier and Walter 1991; OECD 1991). State rules and restrictions (e.g., legally permissible levels of pollutants) or environmental impact reports will continue to play a role, but can efficiently be supplemented by such charges and tradable vouchers to help reduce state expenditure.

Charges resulting from environmental directives must not be confused with taxes. The latter are the source of general financing of the state, whereas charges are levied for special directive purposes (transparency) and can be managed in a fiscally neutral manner by per capita refunds (an ecological bonus with incentives for cooperating). Such charges have three goals: preservation of the environment, a lean state and legitimacy. We cannot discuss in great detail the broad possibilities offered by environmental directive charges here (see Meier and Walter 1991), which include energy charges preserving scarce resources and reducing the emission of damaging substances (e.g., carbon dioxide), directive charges for substances which damage the environment and can easily be traced (e.g., fertilizers, pesticides, volatile organic compounds), and preventive charges for waste disposal to guarantee the proper disposal of toxic substances.

In addition, tradable environment vouchers or pollution permits can fulfill an important function. The basis for such vouchers lies in defining critical limits for environmentally damaging substances. These values are determined by scientific research and then agreed upon politically. The total tolerable amount of pollution is then divided into environmental vouchers or pollution permits, which thus constitute a right to pollute the environment. Such vouchers must not only be issued to enterprises; all citizens must also receive them so that the result of this ecological bonus is redistributive. Citizens may either use (sell) these vouchers or keep them for environmental reasons. By buying and retaining these vouchers, social movements and environmental organizations can partially engage in politics by way of the market.

Because of its more economical use of energy, the new technological style is more compatible with the environment than its predecessor. Even though there will be an increasing relative reduction in the use of resources, because their aggregate use keeps rising environmental problems can hardly be solved. If world society is to be stabilized socially, it must be able to participate more fully in what has become natural in the North. However, with respect to the primary source of energy, the world is limited.

Therefore, a new energy source must become predominant in the future technological style. With the present state of technology, should the rest of the world reach the density of automobiles already found in the West, the ecological burden would be enormous and no longer bearable. Even if such damage could be repaired at all by environmental technology, the cost of petroleum might rise to a level that reverses its historical cost advantage into a disadvantage. Keeping in mind the ensuing and external costs, neither petroleum nor nuclear power will be the energy sources of the future. Instead, solar hydrogen energy may play this role (Bornschier 1988: 106-110; Seitz 1991: 13-15).

How can the central role of petroleum be reduced? How can the path to solar hydrogen energy as the basis for the new technological style be opened up? Carbon dioxide levies, aimed at reducing atmospheric pollution from the burning of fossil fuel and favoring new and less dangerous energy sources, have been under discussion for some time. In the European Union the Commission already took the initiative on this issue in 1991 but it has not yet succeeded in implementing relevant measures.

To date, the climate convention negotiated at the United Nations conference in Rio (ratified March 21, 1994) is a very weak instrument which will hardly bring about coordinated international action in the immediate future because it lacks a binding deadline for the stabilization of emissions causing the green-house effect. In a supplementary declaration, the European Union (together with Switzerland and Austria) has agreed to stabilize the emission of damaging pollutants by the year 2000. But it is doubtful whether an energy policy aimed at the future will really be implemented so long as Western Europe has not overcome its comparative economic weakness vis-à-vis the United States and Japan. And as long as the United States can reap advantages in the form of low prices and a secure supply from the petroleum economy which it largely controls, a change in American energy policy is hardly conceivable. Until recently, the prospects for an innovative energy policy seem to have been brightest in Japan, which is extremely dependent on imported petroleum, and whose oil industry does not have a dominant position in the political economy. Also, Japan's leadership in the new technological style would facilitate facing the high starting costs during the transition to new energy sources. In reality, however, it was the Scandinavian countries, particularly Sweden, which became the forerunners of environmental directive charges on energy and carbon dioxide emissions.

The chances of countering the predominant role of the oil industry are poor so long as the big core countries do not combine their efforts. The example of Italy, which imposes by far the highest fiscal burden on petroleum based energy products shows that a change in relative prices does not necessarily favor alternative energy sources. Thus, despite all the praise showered on market directive mechanisms, we stress that they do not bring about "clean" transport action systems automatically. Since such systems are the medium-term goal, further measures must be contemplated. The market always needs political direction; such direction cannot be restricted to relative pricing policies, because the market alone cannot save society from its long-term self-destructive tendencies. In particular, the market cannot assume society's strategic decisions regarding future ideals; despite its importance, the market always remains politically and morally embedded. To be clear: even if we admit that we do not exactly know to what extent our fears, such as of global warming, will turn out to be justified in the long run, politics has to solve the problem of insecurity in the present and to do so in a preventive way.

A New Approach to the Claim to Equality

The upgrading of liberty in the new societal model does not have to conflict with the claim to equality. The project of modernity can also be continued with reference to equality. In connection with our discussion of efficiency we have already pointed to features of the new technological style that also meet the claim to equality. Once again, mention must be made of the flattening of hierarchies and new group-centered work models.

The three directions in the interpretation of the claim to equality already mentioned in chapter 2 may take the following forms. The requirement for the democratization of freedom is basic equality, i.e., a de facto basic income and broad mass education. Beyond this minimum guarantee work groups and elites may then compete for opportunities. This, however, must be accompanied by an improved guarantee of equal opportunities. Thus, secured basic equality and improved equality of opportunity can readily be brought into line with greater freedom.

Equality as a basis for truly equal opportunities and not merely for equal starting points also maintains its importance, as shown by the disputes surrounding the relationship between the sexes. Since the classical labor issue has more or less been resolved, the obstinate inequality between women and men is on the agenda of the new societal model. Here we refer to the emphasis to be given to the interpretation of equality in terms of outcomes (gender quotas, wages for housework, etc.). Equal rights and possibilities for development for both sexes will emerge to a hitherto unprecedented degree in the new societal model and constitute as big a leap as the welfare state during the Keynesian model, since they improve the situation of half the population.

De facto basic income. For many years now a basic income has been called for by innovative thinkers; politicians, however, have only hesitatingly begun to include it in their agendas. A basic income is functional for the new technological style because it creates purchasing power and helps tackle the problem of unemployment. Despite this fact and although a stronger anchoring of equality in outcomes represents a legitimacy-generating parallel to the revalorization of the market, the reasons for hesitation are obvious—it breaks a taboo. In a market society centered on achievement, unearned incomes are suspect, even though they are enjoyed by the wealthy. In order to take this further step in the direction of decoupling income (life chances) and work, an acceptable new terminology should be adopted, which is why we are using the term de facto basic income.

In an article published in 1981 we discussed basic income as a solution for the future and indicated a moral foundation for it:

> Basic income must not be misunderstood as charity; rather it is a dividend from the unfolding of productive forces paid to all. At the same time, the basic income is the condition and the basis for voluntary, socially useful, and unalienated work, which may also unfold in arenas where the input of labor according to market criteria would not lead to an optimal satisfaction of needs (Bornschier 1981: 236).

Thus, to promote the acceptance of what is functionally needed, a new terminology should be used. Life chances (income and educational vouchers) should increasingly be seen as claims which are not rooted solely in actual participation in the work process. All members of society (not only wealthy people) are heirs to the unfolding of present and future collective productivity. For political reasons the whole population must profit and not only the owners of wealth and the employed. Otherwise, social revolutions would very soon endanger the privileged members of society.

An additional basis for such claims to equality is the recognition of what must be done for society as a whole but cannot (or not optimally) be supplied through the market. An example is the direct payments to farmers, which are increasingly prominent in the European Union, but also in other countries like Switzerland. The income of farmers is no longer primarily determined by fixed prices and quantities, the new policy being justified by the services rendered by them for the environmental protection of the countryside. Such payments also include compensations for domestic work and taking care of people. In Sweden, such compensation will be introduced in 1995.

The desired effects of such measures are an unburdening of the labor market and a privatization of social welfare:

> Income for all will make available an option desired by many people: not to supply labor on the market but to do work that is useful for oneself and for society. This kind of self-chosen work would also improve the quality of life and facilitate the broadening of social services, which would no longer primarily remain in the hands of the state and the public bureaucracies (Bornschier 1981: 236).

A further, third justification of the claim to equality would be the burdening of the entire population with environmental damage in general and carbon dioxide emissions in particular. Citizens have a right to be protected against the damage done by environmental pollution. This compensation can be financed by environmental directive charges (carbon dioxide levies) and be equally distributed among all members of society. Karl-Heinz Mathieu (1993) has put forward this proposal and calculated that it would lead to gains in welfare for all. In addition, because of increased consumption, there would be an increase in employment, thus lightening the burden of unemployment at the onset of the new technological style.

Finally, we have advanced the idea of the taxation of microchips aimed at financing the new social pact under the title "More Market Thanks to Social Security." The justification is that it makes sense and is fair to tax the sources of special productivity. Chips as the basic material of the new technological style are spreading very fast and are constantly becoming cheaper, so skimming off some of their productivity would not impede progress.

On the basis of a de facto basic income that slowly reaches a level that guarantees existence—the level and financing of which would, as usual, be the subject of intense political debate regulated by a model of political negotiation—the unfolding of efficiency can increasingly be entrusted to the markets: "More Market Thanks to Social Security" can be wrapped into a package that at the same time creates legitimacy and is in line with environmental security concerns, thereby impelling the social market economy in the direction of an eco-social market economy.

Nowadays, basic equality as a condition for access to opportunities in society is no longer merely a question of income but also of education. The revolution in microelectronics is invading all spheres of life and threatening to split society: the majority is bound to be delinked from the new technological style. Simple supply-side measures such as, for example, deregulation and technological corporatism no longer suffice. Rather, demand-oriented measures are needed to restore balance. Whereas these were mainly involved the redistribution of income and a growing state demand under the Keynesian societal model, during the next societal model they will have to be founded on the idea that the gap in knowledge in the population at large must be reduced to allow for broad inclusion and thus the stimulation of supply and demand. Educational policy is therefore an important dimension of such a demand-oriented policy, based on a new educational concept that prepares a new societal model by creating the conditions for the use of new technologies and the related life styles also outside the work sphere. The core of such a concept is "life-long learning" (see also conclusion of chapter 9).

To bring the new wave of educational expansion into line with the lean state, the supply of continuing education and training should be subject to the principle of the market. Doris Aebi (1995) has discussed continuing training in the context of state and market and evaluated the efficacy of different directing principles. In her preferred solution, directing the supply of continuing education and training would be the task of the state, which would be responsible for quality norms and the regulation of the suppliers. Vouchers for continuing training would be a possibility for financing demand (see Aebi 1995). The introduction of such measures implies turning from a mere supply orientation towards a demand orientation in the educational system. Educational vouchers, which we have previously discussed, should be part of the movement towards basic equality. Like basic incomes, vouchers originated with earlier innovative thinkers, who in both cases are distributed over the whole left-right political spectrum.

Thus, for the next societal model, equality as the basis for equal opportunities also refers to education, for only in this way can the promises of information society be converted into a stable upswing. In this connection, the Commission of the European Union, too, speaks of an accompanying and encompassing state strategy aimed at the "preparation of the transition to a society in which information is seen as a basic material which is used in agreement between the social partners and on the basis of corresponding educational offers" (Commission of the EC, 1991: 10). The important role of education also is obvious in the Commission's December 1993 White Paper, in which education is seen as a catalyst for a changing society (Commission of the EC, 1993: 129), an adaptation of the educational system being consequently required. This claim is not unrealistic, since the comparatively low average educational level in the European Union has been listed as one of the "drawbacks" in competition within the triad by the Commission.

THE LEAN STATE

Currently, the transformation towards a "lean state" and thus a genuine new beginning is on the agenda. Everywhere awareness is becoming keener that it is time for reforms. After the fundamentalist discourse in the early 1980s, the debate on what the market can and cannot do has once again become more substantial. The new doctrines place more trust in the self-regulatory capacity of the market than was the case with the formerly dominant doctrine of Keynesianism. Still, the renaissance of the market is in need of a new concept of the role of the state, different aspects of which have already been discussed here.

The new model stresses the qualitative role of the state, the setting of priorities, and the communication of visions able to capture the imagination, to give people a feeling of social security and of future development that is in line with environmental demands. Therefore, quantitative size of the public sector will no longer be a sign of strength for the lean state, which will primarily engage in basic programs of action and strategic planning, also extending to realms that used to lie beyond its reach: technology as a production factor and the environment as a scarce resource. In addition, a recasting of the welfare state is required to guarantee social security and the supply of basic needs, including both income and education, in a less bureaucratic way.

During the Keynesian societal model the mediation of interests among capital, labor and the state was a marked institutional innovation. Today—and since technology has become the most important competitive factor—the mediation process among the state, the economy, and science is becoming important, and quasi-corporatist elements are spreading to new spheres.

With the relief provided through market mechanisms for directing the economy, the lean state can distinguish itself by being closer to citizens and responding flexibly to their needs. Apart from being the mediator of visions, the state is to be a moderator of societal issues—ideally in a federalist and subsidiary way. Finally, the state is to become more civilian, i.e., military expenditure will play a less important role. A certain resistance by civil servants to such innovations is nevertheless to be expected.

The reshaping and shrinking of the state are very difficult tasks, as is evidenced by history. But the intensified competition in the world political economy will force states to slim down. In this process, the revalorization of the market must be seen realistically against the background that the "market and competition can only unfold their capacity to produce and distribute goods optimally in the framework and on the basis of a regulating and legitimate political order" (Kohler 1994: 58). Politics can never be reduced to economics, but the political logic of economic action does not have absolute supremacy. It remains embedded in the competition of states at the level of the world political economy, implying the economic logic of political action. In Western core society, such competition will not lead to a minimal state, but rather to a lean state that acts economically and, at the same time, optimizes legitimacy.

Tasks Ahead

For a successful crystallization of the new technological style, the gap between productive possibilities and consumption must be closed by the creation of additional purchasing power as well as by improved access based on education; during the transition structural unemployment will have to be countered by more continuing education and training. At the same time, the environment will have to be taken into account and in the long term a solar hydrogen energy base will have to be created. Despite these huge tasks, the state can become leaner and more democratic. Some relevant instruments have been mentioned, and we stress that a lean state must not be mistaken to mean laissez-faire.

The new technological style is potentially more consistent with environment protection, but will not solve the important ecological issues of the future automatically. The indispensable institutional framework calls for spirited steps pointing far into the future—a guiding regulation coupled with a vision. Today, a renewal of the social contract must reduce tensions along the lines of humankind/nature and North/South. Thus, a coordination of state regulations is needed. This, in turn, requires time at the level of world society. In their own interest, the United States, Western Europe and Japan must give momentum to this process. As is generally the case with innovations, pioneers also reap advantages, however.

NOTES

1 By the end of 1994 many observers are less confident about Clinton's ability to achieve his declared ends, as shown by the fate of his health care reform and the victory of the Republicans at the mid-term elections.

2 Again, one year after working on this chapter one has to add that if the Brundtland report and the Rio conference put the environment solidly on the world agenda, the 1994 Cairo Conference on Population and Development did as much for population and adopted—against considerable objections—a Plan of Action that has very serious implications. (Peter Lengyel reminded us to mention this before the book goes to press, and we would like to thank him.) That a consensus was reached at Cairo is just as remarkable as what occurred in Rio, if not more so, given the deeply controversial nature of the issues.

16
Hegemonic Conditions Without a Hegemon

Changes and Discontinuities of the 1980s

Although our analyses are guided by a world system perspective which is evident from the central mechanism of competition between social arrangements in the world political economy, this book addresses only one specific societal type, i.e., Western society at the core. To reflect the future of hegemonic rivalry in this chapter some introductory reflections on the changes and discontinuities of the 1980s and early 1990s in the system wherein Western society is on top are appropriate. During the 1980s, history accelerated enormously. As a result, world society has, in various ways, changed substantially. What had seemed stable and accountable for decades underwent remarkable transformations so that it is appropriate to speak of the end of the postwar era (Bornschier and Lengyel 1992). At the core of the world system, the whole decade was characterized by technological thrusts and political transitions. Against the background of the relative economic decline of the United States, the hegemonic power of the postwar era, the further economic rise of Japan was remarkable, but also Western Europe's integrational thrust came quite unexpectedly after long years of "Euro-sclerosis".

During the 1980s, these changes were accompanied by a dramatic geopolitical transition of the postwar order. The existing structure—for decades conflictive but also stable—vanished. In Central and Eastern Europe the counter-core with an ideological claim to possess the superior answer imploded in a way that would have been thought impossible shortly before. The collapse of the ideological orthodoxy that had for long been imposed upon the hegemonial reaches of the Soviet Union delegitimized the Soviet domination of Central and Eastern Europe and of the nationalities within the Soviet Union. The revolutions which started in Poland, Hungary, the former German Democratic Republic and Czechoslovakia were the result of Gorbatchev's reforms from 1985. Revolutions are violently discontinuous social processes and occur thanks to the explosive power of basic values and to the important role played by legitimacy, which can only temporarily and at the cost of regressing in the world system be substituted by force and coercion.

The past decade and our present one are not only characterized by discontinuities but also by departures. This epoch will be remembered in the annals of world history as that of the democratic thrust in the East and the South which confirms the long overdue insight that democracy is not just a mere consequence of wealth but one of its most important requisites.

As a result of the dramatic changes in Central and Eastern Europe, the relative and absolute poverty of world populations have been neglected for some time. As we all know, the promises held out by modernization theory have remained unfulfilled for the majority of humanity after decades of patience. And yet, a small number of societies, which grew during the 1980s, achieved what was considered impossible by critical theories. They underwent a belated industrial modernization which allowed them, in a short time, to move from peripheral to semiperipheral status. Some are even poised to become members of the core with South Korea and Taiwan as well as the city-states of Hong Kong and Singapore at the spearhead. On the other hand, the majority of societies experienced the fate foretold decades ago by dependency theorists even if the most dependent of them were not necessarily the worst cases.

How can stagnation in some cases and developmental dynamism in others be explained? We suggested an answer in terms of state-generated order and protection. Such mechanisms select institutions which reconcile the use of capital and the supply of goods with legitimacy and claims. Why such mechanisms, which clearly occasioned the historical success of capitalism, the curbing of the state and social egalitarianism at the core did not function elsewhere was briefly explained, too. Rents from raw materials, from the exploitation of the East-West conflicts and from compassion ("development aid" delivered into the hands of elites) allowed the holders of power to remain self-privileging and unproductive state classes blocking the way towards catching up developmentally. The hitherto exceptional success in industrializing, the raw material deficient semiperiphery, shows that such blockage was absent: thus, important components of the dependency model were lacking.

Still, examples of successful late industrialization have remained exceptions in the postwar era. In the future, many more cases may be expected for reasons of systemic transformation. The end of the East-West confrontation spells the cessation of rents drawn from threats to shift alliance. The new technological style leads towards an information society diminishing the strategic value of raw materials. The connected, intensified level of economic globalization leads to greater rivalry for industrial sitings, the competitiveness of which must initially be politically and socially secured through appropriate institutional arrangements.

Two questions now arise: will the West remain "Western"? and what impact will successful late industrialization have on future rivalry for hegemony? The cultural legacy of the West shaped those institutions which incontrovertibly determine core status: the market and social egalitarianism, the rule of law along with the sharing of power and political counterweights, economic enterprise and systems of skill classification. That functionally equivalent or even competitively superior formations can evolve is demonstrated by cases of successful late industrialization, with Japan as the model, the cultural legacy being equally significant. Apart from less individualistic and more group-oriented criteria of efficiency the following may be noted. Non-parasitical administrative and political elites, devoted to the common good and basic equality, which may well guide capitalism through a strategic planning framework thereby not throttling but rather promoting development can at present be found in certain Asian countries, if not yet in Africa. The bulk of Latin America has to date suffered from the corruption and perversion of inherited Western culture so that only some countries now show signs of emerging developmentally after a relapse from formerly achieved levels. Furthermore, Asian countries, again led by Japan several decades ago, have shown willingness to adopt even forcible measures to limit their population growth (as India and China), an unexpectedly successful liberal example being Thailand. In Latin America and especially in Africa exponential population growth has weighed heavily on economic performance. That is the situation at present, but in the perspective of several decades ahead the

Western core, along with the Asian late industrializers and the formerly communist bloc, will face problems of ageing and declining populations while more youthful and dynamic parts of the world can reap comparative advantages. Such demographic trends partly underlie the predicted shift of the world economic center to the Pacific rim. In the more distant future, it may be the turn of another region.

Cultural legacies contributing to the shaping of modern institutions can therefore be factors which partly determine success or failure. They can thus surely be combined with modern institutions to produce functionally equivalent or even results superior to those rooted in the traditions of the Atlantic West. That is why classic modernization theory must be overhauled. The core will in future include more societies than merely those belonging to the Atlantic West. The multi-culturalism already so prevalent in Canada, the United States, Western Europe and Australasia is not to be interpreted as potentially diluting Western values but rather as a process of recruitment to them and a stimulus to competitiveness through the high motivation of many immigrant groups.

The answer to the first question is also meaningful for the second. After the collapse of the communist counter-core, the arena for hegemonic rivalry will be the core itself which is expanding by incorporating new members from Central Europe and East Asia. And only now, after the elimination of the Soviet Union, is it possible to speak of a core-triad of about similarly powerful actors on the world stage. What about challengers from beyond the core? Industrial powers like Russia, China and India are impressive, but only in sheerly absolute terms and for the near future are not challenging competitors in the information society. If competition for hegemony will rather be confined to the expanding core itself, will the rise and decline of hegemonic powers—to date the central elements of hegemonic rivalry—continue? This is the question we address in what follows, backed by ideas examined so far.

SOCIETAL MODELS AND THE RISE AND FALL OF HEGEMONS

In this book we have addressed the sequence and course of societal models, which constitute hegemonic social practices linking normative theory, technological style, and a politico-economic regime, whose duration is usually of about two generations. Within this central formation core states of differing strength may exist, which is in fact the starting point for the theories of hegemonic and leadership cycles discussed in chapter 6 (see also the overview in Bornschier and Suter 1992, as well as Rapkin 1990). Common to all cycle theories is the idea that the concentration of resources as the basis for hegemony—either of the economic or political variety—fluctuates with some regularity in the world system. In describing phases of high concentration of these power bases, researchers speak of hegemony or leadership; periods marked by the absence of such high concentration are by contrast symptomatic of a multicentric structure, of unstable and conflictive phases without a hegemon or leader.

Here we cannot discuss in detail the most important contributions to this lively debate, in which North American social scientists are most prominent. We propose instead to address the relationship between a change of hegemonic social practices and hegemonic or leadership cycles. That it is possible to combine ideas from both theoretical perspectives in a constructive way is shown by our account of the emergence of the European Union in chapter 14. With the rise of the European Union, three powerful actors have emerged on the world stage, and many contemporary observers are asking: Who will ultimately prevail in the competition? Which state will be the next hegemon?

Such thinking leads us in the wrong direction. It is true that over the time under discussion—the second third of the nineteenth century until the present—states were decisive for the emergence of a new hegemonic practice in two instances. Yet these were due to special historical power structures and systemic forces operating at the core of the world system, and it is doubtful whether such constellations will arise again in similar form.

The existing studies regarding the rise and decline of hegemonic core powers raise questions concerning the interpretation of power constellations on the eve of the next century. The differentiation of the relative positions of the competitors and the systemic transition in the functioning of the world market for protection have not been sufficiently taken into account. Three typical approaches may be mentioned: one centered on the economy (Wallerstein 1984); one centered on politics (Modelski 1987; Kennedy 1987); and one combining economics and politics (Chase-Dunn 1981, 1989).

According to the economic variant of hegemony theory in the tradition of Immanuel Wallerstein and his school (see Bornschier and Suter 1992), the simultaneous coincidence of productive, organizational, commercial and financial leadership characterizes the "mature hegemony" of a dominant nation-state. This is conceived as a comparatively short and transitory phase in the historical transformation of the world political economy; in the case of the United States it is viewed as having already ended. An extrapolation of this explanatory scheme would, in view of the Japanese success, predict a "Pax Nipponica" following the "Pax Americana." Although such a development may be predicted, it is quite unrealistic. While the attraction of the "American way of life" has lost much of its fascination worldwide, there is not the slightest sign of a similar coming attraction of a Japanese way of life. Furthermore, the claim to world leadership is not an automatic result of command over material resources. In the case of Japan, this claim to ideological leadership is not only delayed, as was the case of the United States between 1918 and 1945, but is also hardly realistic due to Japan's isolated and not easily universalizable culture. Japan's industrial success cannot simply be projected into the future (see chapter 12). In a world in which "software" is becoming more and more important, the current high performance of a certain "hardware" is of only limited value. Cultural opening as a precondition for the next round of competition is what is needed. Otherwise, the most successful competitor becomes merely the best technician, and as such one who never sets the pace. The present crisis in Japan has affected its society's self-confidence and exposed the rotten pillars of the postwar order. The years of extreme self-confidence are over and Japan has entered a phase of deep self-doubt: it is moving from being a special case of the postwar era to being a normal case of discontinuous development at the core.

The politico-military variant of hegemony theory (world leadership cycles), suggested by George Modelski and his school and Paul Kennedy (see Bornschier and Suter 1992) emphasizes the ability of a powerful nation-state to generate order on a global scale, an ability which is not closely linked to economic performance, but which—at least at the outset—provides advantages for the political world leader. According to Modelski the United States—despite its economic troubles—remains the hegemonic power for the time being. No rival in the foreseeable future would be in a position to challenge Washington's politico-military superiority and, after a decisive global struggle, supplant the United States, which is the only remaining superpower with global reach. During the Gulf War, the United States reminded the world community that, with the elimination of the former Soviet Union, it remains the only true world power. Even if this role is no longer easily supported by economic performance, the current policy of the United States shows clearly that Washington does not propose to relinquish superpower status. But the emphasis by the United States on its role as superpower promises no advantages in the long run, quite the contrary. With the end of East-West confrontation, military overkill capacity has lost its importance. This creates advantages for the two "free-riders," Japan and the European Community, even if they will be forced to pay more frequent tribute to America as world policeman in the future or possibly take part in its military interventions. Military technology is becoming less relevant today as an advantage for production in non-military areas, and the latter are of increasing worldwide importance. Thus military strength can become a disadvantage in the end if the U.S. administration does not make serious efforts to counter it.

Christopher Chase-Dunn (1981, 1989) has attempted to overcome the shortcomings of these two lines of explanation by conceiving the economic and politico-military capabilities as linked in a complex way—as processes representing two sides of the same coin (see Chase-Dunn, 1989 for a recent statement). His perspective is thus quite similar to our conceptualization of the world political economy. Chase-Dunn's definition of hegemony becomes more complex from this point of view, yet also more realistic. Hegemonic powers must combine economic superiority, in the sense defined by Wallerstein, with politico-military prominence. Such a combination is not in sight, however. Under the military protection of the United States, Japan became an economic and financial power, but it is still without geopolitical ambition, culturally amorphous and without vision for the world. The European Community shares with Japan a helpless role in geopolitical events.

By contrast to Japan, however, Western Europe harbors a cultural mission with clear claims to leadership. The project of a multicultural, lean state could indeed become attractive even to wider world society. By comparison with the United States, Western Europe's social fabric is only slightly damaged and the European Community can easily build on the strategic advantage of its postwar model, the welfare state. With its goals of cohesion and convergence as well as human rights and "social market economy," it may be able successfully to show the way even if it does not attain the top economic and politico-military positions. From this perspective and despite its lack of politico-military backing, the self-confident presentation of the European Community at Seville's Expo '92 becomes understandable: "The European Community is now a magnet for the newly democratic countries of Central and Eastern Europe which seek a new identity as part of the Community.

Brussels has replaced Moscow as the center of their world" (Commission of the EC, 1992: 6).

The enlargement of the European Union through the inclusion of most of the European Free Trade Association (EFTA) states is already fairly advanced. Furthermore, numerous Central and Eastern European countries formerly under the influence of the Soviet Union as well as countries like Turkey have demonstrated their desire to join the European Union. At the moment about a dozen states—possible future candidates from Maghreb not included—knock at the door of the European Union. This demonstrates the existing attraction of the grouping. Such striving for power by way of enlargement is in line with the traditional expansion process of the European Union, but it does not resolve the economic problems and will not create a political structure capable of making the European Union the most important actor of the triad.

The fact that the blocs within the triad can learn quickly from each other nowadays is shown by the fact that American firms were able successfully to meet Japan's economic challenge. In addition, a remarkable turn away from the mistakes of the 1980s is at least being attempted under President Clinton, and there are efforts of a social-democratic and ecologically inspired transition in this still leading country which—if successful—may match the social dimension in the Western European model in the future. Finally, Western European integration has quickly found a match on the other side of the Atlantic: North America, under the leadership of the United States, has created a common market together with Mexico and Canada, and thus confronts the European Union with respect to markets and resources.

SYSTEMIC CHANGES AND NO RETURN TO THE PAST

When we maintain that a future hegemonic state or even group of states within the core is unlikely, we base our arguments on systemic change concerning the functioning of the world market for protection (see chapter 3). A necessary condition for hegemony or leadership, according to cycle theories, is a very unequal distribution of resources among actors within the world market for protection. This structural condition may be converted into hegemony if it is supplemented by the agreement of the other powers to allow the hegemon to provide collective security and to regulate the world political economy.

In the distant past, the dominant position of a state was not necessarily linked to that state playing the role of a hegemon in the world system. Venice, North Holland, and Britain before the "Georgian transition" (Modelski 1990) were dominant in the emerging world economy and were the defenders of the principles of Western society. But they played no leadership role like that of Great Britain in the nineteenth century or the United States after 1941. The reason is the different character of the core powers in economic and politico-military competition. The powers which were economically marginalized by the predecessors of capitalist unfolding and which therefore, and for reasons of internal stabilization of power, were their adversaries challenging them with politico-military means, did not form part of the societal type that finally prevailed. They were counter-cores which were dangerous in military terms but always remained inferior in economic terms. For that reason, those leading in industrialization were always able to prevail in the long run. Thus, the world market for protection worked, albeit slowly and indirectly. The counter-cores did not adapt or only adapted insufficiently to capitalist logic; more typically they collapsed after revolution or lost wars. The latest spectacular case in this line of challengers is the breakdown of the Soviet Union shortly after 1989. The fact that today only democratic market societies compete for core status permits the world market for protection to react more quickly and more directly than has been the case in the past. The competitors are a lot quicker in learning to assimilate the relative advantages of their rivals.

The type of state is not the only thing that has changed: the transnational economy, as the second component in government competition, has also done so. Transnational corporations have the ability to shift business from one state to another or at least threaten to do so (see Bornschier and Stamm 1990). For that reason they have more power to affect state behavior than most firms. By looking at the relative proportion of business controlled by transnationals in the world economy we have an indication of the relative strength of business vis-à-vis political undertakings in general. Of course, transnationals differ across sectors and time in the degree to which they rely directly on state-generated business opportunities. Transnationals with competitive advantages in knowledge and organization are less dependent on business opportunities created by state intervention or consumption. The economic globalization at the end of this century, initiated by the approximately 35,000 transnational corporations, is quantitatively as well as qualitatively a historical novelty. It strengthens the world economy at the cost of states and produces much more direct and immediate reactions of the world market for protection.

A further structural feature of the world market for protection is the relative strength of populations and workers vis-à-vis states and firms. The strength of the people depends upon the degree to which they have a say in politics (i.e., the extent of democracy) and the degree to which unions are free to articulate the interests of their members. The more pronounced the relative strength of the people the less delayed and the more encompassing government and business reaction to their demands will be. Again, this has an effect on the speed of reaction and the direction of compensation through the mechanism of the competition of societal orders in the world market. In addition, education (universal values) and networks of civil society strengthen the cause of the people.

Even under such conditions, however, the power of firms and to a lesser degree of states vis-à-vis the citizenry, is always considerable, since they distribute the means of subsistence—wages and salaries as well as welfare benefits. In a transnational or even globalized world, the people would appear to be handicapped in pressing their claims, since they lack the resources for organizing effectively at the level of world society. This should not lead us to underestimate the impact people can and do have, however. They act efficiently by influencing the actions of particular states. Under political democracy, they also directly affect the parameters of the world market for protection to a greater extent than in the past.

The arguments sketched so far imply that the world market for protection today functions much more directly and influences societal development much faster than it did at any other time in the history of the capitalist system. Before discussing our thesis concerning a new beginning in the absence of a new hegemonic power, we would like to add some brief remarks regarding the two hegemonies of the past two centuries, which were based on special circumstances that no longer exist and thus preclude a superficial and mechanistic learning from history.

Britain's hegemonic position, which peaked in the mid-nineteenth century, was the result of the prior military defeat of its main contender, France. Further, Britain's superior industrial performance was one of the factors triggering the liberal revolts and revolutions of 1830 and 1848 on the continent. Germany, the emergent challenger, was not yet united and Russia was defeated in the Crimean War. The power structure in Europe, at that time the core of the world, was therefore highly skewed in favor of Britain, and as a result its position as the ideological (laissez-faire and free trade), economic (England as the workshop of the world), and military (particularly with reference to its navy) hegemon remained unchallenged for decades.

The hegemony of the United States, too, was the result of a special situation. After two world wars the two authoritarian challengers, Germany and Japan, were virtually ruined; America's allies were exceptionally weakened by the war and problems in connection with their colonial empires. In addition, the United States was the only power able to contain the counter-core of the USSR. In this constellation it became possible for the United States to assume the role of the protector of the West. Immediately following the war, the United States produced half the world's goods and services and took a keen interest in expanding the capitalist world economy.

Here, the new societal model of the Keynesian era—and also the new regulation systems of the world economy—did not spread by imitation but were rather a creation of the United States throughout the core. This is not to deny the importance of the two European pioneers—neutral Sweden and Switzerland—which have been discussed in this book. But without the victory of the Allies (the initial nucleus of the United Nations at its founding in 1945) led by the United States in the war against the Axis powers, no broad new beginning on a democratic basis would have been possible—particularly because it was not only Hitler's Germany but also Stalin's Soviet Union that threatened Western Europe.

GLOBAL HEGEMONY AND COMPETITION OF SOCIAL ORDERS

Britain's hegemony, which reached its peak around 1850, and that of America, which reached its peak around 1950, both illustrate the exceptional character of hegemonic positions in the last two hundred years. We have already outlined reasons why a similar configuration is unlikely to recur in the foreseeable future. Thus, the rise and decline of past hegemonic core powers must not be extrapolated mechanistically as a cycle theory into the future. The following considerations lead us to this conclusion:

(1) One can, on the basis of prior experience, argue that the global cycle of war, by producing victors and vanquished, could lead to significant inequality in power between core countries in the future. This, however, fails to account for the fact that systemic conditions have fundamentally changed. Today, all competing core powers are democratic. Here, for a start, is a

completely different environment for the initiation of a new societal model. What follows from this? A regularity, one could even say a social scientific law, that knows no exception: democracies do not wage war against each other, as most recently substantiated by Bruce Russet (1993, 1994).

(2) In the past, economic advantages could accumulate as a result of a superior social order in a particular society, and over time give rise to a considerable imbalance in economic power. In the future this might only recur with great difficulty due to globalization and the democratization of the core. Societies today learn much more quickly from one another because the effects of competition for a superior social order have grown so much more marked.

(3) The balance of power has long been a powerful mechanism to check the ambition of one power seeking to dominate others. In the future, however, this mechanism will be even more effective. Western Europe's innovation in competition among the core powers is that since the Single European Act of 1986, the European Union has, so to speak, increased state power through the fusion of different national states in the same way as companies increase their market power through mergers. As a result, Western Europe is destined to become a serious player in the triad. At the same time, this will also have a certain effect on the balance of power at the core.

(4) In the heyday of the British and American hegemonies, their respective leadership roles, solidly underpinned by military power, were functionally important in the defence of the principles of Western society because the most important challenger to their power was more or less hostile to these principles. By contrast to these historical constellations, the principles of Western society are today firmly anchored in about two dozen societies.

(5) A substitute for the services of a hegemon in the creation and maintenance of collective goods (in particular international regimes) has for some time now been in sight. The social basis for this replacement is a globally oriented civil society as reflected, for example, in the annual meetings of the World Economic Forum in Davos (Switzerland) or in the work of the Trilateral Commission (Gill 1990). The World Economic Forum is a foremost institution integrating the leaders from business, government and the sciences into a "global partnership for economic and social progress." Trilateralism as a method of conflict resolution was practiced under both Presidents Ford and Carter, and world economic summits have, since the mid-1970s, been instruments for conflict settlement through the personal exchange of information and negotiation (Putman and Bayne 1985). The

unexpected breakthrough in the effort to regulate world trade, and the foundation of the World Trade Organisation in December 1993 are indications that, even in a multipolar world, cooperation and the settlement of disputes are possible in the absence of a hegemon to guarantee the order. This is clearly in contrast to the position which is erroneously put forward in earlier theories of hegemonic stability.

(6) Lastly, since the victory of the market over its historical adversary, the command economy, the guaranteeing of security by a hegemon is no longer as necessary as it once was. Threats from a new potential counter-core (Islamic fundamentalism with increasing state power and oil as a weapon), or from the remaining once socialist counter-core states (possibly China, or also Russia following a successful coup) will be confronted under the leadership of America acting as a sort of world policeman supported by all the other core powers and the United Nations. America's continuing impressive military thus might well take on a specialized role for security of the entire core. This is, however, different from what is understood by a hegemon, a state which possesses clearly superior power in *all* realms.

REFORM AND UTOPIAN SCHEMES

The revitalization of democratic market society after the collapse of the former Soviet empire will lead to a global hegemony of capital, supported by transnationally oriented management in firms, professions and state administrations. In this structure, ordinary people can express their needs and preferences only indirectly by influencing state regulation. This may seem today to be an insignificant consideration. But one should not forget that the royal road to capitalist development was in part paved by paying more attention to the needs of ordinary citizens than the losers did in this competition. All leading societies (in the case of Europe, beginning with Venice in the pre-modern period) offered greater opportunities for their people (see chapters 10 and 13; Modelski 1990) than did the societies that were left standing at the side of the road. This pattern will also continue in the future, since legitimacy not only implies respect for basic values, but is also a productive factor in the hunt for "filthy lucre". For that reason, the competition of orders works like the cunning of rationality.

Basically, Western society is utopian and, at the same time, always contradictory. There is no way out of its external and internal contradictions other than by flight into the future. Through renewed social contracts, a little more of the utopia is brought forth by power struggles, while at the same time it is limited by established power and the market as a steering mechanism. With the dialectical evolution of societal models, the coupling of utopian schemes and reform is committed by its past to break into the future. However, this societal type will only survive if it manages to keep its promises, not only to that fraction of humanity living within the borders of the core, but also to the masses of humanity in other parts of the world. Its survival equally depends on whether its drive for expansion can take place without permanently impairing our planet's capacity to sustain us.

LIST OF TABLES AND FIGURES

Tables

Figures

BIBLIOGRAPHY

A

Abegglen, James C. 1958. *The Japanese Factory*. Glencoe, Ill.: Free Press.
Aebi, Doris. 1995. *Weiterbildung zwischen Markt und Staat: Zur Wirksamkeit von Steuerungsprinzipien in der schweizerischen Bildungsspirale*. Chur: Rüegger.
Aglietta, Michel. 1979. *A Theory of Capitalist Regulation: The U.S. Experience*. London: New Left Books.
Alber, Jens. 1982. *Vom Armenhaus zum Wohlfahrtsstaat*. Frankfurt: Campus.
Allen, Michael Patrick. 1981. "Power and Privilege in the Large Corporation: Corporate Control and Managerial Compensation." *American Journal of Sociology* 86: 1112-1123.
Alston, Jon P. 1983. "Japan as Number One? Social Problems of the Next Decades." *Futures* 15 (5): 342-356.
Altvater, Elmar, and Jürgen Hoffmann. 1980. "Marxistische Ansätze zur Interpretation historischer Wachstumszyklen." Pp. 372-403 in Dietmar Petzina and Ger van Roon (eds.), *Konjunktur, Krise, Gesellschaft: Wirtschaftliche Wechsellagen und soziale Entwicklung im 19. und 20. Jahrhundert*. Stuttgart: Klett-Cotta.
Anderson, James (ed.). 1986. *The Rise of the Modern State*. Atlantic Highlands, N.J.: Humanities Press International.
Anderson, Perry. 1974. *Lineages of the Absolutist State*. London: New Left Books.
——— 1986. *The Bourgeois Revolutions*. Chapter 11 of *State Formation in the World-System*. Report to the World Society Foundation (Zürich).
Archer, Dane, and Rosemary Gartner. 1984. *Violence and Crime in Cross-National Perspective*. New Haven: Yale University Press.
Arendt, Hannah. 1960. *Vita activa oder vom tätigen Leben*. München: Piper.
Ashford, Douglas E. 1986. *The Emergence of the Welfare State*. New York: Basil Blackwell.
Averitt, Robert T. 1968. *The Dual Economy. The Dynamics of American Industry*. New York: Norton.

B

Bairoch, Paul. 1982. "International Industrialization Levels from 1750 to 1980." *Journal of European Economic History* 11 (2): 269-333.
——— 1986. "Historical Roots of Economic Underdevelopment: Myths and Realities." Pp. 191-224 in Wolfgang J. Mommsen and Jürgen Osterhammel (eds.), *Imperialism and After. Continuities and Discontinuities*. London: Allen & Unwin.
Baron, James N. 1984. "Organizational Perspectives on Stratification." *Annual Review of Sociology* 10: 37-69.
——— and William T. Bielby. 1984. "The Organization of Work in a Segmented Economy." *American Sociological Review* 49: 454-473.

Barr, Kenneth. 1980. "Long Waves and Cotton-Spinning Enterprise 1789-1949." Pp. 84-100 in Terence K. Hopkins and Immanuel Wallerstein (eds.), *Processes of the World-System*. Beverly Hills: Sage.

Beck, Ulrich. 1983. "Jenseits von Klasse und Stand? Gesellschaftliche Individualisierungsprozesse und die Entstehung neuer sozialer Formationen und Identitäten." Pp. 35-74 in Reinhard Kreckel (ed.), *Soziale Ungleichheiten*. Special issue no. 2 of *Soziale Welt*. Göttingen: Schwartz.

——— et al. 1980. *Bildungsexpansion und betriebliche Beschäftigungspolitik*. Frankfurt: Campus.

Bell, Daniel. 1976. *The Cultural Contradiction of Capitalism*. London: Heinemann.

Bell, Martin. 1972. *Changing Technology and Manpower Requirements in the Engineering Industry*. Sussex: Sussex University Press.

Bendix, Reinhard. 1956. *Work and Authority in Industry*. New York: Harper and Row.

Bergesen, Albert. 1985. "Cycles of War in the Reproduction of the World-Economy." Pp. 313-331 in Paul M. Johnson and William R. Thompson (Hg.), *Rhythms in Politics and Economics*. New York: Praeger.

——— and Chintamani Sahoo. 1985. "Evidence of the Decline of American Hegemony in World Production." *Review* VIII (4): 595-611.

——— and Ronald Schoenberg. 1980. "Long Waves of Colonial Expansion and Contraction." Pp. 231-277 in Albert Bergesen (ed.), *Studies of the Modern World System*. New York: Academic Press.

Berle, Adolf A., and Gardiner C. Means. [1932] 1967. *The Modern Corporation and Private Property*. New York: Harcourt, Brace & World.

Bhagwati, Jagdish. 1989. "Is Free Trade Passé After All?" *Weltwirtschaftliches Archiv* 125: 17-44.

Biermann, Benno. 1971. *Die soziale Struktur der Unternehmerschaft*. Stuttgart: Enke.

Bieshaar, Hans, and Kleinknecht, Alfred. 1984. "Kondratieff Long Waves in Aggregate Output? An Econometric Test." *Konjunkturpolitik* 30 (5).

Blau, Peter M. 1970. "A Formal Theory of Differentiation in Organizations." *American Sociological Review*, 35: 201-218.

——— 1974. "Parameters of Social Structure." *American Sociological Review* 39: 615-635.

——— and Richard A. Schoenherr. 1971. *The Structure of Organization*. New York: Basic Books.

Bloch, Marc. 1982. *Die Feudalgesellschaft* (translated from French). Frankfurt: Propyläen.

Boli-Bennett, John. 1980. "Global Integration and Universal Increase of State Dominance, 1910-1970." Pp. 77-107 in Albert Bergesen (ed.), *Studies of the Modern World System*. New York: Academic Press.

——— and Francisco O. Ramirez. 1985. "World Culture and the Institutional Development of Mass Education." In John G. Richardson (ed.), *Handbook of Theory and Research in the Sociology of Education*. Westport: Greenwood Press.

———, Francisco O. Ramirez and John W. Meyer. 1985. "Explaining the Origins and Expansion of Mass Education." *Comparative Education Review* 29: 145-170.

Bolte, Karl Martin, and Stefan Hradil. 1984. *Soziale Ungleichheit in der Bundesrepublik Deutschland*. Opladen: Leske & Budrich.

Boltho, Andrea. 1975. *Japan: An Economic Survey*. London: Oxford University Press.

Bombach, G., H.-J. Ramser, M. Timmermann, and W. Wittmann (eds.). 1976. *Der Keynesianismus*. Vol. I. Berlin: Springer Verlag.

Borner, Silvio, et al. 1983. *Die Internationalisierung der Industrie und die Schweiz als Unternehmungsstandort*. Report to the Swiss National Science Foundation.

Bornschier, Volker. 1976. *Wachstum, Konzentration und Multinationalisierung von Industrieunternehmen*. Frauenfeld: Huber.

——— 1977. "Arbeitsteilung und soziale Ungleichheit." *Kölner Zeitschrift für Soziologie und Sozialpsychologie* 29 (3): 438-460.

——— 1981. "Technik und Gesellschaft." Pp. 225-238 in Hardi Fischer (ed.), *Technik wozu und wohin?* Zürcher Hochschulforum, Vol. 3. Zürich: Artemis-Verlag.

——— 1982a "Bildung, Beruf und Arbeitseinkommen: Theoretische Verknüpfungen zwischen Aspekten der sozialen Schichtung." *Zeitschrift für Soziologie,* 11 (3): 254-267.

——— 1982b. "Segmentierung der Unternehmen in der Wirtschaft und personelle Einkommensverteilung." *Schweizerische Zeitschrift für Soziologie* 8 (3): 519-539.

——— 1983a. "The Division of Labor, Structural Mobility and Class Formation. A Theoretical Note." Pp. 249-249 in Donald J. Treiman and Robert V. Robinson (eds.), *Research in Social Stratification and Mobility.* Volume 2. Greenwich (Conn.): Jai Press.

——— 1983b. "Einkommensungleichheit im internationalen Vergleich. Weltwirtschaft versus Entwicklungsstand als Erklärung." Pp. 321-346 in: Reinhard Kreckel (ed.), *Soziale Ungleichheiten.* Special issue 2 of *Soziale Welt.* Göttingen: Schwartz & Co.

——— 1983c. "Eigentum und Verfügungsmacht. Zum korporativen Eigentum." Pp. 161-197 in: Helmut Holzhey and Georg Kohler (eds.), *Eigentum und seine Gründe.* Supplementum 12 of *Studia Philosophica.* Bern: Haupt.

——— 1983d. "Duale Wirtschaft, Statuszuweisung und Belegschaftsintegration." *Soziale Welt* 34 (2): 188-200.

——— 1984. "Zur sozialen Schichtung in der Schweiz." *Schweizerische Zeitschrift für Soziologie,* 10 (3): 647-688.

——— 1986. "Social Stratification in Six Western Countries. The General Pattern and Some Differences." *Social Science Information* 25 (4): 798-824.

——— 1988. *Westliche Gesellschaft im Wandel.* Frankfurt: Campus.

——— 1989. "Legitimacy and Comparative Success at the Core of the World System." *European Sociological Review* 5 (3): 215-230.

——— 1990. "Gesellschaftsmodell und seine Karriere. Eine Anwendung auf die Weltgesellschaft." Pp. 21-54 in Volker Bornschier, Manuel Eisner, Kurt Imhof, Gaetano Romano, Christian Suter (eds.), *Diskontinuität des sozialen Wandels. Entwicklung als Abfolge von Gesellschaftsmodellen und kulturellen Deutungsmustern.* Frankfurt: Campus.

——— 1991. "Soziale Schichtung im keynesianischen Gesellschaftsmodell." Pp. 37-72 in Volker Bornschier (ed.), *Das Ende der sozialen Schichtung? Zürcher Arbeiten zur gesellschaftlichen Konstruktion von sozialer Lage und Bewusstsein in der westlichen Zentrumsgesellschaft.* Zürich: Seismo.

——— 1992. "Politökonomische Regimes: Das Zusammenspiel langer Wellen in Politik und Wirtschaft." Pp. 328-357 in Heidrun Abromeit and Ulrich Jürgens (eds.), *Die politische Logik wirtschaftlichen Handelns,* Berlin: Edition Sigma.

——— 1994. "The Rise of the European Community. Grasping Towards Hegemony or Therapy Against National Decline in the World Political Economy?" Pp. 55-82 in Max Haller und Rudolph Richter (eds.), *Toward a European Nation? Political Trends in Europe.* New York: Sharpe.

——— and Doris Aebi. 1992. "Rolle und Expansion der Bildung in der modernen Gesellschaft – Von der Pflichtschule zur Weiterbildung." *Schweizerische Zeitschrift für Soziologie* 18 (3): 539-567.

——— and Nicola Fielder. 1995. "The Genesis of the Single European Act. Forces and Protagonists Behind the Relaunch of the European Community in the 1980s: The Single Market." Paper presented at the Second European Conference of Sociology, August 30-September 2, 1995, Budapest.

——— and Peter Heintz. 1977. "Statusinkonsistenz und Schichtung – Eine Erweiterung der Statusinkonsistenztheorie." *Zeitschrift für Soziologie,* 6 (1): 29-48.

——— and Peter Heintz (eds.) 1979. "Data Compendium for World System Analysis." Zurich: *Bulletin of the Sociological Institute of the University of Zurich.* Special Issue, March.

——— and Felix Keller. 1994. "Statusgruppenschichtung als Quelle von Konflikt und Devianz." *Schweizerische Zeitschrift für Soziologie* 20 (1): 83-112.

——— and Peter Lengyel. 1990. "Notions of World Society." Pp. 3-15 in Volker Bornschier und Peter Lengyel. (eds.), *World Society Studies.* Vol. 1. Frankfurt: Campus.

——— and Peter Lengyel. 1992. "The End of the Post-War Era." Pp. 3-12 in Volker Bornschier and Peter Lengyel (eds.), *Waves, Formations and Values in the World System.* New Brunswick (NJ): Transaction Publishers.

——— and Peter Lengyel. 1994. "Emergences and Conflict Dynamics in World Society." Pp. 3-17 in Volker Bornschier and Peter Lengyel (eds.), *Conflicts and New Departures in World Society.* New Brunswick (NJ): Transaction Publishers.

——— and Michael Nollert. 1994. "Political Conflict and Labor Disputes at the Core. An Encompassing Review for the Postwar Era." Pp. 377-403 in Volker Bornschier and Peter Lengyel (eds.), *Conflicts and New Departures in World Society.* New Brunswick (NJ): Transaction Publishers.

——— and Hanspeter Stamm. 1990. "Transnational Corporations." Pp. 203-229 in Alberto Martinelli and Neil J. Smelser (eds.), *Economy and Society: Overviews in Economic Sociology.* London: Sage Publications.

——— and Christian Suter. 1992. "Long Waves in the World System." Pp. 15-49 in Volker Bornschier and Peter Lengyel (eds.), *Waves, Formations and Values in the World System.* New Brunswick: Transaction Publishers.

——— et al. 1993. "Die Europäische Gemeinschaft. Die Beschleunigung der westeuropäischen Integration als Teil des sozialen Wandels im Zentrum der Weltgesellschaft." Research report. Zürich: Soziologisches Institut.

Boswell, Terry, and Mike Sweat. 1991. "Hegemony, Long Waves, and Major Wars: A Time Series Analysis of Systemic Dynamics, 1496-1967." *International Studies Quarterly* 35: 123-149.

Bourdieu, Pierre. 1983. "Ökonomisches Kapital, kulturelles Kapital, soziales Kapital." Pp. 183-198 in Reinhard Kreckel (ed.), *Soziale Ungleichheiten*, special issue 2 of *Soziale Welt.* Göttingen: Schwartz.

——— and Jean-Claude Passeron. 1970. *La reproduction.* Paris: Editions de Minuit.

Bousquet, Nicole. 1980. "From Hegemony to Competition: Cycles of the Core?" Pp. 46-83 in Terence K. Hopkins and Immanuel Wallerstein (eds.), *Processes of the World-System.* Beverly Hills, Ca.: Sage.

Boyer, Robert. 1984. "L'introduction du Taylorisme en France à la lumière de recherches récentes." *Travail et Emploi* 18 (Oct-Déc.): 17-41.

——— 1986. *La théorie de la régulation: une analyse critique.* Paris.

Brand, Karl-Werner. 1982. *Neue soziale Bewegungen – Entstehung, Funktion und Perspektive neuer Protestpotentiale: Eine Zwischenbilanz.* Opladen: Westdeutscher Verlag.

——— 1990. "Zyklische Aspekte neuer sozialer Bewegungen." Pp. 139-164 in Volker Bornschier, Manuel Eisner, Kurt Imhof, Gaetano Romano and Christian Suter (eds.), *Diskontinuität des sozialen Wandels.* Frankfurt: Campus.

Braudel, Fernand. 1979. *Cilivisation matérielle, économie et capitalisme, XVe-XVIIIe siècle. Le structure du quodidien: Le possible et l'impossible.* Paris: Librairie Armand Collin Colin.

——— [1979] 1984. *The Perspective of the World.* Vol. 3 of *Civilization and Capitalism 15th-18th Century.* New York: Harper and Row.

Braverman, Harry. 1974. *Labor and Monopoly Capital. The Degradation of Work in the 20th Century.* New York: Monthly Review Press.

Buchanan, James M. 1980. "Rent Seeking and Profit Seeking." Pp. 3-15 in James M. Buchanan, Robert D. Tollison, and G. Tullock (eds.), *Towards a Theory of Rent-Seeking Society.* College Station: A & M University Press.

C

Cain, P.J., and A.G. Hopkins. 1986. "Gentlemanly Capitalism and British Expansion Overseas. I. The Old Colonial System, 1688-1850." *Economic History Review*, 2nd ser., XXXIX (4): 501-525.

Cameron, David R. 1978. "The Expansion of the Public Economy: A Comparative Analysis." *American Political Science Review* 72 (4): 1243-61.

——— 1992. "The 1992 Initiative: Causes and Consequences." Pp. 23-74 in Alberta M. Sbragia (ed.), *Euro-Politics: Institutions and Policymaking in the EC.* Washington D.C.: Brookings Institution.

Carneiro, Robert L. 1973: "Eine Theorie zur Entstehung des Staates." Pp. 153-174 in Klaus Eder (ed.), *Seminar: Die Entstehung von Klassengesellschaften.* Frankfurt: Suhrkamp.

Chandler, Alfred D. Jr. 1962. *Strategy and Structure. Chapters in the History of the American Industrial Enterprise.* Cambridge, Mass.: The M.I.T. Press.

——— 1977. *The Visible Hand. The Managerial Revolution in American Business.* Cambridge, Mass.: Harvard University Press.

Chase-Dunn, Christopher. 1978. "Core-Periphery Relations: The Effects of Core Competition." Pp. 159-176 in Barbara H. Kaplan (ed.), *Social Change in the Capitalist World Economy.* Beverly Hills: Sage.

——— 1981. "Interstate System and Capitalist World Economy. One Logic or Two?" *International Studies Quarterly* 25 (1): 19-42.

——— 1989. *Global Formation: Structures of the World-Economy.* New York: Basil Blackwell.

——— 1992. "The Changing Role of Cities in World-Systems." Pp. 51-87 in Volker Bornschier und Peter Lengyel (eds.), *Waves, Formations and Values in the World System.* New Brunswick: Transaction Publishers.

——— and Thomas D. Hall (forthcoming). *Rise and Demise: The Transformation of World-Systems.* Boulder: Westview

Child, John, and Alfred Kieser. 1979. "Organization and Managerial Roles in British and West German Companies: An Examination of the Culture-Free Thesis." Pp. 250-271 in Cornelis J. Lammers und David J. Hickson (eds.), *Organizations Alike and Unlike. International and Interinstitutional Studies in the Sociology of Organizations.* London: Routledge & Kegan.

Cipriani, Roberto (ed.). 1987. "The Sociology of Legitimation." Special Issue of *Current Sociology* 35 (2): 1-179.

Clark, John, Christopher Freeman, and Luc Soete. 1981. "Long Waves, Inventions and Innovations." *Futures* 13 (4): 308-322.

Coakley, John. 1986. "Cycles of Nationalist Mobilization in Europe: Some Preliminary Remarks." Paper presented at the workshop on "Cycles of Politics." Annual Meeting of the European Consortium for Political Research, at the University of Gøteborg.

Cohen, Benjamin J. 1983. "Balance-of-payments Financing: Evolution of a Regime." Pp. 315-336 in Stephen D. Krasner (ed.), *International Regimes.* Ithaca and London: Cornell University Press.

Cole, Robert E. 1980. *Work, Mobility, and Participation: A Comparative Study of American and Japanese Industry.* Berkeley: University of California Press.

Coleman, James S. 1974. *Power and the Structure of Society.* New York: Norton.

Commission of the European Communities. 1990. *Europa 92. Die Soziale Gemeinschaft: Informationen über sozialpolitische Programme und Initiativen. Für Arbeitnehmer und Verbraucher.* Brussels. Brochure, November 1990.

——— 1991. *Informations- und Kommunikationstechnologien. Die Rolle Europas.* Brussels: General Directorate XIII.

——— 1992. *Europe on the Move. The European Community in the 1990s.* Booklet for the Universal Exposition in Seville 1992. Brussels: Publications Unit.

——— 1992. *Europa der Bürger.* Brochure. Luxembourg. Amt für amtliche Veröffentlichungen der Europäischen Gemeinschaften.

——— 1993. *White Paper: Growth, Competitiveness, Employment: The Challenges and Ways Forward into the 21st Century.* Brussels and Luxembourg: Office for Official Publications of the European Communities.

Conze, Werner, Christian Meier, Jochen Bleicken, Gerhard May, Christof Dipper, Horst Günther, and Diethelm Klippel. 1975. "Freiheit." Pp. 425-542 in Brunner, Otto, Werner Conze, and Reinhard Koselleck (eds.), *Geschichtliche Grundbegriffe.* Vol. 2. Stuttgart: Klett.

Coombs, Rod. 1984. "Long Waves and Labor-Process Change." *Review* 7 (4): 675-701.

Coser, Lewis A. 1956. *The Functions of Social Conflict.* New York: The Free Press.

Cronin, James. 1980. "Stages, Cycles, and Insurgencies: The Economics of Unrest." Pp. 101-118 in Terence K. Hopkins and Immanuel Wallerstein (eds.), *Processes of the World-System.* Beverly Hills: Sage.

Cummings, William K. 1980. *Education and Equality in Japan.* Princeton: Princeton University Press.

Curtin, Phillip. 1984. *Cross-cultural Trade in World History.* Cambridge: Cambridge University Press.

D

Dahl, Robert. 1971. *Polyarchy. Participation and Opposition.* New Haven: Yale University Press.

Dahrendorf, Ralf. [1961] 1967. "Über den Ursprung der Ungleichheit unter den Menschen." In Ralf Dahrendorf, *Pfade aus Utopia. Arbeiten zur Theorie und Methode der Soziologie.* München: Piper.

——— 1979. *Lebenschancen.* Frankfurt: Suhrkamp.

——— 1983a. *Die Chancen der Krise: Über die Zukunft des Liberalismus.* Stuttgart: Deutsche Verlagsanstalt.

——— 1983b. "Grenzen der Gleichheit: Bemerkungen zu Fred Hirsch." *Zeitschrift für Soziologie* 12 (1): 65-73.

——— 1992. *Der moderne soziale Konflikt.* Stuttgart: Deutsche Verlags-Anstalt (extended version of the English-language edition *The Modern Social Conflict,* 1988).

Dann, Otto. 1975. "Gleichheit." Pp. 997-1046 in Brunner, Otto, Werner Conze, and Reinhard Koselleck (eds.), *Geschichtliche Grundbegriffe.* Vol. 2. Stuttgart: Klett.

Davis, Kingsley. 1961. "Social Change Affecting International Relations." In James N. Rosenau (ed.), *International Politics and Foreign Policy: A Reader in Research and Theory.* New York: The Free Press.

Day, R. 1976. "The Theory of the Long Cycle: Kondratiev, Trotsky, Mandel." *New Left Review* 99: 67-82.

De Greene, Kenyon B. 1988. "The Kondratiev Phenomenon: A Systems Perspective." *Systems Research* 5 (4): 281-298.

de Vroey, Michael. 1975. "The Separation of Ownership and Control in Large Corporations." *The Review of Radical Political Economics* 7 (2): 1-10.

Delors, Jacques. 1991. "Wir müssen Grossmacht werden." Interview. *Der Spiegel*

Dipper, Christoph. 1975. "Der Freiheitsbegriff im 19. Jahrhundert." Pp. 489 in Otto Brunner, Werner Conze, and Reinhard Koselleck (eds.), *Geschichtliche Grundbegriffe.* Vol. 2. Stuttgart: Klett.

Dörmann, Uwe. 1991. "Internationaler Kriminalitätsvergleich." Pp. 9-49 in Hans-Heiner Kühne und Koichi Miyazawa (eds.), *Kriminalität und Kriminalitätsbekämpfung in Japan.* 2nd edition Wiesbaden: Bundeskriminalamt.

Duby, Georges. 1981. *Die drei Ordnungen. Das Weltbild des Feudalismus.* Frankfurt: Suhrkamp.

——— 1984. *Krieger und Bauern.* Frankfurt: Syndikat Verlagsgesellschaft.

Durkheim, Emile. [1897] 1983. *Der Selbstmord* (translated from French). Frankfurt: Suhrkamp.

E

Easton, David. 1965. *A Systems Analysis of Political Life.* New York: John Wiley.

Effinger, Manfred, Volker Rittberger, Klaus Dieter Wolf, and Michael Zürn 1990. "Internationale Regime und internationale Politik." Pp. 263-285 in V. Rittberger (ed.), *Theorien der internationalen Beziehungen.* Special issue no 21 of *Politische Vierteljahresschrift.* Opladen: Westdeutscher Verlag.

Eisenstadt, Shmuel N. 1987. *European Civilization in a Comparative Perspective.* Oslo: Norwegian University Press.

Eisner, Manuel. 1990. "Long-term Dynamics of Political Values in International Perspective: Comparing the Results of Content Analysis of Political Documents in the USA, GB, FRG and Switzerland." *European Journal of Political Research* 18: 605-621.

——— 1991. *Politische Sprache und sozialer Wandel. Eine quantitative und semantische Analyse von Neujahrsartikeln in der Schweiz von 1840 bis 1987.* Zürich: Seismo.

——— 1992. "Long-term Fluctuations of Economic Growth and Social Destabilization." *Historical Social Research/Historische Sozialforschung:* 70-98.

——— 1994. "Gewaltkriminalität und Stadtentwicklung in der Schweiz, ein Überblick." *Schweizerische Zeitschrift für Soziologie* 20 (1): 179-204.

Eklund, Klas. 1980. "Long Waves in the Development of Capitalism?" *Kyklos* 33 (3): 383-419.

Elias, Norbert. [1969] 1976. *Über den Prozess der Zivilisation.* Vol. 2. "Wandlungen der Gesellschaft." Frankfurt: Suhrkamp.

——— 1987. *Die Gesellschaft der Individuen.* Frankfurt: Suhrkamp.

Elsenhans, Hartmut. 1981. *Abhängiger Kapitalismus oder bürokratische Entwicklungsgesellschaft: Versuch über den Staat in der Dritten Welt.* Frankfurt: Campus.

——— [1984] 1987. *Nord-Süd-Beziehungen.* Stuttgart: Kohlhammer.

——— 1992. "The Logic of Profit and the Logic of Rent: Risks in the Transition to a New International Order." *Voice of Peace and Integration* (Jaipur/India) 1 (1): 5-44.

Esping-Andersen, Gøsta. 1990. *The Three Worlds of Welfare Capitalism.* Cambridge: Polity Press.

Evans, Peter B. 1979. *Dependent Development. The Alliance of Multinational, State, and Local Capital in Brazil.* Princeton: Princeton University Press.

———, Dietrich Rueschemeyer and Theda Skocpol (eds.). 1985. *Bringing the State Back In.* Cambridge: Cambridge University Press.

F

Fend, Helmut. 1981. *Theorie der Schule.* München: Urban und Schwarzenberg.

Flora, Peter. 1986. *Growth to Limits. The Western European Welfare State since World War II.* 5 vol. published between 1986-1992. Berlin: De Gruyter.

——— 1993. "Europa als Sozialstaat?" Pp. 754-773 in Bernhard Schäfers (ed.), *Lebensverhältnisse und soziale Konflikte im neuen Europa. Verhandlungen des 26. Deutschen Soziologentags in Düsseldorf 1992.* Frankfurt: Campus.

——— and Arnold J. Heidenheimer (eds.). 1981. *The Development of Welfare States in Europe and America.* New Brunswick: Transaction Books.

——— et al. 1983. *State, Economy, and Society in Western Europe 1815-1975.* Vol. I. Frankfurt: Campus.

Fondin, Jean. 1968. *Das Auto. Ein halbes Jahrhundert Geschichte.* Lausanne: Mondo.

Forrester, Jay W. 1976. "Business Structure, Economic Cycle and National Policy." *Futures* 8: 195-214.

——— 1978. "A Great Depression Ahead?" *The Futurist* : 379-385.

——— 1983. "Innovation and Economic Change." In Christopher Freeman (ed.), *Long Waves in the World Economy.* London: Butterworth.

Freeman, Christopher. 1979. "Determinants of Innovation." *Futures* 11 (3): 206-215.

——— (ed.). 1983. *Long Waves in the World Economy.* London: Butterworth.

——— 1989. "Die Verbreitung neuer Technologien in Unternehmen, Wirtschaftsbereichen und Ländern." Pp. 34-63 in Arnold Heertje (ed.), *Technische und Finanzinnovationen. Ihre Auswirkungen auf die Wirtschaft.* Frankfurt: Campus.

——— John Clark, and Luc Soete. 1982. *Unemployment and Technical Innovation.* London: Frances Pinter.

——— and Luc Soete. 1991. *Macro-Economic and Sectoral Analysis of Future Employment and Training Perspectives in the New Information Technologies in the European Community. Synthesis Report.* Study for the Commission of the European Community. Presented at the EC-Conference in Brussels, October 17-18, 1991.

Fukutake, Tadashi. 1974. *Japanese Society Today.* Tokyo: Tokyo University Press.

——— 1982. *The Japanese Social Structure: Its Evolution in the Modern Century.* Tokyo: University of Tokyo Press.

G

Gabillard, Jean. 1967. "Die wichtigsten Lehrmeinungen der Volkswirtschaft." In *Enzyklopädie der Wissenschaften vom Menschen.* Vol. II. Genf: Kister.

Gagliani, Giorgio. 1985. "Long-term Changes in the Occupational Structure." *European Sociological Review* 1 (3): 183-210.

Galbraith, John Kenneth. [1952] 1967. *American Capitalism: The Concept of Countervailing Power.* Harmondsworth: Penguin.

——— 1967. *The New Industrial State.* New York.

——— 1984. *The Anatomy of Power.* Boston: Houghton Mifflin.

Ganshof, François L. 1977. *Was ist das Lehnswesen*? Darmstadt: Wissenschaftliche Buchgesellschaft..

Gartner, Rosemary. 1990. "The Victims of Homicide: A Temporal and Cross-National Comparison." *American Sociological Review* 55 (1): 92-106.

Garvy, G. 1943. "Kondratieff's Theory of Long Cycles." *Review of Economic Statistics* 25: 203-220.

George, Stephen. 1992a. "Intergovernmentalism, Supranationalism and the Future Development of the European Community." Paper presented to the Pan-European Conference on International Relations, Heidelberg, September 1992.

——— 1992b. *Politics and Policy in the European Community.* Oxford: Oxford University Press.

——— 1993. "Supranational Actors and Domestic Politics: Integration Theory Reconsidered in the Light of the Single European Act and Maastricht." Paper presented to the Political Studies Association Annual Conference, University of Leicester, April 1993.

Gerstenberger, W. 1991. *Impact of Information Technologies on Future Employment in the European Community. Study for the Commission of the European Communities.* Presented at the EC-Conference in Brussels, 17-18 October 1991.

Gerster, Hans Jürgen. 1988. *Lange Wellen wirtschaftlicher Entwicklung: Empirische Analyse langfristiger Zyklen für die USA, Grossbritannien und weitere vierzehn Industrieländer von 1800 bis 1980.* Frankfurt and Bern.

Giesen, Bernhard. 1980. *Makrosoziologie. Eine evolutionstheoretische Einführung.* Hamburg: Hoffmann & Campe.

Gill, Stephen. 1990. "The Emerging Hegemony of Transnational Capital: Trilateralism and Global Order." Pp. 119-146 in David P. Rapkin (ed.), *World Leadership and Hegemony.* Boulder: Lynne Rienner.

Gilpin, Robert. 1987. *The Political Economy of International Relations.* Princeton: Princeton University Press.

Gimpel, Jean. 1975. *La révolution industrielle du Moyen Age.* Paris: Edition du Seuil.

Goldstein, Joshua S. 1985. "Kondratieff Waves as War Cycles." *International Studies Quarterly* 29 (4): 411-441.

——— 1988. *Long Cycles: Prosperity and War in the Modern Age.* New Haven: Yale University Press.

Goldthorpe, John H. 1967. "Social Stratification in Industrial Society." In Reinhard Bendix and Seymour M. Lipset (eds.), *Class, Status and Power.* London: Routledge & Kegan.

Gollwitzer, Werner. 1972. *Geschichte des weltpolitischen Denkens.* Vol. I: *Vom Zeitalter der Entdeckungen bis zum Beginn des Imperialismus.* Göttingen: Vandenhoeck & Ruprecht.

Gordon, David M. 1980. "Stages of Accumulation and Long Economic Cycles." Pp. 9-45 in Terence K. Hopkins and Immanuel Wallerstein (eds.), *Processes of the World System.* Beverly Hills: Sage.

Gorz, André. 1980. *Abschied vom Proletariat. Jenseits des Sozialismus,* Frankfurt: Europäische Verlagsanstalt (translated from French).

Gossen, Heinrich. 1854. *Entwicklung der Gesetze des menschlichen Verkehrs und der daraus folgenden Regeln für menschliches Handeln.* Braunschweig.

Graf, Martin, and Markus Lamprecht. 1984. "Zum Problem der Vergleichbarkeit der Bildungsskalen in der Kölner Acht-Nationen-Studie." Zürich: Sociological Institute, unpublished.

Graham, A.K., and Senge, P.M. 1980. "A Long-Wave Hypothesis of Innovation." *Technological Forecasting and Social Change* 17: 283-311.

Grant, Michael. 1980. *The Etruscans.* London: Weidenfeld & Nicolson.

Grimes, Peter 1985. "Long Waves and International Inequality: A Research Proposal." Paper presented at the 26th Annual Convention of the International Studies Association, Washington D.C., March 5-8, 1985.

Gurr, Ted R. (ed.) 1980. Pp. 297-330 in *Handbook of Political Conflict*. New York: Free Press.

——— 1981. "Historical Trends in Violent Crime: A Critical Review of Evidence." *Crime and Justice: An Annual Review of Research* 3: 295-350.

——— and Erika Gurr. 1983. *Crime in Western Societies, 1945-1974*. Ann Arbor: Inter-university Consortium for Political and Social Research.

Gutenberg, Erich. 1963. *Grundlagen der Betriebswirtschaftslehre*. Vol. 2, *Der Absatz*. Berlin: Springer.

H

Haas, Ernst B. 1964. *Beyond the Nation State*. Stanford: Stanford University Press.

——— 1983. "Words Can Hurt You; or, Who Said to Whom About Regimes." Pp. 23-59 in Stephen D. Krasner (ed.), *International Regimes*. Ithaca and London: Cornell University Press.

Haber, Samuel. 1964. *Scientific Management in the Progressive Era 1890-1920*. Chicago: University of Chicago Press.

Habermas, Jürgen. 1983. *Kommunikatives Handeln und Moralbewusstsein*. Frankfurt: Suhrkamp.

Haire, Mason. 1959. "Biological Models and Empirical Histories of the Growth of Organizations." Pp. 272-306 in Mason Haire (Hg.), *Modern Organization Theory*. New York: Wiley.

Haller, Max. 1980. "Bildungsexpansion und die Entwicklung der Strukturen sozialer Ungleichheit." Pp. 22ff. in Ulrich Beck et al. (eds.), *Bildungsexpansion und betriebliche Beschäftigungspolitik*. Frankfurt: Campus, 1980.

Hanf, Theodor. 1975. "Reproduktionseffekt oder Wandelsrelevanz der Bildung." Pp. 120-138 in Theodor Hanf et al. (eds.), *Sozialer Wandel*. Vol. 2. Frankfurt: Fischer.

Harden, Donald. 1963. *The Phoenicians*. New York: Praeger.

Harenberg, Bodo (ed.). 1984. *Chronik der Menschheit*. Vol. 3. Dortmund: Chronik Verlag.

Hartmann, Jürgen. 1983. *Politik und Gesellschaft in Japan, USA, Westeuropa*. Frankfurt: Campus, 1983

Heath, Anthony. 1981. *Social Mobility*. London: Fortuna Paperbacks.

Heidenheimer, Arnold J. 1981. "Education and Social security Entitlements in Europe and America." Pp. 269-2304 in Peter Flora and Arnold J. Heidenheimer (eds.), *The Development of Welfare States in Europe and America*. New Brunswick: Transaction Publishers.

——— 1993. "External and Domestic Determinants of Education Expansion: How Germany, Japan, and Switzerland Have Varied." *Governance. An International Journal of Policy and Administration* 6 (2): 194-219.

Heintz, Peter. 1968. Einführung in die Soziologische Theorie. 2nd ed. Stuttgart: Enke.

Henry, Andrew F., and James F. Short. [1954] 1964. *Suicide and Homicide: Some Economic, Sociological and Psychological Aspects of Aggression*. Glencoe: Free Press.

Hibbs, Douglas A. 1973. *Mass Political Violence*. New York: Wiley.

——— 1987. The Political Economy of Industrial Democracies. Cambridge, Mass.: Harvard University Press.

Hickson, David, et al. 1974. "The Culture-free Context of Organization Structure. A Tri-national Comparison." *Sociology* 8: 59-80.

Hielscher, Gebhard (ed.). 1984. *Die Frau in Japan*. 2nd ed. Berlin: Schmidt.

Hintze, Otto. [1929] 1964. "Wirtschaft und Politik im Zeitalter des modernen Kapitalismus." Pp. 427-452 in Otto Hintze, *Staat und Verfassung*. Vol. II, *Gesammelte Abhandlungen zur Soziologie, Politik und Theorie der Geschichte*, edited and introduced by Gerhard Östereich. Göttingen: Vandenhoeck & Ruprecht, 2nd edition.

Hirsch, Fred. 1976. *Social Limits to Growth*. Cambridge (Mass.): Harvard Univ. Press.

Hobbes, Thomas. [1641] 1962. *Leviathan*. Edited by William Molesworth. Vol. III. Scientia Aalen.

Hobsbawm, Eric J. 1981. "Die Krise des Kapitalismus in historischer Perspektive." Pp. in Folker Fröbel, Jürgen Heinrichs and Otto Kreye (eds.), *Krisen in der kapitalistischen Weltökonomie*. Reinbek: Rowohlt.

Hoby, Jean-Pierre. 1975. *Bildungssystem und Gesellschaft. Ein Beitrag zu ihrer Interdependenz*. Bern: Lang.

Höhn, Siegfried. 1988. "Just-in-Time in Large Complex Companies." In Uwe Holl and Malcom Trevor (eds.), *Just-in-Time Systems*. Frankfurt: Campus.

Holinger, Paul C. 1987. *Violent Deaths in the United States*. New York: Guildford Press.

Holl, Uwe, and Malcolm Trevor (eds.). 1988. *Just-in-Time Systems and Euro-Japanese Industrial Collaboration*. Frankfurt: Campus.

Hondrich, Karl Otto. 1984. "Der Wert der Gleichheit und der Bedeutungswandel der Ungleichheit." *Soziale Welt* (3): 267-293.

Huijgen, Frans. 1983. "Changes in the Skill Level of Work in The Netherlands 1960-1977." Research Committee on Social Stratification (International Sociological Association), 17.-19. Oktober 1983 in Amsterdam.

Hurrelmann, Klaus. 1975. *Erziehungssystem und Gesellschaft*. Reinbek bei Hamburg: Rowohlt.

I

Imai, Masaaki. [1986] 1992. *Kaizen. Der Schlüssel zum Erfolg der Japaner im Wettbewerb*. München: Ullstein, 1992.

Inglehart, Ronald. 1977. *The Silent Revolution. Changing Values and Political Styles Among Western Publics*. Princeton: Princeton University Press.

——— 1983. "Traditionelle politische Trennungslinien und die Entwicklung der neuen Politik in westlichen Gesellschaften." *Politische Vierteljahresschrift* 24: 139-54.

Inkeles, Alex. 1981. "Convergence and Divergence in Industrial Society." In Mustafa O. Allir, Burkart Holzner und Zdenek Suda (eds.), *Direction of Change: Modernization Theory, Research, and Realities*. Boulder, Col.: Westview Press.

——— and Larry Sirowy. 1983. "Convergent and Divergent Trends in National Educational Systems." *Social Forces* 62 (2): 303-333.

International Labour Office. *Yearbook of Labour Statistics*. Geneva: International Labour Office, various years.

Ishida, Hiroshi. 1971. *Japanese Society*. New York: Random House.

——— 1993. *Social Mobility in Japan*. Oxford: Macmillan.

J

Jagodzinski, Wolfgang. 1983. "Ökonomische Entwicklung und politisches Protestverhalten 1970-1973. Eine kombinierte Quer- und Längsschnittanalyse." Pp. 18-43 in Wolf-Dieter Eberwein (ed.), *Politische Stabilität und Konflikt*. Special issue no. 14 of *Politische Vierteljahresschrift*. Opladen: Westdeutscher Verlag.

Jaun, Rudolf. 1986. *Management und Arbeiterschaft*. Zürich: Chronos Verlag.

Jeker, Robert A. 1991. "Globale Wirtschaft und nationale Politik." *Neue Zürcher Zeitung*, April 6/7, no. 79: 9.

Jenkins, J. Craig. 1983. "Resource Mobilization Theory and the Study of Social Movements." *Annual Review of Sociology* 9: 527-533.

Jenks, Leland H. 1960/61. "Early Phases of the Management Movement." *Admistrative Science Quarterly* 5: 421-447.

Johnston, William Ross. 1981. *Great Britain, Great Empire. An Evaluation of the British Imperial Experience*. St. Lucia: University of Queensland Press.

Jürgens, Ulrich. 1992. *Mythos und Realität von Lean Production in Japan*. Berlin: Wissenschaftszentrum Berlin für Sozialforschung.

——— 1994. "Was kommt nach 'Lean Production'? Zur gegenwärtigen Debatte über 'Post-Lean-Production' in Japan." Pp. 191-206 in Hajo Weber (ed.), *Lean Management–Wege aus der Krise. Organisatorische und gesellschaftliche Strategien*. Wiesbaden: Gabler.

——— T. Malsch, and K. Dohse. 1989. *Moderne Zeiten in der Automobilfabrik.* Berlin: Springer.

K

Kaelble, Hartmut. 1981. "Educational Opportunities and Government Policies in Europe in the Period of Industrialization." Pp. 239-268 in Peter Flora and Arnold J. Heidenheimer (eds.), *The Development of Welfare States in Europe and America.* New Brunswick: Transaction Publishers.

——— 1987. *Auf dem Weg zu einer europäischen Gesellschaft. Eine Sozialgeschichte Westeuropas 1880-1980.* München: Beck.

Katzenstein, Peter J. 1985. *Small States in World Markets. Industrial Policy in Europe.* Ithaca, N.Y.: Cornell University Press.

Kawashima, Takeyoshi. 1985. *Die japanische Gesellschaft: Familismus als Organisationsprinzip.* Munich: Minerva Publikationen.

Kennedy, Paul. 1987. *The Rise and Fall of the Great Powers.* New York: Random House.

Keohane, Robert O. 1984. *After Hegemony. Cooperation and Discord in the World Political Economy.* Princeton: Princeton University Press.

——— and Joseph S. Nye. 1977. *Power and Independence.* Boston: Little, Brown & Company.

Kerbo, Harold. 1982. "Movements of 'Crisis' and Movements of 'Affluence': A Critique of Deprivation and Resource Mobilization Theory." *Journal of Conflict Resolution* 26: 645-663.

——— 1983. *Social Stratification and Inequality. Class Conflict in the United States.* New York: McGraw-Hill.

——— 1991. "Social Stratification in Japan." Pp. 421-459 in H. Kerbo (ed.) *Social Stratification and Inequality.* New York: McGraw-Hill.

——— and John A. McKinstry. 1986. "The Implications of Modern Japan for Western Theories of Social Stratification: Some Preliminary Observations." Paper presented to the Research Committee on Social Stratification of the International Sociological Association, Rome, April.

——— and Meika Sha. 1987. "Language and Social Stratification in Japan." Paper presented to annual meetings of the Eastern Sociological Association, Boston, May 1987.

——— and R. A. Shaffer. 1992. "Lower Class Insurgency and the Political Process: The Response of the U.S. Unemployed, 1890-1940." *Social Problems* 39: 139-154.

——— and John A. McKinstry. 1995. *Who Rules Japan*? New York: Praeger.

Kern, Horst, and Michael Schumann. 1970. *Industriearbeit und Arbeiterbewusstsein.* Frankfurt: Europäische Verlagsanstalt.

——— 1984. *Das Ende der Arbeitsteilung? Rationalisierung in der industriellen Produktion: Bestandesaufnahme, Trendbestimmung.* München: Beck.

Kerr, Clark, J.T. Dunlop, F.H. Harbison, and C.A. Myers. 1960. *Industrialism and Industrial Man. The Problem of Labor and Management in Economic Growth.* Cambridge, Mass.: Harvard University Press.

Keynes, John Maynard. [1936] 1964. *The General Theory of Employment, Interests, and Money.* New York: Hartcourt Brace Janovich.

Kindleberger, Charles P. 1973. *The World in Depression, 1929-1939.* Berkeley: University of California Press.

——— 1986. "International Public Goods without International Government." *American Economic Review* 76 (1), March: 1-13.

Klages, Helmut. 1984. *Wertorientierungen im Wandel. Rückblick, Gegenwartsanalyse, Prognosen.* Frankfurt: Campus.

Kleber, Wolfgang. 1983. "Die sektorale und sozialrechtliche Umschichtung der Erwerbsstruktur in Deutschland 1882-1970." Pp. 24-75 in Max Haller and Walter Müller (eds.), *Beschäftigungssystem im gesellschaftlichen Wandel.* Frankfurt: Campus.

Kleinknecht, Alfred. 1979. "Basisinnovationen und Wachstumsschübe: das Beispiel der westdeutschen Industrie." *Konjunkturpolitik* 25: 320-343.

——— 1981. "Lange Wellen oder Wechsellagen? Einige methodische Bemerkungen zur Diskussion." Pp. 107-112 in Dietmar Petzina and Ger van Roon (eds.), *Konjunktur, Krise, Gesellschaft: Wirtschaftliche Wechsellagen und soziale Entwicklung im 19. und 20. Jahrhundert.* Stuttgart: Klett-Cotta.

——— 1983. "Observations on the Schumpeterian Swarming of Innovations." In Christopher Freeman (ed.), *Long Waves in the World Economy.* London: Butterworth.

——— 1986. "Post World War II Growth as a Schumpeter Boom." Pp. 375 in Ivan Berend and Knut Borchardt (eds.), *The Impact of the Depression of the 1930's and its Relevance for the Contemporary World.* Comparative studies prepared the 9th International Economic History Congress, 24.-29. August in Bern, Switzerland.

——— 1987. *Innovation Patterns in Crisis and Prosperity. Schumpeter's Long Cycles Reconsidered.* London: Macmillan.

Kocka, Jürgen. 1975. "Industrielles Management: Konzeptionen und Modelle in Deutschland vor 1914." *Vierteljahreszeitschrift für Sozial- und Wirtschaftsgeschichte* 65, 1969: 332-372.

——— 1975. *Unternehmer in der deutschen Industrialisierung.* Göttingen: Vandenhoeck & Ruprecht.

Kohl, Jürgen. 1981. "Trends and Problems in Postwar Public Expenditure Development in Western Europe and North America." Pp. 307-344 in Peter Flora and Arnold J. Heidenheimer (eds.), *The Development of Welfare States in Europe and America.* New Brunswick: Transaction Publishers.

——— 1985. *Staatsausgaben in Westeuropa - Analysen zur langfristigen Entwicklung der öffentlichen Finanzen.* Frankfurt: Campus.

——— 1992. "Öffentliche Ausgaben." Pp. 260-273 in Manfred G. Schmidt (ed.), *Die westlichen Länder.* Vol. 3, *Lexikon der Politik* (edited by Dieter Nohlen). München: Beck.

Kohler, Georg. 1977. "Die Rechtfertigung bürgerlichen Ungehorsams." Pp. 165-191 in Otfried Höffe (ed.), *Gerechtigkeit als Fairness.* Freiburg: Alber.

——— 1979. "Naturrecht, Gerechtigkeit, Gleichheit." *Studia Philosophica* 38: 135-151.

——— 1981. "Max Weber und der Begriff der Bürokratie." *Reflexion,* September. Zurich: Liberales Institut.

——— 1986. "Ungehorsam des Bürgers und Staatslegitimität: Zum Problem des Widerstandsrechts in der Demokratie." *Neue Zürcher Zeitung,* 20-21 September.

——— 1994. "War, Politics and the Market: Reflections after the Great Potlatch." Pp. 45-60 in Volker Bornschier and Peter Lengyel (eds.), *Conflicts and New Departures in World Society.* New Brunswick: Transaction Publishers.

Kohler-Koch, Beate (ed.). 1989: *Regime in den internationalen Beziehungen.* Baden-Baden: Nomos.

Kondratieff, Nikolai D. [1926] 1979. "Die langen Wellen der Konjunktur." *Archiv für Sozialwissenschaft und Sozialpolitik* 56 (3): 573-609; Reprinted 1979 as "The Long Waves of Economic Life." *Review* 2 (4): 519-562.

Korn Liss, Peggy. 1983. *Atlantic Empires. The Network of Trade and Revolution, 1713 - 1826.* Baltimore: The Johns Hopkins University Press.

Korpi, Walter. 1983. *The Democratic Class Struggle.* London: Routledge & Kegan.

——— 1985. "Economic Growth and the Welfare State: Leaky Bucket or Irrigation System?" *European Sociological Review* 1 (2): 97-118.

——— and Michael Shalev. 1979. "Strikes, Industrial Relations and Class Conflict in Capitalist Societies." *British Journal of Sociology* 30: 164-187.

Koselleck, Reinhard. 1984. *Vergangene Zunkunft.* Frankfurt: Suhrkamp.

Kowalewski, David. 1991. "Periphery Revolutions in World-System Perspective, 1821-1985." *Comparative Political Studies* 24 (1): 76-99.

Krasner, Stephen D. 1976. "State Power and the Structure of International Trade." *World Politics* 28 (3): 317-347.

——— 1983. "Structural Causes and Regime Consequences: Regimes as Intervening Variables." Pp. 1-21 in Stephen D. Krasner (ed.), *International Regimes.* Ithaca: Cornell University Press.

——— (ed.) 1983. *International Regimes.* Ithaca: Cornell University Press.

Krauss, Ellis S., Thomas P. Rohlen, and Patricia G. Steinhoff (eds.). 1984. *Conflict in Japan*. Honolulu: University of Hawaii Press.

Kriesi, Hanspeter, René Levy, Gilbert Ganguillet, and Heinz Zwicky (eds.). 1981. *Politische Aktivierung in der Schweiz 1945-1978*. Diessenhofen: Rüegger.

Kubicek, Herbert, and Alfred Kieser. 1980. "Vergleichende Organisationsforschung." Columns 1533-1557 in: Erwin Grochla (ed.), *Handwörterbuch der Organisation*. 2nd edition. Stuttgart: Poeschel

Kuznets, Simon. 1930. *Secular Movements in Production and Prices*. New York: Houghton Mifflin.

——— 1940. "Schumpeter's Business Cycles." *American Economic Review* 30 (2): 257-271.

L

Lammers, Cornelis J., and David J. Hickson (eds.). 1979. *Organizations Alike and Unlike. International and Interinstitutional Studies in the Sociology of Organizations*. London: Routledge & Kegan.

Lamprecht, Markus. 1988. *Der Beitrag der Bildungsinstitution zur Reproduktion und Legitimation sozialer Ungleichheit* (MA thesis). Universität Zürich: Soziologisches Institut

——— 1991. "Möglichkeiten und Grenzen schulischer Chancengleichheit in westlichen Gesellschaften." Pp. 126-153 in Volker Bornschier (ed.), *Das Ende der sozialen Schichtung? Zürcher Arbeiten zur gesellschaftlichen Konstruktion von sozialer Lage und Bewusstsein in der westlichen Zentrumsgesellschaft*. Zürich: Seismo.

——— and Hanspeter Stamm. 1994. *Die soziale Ordnung der Freizeit*. Zürich: Seismo.

Landes, David S. 1969. *The Unbound Prometheus. Technological Change and Industrial Development in Western Europe from 1750 to the Present*. Cambridge: Cambridge University Press.

Lane, Frederic C. 1973. *Venice, A Maritime Republic*. Baltimore: Johns Hopkins University Press.

——— 1979. *Profits from Power. Readings in Protection Rent and Violence Controlling Enterprises*. Albany: State University of New York Press.

Lehmbruch, Gerhard. 1984. "Concertation and the structure of Corporatist Networks." Pp. 60-80 in John H. Goldthorpe (ed.), *Order and Conflict in Contemporary Capitalism*. Oxford: Clarendon Press.

——— 1992. "Konkordanzdemokratie." Pp. 206-211 in Manfred G. Schmidt (ed.), *Die westlichen Länder*. Vol. 3 of *Lexikon der Politik*. München: Beck.

Lengyel, Peter. 1990. "Australia and South America: Patterns of Semi-peripherality." Pp. 181-211 in Volker Bornschier and Peter Lengyel (eds.): *World Society Studies*. Vol. 1. Frankfurt: Campus.

Lenski, Gerhard E. 1966. *Power and Privilege. A Theory of Social Stratification*. New York: McGraw-Hill.

——— and Jean Lenski. 1987. *Human Societies. A Macrolevel Introduction to Sociology*. New York: McGraw-Hill.

Levy, Jack S. 1983. *War in the Modern Great Power System*. Lexington: University of Kentucky Press.

Lewin, Ralph. 1982. *Arbeitsmarktsegmentierung und Lohnstruktur. Theoretische Ansätze und Hauptergebnisse einer Überprüfung am Beispiel der Schweiz*. Zürich: Schulthess.

Lipietz, Alain. 1984. "Accumulation, crises et sorties de crise: Quelques réflexions méthodologiques autour de la notion de 'Régulation'." Communication à Nordic Summer University, Helsingor, March 2-4, 1984.

——— 1985. "Akkumulation, Krisen und Auswege aus der Krise. Einige methodische Überlegungen zum Begriff der Regulation." *Prokla* 58: 109-137.

Lipset, Seymour Martin. [1960] 1981. *Political Man: The Social Bases of Politics* (3rd edition). Baltimore: Johns Hopkins University Press.

——— 1985: *Consensus and Conflict. Essays in Political Sociologyy*. New Brunswick: Transaction Publishers.

List, Friedrich. 1841. *Das nationale System der politischen Ökonomie*. Vol. 1: *Der internationale Handel, die Handelspolitik und der deutsche Zollverein*. Stuttgart: Cotta.
Locke, John. [1690] 1967. *Two Treatises of Government*. Edition by Walter Euchner: *Zwei Abhandlungen über die Regierung*. Frankfurt: Europäische Verlagsanstalt.
Lundgreen, Peter. 1981. "Bildungsnachfrage und differentielles Bildungsverhalten in Deutschland 1875-1975." Pp. 61-119 in: Hermann Kellenbenz und Jürgen Schneider (eds.): *Wachstumsschwankungen. Wirtschaftliche und soziale Auswirkungen (Spätmittelalter bis 20. Jahrhundert)*. Stuttgart: In Kommission bei Klett-Cotta.

M

Maddison, Angus. 1982. *Phases of Capitalist Development*. Oxford: Oxford University Press.
Mandel, Ernest. 1980. *Long Waves of Capitalist Development*. Cambridge: Cambridge University Press.
Mann, Michael. 1986. *The Sources of Social Power: A History of Power from the Beginning to a.d. 1760*. Cambridge: Cambridge University Press.
Marschall, Thomas H. 1965. *Class, Citizenship and Social Development*. Garden City: Anchor Books.
Marx, Karl [1859] 1974. *Zur Kritik der politischen Ökonomie*. Berlin: Dietz Verlag, 1974.
Maslow, Abraham H. 1954. *Motivation and Personality*. New York: Harper & Row.
Mathieu, Karl-Heinz. 1993. "Bioeconomics and post Keynesian economics: a search for common grounds." *Ecological Economics* 8: 11-16.
Maull, Hanns W., and Volker Fuhrt (eds.). 1993. *Japan und Europa: Getrennte Welten?* Frankfurt: Campus.
McNeill, William H. 1963. *The Rise of the West*. Chicago: Chicago University Press.
——— [1982] 1984. *The Pursuit of Power*, Chicago: University of Chicago Press. German edition: *Krieg und Macht – Militär, Wirtschaft und Gesellschaft vom Altertum bis heute*. München: C.H. Beck, 1984.
Meier, Ruedi, and Felix Walter. 1991. *Umweltabgaben für die Schweiz. Ein Beitrag zur Ökologisierung von Wirtschaft und Gesellschaft*. Chur: Verlag Rüegger.
Mensch, Gerhard. [1975] 1978. *Stalemate in Technology*. Cambridge, Mass.: Ballinger. German edition: *Das technologische Patt*. Frankfurt: Umschau, 1975.
Menzel, Ulrich. 1989. *Im Schatten des Siegers: Japan*. 4 Vols. Frankfurt: Suhrkamp.
Merton, Robert K. 1949. *Social Theory and Social Structure*. Glencoe: Free Press.
Metz, Rainer. 1984. "Zur empirischen Evidenz 'langer Wellen'." *Kyklos* 37 (2): 266-290.
——— 1992. "A re-examination of long waves in aggregate production series." In A. Kleinknecht, E. Mandel, and I. Wallerstein (eds.), *New Findings in Long-Wave Research*. London: Macmillan.
Meulemann, Heiner. 1983. "Value Changes in West Germany, 1950-1980: Integrating the Empirical Evidence." *Social Science Information* 22 (4/5): 777-800.
Meyer, John W. 1977. "The Effects of Education as an Institution." *American Journal of Sociology* 83 (1): 55-72.
Michels, Robert. [1911] 1949. *Political Parties*. Glencoe, Ill.: Free Press.
Mistral, Jaques. 1982. "La diffusion internationale inégale de l'accumulation intensive et ses crises." Pp. 205-237 in Jean-Louis Reiffers (ed.), *Economie et Finance Internationale*. Paris.
Mitrany, David. 1976. *The Functional Theory of Politics*. New York: St. Martin's Press.
Modelski, George. 1978. "The Long Cycle of Global Politics and the Nation State." *Comparative Studies in Society and History* 20 (2): 214-235.
——— 1987. *Long Cycles in World Politics*. Basingstoke: Macmillan.
——— 1990. "Global Leadership: Endgame Scenarios." Pp. 241-256 in David P. Rapkin (ed.), *World Leadership and Hegemony*. Boulder: Lynne Rienner.
Mommsen, Wolfgang J. 1969. *Das Zeitalter des Imperialismus*. Frankfurt: Fischer.
Monsen, R. Joseph, and Anthony Downs. 1965. "A Theory of Large Managerial Firms." *The Journal of Political Economy* 73 (3), June: 220-235.
Monthly Bulletin of Statistics (periodical of the United Nations). 1986. Various volumes and issues until 1986. New York: United Nations.

Moore, Barrington. 1974. *Soziale Ursprünge von Diktatur und Demokratie.* Frankfurt: Suhrkamp.

Moore, Barrington. 1978. *Injustice. The Social Basis of Obedience and Revolt.* White Plains, N.Y.: Sharpe.

Moravcsik, Andrew. 1991. "Negotiating the Single European Act: National Interests and Conventional Statecraft in the European Community." *International Organization* 45 (1): 19-56.

Moscati, Sabatino. 1988. *The Phoenicians.* Mailand: Bompiani.

Mühlestein, Hans. 1957. *Die verhüllten Götter. Neue Genesis der italienischen Renaissance.* Wien: Verlag Kurt Desch.

Münch, Richard. 1984. *Die Struktur der Moderne. Grundmuster und differentielle Gestaltung des institutionellen Aufbaus der modernen Gesellschaften.* Frankfurt: Suhrkamp

N

Nadworny, Milton J. 1955. *Scientific Management and the Unions 1900-1932.* Cambridge (Mass.): Harvard University Press.

Nakane, Chie. [1970] 1985. *Japanese Society.* Berkeley: University of California Press.

Neal, Larry. 1987. "The Integration and Efficiency of the London and Amsterdam Stock Markets in the Eighteenth Century." *Journal of Economic History* 47 (1): 97-115.

Nelson, Benjamin. 1984. *Der Ursprung der Moderne.* 2nd ed. Frankfurt: Suhrkamp.

Nelson, Daniel. 1975. *Managers and Workers. Origins of the New Factory System in the United States 1880-1920.* Madison: University of Wisconsin Press..

Nicolaysen, Gert. 1991. *Europarecht I.* Baden-Baden: Nomos.

Niedermayer, Oskar. 1991. "Die Bevölkerungsorientierungen gegenüber dem politischen System der Europäischen Gemeinschaft." Pp. 321-354 in Rudolf Wildenmann (ed.), *Staatswerdung Europas.* Baden-Baden: Nomos.

Nobel, Peter. 1978. *Anstalt und Unternehmen.* Diessenhofen: Rüegger.

——— 1980. "Das 'Unternehmen' als juristische Person." Pp. 27-46 in Special Issue of *Wirtschaft und Recht.* Zurich: Schulthess.

Nohlen. Dieter. 1992. "Wahlsysteme." Pp. 518-526 in Manfred G. Schmidt (ed.), *Die westlichen Länder.* Vol. 3 of *Lexikon der Politik* (edited by Dieter Nohlen). München: Beck.

Nollert, Michael. 1989. "How Neocorporatism Calms the Wave: A Research Note on Conflict in the Post-War Era." Paper presented at the 30th Annual Convention of the International Studies Association, London, March 28 - April 1, 1989.

——— 1992. *Interessenvermittlung und sozialer Konflikt.* Pfaffenweiler: Centaurus.

Nutter, G. Warren. 1978. *Growth of Government in the West.* Washington D.C.: American Enterprise Institute for Public Research.

O

O'Brien, Patrick, and Caglar Keyder. 1978. *Economic Growth in Britain and France 1780 - 1914. Two Paths to the Twentieth Century.* London: Allen & Unwin.

O.E.C.D. 1975. *Education, Inequality and Life Chances.* Vol. 1. Paris: OECD.

——— 1985. "The Role of the Public Sector: Causes and Consequences of the Growth of Government." Special Issue of *OECD Economic Studies*, Nr. 4.

——— 1988. *New Technologies in the 1990s. A Socio-economic Strategy,* Paris: OECD Publications Service.

——— 1991. *The State of the Environment,* Paris: OECD.

Ogburn, William F. [1922, 1957] 1964. *Social Change: With Respect to Culture and Original Nature.* Reprinted as Chapter 7 in Otis Dudley Duncan (ed.), *William F. Ogburn on Culture and Social Change.* Chicago: University of Chicago Press.

——— and Jean L. Adams. [1948] 1964. "Are Our Wars Good Times?" Reprinted in Otis Dudley Duncan (ed.), *William F. Ogburn on Culture and Social Change.* Chicago: University of Chicago Press.

——— and Dorothy S. Thomas. 1964. "The Influence of the Business Cycle on Certain Social Conditions." Reprinted in Otis Dudley Duncan (Ed.), *William F. Ogburn on Culture and Social Change.* Chicago: University of Chicago Press.

Olson, Mancur. 1965. *The Logic of Collective Action.* Cambridge: Harvard University Press.

——— 1982. *The Rise and Decline of Nations. Economic Growth, Stagflation, and Social Rigidities.* New Haven: Yale University Press.

Ono, A., and T. Watanabe. 1976. "Changes in Income Inequality in the Japanese Economy." Pp. 363-390 in H. Patrick (ed.), *Japanese Industrialization and its Social Consequences.* Berkeley: University of California Press.

Oppenheim, A. Leo 1967. "A New Look at the Structure of Mesopotamien Society." *Journal of the Economic and Social History of the Orient.* 10: 1-16.

P

Paldam, Martin, and Peder J. Pedersen. 1984. "The Large Pattern of Industrial Conflict. A comparative Study of 18 Countries, 1919-1979." *International Journal of Social Economics* 11(5): 3-28.

Pareto, Vilfredo. 1913. "Alcune relazioni fra lo stato sociale e le variazioni della prosperità economica." *Revista italiana di sociologia* Sept.-Dec.: 501-548.

Parkin, Frank. 1979. *Marxism and Class Theory - A Bourgeois Critique.* New York: Columbia University Press.

Parsons, Talcott. 1964. "Evolutionary Universals in Society." *American Sociological Review* 29: 339-357.

Paulsen, Andreas. 1968. *Allgemeine Volkswirtschaftslehre.* Vol. 1. Berlin: Walter de Gruyter & Co.

Penrose, Edith T. 1968. *The Theory of the Growth of the Firm.* 4th ed. London: Blackwell.

Perez, Carlota. 1983. "Structural Change and Assimilation of New Technologies in the Economic and Social Systems." *Futures* 15 (5): 357-375.

——— 1985. "Microelectronics, Long Waves and World Structural Change: New Perspectives for Developing Countries." *World Development* 13 (3): Pp. 441-463.

Peters, B. Guy. 1985. "The Limits of the Welfare State." Pp. 91-114 in Norman J. Vig und Steven E. Schier (eds.), *Political Economy in Western Democracies.* New York: Holmes & Meier.

Pfister, Ulrich, and Christian Suter. 1987. "International Financial Relations as Part of the World-System." *International Studies Quarterly* 31 (3): 239-272.

Pizzorno, A. 1978. "Political Exchange and Collective Identity in Industrial Conflict." In C. Crouch and A. Pizzorno (eds.), *The Resurgence of Class Conflict in Western Europe since 1968.* 2 vols. London: Macmillan.

Polanyi, Karl. [1944] 1978. *The Great Transformation: The Political and Economic Origins of Our Times* (1944; reprint, Boston: Beacon, 1957). German edition: *Politische und ökonomische Ursprünge von Gesellschaften und Wirtschaftssystemen.* Frankfurt: Suhrkamp, 1978.

Poletayev, Andrey V. 1989. "Long Waves in Profit Rates in Four Countries." Paper presented at the international colloquium on: The Long Waves of the Economic Conjuncture - The Present State of the International Debate, Brussels, January 12-14, 1989.

Porter, Michael E. 1990. *The Competitive Advantage of Nations.* New York: The Free Press.

Pryor, Frederic L. 1973. *Property and Industrial Organization in Communist and Capitalist Nations.* Bloomington: Indiana University Press.

Putnam, Robert D., and Nicolas Bayne. 1985. *Weltwirtschaftsgipfel im Wandel.* Bonn: Europa Union Verlag.

R

Raith, Werner. 1979. *Florenz vor der Renaissance. Der Weg einer Stadt aus dem Mittelalter.* Frankfurt: Campus.

Ramirez, Francisco O. 1981. "Comparative Social Movements." *International Journal of Comparative Sociology* 1-2: 3-21.

Rapkin, David P. (ed.). 1990. *World Leadership and Hegemony.* Boulder: Lynne Rienner.

Rasler, Karen, and Thompson, William R. 1983. "Global Wars, Public Debts, and the Long Cycle." *World Politics* 35: 489-516.

Rawls, John. 1972. *A Theory of Justice.* Oxford: Clarendon Press.

Reijnders, Jan. 1990. *Long Waves in Economic Development.* Aldershot: Elgar.

Research Working Group on Cyclical Rhythms and Secular Trends. 1979. "Cyclical Rhythms and Secular Trends of the Capitalist World-Economy: Some Premises, Hypotheses, and Questions." *Review* 2: 483-500.

Ritter, Gerhard A. [1950] 1967. *Die Neugestaltung Deutschlands und Europas im 16. Jahrhundert.* Frankfurt: Ullstein.

——— 1989. *Der Sozialstaat: Entstehung und Entwicklung im internationalen Vergleich.* Munich: Oldenbourg-Verlag.

Robins-Mowry, Dorothy. 1983. *The Hidden Sun: Women of Modern Japan.* Boulder, Col.: Westview Press.

Robinson, Joan. 1962. *Economic Philosophy.* London: Watts.

Rokkan, Stein. 1975. "Dimensions of State Formation and Nation-Building." Pp. 562-600 in Charles Tilly (ed.), *The Formation of National States in Western Europe.* Princeton. N.J.: Princeton University Press.

——— 1981. "Territories, Nations, Parties: Toward a Geoeconomic-Geopolitical Model for the Explanation of Variations within Western Europe." Pp. 70-95 in Richard L. Merritt and Bruce Russett (eds.), *From National Development to Global Community. Essays in Honor of Karl W. Deutsch.* London: Allen & Unwin.

——— and Lars Svåsand. 1978. "Zur Soziologie der Wahlen und der Massenpolitik." Pp. 1-72 in René König (ed.), *Handbuch der empirischen Sozialforschung*. Vol. 12. Stuttgart: Enke.

Rostow, Walt W. 1975. "Kondratieff, Schumpeter, and Kuznets: Trend Periods Revisited." *The Journal of Economic History* 35: 719-753.

——— 1978. *The World Economy: History and Prospects.* London: Macmillan.

——— 1985. "The World Economy since 1945: A Stylized Historical Analysis." *The Economic History Review* 38: 252-275.

Roth, Siegfried. 1992. "Japanization, or Going Our Own Way?" Pp. 4-71 in Study Group International Labor Relations (ed.), *Japanization, or Going our Own Way? Internalization and Interest Representation.* Düsseldorf: Hans-Böckler-Stiftung, Graue Reihe – Neue Folge 48.

Rousseau, Jean-Jacques. [1755] 1978. "Discours sur l'Origine de l'Inégalité parmi les Hommes." Kurt Weigand (ed.), *Schriften zur Kulkturkritik.* Hamburg: Meiner, third edition.

Rueschemeyer, Dietrich. 1977. "Structural Differentiation, Efficiency and Power." *American Journal of Sociology* 83: 1-25.

Ruggie, John Gerard. 1975. "International Responses to Technology: Concepts and Trends." *International Organization* 29: 570 -590.

——— 1983. "International Regimes, Transactions, and Change: Embedded Liberalism in the Postwar Economic Order." Pp. 195-231 in Stephen D. Krasner (ed.), *International Regimes*. Ithaca: Cornell University Press.

Rushing, Walter. 1968. "Income, Unemployment and Suicide." *Sociological Quarterly* 9: 493-503.

Russett, Bruce. 1988a. "Economic Decline, Electoral Pressure, and the Initiation of Interstate Conflict." In Charles Gochman and Alan Ned Sabrosky (ed.), *Prisoners of War.* Cambridge Mass.: Ballinger.

——— 1988b. "Peace Research, Complex Causation and Causes of War." In Peter Wallersteen (ed.), *Peace Research: Achievements and Challenges.* Boulder, Col.: Westview Press.

——— 1990. "Economic Decline, Electoral Pressure, and the Initiation of Interstate Conflict." Pp. 123-140 in C. Gochman, A.N. Sabrosky (eds.), *Prisoners of War.* Cambridge, Mass.: Ballinger.

——— 1993. *Grasping the Democratic Peace. Principles for a Post-Cold War World.* Princeton: Princeton University Press.

——— 1994. "The Democratic Peace." Pp. 21-43 in Volker Bornschier and Peter Lengyel (eds.), *Conflicts and New Departures in World Society.* World Society Studies Vol. 3. New Brunswick: Transaction Publishers.

S

Samuelson, Paul A. [1939] 1944. "Interaction between Multiplier Analysis and the Principle of Acceleration." In Paul A. Samuelson, *Readings in Business Cycle Theory.* Philadelphia.

Sanderson, Stephen K. 1990. *Social Evolutionism: A Critical History.* New York: Basil Blackwell.

Sandholtz, Wayne, and John Zysman. 1989. "1992: Recasting the European Bargain." *World Politics* XLII (1): 95-128.

Sauer, Jochen, and Heinz Gattringer. 1985. "Soziale, familiale, kognitive und motivationale Determinanten der Schulleistung." *Kölner Zeitschrift für Soziologie und Sozialpsychologie* 37: 288-309.

Scheide, J., and Stefan Sinn. 1989. "How Strong is the Case for International Coordination?" Pp. 397-422 in J.A. Dorn and W.A. Niskanen (eds.), *Dollars, Deficits, and Trade.* Boston: Kluwer Academic Publishers.

Schmidheiny, Stephan, with the Business Council for Sustainable Development. 1992. *Changing Course: A Global Perspective on Development and the Environment.* Cambridge, Mass.: MIT Press.

Schmidt, Manfred G. 1982. *Wohlfahrtsstaatliche Politik unter bürgerlichen und sozialdemokratischen Regierungen: Ein internationaler Vergleich.* Frankfurt: Campus.

——— (ed.) 1983. *Westliche Industriegesellschaften. Wirtschaft – Gesellschaft – Politik.* Vol. 2. *Pipers Wörterbuch zur Politik* (ed. by Dieter Nohlen). München: Piper.

——— (ed.) 1992. *Die westlichen Länder.* Vol. 3, *Lexikon der Politik* (edited by Dieter Nohlen). München: Beck.

Schmiegelow, Henrik, 1993. "Japans strategischer Pragmatismus: Bedrohung oder Modell?" Pp. 505-529 in Hanns W. Maull and Volker Fuhrt (eds.), *Japan und Europa: Getrennte Welten?* Frankfurt: Campus.

——— and Michèle Schmiegelow. 1989. *Strategic Pragmatism: Japanese Lessons in the Use of Economic Theory.* New York.

Schmitter, Philippe C. 1981. "Interest Intermediation and Regime Governability in Contemporary Western Europe and North America." Pp. 285-327 in S. Berger (ed.), *Organizing Interests in Western Europe.* Cambridge: Cambridge University Press.

——— and Gerhard Lehmbruch (eds.) 1979. *Trends Toward Corporatist Intermediation.* London: Sage.

Schneeloch, Norbert H. 1982. *Aktionäre der Westindischen Compagnie von 1674,* Vol. 12. *Beiträge zur Wirtschaftsgeschichte,* edited by H. Kellenbenz and J. Schneider. Stuttgart: In Kommission bei Klett-Cotta.

Schneider, Reinhart. 1982. "Die Bildungsentwicklung in den westeuropäischen Staaten 1870-1975." *Zeitschrift für Soziologie* 11 (3): 207-226.

Schott, Kerry. 1984. *Policy, Power and Order. The Persistence of Economic Problems in Capitalist States.* New Haven: Yale University Press.

Schumpeter, Joseph A. 1918/19. "Zur Soziologie der Imperialismen." *Archiv für Sozialwissenschaft und Sozialpolitik* 46: 1-39 and 275-310.

——— 1939. *Business Cycles.* 2 Vol. New York: McGraw-Hill.

Screpanti, Ernesto. 1984. "Long Economic Cycles and Recurring Proletarian Insurgencies." *Review* 7: 509-548.

Seibel, Hans Dieter. 1980. *Struktur und Entwicklung der Gesellschaft.* Stuttgart: Kohlhammer.

Seitz, Konrad. 1991. *Die japanisch-amerikanische Herausforderung.* München: Bonn Aktuell.

Shannon, Thomas Richard. 1989. *An Introduction to the World-System Respective.* Boulder: Westview.

Silver, Beverly J. 1989. "Class Struggle and the Kondratieff." Paper presented at the international colloquium on: The Long Waves of the Economic Conjuncture - The Present State of the International Debate, Brussels, January 12-14, 1989.

Simmel, Georg. 1890. "Über soziale Differenzierung: Soziologische und psychologische Untersuchungen." *Staats- und Sozialwissenschaftliche Forschungen* (ed. Gustav Schmoller). Vol. 10. Berlin: Duncker & Humblot.

——— 1908. *Soziologie. Untersuchungen über die Formen der Vergesellschaftung.* Leibzig: Duncker & Humblot.

Sinn, Stefan. 1992. "The Taming of Leviathan: Competition Among Governments." *Constitutional Political Economy* 3 (2): 177-196.

Skinner, Quentin. 1978. *The Foundations of Modern Political Thought.* Vol. 1. *The Renaissance.* Cambridge: Cambridge University Press.

Skocpol, Theda. 1977. "Wallerstein's World Capitalist System: A Theoretical and Historical Critique." *American Journal of Sociology* 82: 1075-1090.

Smith, Adam. [1776] 1981. *An Inquiry into the Nature and Causes of the Wealth of Nations.* Glasgow Edition of the Works and Correspondence of Adam Smith 2. Indianapolis: Liberty Press.

Smith, Robert. 1983. *Japanese Society: Tradition, Self, and the Social Order.* Cambridge: Cambridge University Press.

Solo, Robert. 1985. "The Formation and Transformation of States." In W. Ladd Hollist, and F. LaMond Tullis (eds.), *An International Political Economy.* Boulder: Westview Press.

Solomou, Solomos. 1986. "Non-Balanced Growth and Kondratieff Waves in the World Economy, 1850 - 1913." *The Journal of Economic History* 46: 165-169.

Sombart, Werner. 1928. *Der moderne Kapitalismus*, 3 vol. in 6 halves, 2nd ed. Leibzig: Duncker and Humblot.

Spahn, Heinz-Peter. 1976. "Keynes in der heutigen Wirtschaftspolitik." Pp. 211-228 in G. Bombach, H.J. Ramser, M. Timmermann and W. Wittmann (eds.) *Der Keynesianismus.* Vol. I. Berlin: Springer-Verlag.

Spencer, Herbert. [1880] 1969. *Principles of Sociology.* London: Macmillan.

Stack, Steven. 1978. "Suicide: A Comparative Analysis." *Social Forces* 57: 644-653.

Starbuck, William H. 1965. "Organizational Growth and Development." Pp. 451-533 in James G. March (ed.), *Handbook of Organizations.* Chicago: Rand McNally.

Stavenhagen, Gerhard. 1969. *Geschichte der Wirtschaftstheorie.* 4th ed. Göttingen: Vandenhoeck & Ruprecht.

Steensgard, Niels. 1981. "Violence and the Rise of Capitalism: Frederic Lane's Theory of Protection and Tribute." *Review* V (2): 247-273.

Stein, Rokkan. 1975. "Dimensions of State Formation and Nation-Building." Pp. 562-600 in Charles Tilly (ed.), *The Formation of National States in Western Europe.* Princeton (N.J.): Princeton University Press.

Steinmo, Sven. 1989. "Political Institutions and Tax Policies in the United States, Sweden and Britain." *World Politics* XLI (4): 500-535.

Sterman, John D. 1986. "The Economic Long Wave: Theory and Evidence." *System Dynamics Review* 2 (2): 87-125.

Stigler, George J. 1972. "Economic Competition and Political Competition." *Public Choice* 13: 91-116.

Stockmann, Reinhard, Guido Dahm, and Klaus Zeifang. 1983. "Konzentration und Reorganisation von Unternehmen und Betrieben. Empirische Analysen zur Entwicklung der nichtlandwirtschaftlichen Arbeitsstätten und Unternehmen in Deutschland, 1875-1970." Pp. 97-177 in: Max Haller and Walter Müller (eds.), *Beschäftigungssystem im gesellschaftlichen Wandel.* Frankfurt: Campus.

Stoffel, W.A. 1985. "Die Eherechtsreformen im Ausland." Schweizerisches Institut für Rechtsvergleichung, Lausanne. In *Neue Zürcher Zeitung*, Nr. 205, 5.9.1985.

Stohl, Michael. 1980. "The Nexus of Civil and International Conflict." Pp. 297-330 in Ted R. Gurr (ed.), *Handbook of Political Conflict.* New York: Free Press.

Stokman, Frans N., Rolf Ziegler, and John Scott (eds.), *Networks of Corporate Power. A Comparative Analysis of Ten Countries.* Cambridge: Polity Press.

Störig, Hans Joachim. [1957] 1961. *Kleine Weltgeschichte der Philosophie.* Gütersloh: Bertelsmann.

Strange, Susan. 1983. "*Cave! hic dragones:* A Critique of Regime Analysis." Pp. 337-354 in Stephen D. Krasner (ed.), *International Regimes*. Ithaca: Cornell University Press.

Strasser, Hermann, and Robert Hodge. 1986. *Status Inconsistencies in Modern Societies.* Duisburg: Verlag der Sozialwissenschaftlichen Kooperative.

Sumner, William G. 1940. *Folkways*. Boston: Ginn.

Süsterhenn, Adolf. 1961. "Menschenrechte." Pp. 303-308 in *Handwörterbuch der Sozialwissenschaften* (simultaneously new edition of *Handwörterbuch der Staatswissenschaften).* Stuttgart/Tübingen/Göttingen: Fischer/Mohr (Siebeck)/Vandenhoeck & Ruprecht.

Swank, Duane H., and Alexander Hicks. 1985. "The Determinants and Redistributive Impacts of State Welfare Spending in Advanced Capitalist Democracies." Pp. 115-139 in Norman J. Vig, and Steven E. Schier (eds.), *Political Economy in Western Democracies*. New York: Holmes & Meier.

T

Taira, Koji. 1962. "Characteristics of Japanese Labor Markets." *Economic Development and Cultural Change* 10: 150-168.

Tannenbaum, Arnold, and Robert A. Cooke. 1979. "Organizational Control. A Review of Studies Employing the Control Graph Method." Pp. 183-210 in Cornelis J. Lammers, and David J. Hickson (eds.), *Organizations Alike and Unlike. International and Interinstitutional Studies in the Sociology of Organizations.* London: Routledge & Kegan.

Tarrow, Sidney. 1988. "National Politics and Collective Action: Recent Theory and Research in Western Europe and the United States." *Annual Review of Sociology* 14: 421-440.

——— 1989. *Democracy and Disorder. Protest and Politics in Italy, 1965-1975.* Oxford: Clarendon Press.

Taylor, Charles L. 1985. *World Handbook of Political and Social Indicators. Third Edition ZA No. 1130-1132.* Köln: Zentralarchiv für Empirische Sozialforschung.

——— and David A. Jodice. 1983. *World Handbook of Political and Social Indicators.* 3d ed. Vol. II. New Haven: Yale University Press.

Taylor, Frederick Winslow. 1911. *The Principles of Scientific Management.* New York: Harper and Row.

Teichler, Ulrich. 1975. *Hochschule und Gesellschaft in Japan. Volume I: Geschichte und Struktur des japanischen Hochschulwesens.* Stuttgart: Klett.

Telò, Mario. 1988. *Le New Deal européen, La pensée et la politique sociales-démocrates face à la crise des années trente.* Brussels: Editions de L'Université de Bruxelles.

Thomas, George M., and John W. Meyer. 1984. "The Expansion of the State." *Annual Review of Sociology* 10: 461-82.

Tilly, Charles (ed.) 1975. *The Formation of National States in Western Europe.* Princeton, N.J.: Princeton University Press.

——— 1985. "War Making and State Making as Organized Crime." Pp. 169-191 in Peter B. Evans, Dietrich Rueschemeyer, Theda Skocpol (eds.), *Bringing the State Back In.* Cambridge: Cambridge University Press.

——— L. Tilly, and R. Tilly. 1975. *The Rebellious Century, 1830-1930.* Cambridge, Mass.: Harvard University Press.

Tollison, Robert D. 1982. "Rent Seeking: A Survey." *Kyklos* 35 (4): 575-602.

Tominaga, Ken'ichi, and Toshio Tomoeda. 1986. "Trends of Status Inconsistency and their Significance in Japanese Society, 1955-1975." Pp. 349-367 in Hermann Strasser, and Robert W. Hodge (eds.), *Status Inconsistency in Modern Societies*. Duisburg: Verlag Sozialwissenschaftliche Kooperative.

Treiman, Donald J., and Patricia Roos. 1983. "Sex and Earnings in Industrial Society: A Nine-Nation Comparison." *American Journal of Sociology* 89: 612-650.

Tsurumi, Kazuko. 1970. *Social Change and the Individual: Japan Before and After Defeat in World War II.* Princeton: Princeton University Press.

Tylecote, Andrew. 1984. "Towards an Explanation of the Long Wave 1780-2000." *Review* 7: 701-717.

U

Ultee, Wout C. 1980. "Is Education a Positional Good? An Empirical Examination of Alternative Hypotheses on the Connection Between Education and Occupational Level." *The Netherlands Journal of Sociology* 16 (2): 135-153.

UNCTAD. 1976. *Handbook of International Trade and Development Statistics.* New York: United Nations.

United Nations. 1983. *Transnational Corporations in World Development. Third Survey.* New York: United Nations Centre on Transnational Corporations.

——— 1988. *Transnational Corporations in World Development. Trends and Prospects.* New York: United Nations Centre on Transnational Corporations.

V

van Duijn, Jacob J. 1981. "Fluctuation in Innovations over Time." *Futures* 13 (4): 271.

——— 1983. *The Long Wave in Economic Life.* London: Allen & Unwin.

van Dülmen, Richard. 1982. *Entstehung des frühneuzeitlichen Europa 1550-1648.* Vol. 10. *Weltgeschichte.* Frankfurt: Fischer.

Väyrynen, Raimo. 1983. "Economic Cycles, Power Transitions, Political Management and Wars Between Major Powers." *International Studies Quarterly* 27: 389-418.

Vogel, Ezra. 1979. *Japan As Number One: Lessons for America.* Harvard University Press.

W

Wada, Richard O. 1975. *Impact of Economic Growth on the Size Distribution of Income: The Postwar Experience of Japan.* World Employment Programme Research Working Paper 37. Geneva: ILO.

Wagner, Adolf. 1981. "Demographische Ursachen langfristiger Wachstumszyklen? Fragen zur Konzeption ökonomischer Zyklustheorien." Pp. 339-360 in R. Spree, and W. Schröder (eds.), *Historische Konjunkturforschung*. Stuttgart: Klett.

Wallerstein, Immanuel. 1974. *The Modern World System, I.* New York: Academic Press.

——— 1979. *The Capitalist World Economy.* Cambridge: Cambridge University Press.

——— 1980. *The Modern World-System II. Mercantilism and the Consolidation of the European World-Economy, 1600-1750.* New York: Academic Press.

——— 1984. *The Politics of the World Economies. The States, the Movements and the Civilizations.* Cambridge: Cambridge University Press.

Weber, Hajo. 1994. "Die Evolution von Produktionsparadigmen: Craft Production, Mass Production, Lean Production." Pp. 21-44 in Hajo Weber (ed.), *Lean Management–Wege aus der Krise. Organisatorische und gesellschaftliche Strategien.* Wiesbaden: Gabler.

Weber, Max. [1920] 1965. *Die protestantische Ethik und der Geist des Kapitalismus.* Edited by Johannes Winckelmann. Tübingen: Mohr (Siebeck).

——— [1921] 1972. *Wirtschaft und Gesellschaft.* 5th ed. Tübingen: Mohr (Siebeck)

——— [1921] 1964. *The Theory of Social and Economic Organization.* Talcott Parsons (ed.). New York: Free Press.

——— 1923*Wirtschaftsgeschichte. Abriss der universalen Sozial- und Wirtschafts-geschichte.* Edited by S. Hellmann and M. Palyi. Munich and Leibzig: Duncker & Humblot. American edition: *General Economic History.* New York: Transaction Books, 1981.

Weede, Erich. 1994. "Legitimacy, Democracy and Comparative Economic Growth Reconsidered." Paper University of Cologne, forthcoming in *European Sociological Review.*

Weir, Margaret, and Theda Skocpol. 1985. "State Structures and the Possibilities for 'Keynesian' Responses to the Great Depression in Sweden, Britain, and the United States." Pp. 107-163 in Peter B. Evans, Dietrich Rueschemeyer, and Theda Skocpol (eds.), *Bringing the State Back In.* Cambridge: Cambridge University Press.

Wieland, Wolfgang. 1975. "Entwicklung, Evolution." In Otto Brunner, Werner Conze, Reinhard Koselleck (eds.), *Geschichtliche Grundbegriffe*. Vol. II. Stuttgart: Klett.
Wildenmann, Rudolf et al. 1982. *Führungsschicht in der Bundesrepublik Deutschland 1981* (Tabellenband). Mannheim.
Williams, Justin. 1979. *Japan's Political Revolution under MacArthur: A Participant's Account*. Athens: University of Georgia Press.
Williamson, Oliver E. 1967. "Hierarchical Control and Optimum Firm Size." *The Journal of Political Economy* 75 (2): 123-138.
Wilson, Dorothy. 1979. *The Welfare State in Sweden: A Study of Comparative Social Administration*. London: Heinemann.
Witte, Eberhard, and Rolf Bronner. 1974. *Die leitenden Angestellten. Eine empirische Untersuchung*. Volume 1. München: Beck.
Wollnik, Michael. 1980. "Einflußgrößen der Organisation." Colons 599-607 in: Erwin Grochla (Hg.), *Handwörterbuch der Organisation*. 2nd ed. Stuttgart: Poeschel.
Womack, James P., Daniel T. Jones, and Daniel Roos. 1990. *The Machine that Changed the World*. New York: Rawson.
World Bank. 1971. *World Tables*. Mimeographed. Washington (D.C.): I.B.R.D.
——— 1983. *World Bank Atlas*. Mimeographed, computer outprint of data 5/2/83, Washington (D.C.): I.B.R.D.
World Economic Forum and IMD. 1992. *The World Competiveness Report*. Lausanne and Geneva.
World Health Organisation, *World Health Statistics* (various years). Geneva.

Y

Yawata, Yasusada. 1994. "Socio-cultural Background of Competitive Management and Technology in the Western Pacific Rim." Pp. 3-21 in Hellmut Schütte (ed.), *The Global Competitiveness of the Asian Firm*. London: Macmillan.
Young, Oran R. 1983. "Regime Dynamics: The Rise and Fall of International Regimes." Pp. 93-113 in Stephen D. Krasner (ed.), *International Regimes*. Ithaca and London: Cornell University Press.

Z

Zentralarchiv. 1979. *Political Action. An Eight-Nation Study 1973-1975. Zentralarchiv-Study-No 765*. Cologne: Zentralarchiv für Empirische Sozialforschung.
Zimmermann, Ekkart. 1977. *Soziologie der politischen Gewalt*. Stuttgart: Enke.
——— 1980. "Macro-Comparative Research on Political Protest." Pp. 167-237 in Ted R. Gurr (ed.), *Handbook of Political Conflict*. New York: Free Press.
——— 1988. "Political Unrest in OECD Countries: Trends and Prospects." *World Futures* 25: 43-82.
——— 1989. "Political Unrest in Western Europe: Trends and Prospects." *West European Politics* 12: 179-196.
Zink, Klaus J. 1994. "Quality Management und neue Formen der Organisation." Pp. 45-64 in Hajo Weber (ed.), *Lean Management – Wege aus der Krise. Organisatorische und gesellschaftliche Strategien*. Wiesbaden: Gabler.
Zwicky, Heinrich, and Peter Heintz. 1982. "Soziale Ungleichheit, Legitimationsanforderung und Konflikt." *Zeitschrift für Soziologie* 11 (3): 268-278.

AUTHOR INDEX

J

K

L

M

N

Name and Historic Event Index

O

P

R

S

Subject Index

M

N

O

Q

R

V

W

Y

Z

For Product Safety Concerns and Information please contact our EU representative GPSR@taylorandfrancis.com
Taylor & Francis Verlag GmbH, Kaufingerstraße 24, 80331 München, Germany

www.ingramcontent.com/pod-product-compliance
Lightning Source LLC
Chambersburg PA
CBHW060127280326
41932CB00012B/1452

9781138517837